Rationality and
the social sciences

Rationality and
the social sciences

Contributions to
the philosophy and methodology
of the social sciences

edited by
S.I. Benn
and
G.W. Mortimore

Routledge and Kegan Paul
London, Henley and Boston

First published in 1976
by Routledge & Kegan Paul Ltd
76 Carter Lane,
London EC4V 5EL and
Reading Road,
Henley-on-Thames,
Oxon RG9 IEN and
9 Park Street,
Boston, Mass. 02108, USA
Text set in Monophoto Times New Roman
Photosetting by Thomson Press (India) Limited New Delhi
and printed in Great Britain by
Unwin Brothers Limited
The Gresham Press, Old Woking, Surrey

ISBN 0 7100 8170 7

Contents

Contents

Contributors

R.P. Abelson
Professor of Psychology, Yale University

S.I. Benn
Professorial Fellow in Philosophy, Australian National University

R. Brown
Professorial Fellow in the History of Ideas, Australian National University

P.S. Cohen
Professor of Sociology, London School of Economics

Q. Gibson
Associate Professor of Philosophy, Australian National University

J.B. Maund
Research Fellow in Philosophy, Australian National University

G.W. Mortimore
Adviser (Part-time Studies), Formerly Research Fellow in Philosophy, Australian National University

Contributors

P.H. Partridge
Professor of Social Philosophy, Australian National
University

R.S. Peters
Professor of Philosophy of Education, Institute of
Education, University of London

C.A. Tisdell
Professor of Economics, University of Newcastle,
New South Wales

O.R. Young
Professor of Government, University of Texas at Austin

Preface

Early in 1971 the Philosophy Department of the Research School of the Social Sciences in the Australian National University decided to sponsor a seminar in the philosophy of the social sciences, and a planning group hit on rationality as a promising theme. Though only six papers were contributed, they seemed interesting enough to warrant making them the nucleus of a larger collection, which the present editors were commissioned to prepare. The collection grew from six to fifteen papers, in part by the addition of new ones contributed at our invitation by four social scientists and philosophers from overseas, in part by splitting and expanding the original six. Of the present contributors, two have held visiting fellowships in the ANU; all but two of the remainder are (or were until recently) faculty members of the ANU. Because we were able to work so closely with most of our fellow contributors, we could hope to achieve an integrated, structured collection, organized around certain key ideas, rather than be content with a parcel of uncoordinated odds and ends. There were, of course, disagreements between editors and authors on substantive questions that could not be resolved; the reader will discover these for himself. Nevertheless, the editors wish to record their appreciation of the patience and good-humoured tolerance exhibited by their colleagues, both local and across the world, in the face of what must sometimes have appeared to be pernickety fault-finding or impertinent invasions of authorial prerogative.

While conscious of the need to avoid tiresome repetition, we have aimed to make each paper self-contained, to the extent at least that a reader interested in the particular field that it surveyed could profit from it without having to read all the preceding ones first. Where reference to another paper would help him, an indication appears either in the text or in the notes. Should these prove inadequate, the selective reader is recommended to go to the Index, which will help him to track down a technical term not fully explained at the point he is at, or assist him in following up a topic treated in several papers.

Nevertheless, because the collection is conceived as a structured whole, the papers will make better sense if read in order. The Introduction lays out certain key distinctions which form the integrating scheme. Chapters 1, 4, 7 and 11, written by one or both of the editors, provide the reader with a conceptual guide to the different parts of the collection.

Mr David Dumaresq helped to compile the Index, and, with Mrs Jan Murray, Mr Stephen Holt, and Mrs Jean Norman, gave invaluable help with the tiresome work of checking typescripts, quotations, sources, and proofs. Miss Isabel Sheaffe, Mrs Diane Schmidt, and Mrs Marie Adamson typed and re-typed our manuscript, patiently reaching for clean paper as they watched us ruin their elegant work with a foul scribble of afterthoughts. To all of these we wish to acknowledge our indebtedness.

Canberra   S.I. BENN
May 1974   G.W. MORTIMORE

Introduction

S.I. Benn and G.W. Mortimore

(a) This collection of papers is about the concepts of rationality social scientists use in formulating hypotheses, models, and explanations. Its aim is twofold: first, to display the variety of these concepts, and to analyse, compare, and relate them to one another; second, to show the different roles such concepts play, in theories of very different kinds over a wide variety of fields, and to assess the explanatory and predictive power (or, in the cases of two papers, the evaluative power) that a theory can draw from such concepts. Of course, these aims are not pursued independently; because scientists devise new concepts or modify those of ordinary discourse for the task in hand, one would expect to find that the differences between the concepts or models of rationality used in different areas of inquiry will correspond to the different tasks for which the theories themselves are designed. For instance, we shall find that rationality requirements may range from very strong conditions that one would expect to find fully satisfied only very rarely in real life, to conditions so weak that any intentional behaviour would satisfy them. Strong accounts tend to be used for theories intended to have strong explanatory and predictive power; they may be used perhaps to formulate a theory that sets up an ideal type to which actual conditions may approximate, but which they never fully instantiate. Weak concepts commonly figure in schemata wide-ranging in scope, but having little predictive or explanatory force precisely because they exclude very little observable behaviour; such schemata require to be supplemented, therefore, with further postulates to make them operationally effective.

(Such methodological differences are discussed, for instance, in Chapters 4, 5, 7 and 10.) Whether human beings have rational beliefs or behave rationally is not, therefore, a question that can be usefully asked out of theoretical context; for the answer will depend on the concept of rationality employed in the theory, and the concept itself on the theory's general structure and function.

This collection is not a random package. It has an underlying structure, corresponding to the different kinds of subject to which the rational/non-rational distinction can be applied. The papers in Parts One and Two deal respectively with the notions of rationality that are applied to an individual's beliefs and actions. Part Three deals with the rationality of persons in respect of both their actions and their beliefs. The last two papers, forming Part Four, consider the use of notions of rationality to assess social institutions, social choices, and societies themselves.

(b) Central to the collection is the notion of rationality as exhibited in an individual's holding a belief or performing an action for reasons that he correctly or reasonably regards as good reasons. There are, however, two related senses in which beliefs and actions can be called rational. One calls them rational in the first sense if one means that the individual believes or acts for reasons which he regards as good reasons. Rationality is then being ascribed to the individual, or rather, to the manner of his believing or acting. To call beliefs or actions rational in the second sense, however, is to judge that there are reasons to support them; this is the sense in which one says that something 'was, or would be, the rational thing to do (or believe)'. So one can intelligibly assess the rationality even of a belief that nobody has entertained or an act that has not been performed. Equally, an individual who holds a belief that is rational in this sense may not hold it in a manner that is rational; he may believe it for bad reasons, even though there are good reasons why it should be believed.

(c) With what are 'believing rationally' and 'acting rationally' (i.e. rationality in the first sense) contrasted? For simplicity's sake we shall refer, just for the moment, to action, though *mutatis mutandis* the argument applies equally to belief. There are three ways of expressing a contrast with 'rational action'; we may say it is 'not rational', 'non-rational', or 'irrational'.

An individual is said to act irrationally if he does something without a reason when it is thought that he should have had a reason; or if he does something for a bad reason; or if there was a good reason for doing something else that the agent knew about, or might reasonably have been expected to know about. To say of an act that it is irrational is to evaluate it as failing to come up to some standard of appropriateness. A person who acts irrationally is not acting well from *some* point of view.

To describe an act as 'non-rational' puts it, by contrast, outside the scope of rationality assessments; it is to say, as of an act done under deep hypnosis, that in the circumstances in which it was done, the subject either could not have had a reason for doing it, or that to assess it in terms of reasons is somehow out of place. To say that an action was 'not rational' means sometimes that it was irrational, sometimes non-rational.

The fact that 'rational' may be used evaluatively does not mean, of course, that there are no descriptive criteria for ascribing it; if that were the case, it would have no explanatory power at all. The social scientist who explains an action as rational is saying, at the least, that a certain kind of relation holds between the agent's action, his beliefs about his situation and options, and the end-states he wishes to bring about. Lurking behind any explanation having this form is the implication that, had the action not been related in this way, it would have been irrational. The concept of irrationality as such, however, has no explanatory or predictive power, precisely because there are so many ways of getting something wrong. So the procedure for dealing with apparent irrationality is either to revise the account of the agent's beliefs or his ends in order to re-establish the relationship of rationality, or to explain the deviant behaviour in non-rational terms—as caused, for instance, by unconscious drives, by hypnotic suggestion, or by physical disease. Consequently, though the concept of rationality figures large in explanatory theories in the social sciences, irrationality appears either diagnostically, to identify a malfunction requiring special explanation (see Chapter 13 for examples of this usage), or evaluatively, to characterize the inadequacy of actions, traits, or institutions.

(d) The only papers in this collection that are concerned specifically with the evaluative implications of ascriptions of rationality (contrasted with irrationality) are Chapters 14 and 15, which discuss the rationality of social institutions, social decision processes, and social choices. In the kinds of discussion with which these papers deal, to say of an institution that it is not rational is almost always to condemn it. But there are other papers, too, that have a more oblique bearing on the evaluative uses of 'rationality'. For instance, the reluctance of some anthropologists to make intercultural comparisons of rationality (see Chapter 3) is prompted in part by the belief that such comparisons are not simply neutral descriptions of cultural traits; because these anthropologists believe that there are no culturally-independent standards of rationality, they hold that such comparisons really amount to appraisals of one culture by the standards of another. Again, Chapters 11 and 12 both concern themselves with the question whether rational traits are, in some sense, natural to man, or constitute the highest stage of human development.

(e) A fundamental distinction that crops up in many of these papers is that between epistemic and practical rationality. Epistemic rationality is exhibited only in belief. The standards of epistemic rationality can be understood to depend on a conception of the proper epistemic concerns for a credent—the concern to believe what is true and to avoid false belief, and the concern to understand. Thus, on one common account of epistemic rationality, the rational man's reasons for belief must bear on the truth of his beliefs and provide a justification for them: a paradigm instance of epistemic rationality, on this view, is a belief validly inferred from other rationally held beliefs. The conception of the proper epistemic end in complex activities like the natural sciences may, however, be spelt out as the properties desirable in a theory—for example, that it should explain phenomena, solve theoretical problems, bring a wide range of diverse phenomena within one explanatory system, and so on. And, as we shall see, in one account of epistemic rationality the concern for truth is played down and replaced by an emphasis on avoiding theories which cannot survive tests.

The notion of practical rationality can be best understood perhaps as a component of the ordinary notion of rationality in action. The notion of rationality in action is a complex one which embraces three requirements: that the agent acted on beliefs (his reasons for action), that his beliefs were rational, and that his reasons for action were good reasons. We shall say that an agent exhibits practical rationality if he satisfies the last condition. In deciding whether a man's reasons were good ones, we may require (i) that the beliefs on which he acted were true and (ii) that, given his beliefs, he had reasons for action sufficient to pick out *this* action as the one *to be done*. Only the second requirement, of course, is a requirement of rationality; and this we shall say is the basic requirement of practical rationality.

The practical rationality exhibited by an agent does not require, therefore, that the beliefs on which he acted be either rational or true. It depends on whether he acted for reasons which were good, in the sense of satisfying requirement (ii) above. Or, to put it another way, it depends on how far he acted out of a belief that his action was better, in terms of his ends, than any of the alternatives. We shall use 'x was the best of the alternatives' and 'there were good reasons for choosing x' interchangeably.

A paradigm of a reason for action is a proposition asserting a relationship between an agent's ends, i.e. the states of affairs he is disposed to pursue, and the action he performs; and the standard instance of a good reason for action is that the action will produce a better outcome, in terms of his ends, than any alternative. Much of Chapters 4 and 7 are concerned with the possibility of unpacking this notion into a set of canons for appraising an agent's reasons for action. Whether there can be good practical reasons of other kinds— for instance, that an action conforms to a norm—is a subject of controversy. Controversial, too, is the question whether there are substantive limitations on the content of the ends it is rational to pursue. If not, practical rationality must be a purely formal notion relating the agent's choice to his ends irrespective of their content. The models of rational action discussed in Chapters 7–10 consist of a set of conditions for formal practical rationality supplemented by substantive restrictions on the content of the agent's ends which are simply stipulated. Chapter 11 explores the general question whether there are any restrictions on the ends it is *rational* to pursue.

A further controversial question is whether practical rationality can be exhibited in a person's believing something to be the case. For that depends on whether beliefs are thought to be within a person's control; if one can *decide* what to believe, then one can have reasons that are not epistemic reasons for choosing between beliefs. So one might choose to believe *p* if that relieves one's anxiety—and if relieving one's anxiety ranks high among one's ends, it could be practically rational to believe *p* for that reason, however epistemically irrational it may be. Of course, believing *p* may be practically irrational, too, if one's anxieties are well-founded, and there is some course one can take to avert the disaster that would occur if *not-p* were the case. For then to believe *p* would prevent one's taking precautions. But if there is nothing one can do, and if one is indeed able to choose what to believe, choosing the epistemically irrational belief might be practically rational.

It will be clear from this discussion that the distinction between epistemic and practical rationality is not the same as that between rationality in belief and rationality in action. It is true that when one talks about rationality in belief, it is usually with reference to epistemic rationality, but our example above is an illustration of another possibility; and some anthropologists try to save the rationality of other cultures by explaining epistemically irrational beliefs as practically rational given the credents' ends. Examples of such arguments are discussed by Barry Maund in Chapter 2.

Just as discussion of rationality in belief generally centres on epistemic rationality, theoretical discussion of rationality in action generally centres on practical rationality. The ordinary concept of rational action is, it is true, a complex one that includes the condition that the action be grounded on epistemically rational beliefs. For reasons discussed, however, in Chapters 4 and 7, theories in the social sciences that operate with more or less technical accounts of rationality to explain individuals' actions, or social phenomena like market prices that result from the interaction of individuals' actions, commonly omit the condition that agents act on rational beliefs.

(f) Some social scientists—many historians, for instance—work with rationality requirements no different from, and no more precise than, those of ordinary discourse. However, technical accounts, particularly of rationality in action, figure prominently in theoretical explanations and predictions of economic behaviour; and analogues of the technical models elaborated by economists have been devised for use in a number of other fields (Chapters 7–10 deal with economic and analogous models). These accounts may attempt to spell out the criteria implied in the ordinary notion as standardly employed, as a set of precisely formulated requirements. This process itself necessarily results in a conceptual change, since the ordinary notion is unlikely to be tidy and coherent enough to yield the determinate and unambiguous inferences that the social theorist is looking for. Indeed, the interests of theory-construction may lead him to disregard altogether certain ordinary requirements where this will provide a theory capable of being applied more widely. We have already noted that some technical notions omit epistemic requirements in this way.

Another feature of technical notions of rationality in action is their tendency to stipulate among their requirements special restrictions on what are admissible as ends. These may be very general: a common condition restricts the rational agent's ends to some valued future state that his action is designed to bring about, thereby ruling out not only purely expressive acts, but actions prompted by normative considerations. Or the restrictions may be quite specific, such as, that an entrepreneur be deemed rational only if he is aiming to maximize his profits, or a voter if he is aiming to elect a government whose policies will benefit him (see the discussion of Anthony Downs's theory of democracy in Chapter 10).

To avoid misunderstanding, the point needs to be made that none of these papers is concerned with the degree of rationality that social scientists themselves exhibit or might aspire to in constructing theories, observing human behaviour, or advising governments. The difficulties that social scientists may have in preserving their objectivity, and the problems of defining conditions for epistemic rationality in fields where the topics studied are not only ideologically highly charged, but where, according to some writers, no observation could be impersonal—such matters are dealt with at most incidentally. This book is about the concepts of rationality that social scientists use, not about the degree of rationality they can, or might achieve.

Bibliography

Each essay in the collection has a bibliography relating specifically to its own subject matter. The following is a selection of works providing a more general background to the philosophy of the social sciences, or to the analysis of the concept of rationality. Works marked with an asterisk have useful bibliographies.

BENNETT, J. (1964), *Rationality*, London.

BORGER, R. and CIOFFI, F. (eds) (1970), *Explanation in the Behavioural Sciences*, Cambridge.

*BRODBECK, M. (ed.) (1968), *Readings in the Philosophy of the Social Sciences*, New York.

BROWN, R. (1963), *Explanation in Social Science*, London.

DEARDEN, R.F., HIRST, P.H. and PETERS, R.S. (eds) (1972), *Education and the Development of Reason*, London, Part 2—'Reason'.

EDGLEY, R. (1969), *Reason in Theory and Practice*, London.

EMMET, D. and MACINTYRE, A. (eds) (1970), *Sociological Theory and Philosophical Analysis*, London.

GIBSON, Q. (1960), *The Logic of Social Enquiry*, London.

*KRIMERMAN, L.I. (ed.) (1969), *The Nature and Scope of Social Science: a Critical Anthology*, New York.

LUKES, S. (1970), 'Some problems about rationality', in Wilson, B.R. (ed.), *Rationality*, Oxford.

NAGEL, E. (1961), *The Structure of Science*, London, Chapters 13–16.

NATANSON, M. (ed.) (1963), *Philosophy of the Social Sciences: a Reader*, New York.

PETERS, R.S. (1971), 'Reason and passion', in *Royal Institute of Philosophy Lectures, vol. IV, 1969–70,—The Proper Study*, London.

RICHARDS, D.A.J. (1971), *A Theory of Reasons for Action*, Oxford.

*RYAN, A. (ed.) (1973), *Philosophy of Social Explanation*, London.

STRETTON, H. (1969), *The Political Sciences*, London.

TOULMIN, S. (1972), *Human Understanding*, vol. I., Oxford.

Part One
Rationality in belief

1

Rationality in belief

G.W. Mortimore and J.B. Maund*

A Introduction

This paper will be concerned with belief, in the very broad sense which embraces religious convictions, 'common-sense' beliefs about the natural and social world, business expectations, and the acceptance of a theory by a scientist. Admittedly, in accepting a theory a scientist's epistemic attitude may be more tentative than *accepting as true*; nevertheless it will be convenient to use 'belief' to cover such cases.

Concerns with rationality in belief are broadly of two kinds. The social scientist may be concerned to characterize and explain rationality in belief as an individual or cultural trait. Examples are Piaget's developmental account of rationality in belief,[1] and anthropologists' accounts of the degrees of rationality in belief to be found in non-European cultures[2] (discussed by R.S. Peters and J.B. Maund respectively in Chapters 12 and 2). Alternatively, the social scientist may be interested in characterizing and explaining individual beliefs; and here he may be concerned with any of three questions. He may be interested in how individuals *extend their range of beliefs*; how, for instance, an entrepreneur forms his expectations for the next planning period about likely market conditions and the consequences of certain pricing policies.[3] A social psychologist, by contrast, may be concerned with how individuals *adapt existing beliefs* which are perceived to conflict in some way with 'incoming' experience or information, with other

*Sections A and B are by G.W. Mortimore and Section C by J.B. Maund.

areas of belief, or with attitudes and actions.[4] Third, anthropologists are interested in how individuals *continue to hold beliefs* such as beliefs in witchcraft that survive unfulfilled prophecies and inefficacious spells.[5]

The aim of this paper is to explore the content of some historically prominent conceptions of rationality in belief that are methodologically relevant to the social scientist. We shall concentrate on the ways in which individual beliefs may be characterized and explained as rational. This will also provide the broad lines of an account of rationality in belief as an individual and cultural trait.

We can distinguish two ways in which we might assess the rationality of a man's beliefs. We can first assess the degree to which an individual has practical reasons for his activities in adapting or retaining his beliefs, and for holding such beliefs. Consider a man who, in order to preserve his reputation, desperately embraces a series of *ad hoc* hypotheses to save a theory that experiment after experiment suggests is false. Given his wish to preserve his reputation and his belief that his reputation hangs on the theory's survival, he has reasons to act and believe as he does. To be sure, they are not reasons which bear on the truth of his beliefs, for they are practical reasons—propositions about the relationship of activities and belief to his ends. The notion of a person's exhibiting practical rationality in choosing on the basis of good practical reasons will be discussed in Chapter 4. Some would object that the notion cannot happily be extended to belief, since an individual cannot choose to believe *p* rather than something else. We shall not pursue this issue, however, since our concern is with a second notion of rationality in belief—epistemic rationality. The degree of epistemic rationality which a man exhibits is wholly independent of the ends he may happen to have. The standards of epistemic rationality can, however, be understood to depend on a conception of the *proper* epistemic concerns for a credent—the concern to believe what is true and to avoid false belief, and the concern to understand.

We shall be considering two extremely influential accounts of epistemic rationality. On the justificationist view (discussed in section B), rationality in belief consists in believing for reasons which provide a certain kind of justification for the belief; the credent's reasons must bear on the truth of his beliefs, unlike the practical reasons considered above. On the falsificationist view (discussed in section C) rationality in belief consists in the credent's adopting towards his beliefs certain attitudes and policies.

B   The justificationist view

1   Reasons for belief

It will be convenient to expound the justificationist view as a view about rationality in *forming a belief*, either through extending one's range of beliefs or adapting an existing belief; the account can be readily extended to cover rationality in continuing to hold a belief. On the justificationist view, coming to believe *p* is taken to involve accepting *p as true*, and we assess the credent's rationality in coming to believe *p* by examining the reasons why he believes, and considering whether those reasons provide an epistemic *justification* for his belief. There has been continuing philosophical controversy over what kinds of reasons for belief do provide grounds for an ascription of epistemic rationality. In this paper I shall concentrate on an historically influential account with which the justificationist view is often associated.[6] On this account, there are two ways in which we can display the rationality of a credent's beliefs by characterizing the reasons why he believes.

(a) We may first indicate something about the credent's grasp of the status or content of *p*. Thus, we might attempt to show that his belief is rational by displaying the logically necessary truth of *p*. The least controversial case is that of a man's accepting a proposition such as 'Every triangle has three sides', which is true by virtue of the content or definition of its terms.

(b) Alternatively, we can describe the credent's reasons for believing *p*, referring to either of two kinds of reason:

   (i) *Experience*   Where an individual believes *p* because he has seen, heard, smelt, etc. that *p*, I shall say that he holds an experiential belief.

   (ii) *Antecedently believed propositions*   Where he believes *p* because he inferred *p* from *m* and *n*, I shall say that he holds an inferential belief.[7]

Experiential beliefs figure in a variety of ways in the social sciences. A social scientist who takes the description of what is there to be experienced as unproblematic may be interested in accounting for the degree of match with what has actually been experienced; or he may try to account for the degree of match between what has been experienced and what is reported by the observer. A typical experiment will explore the ways peer group pressures or expectations influence the sincere reports of individuals who have witnessed a violent crime.[8] Other studies are concerned with the ways the perceptions of individuals in a given culture are conditioned by their linguistic resources, norms, or background beliefs.[9]

Alternatively, the social scientist can explore the more radical question of whether what is there to be experienced is itself a function of such factors as the credent's conceptual scheme and resources, or his expectations. In Chapter 2, Barry Maund explores the view that radically different conceptual schemes structure different realities, and that beliefs formed within any given conceptual scheme are to be appraised only in terms of the reality associated with it. In this paper, however, I shall concentrate on the justificationist account of inferential belief and (in section C) Barry Maund will discuss the falsificationist alternative to it.

2 Rational inferential belief

On the justificationist view, to explain a belief in p as the outcome of a rational inference is to attribute the belief to:

(i) the credent's antecedently believing a set of propositions A (let us call this the credent's propositional base);

(ii) his grasping that A provides adequate support for p;

(iii) (an implication of (ii)) his grasping that A constitutes an adequate reason for believing p.

In characterizing his inference as rational, we also *endorse* his judgments under (ii) and (iii). For the belief to be rational, moreover, the beliefs in A must also be rational. This condition seems to threaten a regress. We will not here pursue the question of how the justificationist might terminate it; though one obvious possibility would be to require that the regress ends with a rational experiential belief.

The justificationist requirement outlined above, that the agent's reasons adequately support his belief, may seem to be too strict. For surely, it might be suggested, a man's belief in God may be rational even though the arguments that led him to that belief are invalid, as long as he has given adequate consideration to counter-arguments and as long as his logical errors are of a fairly sophisticated rather than an elementary kind. It seems that we need the looser condition that it was *reasonable* for him to regard his reasons for belief as good ones. I shall suggest, however, that there are advantages in conceiving of epistemic rationality more strictly than this—as requiring that the credent has made no error in regarding certain considerations as good reasons for belief. For we can then understand the standards for rationality *in belief* to embrace standards of both epistemic and practical rationality. Our standards for rationality in belief *are* less strict precisely because we allow that it may be practically rational for a credent to give less critical attention to counter-arguments than is necessary for full epistemic rationality. The looser condition that it be reasonable for him to regard his reasons for belief as good reasons is, then, sufficient condition for rational belief, though not for epistemic rationality, and the standards of reasonableness largely concern the degree to which a reasonable man can justifiably fall short of full epistemic rationality because of its costs in terms of time, energy, resources and foregone ends.

(a) Rational activity prior to belief

We cannot think of the standards of epistemic rationality as solely concerned with the degree of support given to propositions by antecedently accepted premises. They also demand, at least in cases of belief about fairly complex matters, a variety of activities (let us call them *research activities*) prior to the formation of belief:

(i) increasing the number of possibly relevant considerations which the credent has at his disposal—for example, by research, the collection of data, inference from what he already knows or believes;

(ii) expanding his view of the possible relevance of such considerations—for example, by informing himself of arguments which have been advanced on the question;

(iii) widening the range of propositions which are candidates for belief—for example, by considering alternative positions or constructing and exploring hypotheses.

Consider the entrepreneur attempting to form rational expectations about the consequences of alternative pricing or investment policies. His research activities in seeking and processing information and arguments bearing on his problem will determine the content of the considerations from which his belief is inferred, and the manner in which those considerations influence his belief. The activities themselves will be determined by (i) the level of certainty in expectations which the entrepreneur aims to develop, and (ii) his conception, as an epistemically rational man, of the activities and the range of considerations which would make it rational to entertain expectations with that level of certainty.

To exhibit the fullest, most active kind of epistemic rationality, then, a man must work with a set of norms that prescribe:

(i) the kinds of propositional base which, in the context of the credent's preceding research activities, can license inference to conclusions with varying degrees of certainty;

(ii) the kinds of research activities which are necessary to provide propositional bases of different kinds.

The precise content of these norms will depend on a variety of factors—on the individual's conception of truth, his beliefs about human capacities to attain it, and his beliefs about the possibilities of error given the complexity of the matters on which beliefs are sought.

As we have seen, the degree of epistemic rationality that an individual displays may be limited by practical considerations. The costs, in terms of his other ends, of information-search may make it practically rational for him to engage in a highly restricted search. Similarly, wishful thinking or a desire to protect his personal prestige may lead him to concentrate his investigations on certain options when there is no epistemic reason to believe that they warrant particularly intensive investigation. However, it is possible to overestimate the ways in which practical reasons can reduce a credent's epistemic rationality. For instance, a decision-maker may not set out to form expectations with a predetermined level of certainty, and then put himself in a position rationally to form such expectations; he may have the more modest aim of narrowing uncertainty so far as he can without undue cost. His restricted research activities will not then count against his epistemic rationality, provided the certainty with which he invests his expectations does not exceed what his epistemic situation warrants.

Most cases of belief-formation do not, of course, involve such activities. Most inferences are either simple responses to a small range of propositions forced on the credent's attention; or are the outcome of a brief selection of a few conspicuous considerations from the credent's propositional resources. In these cases the activity of the credent is minimal or non-existent; at the extreme he can be understood as passively responding to stimuli. But while less common, cases in which the credent is active in the ways described above are significant in the sociology and history of science, and in those areas of the social sciences which concern themselves with complex decision-making.

Theoretical accounts in economics of the influence of belief-activities on the expectations of economic agents are still relatively undeveloped. For one thing, economic models of the rational agent traditionally assumed complete knowledge about the outcomes of alternative decisions, or, at least, complete knowledge of the probability distribution of those outcomes. Further, entrepreneurial decisions are widely based on rules of thumb such as cost-plus pricing which do not require the activities we have been discussing. Where decisions can be treated as based on inferential beliefs, writers have been disposed to treat the beliefs as more or less passive responses to a limited range of considerations—as expectations of price levels in the future might be based on a fairly un-reflective extrapolation of recent price levels. There is, however, a growing body of work on what determines information-search prior to decision, and on rational search methods;[10] and theorists are developing models of entrepreneurs' decision-making activities which postulate a degree of epistemic rationality modified and limited by practical rationality, and by such other influences as the conspicuousness of certain alternatives.[11]

(b) The inference

An adequate account of the justificationist notion of a rational inferential belief thus requires attention to the research activities which precede belief-formation; and to complete the account of rational belief-formation, we need to examine how a rational credent infers his new belief from the range of considerations which finally influence it. As we noted earlier, if the credent is responding passively to information-stimuli that force themselves upon his attention, or is doing nothing more than attend to a limited range of considerations, an account of how he infers his beliefs from such material can be sufficient to account for them. These are the types of cases with which social psychologists working on inferential belief are mainly concerned.[12]

On the justificationist account, a credent's belief in p is a rational inference from a set of propositions A if (i) we attribute his belief to his regarding A, at some level of consciousness, as grounds for p, and (ii) we are prepared to endorse this as a reasonable, if not true, judgment. Is this notion of any use to the social psychologist attempting to understand belief-formation and change? The extreme form of a negative answer would run as follows: All that is required for a theoretical understanding of belief is the formulation of 'mental processing rules' which accurately characterize the ways in which individuals move from a set of propositions to a further proposition. The notion of regarding a consideration as a reason or ground adds nothing to the explanatory or predictive force of a theoretical account. We will find in fact that the rules governing belief-formation do not coincide with the rules of formal logic; in any case, it is not the business of the social psycho-logist to endorse or reject the rules which govern systematic pro-cesses of belief-formation.

Robert Abelson suggests in Chapter 3 that many theories of belief can get by happily with a concept of 'subjective rationality', where a credent is subjectively rational if his beliefs can be under-stood as the outcome of the application of predictable mental processing rules which may happen not to conform to the rules of formal logic. Similarly, these theories need only a notion of 'psychological implication' where 'imply' means only 'initiate cognitive processes tending over time to produce...'.[13]

It is worth commenting first on Abelson's contention that the rules of belief-formation he and his colleagues have isolated do not coincide with the rules of formal logic. The rules which Abelson ultimately states turn out to be general statements about the world: a statement about the tendency of love to generate romantic rivalry is said to underpin the disposition of credents to move from 'Joe loves Ann' and 'Ann loves Harry' to 'Joe hates Harry'.[14] But now, it seems, this *can* be represented as an application of a rule of formal logic, for the generalization about the origins of romantic rivalry can be readily understood as a background premise in the credent's argument. Such theories of subjective rationality thus turn out to be theories of rational inference from a series of general propositions about the way the world is.

Still, it might be said, whether the rules in question are those of classical logic or not, all the theoretician needs for his account of belief-formation is the notion of a mental processing rule. The burden of this assertion is that it is not of central importance to the theoretician whether:

(i) the credent regards the considerations which generated his belief as reasons for belief;

(ii) the mental processing rules do or do not coincide with 'the rules of logic'.

Let us examine each of these contentions in turn.

Consider a typical experiment designed to elicit *associative* processes of belief-formation, in which test subjects evaluate a passage more favourably when they think it was written by a writer of high repute. The associative explanation is that the prestige of the author gets transferred by association to the passage. This is surely different from explaining the belief as the outcome of an inference involving the background generalization that the works of writers of high repute are likely to be of high quality. In the second explanation, the credent's belief is the outcome of his regarding the proposition about the passage's authorship as having a bearing on the truth of the proposition about the quality of the passage. Yet the 'mental processing rule' is the same in both cases. This distinction is surely important; for once we attribute a credent's belief to his view of the support relationships between propositions, we locate it within a complex web of norms of belief. And we attribute to the credent himself the disposition to regard his own reasons for belief as reasons for anyone in his situation to believe as he does. This is a disposition manifested in the range of normative activities which include justification, criticism and advice.

Turning to contention (ii) above, does it matter to the theoretician whether the credent's mental processing rules coincide with what the theoretician regards as *the* acceptable canons of inference—say, the classical canons of deductive logic? The logician's accounts of these canons do, of course, provide the theoretician with useful bodies of 'mental processing rules'; and the hypothesis that these rules govern individuals' inferences and beliefs can be experimentally tested. Thus, social psychologists have sought to determine how far inferences about the probabilities of outcomes satisfy the axioms laid down by probability theorists. But the question at issue is whether it is ever important to the descriptive or explanatory force of a theoretical account to identify the credent's mental processing rules as *the* rules of logic. Another way of putting this question is to ask whether it can ever be important to a theoretical account to decide that the agent's reasons for belief are *logically good* reasons.

It might be suggested that if the agent's reasons are logically good ones the explanation of his belief is complete; whereas belief for no reasons, or for bad reasons, poses a further explanatory question about the factors which inhibited or interfered with the exercise of epistemic rationality. On this view, there is a presumption that it is normal to operate according to 'the laws of logic' and that deviations from these rules require explanation. This raises two questions:

I Does a child develop a grasp of the central norms of logic as a consequence of certain very basic and pervasive features of his social situation and experience, so that, other things being equal, individuals will develop a grasp of these norms? Richard Peters sketches the outlines of such an account in Chapter 12, in the course of a discussion of Piaget's theory of epistemic rationality. If such an account could be satisfactorily developed, it would follow that systematic deviations from the norms of logic would require special explanation. It would therefore be very much to the theoretical point to establish whether an individual's reasons for belief were good ones.

II To what degree can we suppose every individual to have a grasp of the basic norms of logic? Some philosophers have recently discussed the links between the grasp of certain basic logical norms and the conditions for the successful use of language.[15] If the use of language itself presupposes a sense of certain fundamental logical normative demands, then a failure to conform to their requirements in inference and belief would require special explanation in terms of inhibiting or interfering factors; and it would again be of theoretical importance to establish whether an individual's beliefs did or did not conform to the laws of logic.

3 Deviations from epistemic rationality

According to the justificationist account expounded in section 2, a rational inferential belief is one held for reasons which the credent reasonably regards as good ones, having engaged in a range of activities appropriately designed to provide him with good reasons. This does not imply, however, that the justificationist account cannot accommodate the ordinary notion that there can be degrees of rationality in belief falling short of full rationality. The beliefs of someone who carried through some but not all of the activities necessary to forming a rational belief on a complicated matter would not be thought wholly irrational. And the grounds from which his beliefs were inferred may lend them some, even though not adequate, support. So the justificationist could say, of the experiment described in Robert Abelson's paper in which credents generalized from a biased sample (pp. 81–2), that the instances lent some support to their beliefs, but not enough to make them fully rational.

It should be clear, then, that the pervasiveness of deviations from full rationality does not imply, as many social psychologists seem to think, that the justificationist concept of epistemic rationality is heuristically expendable. For their explanatory postulates may in fact attribute only weak rationality to credents, as in the experimental situation referred to above. Thus, the mental processing rules detected by the social psychologist in such cases can be understood as conditions of standard epistemic rationality (on the justificationist account), albeit of a rather weak kind.

Deviations from canons of acceptable inference may be understood in either of two ways. On the one hand, they might be treated as pervasive forms of fallacious reasoning, representing a widespread sub-culture of deviant logical norms, governing what count as reasons for belief.[16] On the other hand, they can be understood as the result of factors interfering with standard logical inference. Thus, recent work on propaganda has explored the ways in which the order of presentation of arguments affects belief-formation,[17] or the ways in which an individual's desire to preserve his self-esteem influences his causal ascriptions (as experiments described by Abelson in Chapter 3 suggest). In the latter case, as we have seen, the credent has a practical reason for belief.

4 Beliefs, attitudes and actions

Much of the work Abelson discusses is concerned with the inter-action between an individual's beliefs, attitudes and actions. According to the balance principle, for instance, individuals will not believe that objects which they evaluate positively are 'bonded' to objects they evaluate negatively. Thus, in the Fenwick experiment described by Abelson, one group of experimental subjects was disposed to accept the proposition that modern art exhibitions help rather than damage a store's sales, thereby bringing into balance their positive evaluative attitudes to a manager who was planning such an exhibition, the art exhibition itself and the pros-pective increase in sales (pp. 65–7).

But while the balance principle covers such cases, does it explain them? We might explore two underlying explanations of the experimental subjects' disposition to believe. We might take liking or positively evaluating something to be an instance or expression of a pro-attitude, and then understand having a pro-attitude to something as conceptually linked with the pursuit of certain ends—for example, promoting the well-being of the object of the pro-attitude. In so far as one evaluates the manager and the art exhibition positively, one wants them to do well. Believing that the manager's exhibition would promote sales would then appear to be a case of wishful thinking—believing that what one wants to be the case is the case. Alternatively, we might explain the subjects' beliefs in terms of the background generalization that successful managers are not likely to devise unsuccessful sales promotions. In this case, their beliefs would manifest a degree of epistemic rationality.

The social psychologist will not, of course, ask these further explanatory questions as long as he is satisfied to have identified a mental processing rule which accurately characterizes the systematic process of belief-formation he is studying. He *cannot* ask them without deploying the distinction between practical rationality and epistemic rationality (on the justificationist account), and without taking account of the possibility that beliefs can exhibit a weak degree of epistemic rationality. Unwillingness to operate with these conceptual resources can thus lead the theorist to ignore real explanatory questions, and to give a uniform theoretical account to cases which require radically different explanations.

C   Falsificationism and methodology

Quite a different approach, one which appears to challenge the justificationist account of rational belief, is presented by Popper[18] and a circle of neo-Popperians, the most prominent of whom are Lakatos[19] and Feyerabend.[20] According to the Popperian account the distinguishing mark of the rational believer is the attitude or policy he adopts towards the theories which he believes or accepts. The set of policies and attitudes advocated by Popper and his followers commit one to such activities as making bold theories, expressing one's theories in a highly falsifiable form, subjecting them to criticism and attempts to falsify them, seeking alternative theories and examining rival explanations. We shall refer to this as falsificationism. Popper argues that there has been no shortage within science (and non-science) of well-confirmed theories. By appending *ad hoc* hypotheses to our theories to accommodate any phenomena which apparently do not conform, we shall have little difficulty in confirming almost any theory. What is required for a scientific theory to be truly rational is that it can be accepted in a truly rational way, i.e. that it be subjected to attempts to falsify it.[21] In the Popperian account, to accept a theory is to make a decision about its suitability for a certain purpose, e.g. for being tested, for being persisted with as a working hypothesis, for use in the interpretation of experimental phenomena, for use in devising technological gadgetry, and so on. The Popperians try to dispense with acceptance *tout court*, not least because in this way they hope to avoid the knotty problems about the rationality of acceptance *tout court* raised by Hume's doubts about inductive inference.[22] The rational scientist is held to order different theories along scales of boldness, testability, and corroboration or falsification of predictions. On the basis of this ordering, he then decides whether to accept a theory for testing, whether to continue working with and exploring it, or whether to reject it.

It is thus possible to distinguish two types of rules in the Popperian methodology:

(a) rules governing policies and attitudes towards theories;

(b) criteria for the appraisal, i.e. for the acceptance and rejection, of theories: Are they bold? Do they lead to novel predictions? Have they been submitted to severe tests? Have they been falsified?

Lakatos has amended these criteria in an important way, emphasizing that rival theories are in competition.[23] So what is important in evaluating theories is their *comparative* boldness, novelty of prediction, and degree of corroboration. Because Lakatos's impressive studies represent a natural development of the basic Popperian framework, I shall concentrate on his exposition. Nevertheless, the account ought still to be called Popperian.

To evaluate properly the falsificationist account of rationality we shall need to examine separately: (i) the falsificationist *policy*, and its relationship to the qualities of theories which are taken to be rationally desirable; and (ii) the falsificationist standards for appraising theories.

1 The rationality of the falsificationist policy

In this section, I consider four questions about the rationality of falsificationist policies:

(a) How much of scientific activity would we need to call non-rational on the falsificationist account?

(b) Can the falsificationist policies be justified as tending to produce theories with the theoretical qualities which falsificationists value?

(c) Why are these theoretical qualities desirable?

(d) Can the falsificationist standards be applied without regard to the historical context?

(a) The methods employed by scientists

According to the Popperian account, the less than fully rational believer adopts the policy of merely seeking confirmation for his belief-system, by articulating, reforming, and extending it without questioning any of its basic assumptions or concepts. Yet, according to Thomas Kuhn,[24] in the periods between major theoretical upheavals, this is precisely the policy that scientists follow, instead of attempting to upset or falsify the belief-system in the way the Popperian model leads us to expect. Newtonian physics and quantum physics provide good examples of such periods. If we substitute for Kuhn's temporal dichotomy between revolutionary and normal science, an a-temporal characterization of different aspects or types of science, the Kuhnian account, though oversimplified, can be recognized as a worthwhile *description* of science as it is actually practised. It is especially relevant for us, however, because it provides an alternative to the policy advocated by Popper, and thus raises the question of what criteria may be used in the rational comparison of such different policies.

(b) Falsificationist policies and ends

As we have seen, the falsificationist methodology lays down rules of two types—those governing strategies to be adopted towards one's theories, and rules for the appraisal of theories. Are the former to be justified in terms of the latter, i.e. in terms of the theoretical ends or goals which the enquirer is pursuing?

Now the rules governing the rational strategy are not entirely independent of the rules of rational appraisal—for it is built into the falsificationist account that a theory's having been subject to the falsificationist strategy is one of the rationally desirable features of a theory. It is a truism, then, that following such a strategy would be a rational way of going about producing such a theory. Nevertheless there are other virtues that a rational theory ought to have—even on the falsificationist account. It seems important that it should explain phenomena and provide understanding, that it solve theoretical problems, that it bring a wide range of diverse phenomena within one explanatory system, that it does not generate further major problems, or false predictions. Are falsificationist policies necessarily the best way of producing theories with such qualities?

In some situations at least, a confirmatory policy could be the best way of achieving a scientist's theoretical goals. To develop an adequate explanatory system scientists may have to devote themselves to exploring one major belief-system rather than engage in controversy between rival belief-systems. In Ancient Greece, for example, there was no shortage of rival theories to explain the world: Plato, Aristotle, Thales, Anaxagoras, Anaximander, Pythagoras, Parmenides, Democritus and others developed major rival systems with varying degrees of explanatory adequacy. In this epoch there was considerable comparative criticism of rival theories; but it was not as fruitful as the post-Newtonian era when physicists worked to a large extent within the limits of the Newtonian framework.

(c) The ultimate falsificationist goal

According to the Popperian account, science is an activity of conjecture, hypothesizing, testing, conventional acceptance and tentative acceptance of theories. Why engage in it? To be sure the activity results in a range of theories which at any given end-point can be ordered and compared along several dimensions; but why should that ordering and comparison be of any greater merit than the orderings that might result from alternative methodologies? Are the falsificationist policies intended to bring the scientist closer to the truth?

There are two very different strands of thought in the Popperian position. First, by emphasizing method and policy the Popperians hope to sidetrack Humean doubts about inductive inference. If Hume is right, no claim about the truth of any scientific theory can be justified because it will involve inductive inference.[25] An account of scientific rationality that relates rationality not to claims about the truth of theories but instead (a) to claims about acceptance-for-a-purpose and (b) to attitudes and policies, will have a clear advantage. But on the other hand, the ordering of theories according to the Popperian methodology is also said to be related to their verisimilitude or nearness to truth. This statement involves a metaphysical claim; for we have no independent knowledge of the nearness to the ultimate truth of various scientific theories (and hence no way of checking on the statement that the Popperian methodology orders scientific theories along the dimension of verisimilitude). It is ironic that the Popperian account of methodology, which was meant to demarcate science from non-science, and in particular from metaphysics, itself rests on an implicit metaphysical assumption.

What is of particular importance for our purpose, however, is to see that the essential aim of the strategy recommended in the falsificationist methodology is to generate theories which have the best prospects of approaching the truth.

(d) Falsificationist standards and the historical context

In applying falsificationist standards, we surely need to consider the enquirer's policies in the light of the alternative theories which are conceptually available to him, bearing in mind that their range may be severely limited. There was certainly no effort on the part of physicists prior to the nineteenth century either to attempt to falsify the Euclidean physical geometry they used or to develop rival systems. But since it is at least plausible to say that it was conceptually impossible for physicists, equipped only with the concepts then available, to conceive of any alternative to Euclidean geometry, it could hardly have been irrational for them not to have attempted to develop one.

Perhaps, however, a person should be evaluated as displaying a lower degree of rationality to the extent to which he takes no steps to increase his conceptual resources and hence his conceptual options. However, there are constraints, outside a scientist's control, on his capacities to increase the number of his conceptual options. A thinker may, for example, be only able to develop an alternative to the prevailing conceptual scheme by incorporating elements taken from another discipline or field of study in which he is not an expert. Much of modern physics has required the prior development in pure mathematics of, for example, group and tensor theories. In the case of physical geometry, the development of alternatives to Euclidean geometry was possible only after independent logical-mathematical work in pure geometry—viz. the long sequence of studies in pure Euclidean geometry which culminated in the work of Riemann and Lobatchevsky.

Thus whether or not it is rational to attempt to falsify or develop alternatives to central and important elements in one's conceptual scheme will vary from one historical context to another. Nevertheless, the belief-system of a culture is rated the more rational for its having been subjected to a policy of falsification and comparison with rivals, and is the more rational, too, for having been subjected to either policy rather than to any other.

Such considerations suggest that a scientist, or a community of scientists, would be rational to follow a hybrid strategy that combines falsificatory and confirmatory policies. Lakatos attempts to describe the rules that would guide the composition of such a mixed strategy.[26] For Lakatos, the progress of science is marked by the successive rise and demise of research programmes. Each is said to have two constituents: a negative heuristic consisting of a set of assumptions and theories which one decides by fiat are to be left untouched by recalcitrant and falsifying phenomena; and a positive heuristic, consisting of statements specifying a range of hypotheses for study, a set of problems, and plausible types of solutions, which provides the resources for generating auxiliary saving hypotheses in the case of falsification.

Lakatos prescribes as rational the policy that one pursue a mixed strategy towards one's research programme while it is progressing: to make no attempt to falsify or revise the negative heuristic, whilst adopting a more standard falsificatory policy towards the contents of the positive heuristic. It is difficult, however, to determine when, according to Lakatos, it is rational to attempt to falsify the negative heuristic (i.e. to look for new research programmes). On the one hand he holds that it is rational for a scientist to persist with a programme even if there are phenomena which 'falsify' it, as long as the programme is progressing; and also that it is rational for a scientist to abandon a programme if it loses its progressiveness and stagnates. But on the other hand, if only these policies were followed, the proliferation of rival research programmes which is held by Lakatos to be both desirable and essential for scientific progress would not arise. In order to achieve this proliferation, some scientists at least, would need to introduce new research programmes before the established one had stagnated (i.e. while it is progressive).

We should therefore interpret Lakatos as prescribing as rational the policy of persisting with a research programme while it is progressing, while also recognizing that from the standpoint of the general advancement of scientific knowledge, a scientific community could be thought more rational if its organization and prevailing attitudes encouraged some scientists, but not all, to start looking for alternative paradigms even before the prevailing ones have well and truly stagnated. Hence the rationality of the organization of a scientific community could well depend on some scientists' disposition to explore new research programmes even when the old ones still have fruit to bear.

2 Rational appraisal of theories

(a) Rules of the falsificationist account

But do the rules of the falsificationist account provide criteria hard and sharp enough for the clear-cut evaluation of theories? For the selection of theories within a research programme, criteria are specified for three sorts of situation: selecting a theory (i) as worthy of testing; (ii) as worthy of being persisted with even in the face of falsifying phenomena and awkward problems; and (iii) as worthy of being eliminated in favour of a rival. With respect to research programmes analogous sorts of situation arise, but while the falsificationist account offers reasonably sharp criteria for evaluating theories within research programmes, the criteria for selecting and eliminating research programmes themselves waver between vagueness and excessive strictness. The question of the rational elimination of research programmes is important not least because it is by such means that the important set of theories composing the negative heuristic (i.e. the set of presupposed and assumed background theories) are eliminated and altered.

According to Lakatos a research programme supersedes and therefore ought to replace a rival if it is theoretically and empirically progressive while the other is stagnating. In practice, however, one is seldom confronted with a choice between research programmes one of which is flourishing and the other completely stagnant. Often each programme has both its special troubles and its special triumphs, and different scientists may assess their relative significance differently. Or different scientists may make different overall assessments of the respective merits of competing research programmes. Thus, in most situations Lakatos's set of criteria simply cannot be applied for the elimination of research programmes. But what *are* the criteria offered for rational choice in such situations? It is instructive to consider one of Lakatos's own examples.[27] In the case of the chemist Prout who proposed a bold hypothesis to support his faltering research programme, the

27

majority of the best scientists who rejected Prout's programme are taken to task by Lakatos for being too rash in their rejection. Prout's rationality, by contrast, is applauded; yet the reason why Prout is praised as rational in contrast to someone like Lorentz with his ether-dependent relativity theory, seems to be that eventually the former's hypothesis triumphed, i.e. it 'came good', while the latter's has remained barren. But at the time that Prout advanced his hypothesis, there seemed no way of telling whether it would be fruitful or not. It would seem that, in most actual situations of choice between rival research programmes, Lakatos's account either allows any choice to be 'rational', or implies that which is the rational choice depends on the eventual success or failure of the respective programmes. In either case, this account of rationality seems useless for assessing scientific theories. The liberality of the first interpretation seems in addition to abandon falsificationism. It is remarkable that this same issue stands out in the work of another historian of science, Thomas Kuhn.

(b) Kuhn and irrationalism

Thomas Kuhn's work has been widely interpreted as denying that scientists can have reasons for selecting one from a range of alternative theories in periods of revolutionary science.[28] In a period of normal science, the community of scientists can be characterized as sharing a set of values, standards, and presuppositions which determine the set of interesting problems to be studied, the range of plausible hypotheses from which selection is to be made and the criteria of adequacy of evidence. These scientists share a common conception of what is a good type of hypothesis and of what is a good reason for accepting a hypothesis. Revolutionary science, on the other hand, marks a transition period during which the old set of values, standards, and presuppositions (what Kuhn calls 'a paradigm') comes under challenge. When it is replaced by a new set we have embarked on a new period of normal science.

Particularly controversial in this account is Kuhn's explanation of the change from one paradigm to another. Some of his remarks suggest that he takes the change to be non-rational. Choice between rival paradigms is seen as different from choice between minor theories in a period of normal science. To explain the major change, it seems we must refer to non-rational or irrational factors: mob-psychology, authority-figures, persuasion (pragmatic and rhetorical rather than logical), and so on.

At other times, however, and especially in his later comments, Kuhn appears to be saying that the change between rival paradigms is rational and can be explained in terms of the reasons held by the participants to the dispute: what distinguishes the dispute from a standard dispute in normal science is that the values and standards appealed to in the revolutionary period are more like those employed in philosophical disputes than those employed in normal scientific disputes. So there are good reasons for theory choice, 'reasons of exactly the kind standard in philosophy of science: accuracy, scope, simplicity, fruitfulness, and the like'.[29] Furthermore, scientists share these values but 'nevertheless make different choices in the same concrete situation', since different people may place different relative weight on different values and, more importantly, 'simplicity, scope, fruitfulness, and even accuracy can be judged quite differently (which is not to say they may be judged arbitrarily) by different people'.[30]

Although Kuhn has been severely criticized by Popper and Lakatos, this particular feature of his account, viz. the indeterminacy of rational criteria in situations of revolutionary science, is compatible with the falsificationist account. For Kuhn's 'revolutionary science' situation corresponds to Lakatos's situation of choice between rival research programmes, and it seems that in the latter situation criteria cited by Kuhn are employed: simplicity, scope, fruitfulness. This comes out both in Lakatos's emphasis on the need for the scientist's conventional acceptance of theories as background knowledge and by his admission that the falsificationist rules for appraisal of theories provide hard, determinate criteria for theory-choice only in the special circumstance that one theory is a sub-theory of the other.

3 Rationality and the history and sociology of science

The issues raised in the discussion of Kuhn and Lakatos raise some important questions for those interested in the history and sociology of science. In an illuminatingly titled article,[31] 'Logic of discovery or psychology of research?', Kuhn writes of a major unsolved problem, that of explaining why science—our surest example of sound knowledge—progresses as it does. In discussing the nature of this explanation he writes:[32]

> the explanation must, in the final analysis, be psychological or
> sociological. It must, that is, be a description of a value system,
> an ideology, together with an analysis of the institutions
> through which that system is transmitted and enforced.
> Knowing what scientists value, we may hope to understand
> what problems they will undertake and what choices they will

29

make in particular circumstances of conflict. I doubt that there is another sort of answer to be found.

Lakatos and Popper, on the other hand, seem to regard their accounts of the methodology of science (the logic of discovery) as unrelated to the psychology and sociology of knowledge and indeed write of the latter fields of study in almost contemptuous terms.[33] Their disagreement with Kuhn, however, may be more apparent than real. For a lot depends on just what counts as psychology or sociology of knowledge; what Lakatos, in particular, attacks is one way of doing sociology (he cites the sociological observer at a scientific seminar who pays attention not to what is said but rather to the seating arrangements, the frequency and duration of speeches, the mode of talking, etc.). But this is not the only way of doing sociology. Winch, for example, in his *Idea of a Social Science*,[34] argues for a sociology in which one makes intelligible the practices and beliefs of a social community only by seeing the point of the rules followed by the people in the community. The observer must see the point of an activity by becoming a participant or rather by becoming one who is capable of participating—he can understand the distinctions made, the categories employed, the judgments made 'from the inside'. Such an internal sociology contrasts sharply with the externalist one attacked by Lakatos, but may very well meet Kuhn's requirements. In other words, explaining how science progresses may very well require, as Kuhn suggests, a psychological and sociological study of what scientists do—but that study itself may only be fruitful if one has the understanding of the point of the scientists' activities, an understanding which is provided by the work of Lakatos and Popper on the methodology of science.

But even on Lakatos's and Popper's account, the methodology of science is sufficient to explain neither the decisions that scientists do take in such situations, nor, therefore, the course that science subsequently follows. For according to their account, if science is to proceed, a large proportion of scientists' decisions must be taken in situations in which either (a) the right decision is conventional or (b) there is no one decision which is 'the' rational decision; rather there are a variety of decisions each of which may be reasonable. So if we are to restrict the term 'rational' to the set of criteria and rules described in the methodology, the explanation of the progress of science will, *in part*, need to have recourse to non-rational factors.

To avoid misunderstanding, it should be stressed that to say that an explanation of a paradigm-choice may require recourse to non-rational factors, is not incompatible with saying that the scientist has reasons for adopting (or rejecting) a paradigm. But since the reasons cannot be sufficient or conclusive for a uniquely rational choice, the account of rationality cannot explain a decision between two paradigms as *the* rational decision to make in the situation. So though a given scientist's reasons may still figure in an explanation of a paradigm change, we may need a further explanation of why, for instance, Einstein took cognizance of one set of reasons in choosing an ether-dispensing relativity and Lorentz took cognizance of a different set, in choosing an ether-assuming relativity theory. An adequate explanation would not exclude reasons; but it would have to include other factors besides reasons.

Notes

1 Piaget, J. and Inhelder, B. (1958), Ginsburg, H. and Opper, S. (1969).
2 Wilson, B.R. (1970).
3 Ozga, S.A. (1965).
4 Abelson, R.P. (1968).
5 Wilson, B.R. (1970).
6 Hume, D. (1964), Passmore, J.A. (1968), Flew, A.G.N. (1961), Price, H.H. (1969).
7 It will be apparent that the notion of a rational inferential belief leaves out of account the case where a man does not come to believe *p* by a process of rational inference, but later appreciates that *p* can be inferred from and justified in terms of *m* and *n*, and continues to believe *p* because he sees that *p* follows from *m* and *n*. The account of rational inferential belief can, however, be easily adapted to cover such cases.
8 Graham, D. (1962).
9 Tajfel, H. (1968).
10 Koopman, B.O. (1956), Lamberta, D.M. (1971).
11 Cyert, R.M. and Welsch, L.A. (1970).
12 Abelson, R.P. *et al.* (1968), Festinger, L. (1957) and Festinger, L. (1964). See also the bibliography to Zajonc, R.B. (1968).
13 Abelson, R.P. (1968), p. 133.
14 Ibid., p. 135.
15 Lukes, S. (1970), Hollis, M. (1970).
16 Abelson, R.P. and Rosenberg, M.J. (1958), Henle, M. (1962). See also the bibliography to Johnson, D.M. (1968).
   It should be noted that these deviant mental processing rules cannot be represented as background world views or ideologies as Abelson suggests (see Abelson, R.P. (1968) and pp. 71–2 above)
17 Hovland, C.I. *et al.* (1953) and Hovland, C.I. (1957).
18 Popper, K.R. (1959) and (1968).
19 Lakatos, I. (1968), (1970a) and (1970b).
20 Feyerabend, P.K. (1965).

21 The implications of falsificationism for anthropology are discussed in Jarvie, I.C. (1964), pp. 131–52.
22 In section 1(c) I express doubts about the consistency of the Popperian account on this matter.
23 See Lakatos, I. (1970a) and (1970b).
24 Kuhn, T. (1962).
25 See Stove, D. (1973) for a recent criticism of Hume's sceptical argument on induction.
26 Lakatos, I. (1970a), pp. 132–8.
27 Ibid., pp. 138–40.
28 Kuhn, T. (1962).
29 Kuhn, T. (1970b), pp. 261–2.
30 Ibid., p. 262.
31 Kuhn, T. (1970a).
32 Ibid., p. 21.
33 For example, see Lakatos, I. (1970a), p. 174.
34 Winch, P. (1958).

Bibliography

Sections A and B

ABELSON, R.P. (1968), 'Psychological implication', in Abelson, R.P. *et al.* (eds) (1968).

ABELSON, R.P. and ROSENBERG, M.J. (1958), 'Symbolic psycho-logic: a model of attitudinal cognition', *Behavioral Science*, III, pp. 1–13.

ABELSON, R.P. *et al.* (eds) (1968), *Theories of Cognitive Consistency: A Sourcebook*, Chicago.

CYERT, R.M. and WELSCH, L.A. (eds) (1970), *Management Decision Making*, London.

FESTINGER, L. (1957), *A Theory of Cognitive Dissonance*, Evanston, Illinois.

FESTINGER, L. (1964), *Conflict, Decision and Dissonance*, Stanford.

FLEW, A.G.N. (1961), *Hume's Philosophy of Belief*, New York.

GINSBURG, H. and OPPER, S. (1969), *Piaget's Theory of Intellectual Development*, Englewood Cliffs, New Jersey.

GRAHAM, D. (1962), 'Experimental studies of social influences in simple judgement situations', *Journal of Social Psychology*, LVI, pp. 245–69.

HENLE, M. (1962), 'On the relation between logic and thinking', *Psychological Review*, LXIX, pp. 366–78.

HOLLIS, M. (1970), 'The limits of irrationality', in Wilson, B.R. (ed.) (1970).

HOVLAND, C.I. (1957), 'The order of presentation in persuasion', in *Yale Studies in Attitude and Communication*, vol. I, New Haven.

HOVLAND, C.I. *et al.* (1953), *Communication and Persuasion*, New Haven.

HUME, D. (1964), *Treatise of Human Nature*, ed. Selby-Bigge, L.A., Oxford.

JOHNSON, D.M. (1968), 'Reasoning and logic', in *International Encyclopedia of the Social Sciences*, vol. 15.

KOOPMAN, B.O. (1956), 'The theory of search', *Operational Research*, IV, pp. 324–46.

LAMBERTA, D.M. (1971), *Economics of Information and Knowledge*, Harmondsworth.

LUKES, S. (1970), 'Some problems about rationality', in Wilson, B.R. (ed.) (1970).

OZGA, S.A. (1965), *Expectations in Economic Theory*, Chicago.

PASSMORE, J.A. (1968), *Hume's Intentions*, rev. edn, New York.

PIAGET, J. and INHELDER, B. (1958), *The Growth of Logical Thinking from Childhood to Adolescence*, London.

PRICE, H.H. (1969), *Belief*, London.

RUNCIMAN, W.G. (1970), 'The sociological explanation of religious belief', in Runciman, W.G., *Sociology in its Place*, Cambridge.

TAJFEL, H. (1968), 'Social perception', in *International Encyclopedia of the Social Sciences*, vol. 11.

WILSON, B.R. (ed.) (1970), *Rationality*, New York.

ZAJONC, R.B. (1968), 'Thinking', in *International Encyclopedia of the Social Sciences*, vol. 15.

Section C

FEYERABEND, P.K. (1965), 'Problems of empiricism', in Colodny, R. (ed.), *Beyond the Edge of Certainty*, Englewood Cliffs, New Jersey, pp. 145–260.

JARVIE, I.C. (1964), *The Revolution in Anthropology*, London.

KUHN, T. (1962), *The Structure of Scientific Revolutions*, Chicago.

KUHN, T. (1970a), 'Logic of discovery or psychology of research?', in Lakatos, I. and Musgrave, A. (eds), *Criticism and the Growth of Knowledge*, Cambridge, pp. 231–78.

KUHN, T. (1970b), 'Reflections on my critics', in Lakatos, I. and Musgrave, A. (eds), *Criticism and the Growth of Knowledge*, Cambridge, pp. 231–78.

LAKATOS, I. (1968), 'Changes in the problem of inductive logic', in Lakatos, I. (ed.), *The Problem of Inductive Logic*, Amsterdam, pp. 315–417.

LAKATOS, I. (1970a), 'Falsification and the methodology of research programmes', in Lakatos, I. and Musgrave, A. (eds), *Criticism and the Growth of Knowledge*, Cambridge, pp. 91–196.

LAKATOS, I. (1970b), 'History of science and its rational reconstructions', in Cohen, R.S. and Buck, R.C. (eds), *Boston Studies in the Philosophy of Science*, vol. 8, Dordrecht, pp. 91–136.

POPPER, K.R. (1959), *The Logic of Scientific Discovery*, London.

POPPER, K.R. (1968), 'Epistemology without a knowing subject', in Rootselaar, B. van and Staal, J.F. (eds), *Proceedings of the Third International Congress for Logic, Methodology and Philosophy of Science*, Amsterdam, pp. 333–73.

STOVE, D. (1973), *Probability and Hume's Inductive Scepticism*, Oxford.

WINCH, P. (1958), *The Idea of a Social Science*, London.

2

Rationality of belief—intercultural comparisons

J.B. Maund

A Introduction

To an observer from a western culture, in particular to one with a scientific background, many beliefs and practices of people in other cultures appear irrational. Their beliefs about the types of forces operating in the world and their actions intended to procure rain or guard against sickness seem to run counter to normal standards of rationality. Magic, witchcraft and primitive religions are belief-systems which commonly provide the background for such seemingly irrational beliefs and practices.

However, many find this account, which might be called the naïve Intellectualist view, most unsatisfactory. One source of the uneasiness is the fear that ethnocentric bias may be distorting the western observer's view. Could it be that to assess the beliefs and practices of these cultures by any criteria of rationality is mistakenly to suppose them to be similar in kind and in function to the beliefs and practices of our own culture; or that these cultures, far from being irrational, sustain different standards of rationality from our own; or that they attach little importance to rationality as a value? I propose in this paper to examine two important views which take up these suggestions: first, the Symbolic/Expressive account which interprets magic and religion as non-rational; and second Peter Winch's suggestion that other cultures may subscribe to alternative standards of rationality. In the course of the discussion, and in the concluding section, I shall be proposing a modified Intellectualist view which can meet the objections brought against the naïve view.

B The dramatic-expressive model

1 Characterization of the model

The Intellectualist model presupposes that we can make a clear distinction between ritual actions and ritual beliefs.[1] The latter comprise a belief-system presupposed by the ritual actions and justify or make intelligible particular actions. The ritual belief-system can be evaluated by normal criteria of rationality and can be compared with other belief-systems, religious, magical, or scientific. Expressions of belief either make or presuppose truth-claims about the existence of a range of entities (e.g. spirits, gods, witchcraft substance, souls) and about causal relationships between these entities and the objects of the person's natural environment.

Anthropologists such as E.R. Leach[2] and J.H.M. Beattie[3] reject this model, taking ritual actions and beliefs to be symbolic, dramatic or expressive. According to Beattie, for example:[4]

The man who consults a rain-maker, and the rain-maker who carries out a rain-making ceremony, are stating something; they are asserting symbolically the importance they attach to rain and their earnest desire that it shall fall when it is required.

There are two separate claims implicit in the Symbolic/Expressive account:

(i) Ritual utterances are not to be interpreted literally, as asserting descriptive or explanatory hypotheses, but are primarily expressive, e.g. of a person's commitment to a social system or to a set of moral, aesthetic, social or political values.

(ii) Ritual practices are not intended as practical techniques for bringing about certain desirable ends but are primarily symbolic and expressive of social, moral, political or aesthetic values.

These claims are logically independent and ought not to be conflated. It does not follow from the fact that ritual practices have symbolic and expressive functions that it would be improper to evaluate ritual belief-systems by the criteria appropriate for evaluating the rationality of scientific belief-systems.

Even acts that express emotions, feelings, moods, etc., are performed within the framework of a particular belief-system: they presuppose specific beliefs about the existence (or hypothetical existence) of objects of love, hate, or fear, and about ways of behaving with regard to those objects. Thus, to express gratitude for a gift, one must believe that a certain object is a gift, that there exists a certain person who presented the gift, and that the other person intended to give the gift.

Even if it were true, therefore, that many actions in religious and magical contexts are the acting out of desires or the expression of feelings or values, a belief-system with cognitive content might still be a precondition for the practices. The nuns of Aldous Huxley's *The Devils of Loudun*,[5] by performing lewd acts, uttering obscenities, and having fits, acted out their sexual fantasies. Interpreting their behaviour as evidence that they were possessed by devils, they were able to shift blame and responsibility for their behaviour on to the devils, and so release themselves from their sexual repressions. They could do this, however, only because it was believed that there were devils who could force their victims to do things they would not do otherwise. The victims' emotional needs could not have been satisfied had the beliefs not had the cognitive content that they did.

The second claim of the Symbolic/Expressive account is also open to doubt. For consider the distinction between means/end acts (those intended as a means for securing some desired end) and expressive acts (those which express emotions, feelings and moods). The contrast between symbolic and non-symbolic acts cuts across this distinction, for while some symbolic acts are expressive, e.g. the exchange of rings between lovers, other symbolic acts are means/end acts. Linguistic speech acts such as describing, requesting and commanding are symbolic acts intended to achieve certain ends; for instance, that the person addressed shall acquire certain beliefs. What distinguishes this type of symbolic act is the special causal role played by the use of symbols. Because the type of causal relation between symbolic act and desired end is different from the type of causal interaction operating in standard practical techniques, it is easy to draw the mistaken conclusion that it is not a type of means/end act at all.

This point is of some significance for our purposes, since one of the examples upon which Beattie relies to illustrate his thesis is the case[6] in which a group of people, instead of sacrificing an ox, substitute instead a cucumber (an item they can easily afford to lose). Beattie claims that this demonstrates that the people do not regard the sacrifice as a practical technique. But if we distinguish practical techniques from other types of means/end acts, e.g. of the symbolic sort, we can admit that the sacrifice is not a standard practical technique while asserting that the act is done in order to acknowledge the presence and power of a Deity, and to obtain its benevolent intervention.

I have argued, then, that to recognize that many ritual acts are symbolic, dramatic and expressive, leaves entirely open the possibility of assessing the rationality of the belief-system.

2   A belief-system without truth-claims

D.Z. Phillips's account[7] of religious beliefs amounts to a claim that there can be belief-systems which neither consist in nor pre-suppose descriptive or explanatory propositions. If Phillips is right, he has provided a possible model for interpreting belief-systems which could not be adequately understood on the Intellec-tualist model.

Phillips argues that there is a logical distinction between religious beliefs and beliefs which are descriptive or explanatory hypotheses. It is only with regard to the second sort of belief that it is legitimate to apply objective criteria of rationality, consider evidence, test by experiments, and so on. By contrast, many religious beliefs,[8]

> such as belief in the Last Judgement are not testable hypotheses
> but absolutes for believers in so far as they predominate in
> and determine much of their thinking. ... To construe these
> beliefs as hypotheses which may or may not be true is to falsify
> their character.

The belief shows itself in the way a man holds the idea before his mind when he takes any decisions of importance, in the way it determines his attitude to his aspirations, failures and misfortunes. Believing in it 'means, for example, putting one's trust in it, sacri-ficing for it, letting it regulate one's life and so on'.[9] Anyone claiming to have evidence to support such a belief would not be so much mistaken as guilty of a gross misunderstanding.

Phillips's argument seems to turn on a distinction between 'belief-in' and 'belief-that'. But he has not shown that each type of belief has a distinct set of objects, and that hypotheses and theories cannot be the objects of 'beliefs-in'. And surely one can believe in hypotheses and theories. It does not follow, therefore, that a belief-in something must on that account alone be exempt from rational assessment. Phillips needs to show that there can be cases where to believe-in X does not presuppose or imply the truth of beliefs-that about X. But on the contrary, H.H. Price has provided reasons[10] for holding that it is an essential part of having a belief-in attitude at all that one have some beliefs-that. A person who believes in British Jus-tice believes that it will not be corrupt, that it will provide fair trials, and so on. If, then, the holding of a belief-in attitude does entail having some beliefs-that, at least part of the rationality of the belief-in attitude will depend on how rational it is to hold such beliefs-that.

3   Poetic metaphors and scientific models

A third version of the Symbolic/Expressive view holds that ritual utterances are to be interpreted as expressive statements, that such statements presuppose a set of descriptive hypotheses but that the hypotheses can be translated into *non-ritualistic* terms. Putative statements about gods, spirits, witchcraft substance, etc., are thus to be interpreted as metaphors or allegorical ways of expressing the importance of, say, love, courage, good rains, and so on. The making of putative descriptive statements about the Virgin Mary is taken to be a way of proclaiming an ideal of womanly behaviour.

On this view, we can say that religious believers do not believe either that such entities as deities, spirits, or dead ancestors exist, or that such entities have causal powers and capacities. Instead, the entities presupposed by ritual utterances, interpreted expressively, will be ordinary things such as persons, communities, social and family relationships, ideals, rain, and so on. Thus the people in religious and magic cultures will not be presenting large-scale world views that can be seen as plausible rivals to scientific theories, and hence properly judged as inadequate or irrational by scientific standards.

Now such an account may be a plausible rational reconstruction of a religious belief-system as it could be rationally held by a person in a scientifically oriented society; but that it is a correct interpretation of all religious beliefs and of magical beliefs seems highly implausible. A further difficulty in the account is that we need criteria for distinguishing statements which are to be interpreted literally and hence descriptively from ones which are to be interpreted symbolically, allegorically, or metaphorically. We would need to avoid the trap of deciding that an utterance was symbolic merely because, if it were interpreted literally, it would be irrational by scientific standards.

In any case, to accept the view that magical and religious belief-systems are, like poetry, basically metaphorical, does not commit one to the sharp opposition that Beattie takes for granted when he asserts that the myth-makers are on the side of the poets rather than the scientists.[11] A great deal of poetry can be construed as explanatory, or as addressed to questions of truth-and-falsity,[12] even though the medium of expression may be a metaphor or allegory. For instance, the two poetic statements: 'Life is a tale told by an idiot' and 'Life is a play in which every man has his role', certainly appear to be saying things about life that are in conflict. Moreover, science has its poetic overtones too. Explanations in one area of discourse are often put in terms of models and analogues drawn from other areas of discourse—clockwork mechanisms, colliding billiard-balls, planetary systems, water waves, etc. Like a piece of poetry, a new scientific theory may provide a new way of looking at things—each may make a comparison between two sets of phenomena hitherto unrelated, taking one as providing the analogue for the other. Like a model in a good scientific theory, a good poetic image requires the image and what is 'imaged' to have important features in common; and the value of the poetic image often depends on the extent to which the analogue can be extended and thus provide the basis for an even more striking comparison. Of course, there are crucial differences between poetry and science, resting on the scientist's method of testing his explanations and descriptions of phenomena. The poet is usually content to present a novel image; the scientist's image must be elaborated, extended, tested, modified, criticized, and so on. For all that, science relies heavily on the poetic imagination.

To see myth-makers and tellers of magical stories as on the side of the poets is not necessarily then to set them against the scientists. Many scientific theories have developed from origins which were little more than poetic speculations and the importance of poetic imagination in developed scientific theorizing ought not be ignored. It is thus not at all eccentric of the Intellectualists to see certain myths and magical world views as incipient forms of science, however poorly developed the experimental and critical attitudes of those who believe in them.

4 The anthropological evidence

Despite the examples that Beattie cites in support of his model, there are many others for which it is inadequate.

(i) Among the Azande, there are people who are unaware of having performed witchcraft but admit to being witches because certain oracles say that they are. The Azande say that these people have unconscious wishes, and that the witchcraft must have been performed by their souls while they slept;[13] it is hard to see how the Symbolic/Expressive model could account for these beliefs; the notion of the soul acting while the person sleeps certainly seems to be an explanatory device.

(ii) According to Anthony Wallace's description,[14] the Iroquois have a theory of dreams and the unconscious mind not unlike Freud's. They believe that frustration of unconscious desires and wishes can cause mental and physical illness. They often act out in a symbolic way an event in an evil dream; it is believed that a wish, although irrational and destructive, is fateful, and that the only way of forestalling realization of an evil-fated wish is to fulfil it symbolically. We might have taken such behaviour as providing support for Beattie's dramatic-expressive interpretation, except

39

for the nature of the wishes and desires symbolically acted out. For many of these wishes and desires are in themselves irrational or, at least, unpractical. A woman may see herself in her dream eating a certain type of tomato at a particular time; the rest of the tribe will be determined to obtain such a tomato so that the woman can act out her dream. While it may be understandable that a rain-maker's rite may express the importance he and his patron attach to rain, it seems odd to give a similar account of the Iroquois' behaviour; for the evil they are attempting to forestall is completely unknown, and but for their theory of dreams and the forces inspiring them, they would not believe that there was any evil to be avoided.

(iii) It seems to be the case in many societies that magic gives way to a large extent to science and technology when these become available. And this would seem to indicate that these people regard magic as essentially practical rather than dramatic. David Mandelbaum has described[15] how, in many villages in India and Ceylon where the religion used to consist of two complexes, one transcendental, the other concerned largely with very practical matters like illness, weather, and misfortune, the latter is being replaced by science and technology while the transcendental complex continues to flourish.

Though examples enumerated in this way are very inconclusive, they increase nevertheless the plausibility of the Intellectualist model, showing, too, that the dramatic, expressive and symbolic functions of a belief-system may depend on its also having descriptive and explanatory functions.

5 Explanation of the model's use

Beattie sees his account as providing the only way of answering certain questions and of understanding certain practices: '...why people should have come to hold such mistaken views [as magic], and why they should be so slow to relinquish them ... cannot ... be answered unless the symbolic character of ritual is taken into account'.[16] Furthermore, to explain why a society does not attempt to test magic empirically Beattie writes: 'It is simply that there would be no point in doing so, for if and in so far as the central significance of a rite is expressive, it is thus far an end in itself.'[17]

By interpreting the belief-systems as primarily expressive, rather than descriptive and explanatory, we may provide a plausible way of answering such questions. But it is not the only way. For Beattie assumes that it would be easy to falsify a system of magic within the context of a given culture if the believers had a critical attitude to their beliefs. But a comprehensive framework of beliefs (as opposed to specific hypotheses within that framework) could not be conclusively falsified without developing an alternative framework—and that is no easy task. Aristotelian physics did not just fall away; it required the intensive development and articulation of Cartesian and Newtonian frameworks. It is not as if magic is a hopeless explanatory model—it has good confirmation considering the data available. Indeed, to show its empirical inadequacy, a scientist would need to take account of data outside the ordinary experience of people in the magic-culture. Medicine in the West was in a hopeless state in the sixteenth and seventeenth centuries; why should one expect a member of a primitive culture to come up with a more rational alternative than magic, given his limited experience and resources?

Beattie's second assumption appears to be that a belief-system has an explanatory/descriptive role only if the believers have an attitude of attempting to falsify it and of seeking alternatives. I have already argued that this assumption is false. The myth-makers and poets may have explanatory interest even if they do lack this attitude.

One of the chief driving forces behind Beattie's argument appears to be the fear of ethnocentricity. The Intellectualist account is rejected largely because it supposedly entails the irrationality of other cultures; if we take their belief-systems to involve explanatory and descriptive hypotheses, we will be in a position to compare them with our own, by our standards of rationality, and Beattie assumes that the belief-systems of non-scientific cultures must perform badly in such a test. Another model, for example the Symbolic/Expressive account, is then proposed as a way of 'saving the rationality' of the other cultures.

There is, however, another course open to us: to retain the Intellectualist account but revise the judgment of the naïve Intellectualist that most (or all) ritual belief-systems, literally interpreted, are irrational. This judgment may very well be ethnocentric, but so then are writers such as Beattie and Phillips who hold that ritual utterances, if literally interpreted, would be so irrational that this must be a misinterpretation. Let us grant, however, that in our science-oriented societies in which we have highly developed, articulated, and confirmed scientific theories to provide us with a viable alternative, it is irrational to believe in magical and religious systems, interpreted literally. It does not follow that it is irrational in those cultures where there is no scientific alternative and where, indeed, the conditions required for the development of this alternative may not obtain. On the contrary, as we shall see, there may

41

be circumstances in which such belief-systems are highly rational.

C Forms of life and rival criteria of rationality

Let us now consider a second type of attempt to save the beliefs of other cultures from the charge of irrationality. This allows that magical belief-systems can be assessed in terms of their rationality or irrationality, but insists that other cultures may have different criteria of rationality, incommensurable with those standardly employed in western science. This view has been most provocatively presented by P. Winch who challenges the widely held assumption that scientific rationality is the paradigm of rationality.

At various points in his writings[18] Winch develops at least two different accounts of this difference in standards of rationality; and while they are not sharply separated in Winch's discussion, it will be profitable to deal with them separately.

1 Universes of discourse and forms of life

The first of Winch's arguments is that other cultures may have different universes of discourse, associated with different forms of life. Beliefs formed within any given universe of discourse are to be assessed in terms of rationality standards relative to that universe, and different universes of discourse may be associated with different criteria of rationality. A universe of discourse is constituted by a set of linguistic rules and practices which identify a set of sentences that can be meaningfully uttered, as well as specifying procedures for determining which of these sentences there is good reason to believe are true. This use of the term 'universe of discourse' is illustrated in a passage in which Winch asks whether magic, like science, comprises a coherent universe of discourse 'in terms of which an intelligible conception of reality and clear ways of deciding what beliefs are and are not in agreement with this reality can be discerned.'[19]

Winch is insistent that two alternative universes of discourse and the beliefs formulated within them cannot be assessed in relation to reality, conceived as something independent of any universe of discourse or form of life. Winch[20] criticizes Evans-Pritchard for trying to work with a conception of reality which is not determined by its actual use in language. There is no reality independent of a universe of discourse, and to the extent that two universes are significantly different, Winch holds that we have to conceive of the individuals operating within them as in touch with different realities. So no universe of discourse can be dismissed as irrational on account of a putative discrepancy between it and reality.

Winch states his position at other times in terms of differences between forms of life:[21]

> Criteria of logic are not a direct gift of God, but arise out of, and are only intelligible in the context of, ways of living or modes of social life. It follows that one cannot apply criteria of logic to modes of social life as such. For instance, science is one such mode and religion is another; and each has criteria of intelligibility peculiar to itself. So within science or religion actions can be logical or illogical: in science, for example, it would be illogical to refuse to be bound by the results of a properly carried out experiment; in religion it would be illogical to suppose that one could pit one's own strength against God's; and so on. But we cannot sensibly say that either the practice of science itself or that of religion is either illogical or logical; both are non-logical.

Note that in the above passage science is a *form of life*, i.e. a practice informed by a set of aims, norms, and values, whereas in a passage quoted earlier it is a universe of discourse. There is some uncertainty, therefore, whether it is the form of life or the universe of discourse which is the central idea in Winch's work. The notions are clearly interdependent, and I shall deal with each in turn.

(a) Universes of discourse

Though Winch's account of what would constitute a form of life and a universe of discourse is never very explicit, he does offer, as examples of *different* ones, science, religion, and magic. He insists that because Zande magic has its own conception of reality and its own standards of rationality, it is a gross distortion to see such a system as an attempt to provide quasi-scientific understanding of the world. The Azande have nothing like scientific conceptions, nor scientific standards of rationality, so it is absurd to regard a western scientist and a Zande witch-doctor as making truth-claims about the same reality.

Still, the Azande *do* have non-magical beliefs about growing crops, hunting, chickens, persons and so on. When they claim to see a chicken, they are surely making truth-claims about a non-magical reality; and they apply scientific conceptions and scientific standards no more to this reality than to their magical beliefs. Surely then, if Winch is right, their truth-claims about this reality are no more likely to come into conflict with truth-claims by western

43

scientists than their claims about the magical reality. But this is absurd. Their descriptions and explanations of the behaviour of objects in (what we might call) the common-sense reality is surely as much open to challenge, refutation, modification or confirmation as the similar descriptions and explanations made by people in other cultures. Indeed, Steven Lukes[22] and Martin Hollis[23] have argued that it is a precondition of our being able to understand and translate the language of a strange culture (and hence to attribute specific beliefs to people in the culture) that there be a shared reality.

Though the arguments of Lukes and Hollis are persuasive, it may be possible to reconstruct Winch's position so as to meet their objections. For within our own language and culture, mathematics and natural science deal with different realities and establish different types of conclusions. The methods of establishing mathematical truths are different from those of establishing scientific truths; a large part of scientific reasoning is, by the standards of mathematics, logically invalid, involving as it does inductive reasoning. Though the nature of mathematical reality is controversial, it is plausible that mathematical entities (for instance, the natural numbers) are abstract entities. In discussing mathematical logic, K. Gödel argues that classes and concepts may be conceived as real objects, existing independently of our definitions and constructions.[24]

If our language successfully incorporates two such diverse realities, could not an alien culture incorporate two realities, one pertaining to magical thinking, the other to the same reality which is revealed in our culture by scientific (and common-sense) thinking? No doubt there is some sort of connection between the mathematical and scientific realities, but perhaps there is also some sort of connection between the magical world and the scientific (or common-sense) world.

Winch argues that our western culture does not have a form of life similar to the magic of other cultures. And likewise there are some cultures which do not have anything remotely resembling our mathematics. An anthropologist-philosopher of such a culture, were he to use the Lukes-Hollis argument, would conclude that the subject called 'mathematics' as studied in western cultures is absurd and meaningless.

On Winch's view, then, the process of understanding and translating an alien language can require an extension or modification of our language because we have to understand a radically different universe of discourse. And why should not this require that we educate ourselves to an awareness of an aspect of experience of which we have hitherto been ignorant, just as to translate mathematical statements into the language of a non-mathematical culture would require educating the people of such a culture and modifying (and extending) their language? We could hardly claim that western cultures have developed all the possible ways of finding out about all aspects of experience;[25] even were it true, how would we know it to be true? If Winch is claiming only that there *might be* other ways of finding out about aspects of experience it is by no means obvious that he has been refuted by Lukes and Hollis.

(b) Different forms of life

We have seen that the argument by which Winch proposes to establish the incommensurability of religion, science, and magic links the claim that each comprises its own coherent universe of discourse, its own reality and criteria of rationality, with the claim that each constitutes a distinct form of social life, in which the respective practices and beliefs are made intelligible. I shall now argue that this second claim cannot be sustained.

(i) Science and technology Consider the relation between science and technology. Supposing the scientific form of life to be the activity of scientists with mainly theoretical aims and interests, is the form distinct from technology, where practical aims and interests are followed, and where costs, prices, etc., provide the norms for the making of decisions? Or do we take science and technology to comprise one form of life? If they are distinct, how can beliefs which occur in a technological context be evaluated as false or irrational, by reference to beliefs which occur in the scientific context? How indeed can science be applied? How can technologies be improved and aided by science?

To decide, however, that technology and science constitute a single form of life would be to abandon Winch's claim that a form of life is coherent in the sense that the practitioner follows a coherent set of rules and norms in the pursuit of a coherent set of goals. For scientists and technologists are often following different norms. Science has largely been practised through the pursuit of theoretical aims and the solving of theoretical problems; its practical applications have usually come long after the theoretical work was done, and seldom could have been foreseen. Though some scientists, such as Galileo and Huygens, have been interested in practical problems, their interest has generally been in the theoretical implications of those problems—in a mechanism, perhaps, that provided a model or analogue for the theoretical explanation of other phenomena.[26]

(ii) Science and religion   If Winch's position is so weakened that science and technology, by virtue of their interplay, constitute a single 'form of life', then science and religion too must constitute a single form of life—for there has been as much or more interplay between science and religion. Nevertheless it is certainly plausible to see them as distinct forms of life. Thus we might take science to be that activity, the ultimate aim of which is to provide rational understanding of the world, that proceeds by formulating theories that systematize and order phenomena, logically articulating them, and subjecting them to empirical testing. And it is plausible to view religion as concerned not with this sort of rational understanding of the world, but with emotional and spiritual values, the worth of a religion being judged by its success in guiding and inspiring one's life rather than as ordering phenomena in a systematic way.

But while it may be useful to distinguish modern science and modern religion in this way, if we trace the tradition to which each belongs we shall find some of these traditions merging. Historically there has been an extensive interplay between theological and scientific ideas. And moreover, in the traditions from which modern science has developed, its present components were not allied at all.

Clearly the scientific revolution drew heavily on the Platonic tradition with its emphasis on the mathematical method and idealizations: the idealized descriptions (ideal gases, point-masses, perfectly smooth surfaces, etc.) and the use of the language of mathematics as the key to understanding the world were crucial elements in the progress of physics. Yet although Plato was devoted to the pursuit of theoretical and rational understanding of the world, he seems to have held the empirical study of nature in low esteem. Thus we have, in the Platonic tradition, the divorce of these two essential components of modern science. In addition, Plato seems to have shared with the Pythagoreans something of their mystical and religious attitude to mathematics. There was thus in this important tradition not only a separation of two important components of modern science, but also a combination of one of these components with a component of what is usually taken to be distinctive of the religious or mystical universe of discourse.

By contrast, the empirical study of natural processes by experimentation was in medieval times largely carried on by the alchemists, while the Platonic and Aristotelian scholars who bequeathed to modern science a host of theories and theoretical problems of dynamics and astronomy largely ignored it. The alchemists' experimental techniques and low-level empirical knowledge made a large contribution to chemistry, but interestingly, their experimentation and study of nature seems to have been imbued with a religious attitude to nature. In describing natural processes, they used as models and analogues human relationships and relationships between man and God. The interactions between acids and metal, between one substance and another, were described in terms such as marriage, birth, life, death, and so on. Nor can the theological-scientific interaction be viewed as belonging to the pre-history of science 'proper'. The important use made of theological arguments in the Leibniz-Clarke correspondence[27] on the respective merits of absolute and relative space, time, and motion renders that contention suspect.

There thus seem to be three major ways in which the scientific and religious forms of life interacted:

1 scientific activity was one way of worshipping and praising God;

2 religion provided analogies for use in making intelligible the working of natural processes;

3 there was the combined use of theological and scientific arguments; it was thought acceptable to use scientific arguments to support theological beliefs and to use theological beliefs in the valuation of rival scientific theories.

Thus, to speak, as Winch does, of science as a coherent universe of discourse in terms of which an intelligible conception of reality and clear ways of deciding what beliefs are and are not in agreement with this reality can be discerned, is to mask the many differences and tensions that do occur within science. Science has a variety of aims, paradigms, and rules which sometimes conflict; among this variety are features which it shares with non-scientific discourse and activities.

Indeed, the historical context in which science has developed has comprised a variety of traditions of such diversity that until relatively recent times there has been greater inter-penetration of the religious and scientific forms of life than of the scientific and technological forms of life. Consequently if we claim that scientific and religious beliefs are incommensurable, while beliefs from a technological context can be challenged by those from a scientific context, then whether two belief-systems are incommensurable cannot depend upon whether they are associated with distinct forms of life. Thus Winch's argument cannot be sustained.

(iii) Ideal forms of life However, a different interpretation of 'form of life' may yield a more plausible but modified thesis. We may lay down, for instance, a set of aims, norms, and goals which are said to be characteristically scientific and which are requirements

for an activity's counting as scientific. We would then be working with a normative conception of 'proper science' or 'good science'. In a particular social or historical context, we could abstract from the mixture of aims and norms actually pursued by scientists those contained in 'proper science' and treat the others as external to the scientific activity itself. This would be to commit us to a particular methodology of science,[28] e.g. to Inductivism, Conventionalism, Popperian (or neo-Popperian) Falsificationism or some other. Similarly, we may pick out a different set of aims, rules, and norms as characteristically religious and thus define a religious 'form of life'. It would thus be possible for a specific historical activity to have several components, one participating in the religious form of life, another in the scientific form of life.

It should be pointed out that this modification accords poorly with the spirit of Winch's programme. To see a particular historical situation, e.g. the Leibniz-Clarke dispute, as comprising two distinct components, one scientific the other theological, is to impose on that situation a judgment made by an observer from a different historical situation, and one not likely to be shared by those within the original historical situation. In overriding in this way the judgments of the participants in a cultural situation, we appear to break faith with one of the central principles presented in *The Idea of a Social Science*.

Notwithstanding this cost, it may be possible to identify distinct forms of life so different that they involve different criteria of rationality and different realities. But do we have any reason to suppose that this possibility is ever actualized? Is any such characterization of, say, an actual religious form of life forthcoming? Winch does not provide any, although he commends the position adopted by D.Z. Phillips, a position criticized in the first part of this paper. But, on Phillips's account, religious statements are not to be interpreted as making truth-claims about a reality different from that described by scientific theories, but rather as making no truth-claims at all. Still, the possibility of there being different forms of life, whether we have examples available or not, might be sufficient reason for the anthropologist to exercise caution in interpreting alien cultures, and to be alert to the possibility that, in some culture, an incommensurable form of life might be present.

2 Ends and standards of rationality

The argument so far considered began with the contention that forms of life in two societies may be radically different, introduced a doctrine about the relativity of reality to the universes of discourse associated with those forms of life, and drew the conclusion that the universes of discourse and the beliefs formed within them cannot be comparatively assessed by reference to one non-culturally-relative set of rationality criteria.

The second strand in Winch's thinking also starts with the idea of radically different forms of life. But the contention now is that, given the very different ends and interests that may be central to the two forms of life, one society may be willing to tolerate large-scale inconsistencies for the sake of other ends, or may simply lack altogether an interest in a 'rational' activity like testing. Given its members' ends and interests, it is suggested, we cannot criticize them if they give a low priority to meeting a rational standard to which we attach much more importance, or if they altogether lack an attitude which we regard as an essential component of the rational life.

In this section, I shall examine how a society's ends and interests are relevant in assessing whether its beliefs are rational. I shall begin by distinguishing between (a) the process of accepting (and retaining) a belief-system and (b) the adoption of certain policies towards one's belief-system. We can then make further sub-divisions of (b):

b_1: a policy of subjecting belief-systems to criticism, comparison with alternatives, attempted falsification;

b_2: a policy of attempted confirmation of belief-systems: this policy includes the attempt to explore and extend one's belief-system, without necessarily attempting to falsify it;

b_3: a policy of (unreflective) retention of a belief-system.

Clearly, in order to evaluate the rationality of a particular policy towards changing a belief-system, we shall have to examine the ends—the purpose and uses of belief-systems within cultures. These may be theoretical or practical.

(a) Theoretical ends

By adopting a belief-system, one may promote certain theoretical ends—increase one's understanding of the world, provide powerful explanations, make testable predictions. It is by reference to such goals that, standardly, one evaluates and orders belief-systems from the point of view of epistemic rationality. But in the rational appraisal of belief-systems, two other relevant features need to be taken account of: (i) the types of problems that are considered important to solve; and (ii) the ideals of natural order presupposed, i.e. the central paradigms of the way (ways) nature works.

Within science it often happens that a comprehensive theory

49

with a set of significant problems gives way to a different one with a different set of significant problems. Rather than solving all the old problems, the new theory often sets them aside as either unstateable within the new theory, or as excluded by its basic assumptions, or as unworthy of attention. Magic and astrology aim at answering questions like, 'Why was it my fate to have a sickly child when my brother's child is healthy?', while such questions are either simply disregarded by science or else the answer is given that it happens by chance.

A theory may be very successful at solving one range of problems but barren in its attempts to solve a different set. Newtonian mechanics, for example, swiftly eliminated many theoretical problems of astronomy and terrestrial motion, but the attempt in the eighteenth century to extend the Newtonian paradigm to chemistry met with little or no success. To solve these chemical problems, other traditions needed to be drawn upon. Thus a theory may be well ahead of its time; to be successful, a theory needs its problems at the right time and the right place.

To appraise a belief-system we need also to pay attention to its conceptions of how nature works; different ideals of nature adopt different models, mechanisms or phenomena as paradigms for explanation. Clockwork mechanisms and colliding particles have provided mechanistic paradigms, while the personal and intelligent actions of human beings have provided teleological paradigms. There are important differences among belief-systems of the latter sort, depending on which aspects of personal action are taken to be important, for instance, intelligence and goal-directedness, power and activity, or the involvement of emotions such as love, jealousy, anger.

There is no *a priori* reason for regarding the personalized models of magical belief-systems as necessarily absurd or irrational paradigms. Despite the remarkable success of modern science, and in particular of modern physics, in explaining a wider range of phenomena than any alternative theory, it does not follow that because it presupposes a mechanistic depersonalized model, it is therefore rational to adopt such an ideal in all contexts and in all situations. Aristotelian physics, employing a different ideal, was both successful in explaining a wide range of the available phenomena, and was also well-supported by common-sense experience. A wide range of conceptions have become empirically acceptable and respectable in sound physical theories only after developing through an earlier stage in which they were regarded as absurdities or conceptual impossibilities relative to previous conceptual schemes: action-at-a-distance (Newton agrees with Leibniz that it is absurd),

Einstein's relativity of simultaneity, Copernicus's moving earth, Bruno's infinite worlds, Darwin's descent of man from lower creatures, Freud's concept of the sexuality of children, and so on.[29] These and many other examples should make us wary of setting aside the personalized models of magic cultures as obviously absurd.

(b) Practical ends

But belief-systems serve significant practical goals as well as theoretical ones. One obvious practical goal is control over the environment, and for this science is particularly apt; a second is to provide meaning and significance to human life, to give point and direction to our activities. Religious belief-systems and political ideologies like various forms of Marxism provide such problems with answers of varying degrees of adequacy. Another practical goal, related to the last, is relief from agnosticism; a belief-system may satisfy a desire for commitment, the desire varying in intensity from person to person. Again, a belief-system may enable one to cope with illness, misfortune and death, either by coming to terms with them or, to a certain extent, by overcoming them. Some religious belief-systems give suffering a special value; other systems explain and provide apparent means of overcoming it, as in systems of magic and witchcraft; fatalistic belief-systems just account for, or find a place for it.

In addition, belief-systems may serve to preserve social structures, or as Leach[30] and Firth[31] have shown, to reflect existing social pressures and conflicts. Firth, for example, describes how there are variations of the traditional tales of Tikopia which reflect the organizational competition and pressures of present-day clans. The importance assigned to a particular clan in the supposed history of the origins of the society depends on whether the narrator is a member of that clan or another. Each history is meant to provide a justification for social distinctions to be made in present-day society. Empirical research would possibly show that the fact that a belief-system promoted such practical goals provides a far better explanation for the preservation of most peoples' belief-systems than the rational justifications which those people are generally disposed to offer.

(c) Belief policies

We can now relate the goals promoted by belief-systems to the policies of changing or retaining belief-systems. If the prevailing belief-system in a culture serves to furnish a point or direction to people's lives or to provide control over the environment or to enable people to come to terms with sickness and suffering, then there will be little incentive to change the belief-system. Similarly, if a belief-system serves to reinforce the status of particular groups and clans within a society, then it will be in their interest to preserve it intact, using for instance their power over education or their ability to justify the belief-system to other groups within the society.

One important thing to notice is that the belief-system may serve these practical ends even if false. Even control over the environment can be obtained with false theories, since even false theories can yield *some* successful predictions.

Certain attitudes and policies appear better than others for acquiring belief-systems with desirable theoretical qualities (high explanatory power, high empirical content, simplicity, and so on), but it is not at all certain that these policies will be the most practically rational for producing belief-systems which promote desired practical goals. For any society which did not have theoretical interests, at least as part of their ultimate ends, it would not necessarily be practically rational to pursue these policies. If such a society had an established belief-system which handled effectively its most significant practical problems, it would probably be practically rational for the people to retain it, rather than look for alternative systems. It is questionable whether the search for a better alternative would be worth the cost (in time, labour and goods). Although the applied results of modern science are vast and impressive, it was a long time before western science yielded any practical benefit.

A system, while serving practical goals, may also serve theoretical goals, even if the latter are sub-goals. If magic and witchcraft have explanatory roles, then a worthwhile comparison might be made not between magic and, say, physics, but rather between magic and belief-systems such as those of Freudian psychology or Marx's Historical Materialism. Though Popper[32] denies that these theories are scientific they do have claims to be regarded as explanatory. They provide theories from which we can deduce descriptions of a wide range of phenomena, and on this score are comparable with magic and witchcraft. And furthermore, not unlike magic and witchcraft, they have a propensity to absorb contradictions and putative refuting instances. Clearly believers in such systems adopt towards them a confirmatory policy, rather than the falsificatory policy advocated by such writers as Popper and Feyerabend.[33] Other things being equal, the confirmatory policy is to be less highly valued than the other, but there are circumstances where this ordering is reversed.

Moreover, attitudes to the framework of belief may be different from attitudes towards individual beliefs and sub-systems of individual beliefs within the framework. The Azande certainly approach the witchcraft framework with a closed mind, but with respect to individual beliefs they seem to employ sound inductive inferences and make experiments. They have tests by which they appraise the quality of oracles and witch-doctors. Evans-Pritchard described some of the Azande devising impossible questions for a witch-doctor's oracle for the purpose of exposing him as a fraud. Some oracles come to be rejected because of their poor performance, while, on the other hand, many have been introduced from other neighbouring cultures. The Azande seem to be aware that many witch-doctors are frauds and display a strong scepticism towards individual witch-doctors though practically all resort to magic in times of trouble. If we are to make comparisons with respect to the attitude towards beliefs, then Azande magic may compare with some of the practices of navigation and surveying for which even today the astronomy of Ptolemy is more than adequate. Such skills seem aimed more at practical goals than at providing powerful and satisfying explanatory theories.

(d) Some applications in anthropology

Different societies, I suggest, may be usefully compared with respect to the types of theoretical and practical ends which their belief-systems serve. All societies will have some theoretical goals even if they are only sub-goals; they will differ in the relative importance they assign to them. Even such a sharp critic of the Intellectualist doctrine as Beattie concedes that: 'On the cognitive level, they [religious and magical beliefs and practices] provide satisfactory answers to otherwise insoluble questions: they fill gaps in human knowledge and experience and so diminish areas of doubt and uncertainty.'[34]

Levi-Strauss has, perhaps more than anyone else, stressed the importance of such cognitive goals in primitive cultures.[35] They often have classificatory systems, for plants and animals, of a sophistication far in excess of that required to meet practical ends. Furthermore, as examples of cultures having general comprehensive explanatory systems, Horton has described[36] the Kalabari, Middleton[37] the Lugbari, and Hallowell[38] the Ojibwa.

An excellent intercultural comparison is made by S.F. Nadel contrasting the Korongo with the Mesakin:[39]

The Korongo, who have no witchcraft, possess a full and explicit mythology concerned with explaining all the things in

53

the world—the creation of man and animals, the origin of death and disease, the invention of fire. ... The witchcraft-ridden Mesakin ... have nothing of the kind.

These societies seem sharply distinguished by the relative emphasis placed upon theoretical goals. There remain, however, a number of interesting questions: to what extent do the Korongo's explanations of the origins of man, disease, fire, etc., help them in overcoming their practical problems of ordinary life: does the ability to fit death and disease into an explanatory system, or into an explanatory system of a certain type, help to remove anxiety about such matters? Are the Mesakin different because their explanations are directed at solving different problems?

It seems from Nadel's report that the Mesakin belief-system is not practically rational (in at least one important aspect) in that it creates anxiety instead of removing it. However, it may have other consequences:[40]

The accusations of witchcraft *do* deflect tensions and aggressive impulses ... from the maladjusted institutions which cause them ... so that these institutions can continue to operate ... [The] witchcraft beliefs enable a society to go on functioning in a given manner, fraught with conflicts and contradictions which the society is helpless to resolve....

A thoroughgoing comparative examination of belief-systems would need to take into account both types of consequences: those which are practically rational and those which tend to preserve the society and keep it functioning.

Conclusion

This paper has been an attempt to put forward a modified Intellectu-alist view which meets the points made by Beattie and Winch. I argued that Winch's general argument for the thesis that magic-cultures may have alternative standards of rationality cannot be sustained. Nevertheless a modified Winchean position may be true: that there could be components of forms of life in other cultures incommensurable with scientific forms of life, and that to understand and evaluate them would require extending our lan-guage and rationality standards in important ways. But it remains to be established that any such instances exist.

I accept Beattie's point that the belief-systems of many cultures are, in part at least, dramatic and expressive, and are not main-tained because they are regarded as fulfilling theoretical goals analogous to those of science. I have argued, however, that even if religious and magical utterances are to be understood as expressing attitudes, these attitudes themselves presuppose certain beliefs about reality which can only be interpreted on the Intellectualist pattern. For such an interpretation one must appreciate the features which poetry and myth-making have in common with scientific theorizing, despite their obvious and important differences.

For all that, the reason for retaining a belief-system may be that it promotes with some success a range of practical rather than theoretical goals. In many cultures theoretical ends may be given relatively low priority, and may be pursued only because they are thought to promote practical goals. Even within the same culture different groups may put different weights on practical and theoretical ends. Recognizing this fact, we may be better able to evaluate the rationality of the belief-systems of other cultures, as well as to explain why a given culture retains a belief-system unchanged or unexamined. Especially significant for such an evaluation is the extent to which theoretical ends are sub-goals valued for promoting practical ends, e.g. for gaining control of the environment, for coping with misfortune, in providing a meaning to one's life, etc.

Accordingly, it would not be practically rational for many cultures to look for alternatives to their belief-systems, if like Zande magic, their system appears to promote their practical ends fairly satisfactorily. But even from the standpoint of theoretical rationality, and bearing in mind the limited range of phenomena and problems the people can actually know about, primitive belief-systems may have considerable explanatory power.

In any case, to evaluate such a belief-system as an explanatory system is not to criticize the people of such a culture for not following a policy for critically testing and exploring their belief-system. For in western cultures, too, this policy is confined only to small groups (e.g. to the scientific community); it is appropriate to compare the Azande not with western scientists but with other groups in western cultures who engage unreflectively in activities which take the broad scientific framework for granted.

Notes

1 I shall use the term 'ritual' in such a way that religious, witchcraft and magic beliefs (and actions) are all ritual beliefs (and actions).
2 Leach, E.R. (1954).
3 Beattie, J.H.M. (1964).
4 Ibid., p. 203.
5 Huxley, A. (1952), *The Devils of Loudun*, London.
6 Beattie, J.H.M. (1966).
7 Phillips, D.Z. (1971).

8 Ibid., p. 130.
9 Ibid., p. 130.
10 Price, H.H. (1971).
11 Beattie, J.H.M. (1970), p. 261.
12 For an account of poetic truth as comparable to scientific truth, see Hesse, M.B. (1954).
13 Evans-Pritchard, E.E. (1937), p. 136.
14 Wallace, A.F.C. (1967), p. 176.
15 Mandelbaum, D. (1966).
16 Beattie, J.H.M. (1966), p. 64.
17 Beattie, J.H.M. (1964), p. 204.
18 Winch, P. (1958) and (1970).
19 Winch, P. (1970), p. 83.
20 Ibid., p. 82.
21 Winch, P. (1958), pp. 100–1.
22 Lukes, S. (1970).
23 Hollis, M. (1968).
24 Gödel, K. (1946), p. 137.
25 It might be, for example, that some other culture has a belief-system which has as a central paradigm (in Thomas Kuhn's sense) a type of experience or a type of perceived phenomenon that is not normally available to people in our culture.
26 See, for example, Hall, A. Rupert (1970).
27 Alexander, H.G. (ed.) (1956).
28 See Lakatos I. (1970) for an important account of various possible methodologies.
29 See Holton, G. (1965).
30 Leach, E.R. (1968).
31 Firth, R. (1968).
32 Popper, K.R. (1959).
33 Feyerabend, P.K. (1965).
34 Beattie, J.H.M. (1964), p. 238.
35 Lévi-Strauss, C. (1966).
36 Horton, R. (1970).
37 Middleton, J. (1960).
38 Hallowell, A.I. (1969).
39 Nadel, S.F. (1952), p. 27.
40 Ibid., p. 29.

Bibliography

ALEXANDER, H.G. (1956), *Leibniz-Clarke Correspondence*, Manchester.

BEATTIE, J.H.M. (1964), *Other Cultures*, London.

BEATTIE, J.H.M. (1966), 'Ritual and social change', in *Man*, I, pp. 60–74.

BEATTIE, J.H.M. (1970), 'On understanding ritual', in Wilson, B.R. (ed.), *Rationality*, Oxford, pp. 240–68.

BORGER, R. and CIOFFI, F. (eds) (1970), *Explanation in the Behavioural Sciences*, Cambridge.

EVANS-PRITCHARD, E.E. (1934), 'Lévy-Bruhl's theory of primitive mentality',

Bulletin of the Faculty of Arts, University of Egypt (Alexandria), pp. 1–36.
EVANS-PRITCHARD, E.E. (1937), *Witchcraft, Oracles and Magic among the Azande*, Oxford.
FEYERABEND, P.K. (1965), 'Problems of empiricism', in Colodny, R. (ed.), *Beyond the Edge of Certainty*, Englewood Cliffs, New Jersey, pp. 145–260.
FIRTH, R. (1968), 'Oral tradition in relation to social status', in Georges, R.A. (ed.), *Studies on Mythology*, Homewood, pp. 168–83.
GÖDEL, K. (1946), 'Russell's mathematical logic', in Schilpp, P. (ed.), *Philosophy of Bertrand Russell*, Evanston, Illinois, pp. 123–54.
HALL, A. RUPERT (1970), *From Galileo to Newton 1630–1720*, London.
HALLOWELL, A.I. (1969), 'Ojibwa ontology, behavior and world view', in Diamond, S. (ed.), *Primitive Views of the World*, New York and London, pp. 49–82.
HESSE, M.B. (1954), *Science and the Human Imagination*, London.
HOLLIS, M. (1968), 'Reason and ritual', *Philosophy*, XLIII, pp. 231–47.
HOLTON, G. (1965), 'The thematic imagination in science', in Holton, G. (ed.), *Science and Culture*, Boston, pp. 88–108.
HORTON, R. (1970), 'African traditional thought and western science', in Wilson, B.R. (ed.), *Rationality*, Oxford, pp. 131–71.
KUHN, T. (1962), *The Structure of Scientific Revolutions*, Chicago.
KUHN, T. (1970), 'Logic of discovery or psychology of research?', in Lakatos, I. and Musgrave, A. (eds), *Criticism and the Growth of Knowledge*, Cambridge, pp. 1–23.
LAKATOS, I. (1970), 'History of science and its rational reconstructions', in Cohen, R.S. and Buck, R.C. (eds), *Boston Studies in the Philosophy of Science*, vol. 8, Dordrecht, pp. 91–136.
LEACH, E.R. (1954), *Political Divisions of Highland Burma*, London.
LEACH, E.R. (1968), 'Myth as a justification for faction and social change', in Georges, R.A. (ed.), *Studies on Mythology*, Homewood, pp. 184–98.
LÉVI-STRAUSS, C. (1966), *The Savage Mind*, London.
LUKES, S. (1970), 'Some problems about rationality', in Wilson, B.R. (ed.), *Rationality*, Oxford, pp. 194–213.
MANDELBAUM, D. (1966), 'Transcendental and pragmatic aspects of religions', *American Anthropologist*, LXVIII, pp. 1174–91.
MIDDLETON, J. (1960), *Lugbara Religion*, London.
NADEL, S.F. (1952), 'Witchcraft in four African societies', *American Anthropologist*, LIV, pp. 18–29.
PHILLIPS, D.Z. (1971), 'Religious beliefs and language-games', in Mitchell, Basil (ed.), *The Philosophy of Religion*, London, pp. 121–42.
POPPER, K.R. (1959), *The Logic of Scientific Discovery*, London.
PRICE, H.H. (1971), 'Belief "in" and belief "that"', in Mitchell, Basil (ed.), *The Philosophy of Religion*, London, pp. 143–67.
PRICE, H.H. (1972), *Essays in the Philosophy of Religion*, Oxford.
QUINE, W.V.O. (1969), *Ontological Relativity*, New York.
WALLACE, A.F.C. (1967), 'Dreams and the wishes of the soul: a type of psychoanalytic theory among the seventeenth century Iroquois', in Middleton, J. (ed.), *Magic, Witchcraft and Curing*, Garden City, New York, pp. 171–91.
WINCH, P. (1958), *The Idea of a Social Science*, London.
WINCH, P. (1970), 'Understanding a primitive society', in Wilson, B.R. (ed.), *Rationality*, Oxford, pp. 78–111.

3

Social psychology's rational man

R.P. Abelson

A Difficulties with the concept of rationality

The literature in modern academic social psychology rarely mentions 'rationality', despite the very deep concern for cognitive representations and processes which has characterized social psychology since the time of Kurt Lewin.[1] There is a complex of factors responsible for this aloofness. For us, any attempt to understand individual social thinking and social behaviour by investigating the existence and degree of human rationality has seemed—if I may take alliterative licence—too prescriptive, too presumptive, and too pre-emptive.

1 The prescriptive concept of rationality

Because the social scientist usually endeavours to pursue his inquiries according to well-elaborated standards of rationality, it is natural for him to place a generally high value on these standards. He may also feel that since individual and societal problems might be addressed more successfully through rational thought and rational action, an appealing long-range prescription for the improvement of the human condition is to increase the general prevalence of rationality.

From both of these motivations may spring the temptation to confuse prescription with description. Both the hope that man be rational and the despair that he be not, may colour the assessment of the degree to which he is. Social psychologists are especially sensitive to the possibility that values may distort belief (this phenomenon being part of their subject matter), and they are therefore generally sceptical of ideological characterizations of human nature which might impute ubiquity to things seen as good or bad. The Western European cultural tradition has ideologized rationality, and thus social psychologists within that tradition (Americans, mainly) are cautious to a fault not to take a position on the probable degree of extant rationality.

The history of the study of authoritarianism, a psychological constellation so repugnant that the investigators[2] carelessly exaggerated its degree of association with other academically unpopular attitudes such as political conservatism,[3] is a case which has reinforced the impulse to avoid value-laden organizing constructs. The present academic caution is probably overdone, but it is there nonetheless.

2   The presumptive concept of rationality

To achieve full rationality in any given situation, an individual must carry out a number of cognitive tasks: he must bring to mind the relevant considerations, test the credibility of premises subject to doubt, gather further necessary information, calculate the most rational policy, and act if possible so as to implement this policy; furthermore, each of these steps may be subject to frequent revision in light of unanticipated consequences of the implementation.

Social psychologists typically find this succession of steps grossly implausible as a model of standard human functioning. Too many presumptions about cognitive abilities seem necessary to sustain such a model, and the assumption of motivation strong enough to support all this cognitive effort seems gratuitous.

If we subject the possibility of rational habit of mind to rational analysis, we should ask, what is the typical payoff to an individual for being rational? Despite the seemingly obvious advantages in normal life adjustment of what clinical psychologists call 'reality testing', it is not so clear what costs or punishments are incurred by individuals for being non-rational concerning remote events. If a man believes that all the bad storms last winter were deliberately caused by Chinese atom bomb tests, what corrective factors would ever disabuse him of this misapprehension? We might presume that this man would *want* to examine carefully the plausibility of a manipulated connection between bomb tests and weather, but this is merely a presumption. Why should he care? Even if he cares, how would he have the wherewithal to carry out such an examination? There are many events in the world so remotely or indirectly caused that rational access to their analysis is difficult and tedious. A variety of non-rational beliefs in what I like to call 'occult causation' (extrasensory perception, the will of God, the hand of fate, the streak of luck, the unexplained mechanisms of the 'System', the exercise of jinxes and hypnotism, the power of prayer, etc.) maintain their hardy popularity in part because of the virtual impossibility of checking, much less refuting their premises.

Geoffrey Mortimore distinguishes in his essay between epistemic and practical rationality. The latter is consistent with the intrusion into belief-formation of epistemically irrelevant factors or with the omission of epistemically relevant factors, according to the practical decision context of the individual. Thus a person adopting a conclusion against his own better judgment because of the strong feelings of a friend might be said to show practical rationality if the loss of his friend's esteem were worse for him than accepting a more plausible conclusion. Now, even if attention is confined to practical rationality rather than the more stringent demands of epistemic rationality, there still remains an underlying presumption which the social psychologist finds troublesome.

If there is one message above all others that social psychology carries, it is that *individuals are very much more susceptible to the social influence of peers or authority figures than they are ordinarily aware.* This has been demonstrated in many ways,[4] but one of the most striking comes from Milgram's laboratory studies of obedience,[5] in which most people dutifully committed what seemed to be grossly harmful interpersonal acts on instruction by an authoritative experimenter under the façade of a simple experiment on the effects of punishment. Another case in point is Janis's analysis of 'Groupthink',[6] by which small groups of elite decision-makers (e.g. President Kennedy's policy advisers) made wretched policy decisions (the Bay of Pigs fiasco) by suppressing individual doubts in the face of the momentum of cohesive group activity. In both of these phenomena, there was of course some awareness of social pressures, but the awareness was dim and inadequate and the individuals involved were uncomfortable and puzzled in accounting afterwards for their behaviour. Individual standards and social pressures were weighed differently in thought and in action, since the great force of the social pressures was not reflectively appreciated.

This contribution to non-rationality is not neurotic or abnormal. It is true that in many psychotherapeutic procedures (encounter groups, marriage-counselling, sex-counselling, and especially psychoanalysis) it is focal to bring to the individual's awareness his feelings about the attitudes and actions of others. If a person could clearly articulate potential social rewards and costs, then he would be in a much better position to construct a 'balance sheet'[7] for making practically rational decisions. But insufficient awareness of subtle social influence is extremely widespread. The academic reader who is sceptical of this may perhaps convince himself by assigning as a class exercise that each student perform some simple action which strongly violates the social conventions of some group (without violating ethics or the law). Students very typically experience astonishment at how difficult it is to carry out this assignment, despite the anticipation that it might be fun. It disturbs their preconception that they are autonomous agents free from unanticipated social restraint.

3   Rationality as a pre-emptive concept

There is one other consideration that makes social psychologists leery of the rationality concept. We have preferred to concentrate on factors which could be manipulated (or observed to vary) situationally rather than on factors which might reside within persons. Rationality seems a topic from some other discipline's agenda, ill-suited to the generation of interesting empirical research. It is easy to talk about rationality, but hard to do anything to advance our understanding of it directly.

The trouble is that once one starts to talk about rationality, it pre-empts the way we organize our views of human thought and behaviour. We tend to think always in terms of default from a standard—in such-and-such a situation, why do people *not* behave rationally? But searching for the idealization that isn't there is a less productive research strategy than finding out what *is* there. Rationality simply may not be a useful descriptive concept when we look carefully at what is going on psychologically.

A good case in point is the somewhat parallel concept of altruism (also prescriptive, presumptive, and pre-emptive). In the good deal of social psychological research in the area of helping behaviour,[8] the concept of altruism is not very useful in explaining the intriguing array of differences between occasions in which help is offered, and those in which it is not. There are a large number of other motives served by helping or not helping in any given situation.

Similarly there are many mundane (and esoteric) functions served by holding beliefs,[9] other than in the service of rationality. Beliefs may be comforting, may protect against anxiety, may organize vague feelings, may provide a sense of identity, may be the prerequisite for participation in a cause, may provide something to say to avoid seeming uninformed, etc. Similarly there are many motives for action, independent of rationality considerations. It is interesting to contemplate the possible developability of a motive to be rational in thought and action, and I find myself generally sympathetic to Geoffrey Mortimore's discussion of this idea. However, I think it is misleading to be so fixed on the concept of rationality that its presence or absence is the primary governing consideration in the analysis of behaviour or belief. It is particularly bothersome to social psychologists when rationality discussions neglect the rewards of social conformity, and the costs of social deviance.

4 Limited subjective rationality

I have argued that a direct frontal assault on the questions raised by the rational ideal is neither congenial to social psychologists, nor apt to prove empirically rewarding. However, it is possible to piece together from a variety of investigations with other aims, a general conception of the extent and nature of human rationality to which most social psychologists would probably agree. I will refer to this conception as 'limited subjective rationality'.

As I have noted elsewhere,[10] the phrase 'subjective rationality' implies two different departures from objective rationality: the use of reasoning capacity upon a personally distorted picture of reality; or alternatively, the application of predictable mental processing rules which happen not to correspond to the rules of formal logic. These two intrusions of personal calculus into the cognitive realm might also co-occur: predictable but not necessarily fully logical rules might be applied by the individual to a specifiable but not necessarily accurate picture of the world. This is a view which is essentially shared by the 'cognitive consistency theories'[11] in social psychology, which presume a high degree of cognitive order according to as yet only dimly understood principles of what might be called 'psycho-logic'.[12]

The term 'limited' I have appended in order to make clear the view that important considerations which might usefully contribute to a subjective calculus are often filtered out, overlooked, or oversimplified by the individual, and do not contribute properly to his mental processing. The usual item in the 'filtered' category is the unconscious need, but that is not primarily what I intend here. Rather, I would emphasize the tendency, already discussed, for individuals to be blind to the powerful effects of social forces upon their beliefs and behaviour.

The cultural traditions in western democracies stress the over-arching importance of autonomy of mind and independence of action, for without these possibilities there would be no individual freedom. Given an atmosphere of pride in this heritage, there is a natural tendency for us to imagine that we are exercising individual liberty even when we are not. Conversely, to yield to social pressure, whether from spouse, boss, neighbours, union, or whoever, is usually construed as a sacrifice of principle, and we tend to deny that this has happened even when it has. It is clear that we *are* often influenced by others, and the tendency to deny it filters our ability to be (even subjectively) rational. This tendency has been called the 'illusion of choice'.[13] We will discuss some of its curious consequences in detail in section B3.

We are ready now to review specifically a number of social psychological lines of research and theory, as they reflect on the view of rationality stated here. Section B sketches the cognitive consistency principles, and section C the recent work on attribution theory.[14] In section D, a variety of human cognitive limitations are discussed. Cognitive overload—the excess of processing requirements over processing capacity—is another of the major sources of information loss reducing the correspondence between actual thought processes and the rational ideal.

B   The consistency principles

Several principles or theories from a major current within social psychology of the past two decades have postulated forces tending to produce consistency between belief and affect, or between belief and action. We will review three of the streams within this current: the congruity principle, the balance principle, and dissonance theory.

1   The congruity principle

A great deal of attention in social psychology has been given to the study of communication and persuasion. Osgood and Tannenbaum[15] were concerned with rudimentary communication situations in which a liked or disliked communicator (the 'source') endorsed or criticized a concept either liked or disliked by a member of the communication audience. They postulated that in the endorsement case, the audience member would tend to compromise appropriately his evaluation of both source and concept toward equality in sign and intensity. Thus if strongly liked *President Eisenhower* praises weakly disliked *Golf*, there would be a tendency for the recipient of this communication to change his opinion of *Golf* in a favourable direction, and his opinion of *President Eisenhower* in an unfavourable direction. The latter change would be of lesser extent than the former, since a strongly held initial evaluation would be less vulnerable to change than a weakly held initial evaluation.

In the criticism case, the congruity principle specifies that evaluations of source and concept would tend toward opposition in sign, with equality in intensity. For example, if revered *Mao Tse-tung* condemns mildly admired *Lin Piao*, then the evaluation of *Mao* is predicted to drop slightly, but that of *Lin* to tumble disastrously. In a contrasting version of this example, a *Mao*-hater with initially neutral feelings toward *Lin* would end up feeling rather kindly toward *Lin* as a result of an attack by *Mao*.

The situations for which these predictions are designed are limited, to be sure, and the congruity principle of course does not work perfectly in practice. (There is some impressive evidence in its favour, however.[16]) Nevertheless it is a good illustration of a style of principle-formation repeatedly encountered in social psychology. Principles in this style embody limited subjective rationality in that the individual deals with mini-systems of symbolic objects by using a small number of simple rules which 'make sense' for him.

2 The balance principle

A somewhat broader paradigm for affective-cognitive consistency than the congruity principle is the balance principle formulated by Fritz Heider.[17] The simplest version of this principle involves the cognitions of person P about himself in relation to another person O, and about both persons in relation to some object X (which might be a third person). Two types of relations are considered—'sentiment relations', which can be subdivided into positive and negative sentiments, and 'positive unit relations', not further subdivided. The prototypic examples of sentiment relations are 'likes' and 'dislikes'. Unit relations can be variously realized as 'owns', 'belongs with', 'produces', etc.—anything which establishes a conceptual unit bonding two cognitive subjects.

The balance analysis considers the triadic configuration of relationships: P-O, O-X, and P-X. Suppose, for example, that P likes O, that O is bonded to X, and that P despises X. It is intuitively apparent that such a situation would be uncomfortable for P, and that he might attempt some change in a relationship so as to remove the discomfort. He might cease liking O, he might struggle to reassess his feelings toward X, or he might try to deny the connection between O and X. (More elaborate possibilities have been discussed in Abelson.[18]) The P-O-X triad in this example is 'imbalanced', and each of the given relationship changes would have produced a new and 'balanced' triad. Heider's principle is that imbalance initiates psychological forces tending to restore balance.

All possible combinations of unit relations and positive and negative sentiment relations in a complete P-O-X triad can be characterized as balanced or imbalanced. The general rule is that balance occurs when there are no negative relations (a liked other is bonded to a liked X; self and bonded other both like X; etc.) or two negative relations (self and bonded other both dislike X; etc.), whereas imbalance occurs when there is but one negative relation (a liked other is bonded to a disliked X, as above; self and disliked other are both bonded to X; etc.) or—though there has been some theoretical uncertainty about this—when there are three negative relations (self and disliked other both dislike X).

The principle stems from a general view of the individual as attempting to make sense out of his environment by schematic interpretations of incomplete and ambiguous facts within a circumscribed domain. The balance principle is therefore an excellent prototype for what we have called limited subjective rationality. In extensive reviews of the balance principle,[19] there is a spectrum of judgmental data, and a scattering of studies on learning, memory and attitude change, which taken together are quite broadly supportive of the principle, despite certain ambiguities in the details. The principle has been mathematically generalized by Cartwright and Harary[20] and Abelson and Rosenberg[21] to apply to more than three cognitive elements. A brief review of a communication study by Rosenberg and Abelson[22] may give some idea of the implications and limitations of the generalized principle in practice.

In this experiment, the subjects were instructed to imagine that they were profit-hungry owners of a large department store facing a perplexing imbalanced situation. Fenwick, the highly astute and successful manager of the rug department, was said to be planning a huge display of modern art in his department, an action which according to survey information could have a severe negative effect on rug sales because of conservative customer reaction. Three separate beliefs could resolve the puzzle of a competent manager doing such a disastrous thing, and a different vice-president was persuasively communicating one or another to the owner: (1) the survey information was outdated, and in fact modern art displays really help sales; (2) the report of the Fenwick plan was based on insubstantial rumour, and even if true, it was obvious that Fenwick upon informed reconsideration would drop the whole thing; and (3) Fenwick's prior management of the rug department had not been shrewd at all, but rather poor when evaluated by modern competitive criteria for departmental managers. Acceptance of any one of the three beliefs would lead to a theoretically balanced resolution; in the first case, that competent Fenwick will do a helpful thing; in the second, that competent Fenwick will not commit the bad mistake; in the third, that *in*competent Fenwick *will* commit the bad mistake. Each of these, in its way, is perfectly understandable as a statement of characterological consistency. The experiment was designed so as to manipulate conditions disposing toward one rather than another of these three balanced resolutions.

The way this was attempted was to build in three differing sets of affective dispositions, each balanced with respect to only one of the resolutions. There were three different groups of subjects, each provided with different initial attitudes. In Group I, the store owner was said personally to admire both the personality of Fenwick and the aesthetics of modern art. If members of this group accepted the argument that modern art really helps sales (but rejected the other two arguments), they could arrive at the balanced conclusion that shrewd and likeable Fenwick planned a pleasing art display beneficial to sales. In Group II, Fenwick was presented as likeable, but modern art as loathsome. This group, by accepting only the argument that Fenwick would indeed not post the display, could reach closure by believing that shrewd and likeable Fenwick would reject involvement with the ugly and hurtful art show. In Group III, Fenwick was said to be obnoxious and modern art loathsome. By accepting only the communication impugning Fenwick's record, this group could achieve the final formulation that incompetent and obnoxious Fenwick was indeed planning an ugly art display ruinous for store sales.

The experimental predictions about differential *communication acceptance* for the three groups were strongly supported. However, an unanticipated theoretical difficulty revealed by the study was that following exposure to the three communications, the conclusions reached by the subjects about the total situation on a post-questionnaire were frequently not the balanced configurations prescribed by hypothesis. This was not a problem with Group I, whose subjects both accepted the argument about the good effect of a potential art display on sales and maintained the happy vision of good Fenwick performing a good act. However, in Group II, although most subjects were initially willing to accept the argument that Fenwick would not pursue his plan, a number of subjects apparently changed their minds and slipped into the same pleasing pattern as did Group I. With Group III, the final versions of the dilemma were heterogeneous and usually unresolved. The prediction that subjects would resolve the perplexity by blaming the bad plan on bad Fenwick is by hindsight naive. It ignores the obvious fact that a bad action by a bad actor may leave disequilibrium in the victim not because the action is inexplicable but because it is painful.

These irregularities in the data led Rosenberg and Abelson to recognize a dual-motive approach by individuals to their belief-structures: (1) to alter or preserve beliefs about a state of affairs to achieve attitudinal *balance*, wherein there is a harmony between affect and belief in providing a meaningful construction of reality; (2) to follow *hedonism* in belief, by accepting that which is pleasurable, or at least not painful. When a communication suggests an outcome both balanced and hedonic, it is especially welcome, but when balance and hedonism are pitted against each other, the individual may have trouble deciding what to believe.

This point may be visualized readily by encoding the balance principle in one or the other of the two statements—'Good people do good things'; 'Bad people do bad things'—and the hedonism 'principle' in the statement, 'Good things happen to me'. Now we may write the four combinations of balance and hedonism as follows:

Balanced–hedonic:	'Good people do good things for me'
Balanced–antihedonic:	'Bad people do bad things to me'
Imbalanced–hedonic:	'Bad people do good things for me'
Imbalanced–antihedonic:	'Good people do bad things to me'

The first combination is optimal in terms of what one might 'want to believe' about the world, if facts and interpretations could be bent in that direction. The next two combinations are unpleasant and puzzling, respectively. The last combination is bothersome in both respects, and therefore represents the type of configuration which should yield the greatest motivated avoidance. Other results of the Fenwick experiment support this latter statement. The study as a whole illustrates the analysis of the interaction between prior attitude and reaction to a communication, using limited consistency principles.

A slightly different application of the concept of balance is captured by the 'Just World' principle: If something bad happens to someone, then he must have deserved it; if something good happens to someone, then he must have been worthy. The implications of the 'Just World' principle are reviewed elsewhere.[23]

3 Dissonance theory

The most influencial of the consistency principles has been 'cognitive dissonance theory', originally formulated by Festinger,[24] and followed by a very large number of experimental explorations of its attitudinal and behavioural consequences.[25]

The theory begins with a specification of what is meant by a 'dissonant' relation between cognitions. Two cognitions, X and Y, about own beliefs or behaviour, or aspects of external reality, are said to stand in dissonant relation when the opposite of Y 'follows from' X. For example, if X is the knowledge, 'I am standing un-protected in a driving rainstorm', and Y is 'I am not getting wet', a dissonant relation is present because it follows from standing unprotected in the rain that one gets wet. Or if X is 'I am trembling with fear' and Y is 'All objects in the environment are benign', there is dissonance because it 'follows from' being afraid that there is something to be afraid of. There has been considerable discussion in the literature of the potentially very vague phrase 'follows from'. Aronson[26] suggests that it corresponds to 'psychological expect-ancy', and Abelson[27] invokes 'psychological causation'. Irle[28] claims that the individual must have a *hypothesis* in order for dis-sonance to be produced (by violation of the hypothesis). These various interpretations have in common that 'follows from' is intended as a psychological, not a formally logical, construct. If it is typically the case that subjects, when given X as true, agree after time for reflection that Y is also true, we may say that X and Y are related by psychological implication, or that Y 'follows from' X.

Two cognitions would stand in 'consonant' relation if one followed from the other. Finally, two cognitions could simply be irrelevant if they carried no psychological implications for each other.

In any given situation, more than two cognitions will in general be present. The total magnitude of dissonance is defined in terms of the relative number of dissonant to consonant pairs. Dissonance is postulated to induce effort aimed at its reduction, with greater effort the greater the magnitude of dissonance. The simplest means of dissonance reduction is to change one or the other member of a dissonant pair.

This sparse theoretical machinery has been applied to several different situational paradigms. The most often studied and pro-bably most interesting is connected to the 'psychology of insufficient reward'. In an early study by Festinger and Carlsmith[29] subjects were induced for either an insufficient ($1) or more than sufficient ($20) reward to claim to another subject that an impending task was fun when in fact they knew that it was quite boring. To tell a minor falsehood was for most of these college student subjects presumably dissonant with their self-concepts as sincere individuals, but the large reward at least provided some justification for this behaviour. (In the language of dissonance theory, the receipt of an ample reward is consonant with the performance of a solicited behaviour. Behaviour 'follows from' being rewarded.) The individuals receiving only $1, however, had no such justification, and were therefore subject to greater dissonance.

The mode of dissonance reduction most readily available to subjects in this situation was to change their opinions of the boring task. Telling someone that X is true is not insincere if you yourself believe X. The prediction in the Festinger-Carlsmith experiment was thus that individuals paid $1 to talk up the dull task would themselves come to regard it as more interesting than subjects paid $20. The less the reward for persuading another person, the greater the self-persuasion effect! This prediction was well supported by experimental data.

There have been many experimental tests of similar predictions, partly to meet criticisms of the original study, and partly to explore psychological factors crucial to the operation of the paradigm. The self-persuasion effect for insufficient reward has been repeatedly verified in the laboratory, and appears to be strongest under the following conditions: the individual's behaviour has important *consequences* for other people;[30] the individual has high *commitment* to the behaviour;[31] the individual feels he had a *choice* in whether or not to engage in the behaviour.[32]

To find oneself making insincere statements is especially unsettling when other people may be seriously misled by those statements. In a study by Nel, Helmreich and Aronson,[33] the possibility of such serious consequences was introduced by inducing anti-marijuana subjects to make pro-marijuana speeches to a supposedly neutral and potentially corruptible audience. Subjects doing such a thing for ample payment might justify it as an unpleasant job, but subjects making the speech for an insufficient reward—and of their own free will—would have a difficult problem accounting for their own reprehensibility. One resolution is to weaken or alter one's own attitude, so that one's behaviour is not so damaging after all, and this is exactly what the low-reward subjects in this study did, by becoming substantially more pro-marijuana. When the reward was high, or when the audience for the speech was supposedly uninfluencible because they were already strongly pro- or strongly anti-marijuana, this attitude change effect did not occur.

Another resolution to such an awkward dilemma is to suppose that one could later undo or 'take back' what was said, by telling the audience that one didn't mean it. Helmreich and Collins[34] manipulated this commitment factor by establishing 'take back' and 'no-take back' instructions for different groups of subjects making an insincere speech for videotape. The no-take back condition for small reward, a highly committal and very dissonant situation, produced the large attitude change effect predicted by dissonance theory.

The factor of free choice is strongly inherent in the insufficient reward paradigm. If an individual is *forced* to do something he would not ordinarily do, there is little cognitive dissonance, as the applied force provides sufficient justification for the behaviour; however, when he has himself chosen to do something he would not ordinarily do, there is a great deal of cognitive dissonance, as the behaviour is essentially inexplicable. The studies cited above made use of a free choice manipulation: each subject was told before composing his speech arguments that it was up to him whether he wanted to go through with the performance or not.

Almost without exception, when subjects in these psychological experiments are told that they are free to refuse to continue, they consider this offer seriously, and then decide to continue. They often thus agree with surprising good grace to do some rather unpleasant things. The social pressure to complete experimental procedures, whatever they may be, is much stronger than subjects realize, and the proffered free choice is merely an 'illusion of choice'.[35] It is implicit in the social contract of being an experimental subject that one should do what the experimenter asks, and it is surprisingly difficult and embarrassing to reject experimental requests even in the face of disingenuous permission to break the social contract.[36]

We may thus restate the dissonance paradigm for insufficient reward in the following way: A person is subtly pressured to do something contrary to his usual attitudes, but he doesn't realize he has been pressured, thinking that he had a totally free choice of whether or not to engage in the behaviour, even though this commits him to something with unpleasant consequences for his self-esteem. There is very little tangible external justification for his behaviour. He ends up by changing his attitudes so as to provide internal justification for the behaviour. This phenomenon has led dissonance theorists to state that man is not a rational animal, he is a *rationalizing* animal.[37]

Were subjects to realize that they had been pressured into the behaviour, this would provide sufficient external justification, and they would not need to invent internal justification. Paradoxically, then, it is the vanity of assuming one's own freedom from social pressure that leads to the surrender of freedom in the formulation and expression of one's values. Cultural historians might wish to consider whether this is a peculiarly American paradox. As we noted in section A2, the American in life or laboratory seems strongly motivated to conform to others while asserting his own individuality, at the same time trying to preserve a public image as a rational person.[38] Possibly, susceptibility to such contortions may be broadly typical of western culture in general. Not nearly as many dissonance experiments have been done in Europe or Australia as in the United States, and the results abroad may or may not follow the same general pattern.[39] It would be fascinating if the insufficient reward paradigm failed in an oriental culture, because of the absence of an 'illusion of choice', but to the writer's knowledge, appropriate experiments have not been attempted.

4 Imbalances v. dissonances

Our review of these mini-systems for characterizing subjective rationality has left a large, theoretical loose end, namely that there is some lack of correspondence between situations classified as imbalanced and those classified as dissonant. For example, a triad of sentiment relations in which Joe likes George, George dislikes Ed, and Joe likes Ed, is a clear case of imbalance, yet a dissonance theorist would not consider it a case of dissonance. Such a theorist might say, 'Maybe Joe can like both George and Ed even though there is antagonism between two of them. The world is full of examples like that. After all, I wouldn't automatically dislike someone that a friend of mine disliked. Nor would I expect that if I disliked someone, all my friends would uniformly dislike him. There are all sorts of reasons why any two given people might not get along.'

Here the dissonance theorist is rejecting the psychological implication claimed by the balance theorist. Given X (Joe likes George, and George dislikes Ed), he does not agree that Y (Joe dislikes Ed) will follow. This only follows if a certain organizing principle or 'underlying cognition' is present, incorporating the notion that the enemy of a friend is necessarily an enemy. Some people might believe this, and some not.

Consider an individual with the underlying cognition that the struggle for survival in a hostile environment requires decisive classification of every person as either a friend admissible to the in-group gang or as an enemy belonging to the out-group gang ('Anyone not with us is against us'). A dissonance theorist should grant that for a person with this world view it *would* follow from

'Joe likes George' and 'George dislikes Ed' and 'Joe dislikes Ed'. Given the other two premises, it would be dissonant to know that 'Joe likes Ed', as this would recognize the possibility of positive affective bonds across hostile gang boundaries, a possibility as absurd for our hypothetical zealot as a strong perceptual dissonance such as snow during a heat wave.

There is thus the clear conceptual possibility that for some individuals, an affective imbalance based on sentiment relations would also be a dissonance, whereas for others, dissonance would be absent. But consider a second example of a linked set of three relations: Joe plants a time-bomb; the time-bomb causes destruction in a target area; Joe doesn't want destruction in the target area. Would a dissonance theorist say this were dissonant, because it 'follows' from the first two statements that Joe wants destruction in the target area? I think that the answer is now 'yes'. The underlying cognition in this case is: *What a person's knowing actions will primarily cause, he desires.*

Although one may wish to introduce qualifications and subtleties into this straightforward statement of the naive notion of intention, even as it stands it has such strong intuitive appeal that it is difficult to imagine a serious alternative. That people act purposefully, everyone knows, or certainly assumes.[40] It is both imbalanced and dissonant that a person would freely carry out an action he knew would produce nothing he wanted.

Note that even though balance and dissonance theory both encompass this important case of intentional action, the natural 'follows from' statement of dissonance theory is the more specific. If person A carries out (is 'bonded' to) action B, and B causes (is bonded to) action C, one may educe from the balance principle that A will bear some positive relation to C, but no specific interpretation is specified. 'Person A *is responsible for* consequence C' is a sensible albeit not very daring eduction. Other positive relations, though yielding balance in the A-B-C triad, might be vapid or irrelevant, for example, A *recommends* C or A *owns* C. The appropriate A *wants* C is only one of many balanced possibilities, but the dissonance paradigm would presumably demand this possibility uniquely.

Let us consider still another case, one in which balance and dissonance interpretations are sharply different. In a romantic triangle in which Joe loves Ann, and Ann loves Harry, does it follow, as balance theory would seem to require, that Joe likes Harry? This is an evidently awkward example, since intuition and experience clearly suggest that Joe would not like Harry. In some reviews of balance theory[41] this situation has been reinterpreted to try to remove the paradox. Joe, it is said, wants to possess his love object, Ann; but Harry, by alienating Ann's affections, frustrates Joe's intent. Therefore Joe hates Harry, as both balance theory and common sense require. This reinterpretation yields the complex though not unrealistic possibility that the two men may simultaneously respect and hate each other. To the extent that they both share a favourable opinion of Ann, they might have mutual respect as men of comparable good taste; but to the extent that they both compete for the unsharable commodity of unique object of Ann's affections, they should dislike each other.

In contrast to this somewhat tortured re-analysis by the balance principle, a dissonance analysis would probably consist of a no-nonsense appeal to the well understood concept of romantic rivalry. It follows directly from 'Joe loves Ann' and 'Ann loves Harry' that 'Joe hates Harry' because of the underlying cognition, 'Men hate their rivals'.

It may be objected, however, that to state 'the rivalry principle' of psychological implication does not explain why one expects Joe to hate his rival: it merely invokes a common-sense truism to reach the conclusion demanded by common sense. Something follows because it naturally follows. The only way out of this circularity, it seems to me, is by detailed codification of a number of the widespread and robust principles used in 'common sense' rather than by abstract argument over the logic of mental calculi. This is the task I have set myself in recent attempts to develop a model of the structure of belief-systems.[42] It should not be surprising that a number of different underlying cognitions (that is, subjective principles) would be needed, and there is nothing in balance theory, incidentally, which demands that no other cognitive principles ever be operative. Heider in fact urged a multiple principle system, using the piquant metaphor that the flight of birds does not refute the law of gravity.[43]

Of dissonance theory one might say that its model of implication is indeed nothing more than simple common sense, but that its unique contribution consists in the unexpected way that common sense is connected to behaviour, namely that under certain governing conditions it is used non-rationally to justify prior behaviour, rather than rationally to shape incipient behaviour.

C Attribution theory

Recently, a body of research with several unifying hypotheses has grown into what social psychologists call 'attribution theory'. 'Attribution' is the process by which an observer assigns a causal interpretation to a given social event or set of events on the basis of present information and previous assumptions. Usually, there are drastically different causal interpretations potentially available for even the simplest event: a person can be seen to succeed on a task because he has ability (or luck), or because the task is easy; a person can be seen to engage in a behaviour because he wants to or because he is forced to; a person can be seen to feel disturbed because he is neurotic, or because he is harassed by circumstance; and so on. In each of these examples, the first alternative assigns the cause to some factor internal to the person, and the second alternative to some aspect of the external stimuli or circumstances. It is a major chosen task of attribution theory to delimit the conditions for an observer to make a 'person attribution' versus a 'stimulus attribution'. Important consequences for ideas about social reality flow from these alternatives.

Of several theoretical analyses of the factors involved in attribution, that of Kelley[44] is the most rationalistic. To generate a predictive scheme for attributions, he applies Mill's Laws of Difference when a certain actor is observed consistently to give a certain response to a certain stimulus. If other actors do not give the same response to this stimulus (a condition of 'low consensus'), then the actor is seen as the cause of the response. For example, imagine that a certain child consistently cries in the presence of a certain dog. If other children rarely cry in the presence of this dog, it seems reasonable for an observer to exempt the dog from causal responsibility and to focus on the child (especially if he cries to other dogs). If, on the other hand, this child rarely cries in the presence of other dogs (and other children also cry to this dog), then the reasonable observer will assume that the dog is the cause of the crying.

This analysis provides a rational baseline for the attribution process. It is not clear, however, to what extent actual attributions obey the rational model. One difficulty is that the necessary background information may not be available to the observer. Moreover (and of most interest for this paper), there are several factors which may bias the attribution away from the rational baseline. It is not our purpose here to review these factors exhaustively, but the mention of a few will serve to illustrate subjective qualifications on rationality.

McArthur[45] explored Kelley's model by varying the available information on consensus and distinctiveness for several types of events. In general, she found Kelley's analysis supported, except that the particular nature of the situation had great influence when the information was inconclusive. An example of inconclusive information is high consensus and low distinctiveness—when 'everybody does it to every stimulus' there is no logical basis to assign responsibility to either the person or the stimulus. However, in such cases McArthur found that if the situation involved *social performance* or *social action*, there was person attribution; if the situation concerned the expression of *attitudes* or *feelings*, there was stimulus attribution. In other words, we tend to invest people with 'skills' and 'intentions' when they are observed in the performance of directed action, rather than attributing such behaviours to incentives and obstacles in the environment. However, we assume that emotive responses are largely induced by the environment rather than emanating from within the person. (This same conclusion has been anticipated by the philosopher R.S. Peters,[46] operating in a different style and from different premises.)

These curious kinks in a pure logic of causal attribution are mild compared to the attribution bias noted by Jones and Nisbett:[47] individuals tend to attribute the behaviour of *others* to personal dispositions or traits, but rarely tend to use trait attributions in explaining their own behaviour. This is especially the case for negative traits. If the other fellow does something bad, it is because he has bad characteristics, but if I do something bad, it is because of situational pressures or desperate circumstances. This kind of cognitive device could be explained as a motivated bias in defence of self-esteem. A more 'rational' explanation is that the information available to an individual to explain his own behaviour is substantially different from the information available to explain the behaviour of others. For one thing, a person usually can provide numerous falsifications of any potential character trait description of himself from detailed knowledge of past situations in which he did not display dishonesty, laziness, cruelty, or whatever. However, single instances of the behaviour of others are often not viewed in the context of past exceptions because that information is not available.

Another consideration that may account for the attribution bias is that the perceptual information at the moment of the critical behaviour is different from different perspectives. In the behaver's perceptual field, other people and stimuli are much more apparent to the behaver than is the behaver himself; in the passive observer's perceptual field, however, the behaver is the focus of observation. The assumption that causation will be invested in what is best seen (or heard) then leads to the conclusion that the behaver will give a stimulus attribution and the observer, a person attribution. However, this informational explanation of defensive attribution is not completely convincing, as the treatment of information about others appears often to be more superficial and biased than the treatment of the same information about self. The observer often jumps to an unfair conclusion about the behaver. For example, Jones et al.[48] found that failure by others on the early trials of a novel and difficult task tends to be accounted as evidence of their stupidity, but failure by self is interpreted as getting warmed up; unexpected success on later trials of this task tends to be dismissed as mere luck in others, but seen as evidence for emerging skill in self.

It appears that in the attribution process there is typically some compromise between a completely objective use of information and a completely self-serving style in which information is not used at all. The compromise involves selective use of information consistent with self-interest. To be more specific, there is a tendency for individuals to accept information rapidly and off-handedly when it has no personal consequences for them, but to closely examine and favourably reprocess information with personal consequences. The asymmetry is in part based upon human information-processing limitations—it is always inconvenient and often impossible to explore all of the implications flowing from a given information set, or even to digest adequately the information itself, and so the individual must pick and choose where to spend his mental energy (see section D1 on 'information overload').

One final selected topic within attribution theory is 'misattribution' and its applications to so-called 'misattribution therapy'.[49] Suppose that a person has a habit or feeling which he finds disturbing because it reflects badly on his character or personality. He might, for example, have a strong aversion to airplane flights, discomfiting because other people may consider him neurotic and chide him for letting childish fears cloud his appreciation of the obvious practical advantages of flying. If such an individual can be induced to misattribute his aversion, using some psychologically benign stimulus factor, say, the noise of jet engines to which his ears happened to be particularly sensitive, then the stigma and distress of self-blame are removed.

Several experiments have demonstrated the possibility of misattribution. Storms and Nisbett[50] found that insomniacs, after trying for several nights a pill they thought would keep them awake, reported falling asleep sooner than they had without the pill (which was actually chemically inactive). The authors explain this paradox as a misattribution phenomenon: the subjects' difficulties in falling asleep were habitually compounded by worrying that as insomniacs something was seriously wrong with them; with a pill to which they could attribute their sleeplessness, however, this surplus worry was removed and sleep came easier. Davison and Valins,[51] working a similar theme with one more turn, tricked subjects into believing that a particular pill had made them more resistant to electric shock; later, it was revealed that the pill had no physiological effects whatever. Subsequently, the subjects without any pills evidenced genuinely greater tolerance to electric shocks. This phenomenon can be understood as follows: if the initial resistance to shock were not conferred by the inactive pill, then the resistance must have been due to an internal capability; somehow subjects believing themselves capable of higher shock tolerance were thereafter able to display a physiological pattern indicative of less actual sensitivity to shocks.

Physiological symptoms can be used to establish misattribution as well as to measure it. Valins[52] provided bogus feedback which subjects thought represented the amplified sound of their own heartbeats. The experimenter was able to increase subjects' judgments of the attractiveness of particular females by co-ordinating faster heartbeat signals with the display of their photographs. Valins and Ray[53] were able to lower subjects' avoidance reactions to snakes by co-ordinating *non-increase* of heartbeat with slides of snakes, interspersed with increased heartbeat signals when warnings of impending electric shock were shown. A good review of several studies of this general type has been given by Valins and Nisbett.[54]

Although these phenomena may smack of mere trickery, they bear an important lesson in the analysis of human rationality. In general, *individuals seeking an account of their own behaviour seem to prefer unitary explanations to conjunctive explanations.* The photograph viewers do not act as though they believe, 'This girl is really ordinary looking and my heart rate increase is due to something else.' It is mentally much more economical to suppose that physiological and affective reactions are covariant. The insomniac brought to believe that a pill can cause his wakefulness thereby seems to believe that his own neurotic tendencies are less responsible. He does not conclude that since both the pill and the neurosis could very well operate jointly, the presence of the one is irrelevant to the effect of the other.

Another simplifying misattribution to which we have repeatedly referred in other contexts is the tendency to neglect group pressures on behaviour in favour of explanations based on individual initiative. An interesting observation just beginning to make its way into the attribution literature is that when no prior group stereotypes are available, attributions to individual actors almost always dominate attributions to the groups to which the actors belong.[55] For example, the My Lai massacre is widely interpreted by the public in terms of the foolishness or moral weakness of Lieutenant Calley, but not so typically viewed in terms of the dehumanized atmosphere of groups of soldiers on search-and-destroy missions.

Man, the simple explanation-seeker for his own behaviour and the behaviour of others, is often unable to arrive at adequately complex explanations. We next turn to an examination of evidence suggesting how general this penchant for mental economy is.

D Cognitive limitations

1 Limited capacity to process information

In the past twenty years, a number of psychological investigations have emphasized a universal theme: limitation of the human mind in the face of complexity. Psychological interest in this broad area was stimulated by the advent of information theory,[56] which led to a series of experiments on the 'channel capacity' of individuals in processing simple perceptual information. This is a function of the number of reliable perceptual discriminations a person can make (and the rate at which he can respond on the basis of those discriminations).

In a famous paper, 'The magical number seven plus or minus two: some limits on our capacity for processing information', George Miller[57] articulated the somewhat surprising summary statement that individuals could only make from five to nine perceptual discriminations along *any* single stimulus dimension. It is as though there is a fixed amount of attentional energy which individuals can stretch to cover whatever range of possible stimuli presents itself. If the stimuli are closely bunched along the stimulus dimension (e.g. of loudness or brightness), then fine absolute discriminations are made, whereas if the stimuli are widely spread, absolute discriminations become coarse, so that either way, the same 'magical number' of approximately seven stimulus prototypes are reliably distinguished along the stimulus dimension.

There are many qualifications to this basic proposition, which is somewhat too starkly stated here. Nevertheless, the general point for our purposes is that there are clear organismic limitations at the simple level of perceptual processing. One might anticipate that at more complex levels of information processing, limitations would be even more severe. There has been much comment in the general press about the human consequences of the 'information explosion'. Some writers have discussed the impingement of modern technology on urban life[58] so as to produce such 'information overload' that individuals simply cannot cope with the pace of daily life, thereby becoming protectively withdrawn and alienated.

We wish to examine those tangible aspects of cognitive limitation with consequences for subjective rationality. What is often most important is not *how much* information an individual can process, but by *what method* he processes whatever information he can manage to handle. One of the most interesting issues here concerns 'statistical' versus 'clinical' judgment.[59] Judges are given complex case materials to evaluate in order to arrive at classifications or predictions. A number of quantitative cues are available on each case for the judges to use in whatever way they can. The question is whether the information in the cues is utilized in a more or less mechanical way, each cue contributing slightly as an appropriate statistical predictor, or whether idiosyncratic configurations or patterns of cues are noted and skilfully used, as clinicians are wont to claim for the nature of their art. Many studies on this question[60] have come out almost uniformly discouraging to the clinical point of view. Judges attempting to use configural cues make predictions which are in general worse than simple statistical predictions would be (say, by use of multiple regression equations).

What is even more embarrassing, there are strong indications that judges trying to predict on the basis of cue patterns do not in fact even use much pattern information[61]—rather, they simply become ragged statistical processors relying on additive combinations of the several diagnostic cue dimensions, without realizing that they are doing so. One of the sources of evidence for this assertion comes from the so-called 'bootstrap effect'.[62]

Picture the common situation in universities, in which a faculty committee reviews a group of applicants for admission on the basis of a number of presumably relevant bits of information, or 'cues', in each application. From the perspective of a particular faculty judge, he must somehow combine the cues to arrive at a prediction of the prospective degree of future success of every candidate. The judge may not formulate the task to himself in terms of 'combining cues'—he might conceive the evaluation process as one involving global impressions—but we can always analyse his performance as in effect necessitating cue combination. To clarify the analysis, suppose that each of the cues lends itself to quantitative expression (e.g. aptitude test scores), and that the prediction is rendered by the judge on a quantitative scale such as predicted Grade Point Average. Some judges in this situation might give heaviest weight to one cue, some to another, but almost all judges will give some weight also to cues other than the single most important one. The phrase 'give weight to' is more than metaphorical here, for a judge's predictions are themselves statistically predictable as weighted linear combinations of the several cues. The bootstrap effect arises when the linear formula summarizing the judge's prediction scheme is applied to each individual candidate. Paradoxically, these bootstrapped predictions are frequently more accurate in predicting Grade Point Averages than were the original direct predictions by the judge. The explanation for the paradox is that the judge is fallible in applying his own cue weightings to all individual cases, but the statistical weighting removes this fallibility. Furthermore, and more interesting, there is very little useful predictive information in the individual judgments which is not captured by the linear formula.

2 Cognitive algebra

An extensive experimental programme has been conducted by Norman Anderson[63] with the aim of exploring the laws of subjective combination of miscellaneous items of stimulus information. He has concluded that such information integration is typically governed by a kind of 'cognitive algebra' in which the values of stimulus impressions along subjective scales are multiplied by importance weights and then added together. Anderson does not intend this model to be taken as a literal description of the cognitive processes of subjects: nevertheless his experimental subjects yielded data in conformance with algebraic models, as if they were doing the requisite computations.

An early realization of this approach was the study of impression formation from trait adjectives.[64] Subjects were presented with a small number of adjectives describing a person, and asked to rate the degree to which they would feel favourable toward this person. The adjective set might contain, for example, 'intelligent; warm; stubborn', or any of myriad other groupings involving such terms in combinations with others.

This deceptively simple task conceals a fundamental issue. Solomon Asch[65] had contended that some terms such as 'warm' are highly central to impressions of the personality of others, and that other terms would be heavily coloured in meaning by inclusion in combination with a central term. In other words, impressions of other persons are formed configurally. The contrasting view is that impressions are formed by the accretion of separate pieces of information, each making its characteristic contribution to the result. In this view, to be 'warm' is quite favourable, and thus 'warm, intelligent' is extremely favourable; but 'stubborn' is moderately unfavourable, thus 'warm, stubborn' is only a shade better than neutral, if at all. Combinations of three or more terms would work in a similar *additive* way, with no necessity for the assumption of any global configural tendencies. Anderson's data come out massively supportive of the algebraic as opposed to the configural view.[66] Apparently in judgments of this kind, mental operations simulate a kind of statistical clerkship. This line of research is yet another evidence of the tendency toward the use of very low-level rules in subjective judgment.

3   Prediction under uncertainty

Still more striking evidence of cognitive limitation comes from studies of human prediction under uncertainty.[67] It is becoming increasingly clear from recent research that people are typically prone to employ non-rational simplifying biases in their employment of probability concepts. Among these biases are: the misapprehension that outcomes are the more probable the more ways one can subjectively imagine their occurrence; and the notion that a sample sharply deviant in its surface characteristics from the population from which it came, must have been a sample of low probability. The former bias is associated with what Amos Tversky and Daniel Kahneman[68] call 'availability'; and the latter with 'representativeness'. These two factors are hypothesized as ways by which people can deal mentally with the ideas of variability and chance, both very difficult to appreciate objectively.

The concept of 'availability' is illustrated by responses to the following question: 'An English word has been drawn at random from a complete set of common English words of 3 or more letters. Which is more likely—that this word will have a "k" as its *first* letter, or "k" as its *third* letter?' Most people answer this question (or an equivalent version stated in terms of relative frequency rather than relative likelihood) with *first* rather than *third*, despite the objective fact that the latter event is about three times as likely as the former. Tversky and Kahneman explain this result[69] in terms of the way the respondent goes about answering the question. The respondent tries to think of a few words beginning with 'k' and a few with 'k' as third letter. First-letter 'k' words spring readily to mind. Third-letter 'k' words are less 'available' (for reasons which will not concern us here), and, finding their discovery harder, the respondent concludes that they are less frequent in the language.

The availability bias has important implications for practical judgments in the face of important uncertain events. Consider the theoretical assumption[70] that an individual judges the probability of an uncertain event as greater, the higher number of plausible scenarios he can construct including the event. If this assumption is correct, the consequences for rational decision-making models are devastating. There are many ways in which the cognitive availability of event scenarios may deviate from their actual 'availability' in the real world; for example, by having occurred in the particular experience of an individual, or by being especially dramatic or memorable. When considering whether to take out an insurance policy, thus, an individual would try to imagine various pertinent accidents. If many came readily to mind, the insurance would seem worthwhile, because accidents would be deemed probable. If accident scenarios were hard to imagine, the insurance would seem relatively useless. On this basis, people with a gloomy turn of mind and those who had recently suffered from accidents or near-misses would be much more inclined to buy insurance, quite apart from any considerations of price.[71]

An especially intriguing example of the operation of the availability bias arises when an international decision-maker must assess the likelihood of military action by an adversary nation. If his own nation promotes a ready image of the adversary as impulsive and dangerous and/or if there are historical precedents which make it easy to call an enemy attack to mind, then the subjective likelihood of such attack will tend to exceed the objective likelihood. Political scientist Robert Jervis has recently written in detail on the effects of dramatic historical events during the formative career years of diplomats on the later misperceptions by those diplomats,[72] an effect mediated in large measure by the availability bias.

The concept of representativeness is illustrated by responses to this question: 'In a metropolitan area, a sociologist surveyed all the families with six children. He found exactly 72 families in which the birth order of boys (B) and girls (G) was BGGBGB. How many six-child families do you think there were in which the precise birth order was GBBBBB?'

Most people answer this question with numbers around 20. The objectively correct best estimate is 72, based on the principle that the specific order BGGBGB is no more likely than the specific order GBBBBB, despite the appearance of greater regularity in the pattern of three boys out of six than in the pattern with one girl out of six. The three of six pattern might be considered more 'representative' of a population equally divided between boys and girls, producing a bias toward overestimation of the probability of any given sequence displaying three of six.

The representativeness bias seems to account in part for the attractiveness of contrived causal explanations for coincidences.

People in general, even if they are sophisticated in other ways, have great difficulty appreciating the extent to which true randomness is erratic and 'lumpy' rather than smoothly reflective of representative trends. Streaks and apparent patterns of all sorts are frequently taken as evidence for the operation of mysterious forces such as jinxes, ESP, or divine providence. There may be other spurs to such beliefs, but the representativeness bias certainly aids them.

In a recent paper, Tversky and Kahneman[73] have given a number of illustrations of these and other biases in judgment under uncertainty. They make a strong case for the ubiquity of departures from objective rationality. Nevertheless, subjects who fall victim to biases do so under the illusion that they are making reasonable judgments, and thus we can consider them subjectively rational within the limitations of a number of compelling but misleading conceptions about the laws of chance.

E Epilogue

With a variety of contents, this chapter has repeatedly sounded the refrain that rationality as an ideal is very liable in practice to be superseded by strong psychological mini-principles limited in scope and high in subjectivity. Both scope limitation and subjectivization involve many cognitive and motivational forces which psychologists are in the process of trying to unravel. Here we have merely sketched and exemplified these forces. We have pictured the typical individual as overloaded with information which he does not quite know how to process even if he were motivated to invest considerable mental energy. Furthermore (we have asserted) the individual's mental processes are subject to illusion and oversimplification because of biased or misleading experience, motivated self-enhancement, and insufficient awareness of social pressures, even though the individual may honestly try to follow common sense.

For a rationalist, this seems a very gloomy picture. My personal view is not quite as gloomy as the above may sound, in that I am confident that increased rationality can be learned and nurtured. Individuals no doubt can perform more rationally when the appropriate cognitive equipment and motivational circumstances are present. We need to study how this might come about, and it is important in so doing that we be realistic about how far away from full rationality the human condition lies.

Notes

1 Although the content of his major book (Lewin, K. 1951) did not

83

directly dominate the field, many of the major figures in social psychology (Festinger, Kelley, Thibaut, Deutsch, among others) were students of Lewin's, and much influenced by his phenomenology. Fritz Heider, another very influential social psychologist, came also from the European philosophical tradition which looked to cognitive factors and rejected behaviourism.

2 Adorno, T.W. *et al.* (1950).
3 Christie, R. and Jahoda, M. (1954).
4 Abelson, R.P. (1972).
5 Milgram, S. (1973).
6 Janis, I.L. (1972).
7 Janis, I.L. and Mann, L. (1976).
8 Berkowitz, L. (1972).
9 Smith, M.B., Bruner, J.S. and White, R.W. (1956).
10 Abelson, R.P. (1968).
11 Abelson, R.P. *et al.* (1968).
12 Abelson, R.P. and Rosenberg, M.J. (1958).
13 Kelley, H.H. (1967).
14 Jones, E.E. *et al.* (1968).
15 Osgood, C.E. and Tannenbaum, P.H. (1955).
16 Tannenbaum, P.H. (1967).
17 Heider, F. (1946).
18 Abelson, R.P. (1959).
19 Newcomb, T.N. (1968). See also Zajonc, R.B. (1968).
20 Cartwright, D. and Harary, F. (1956).
21 Abelson, R.P. and Rosenberg, M.J. (1958).
22 Rosenberg, M.J. and Abelson, R.P. (1960).
23 Lerner, M.J. (1970).
24 Festinger, L. (1957).
25 Aronson, E. (1969).
26 Ibid.
27 Abelson, R.P. (1968).
28 Martin Irle, University of Mannheim, Germany, personal communication.
29 Festinger, L. and Carlsmith, J.M. (1959).
30 Nel, E., Helmreich, R. and Aronson, E. (1969). See also Collins, B.E. and Hoyt, M.F. (1972).
31 Helmreich, R. and Collins, B.E. (1968).
32 Brehm, J.W. and Cohen, A.R. (1962).
33 Nel, E., Helmreich, R. and Aronson, E. (1969).
34 Helmreich, R. and Collins, B.E. (1968).
35 Kelley, H.H. (1967).
36 This exacerbates the somewhat controversial ethical status of laboratory experiments in which subjects are induced to perform novel or uncharacteristic behaviours. It is important to note that careful 'debriefing' procedures are a standard part of such experiments. Subjects are fully informed in a post-mortem discussion session in which the experimenter explains the situational pressures he used, thereby relieving the subject of the onus of personal responsibility for

uncharacteristic actions. The typical reaction is one of relief combined with interest in having participated in an unusual experience from which they may have learned something about social psychology.

37 Aronson, E. (1972).
38 Lane, R.E. (1962), pp. 134, 338, 376.
39 At the time of writing, the appropriate references were not available to the writer, but Jean-Pierre Poitou of the University of Aix-en-Provence, France, and Joseph Nuttin of the University of Louvain, Belgium, have been working separately on summaries and reformulations of dissonance theory. See Poiton, J.-P. (1974).
40 Many scholars have noted the importance of this assumption in the thinking of Everyman. See Langford, G. (1971). The psychologist Gordon Bear calls the assumption of purposeful action by normal actors the Rationality Schema, and has begun a progress of research to demonstrate its importance in mundane psychological explanation. This research is foreshadowed in Bear, G. and Hodun, S.A. (1975)
41 Newcomb, T.N. (1968).
42 Abelson, R.P. (1973) and (1975).
43 Heider, F. (1958), p. 210.
44 Kelley, H.H. (1967).
45 McArthur, L.A. (1970).
46 Peters, R.S. (1969).
47 Jones, E.E. and Nisbett, R.E. (1971).
48 Jones, E.E. et al. (1968).
49 Ross, L.D., Rodin, J. and Zimbardo, P. (1969).
50 Storms, M.D. and Nisbett, R.E. (1970).
51 Davison, G.G. and Valins, S. (1969).
52 Valins, S. (1966).
53 Valins, S. and Ray, A.A. (1967).
54 Valins, S. and Nisbett, R.E. (1971).
55 Blechman, E.A. (1973).
56 Developments in information theory of consequence for psychology are concisely organized in Garner, W.R. (1962).
57 Miller, G.A. (1956).
58 Milgram, S. (1970).
59 Meehl, P.E. (1954).
60 Goldberg, L.R. (1968).
61 Hammond, K.R., Hursch, C.J. and Todd, F.J. (1964).
62 Wiggins, N. and Kohen, E.S. (1971). See also Dawes, R.M. (1971).
63 Anderson, N.H. (1974).
64 Anderson, N.H. (1966).
65 Asch, S.E. (1946).
66 Anderson, N.H. (1968).
67 Tversky, A. and Kahneman, D. (1971).
68 Ibid.
69 Tversky, A. and Kahneman, D. (1973).
70 Spetzler, C.S. and Stäel von Holstein, C.S. (1972).
71 Price could still affect the decision without direct inclusion in a utility calculus. For example, price could influence the individual's motivation

to think about insurance. For a low price, the individual might think
longer, increasing the operation of the availability factor.
72 Jervis, R. (in press, 1976).
73 Tversky, A. and Kahneman, D. (1974).

Bibliography

ABELSON, R.P. (1959), 'Modes of resolution of belief dilemmas', *Journal of Conflict Resolution*, III, pp. 343–52.
ABELSON, R.P. (1968), 'Psychological implication', in Abelson, R.P. *et al.* (eds), *Theories of Cognitive Consistency: A Sourcebook*, Chicago.
ABELSON, R.P. (1972), 'Are attitudes necessary?', in King, B. and McGinnies, E. (eds), *Attitudes, Conflict, and Social Change*, New York.
ABELSON, R.P. (1973), 'The structure of belief systems', in Schank, R. and Colby, K.M. (eds), *Computer Models of Thought and Language*, San Francisco.
ABELSON, R.P. (1975), 'Representing mundane reality in plans', in Collins, A. and Bobrow, D. (eds), *Representation and Understanding*, New York.
ABELSON, R.P. and ROSENBERG, M.J. (1958), 'Symbolic psycho-logic: a model of attitudinal cognition', *Behavioral Science*, III, pp. 1–13.
ADORNO, T.W., FRENKEL-BRUNSWICK, E., LEVINSON, D.J. and SANFORD, R.N. (1950), *The Authoritarian Personality*, New York.
ANDERSON, N.H. (1966), 'Component ratings in impression formation', *Psychonomic Science*, VI, pp. 279–80.
ANDERSON, N.H. (1968), 'A simple model of information integration', in Abelson, R.P. *et al.* (1968).
ANDERSON, N.H. (1974), 'Cognitive algebra: integration theory applied to social attribution', in Berkowitz, L. (ed.), *Advances in Experimental Social Psychology*, vol. VII, New York.
ARONSON, E. (1969), 'The theory of cognitive dissonance: a current perspective', in Berkowitz, L. (ed.), *Advances in Experimental Social Psychology*, vol. IV, New York.
ARONSON, E. (1972), *The Social Animal*, San Francisco.
ASCH, S.E. (1946), 'Forming impressions of personality', *Journal of Abnormal and Social Psychology*, XLI, pp. 258–90.
BEAR, G. and HODUN, S.A. (1975), 'Effects of an implicational principle on the learning and recall of conformatory, contradictory, incomplete, and irrelevant information', *Journal of Personality and Social Psychology*, (in press).
BERKOWITZ, L. (1972), 'Social norms, feelings, and other factors affecting helping and altruism', in Berkowitz, L. (ed.), *Advances in Experimental Social Psychology*, vol. VI, New York.
BLECHMAN, E.A. (1973), 'Attribution theory and family therapy: attributional impediments to research on family behavior change', Paper delivered at American Psychological Association meeting, Montreal.
BREHM, J.W. and COHEN, A.R. (1962), *Explorations in Cognitive Dissonance*, New York.
CARTWRIGHT, D. and HARARY, F. (1956), 'Structural balance: a generalization of Heider's theory', *Psychological Review*, LXIII, pp. 277–93.

CHRISTIE, R. and JAHODA, M. (eds) (1954), *Studies in the Scope and Method of 'The Authoritarian Personality'*, Chicago.

COLLINS, B.E. and HOYT, M.F. (1972), 'Personal responsibility for consequences: an integration and extension of the "forced compliance" literature', *Journal of Experimental Social Psychology*, VIII, pp. 558–93.

DAVISON, G.G. and VALINS, S. (1969), 'Maintenance of self-attributed and drug-attributed behavior change', *Journal of Personality and Social Psychology*, XI, pp. 25–33.

DAWES. R.M. (1971), 'A case study of graduate admissions: application of three principles of human decision making', *American Psychologist*, XXVI, pp. 180–8.

FESTINGER, L. (1957), *A Theory of Cognitive Dissonance*, Evanston, Illinois.

FESTINGER, L. and CARLSMITH, J.M. (1959), 'Cognitive consequences of forced compliance', *Journal of Abnormal and Social Psychology*, LVIII, pp. 203–10.

GARNER, W.R. (1962), *Uncertainty and Structure as Psychological Concepts*, New York.

GOLDBERG, L.R. (1968), 'Simple models or simple processes? Some research on clinical judgments', *American Psychologist*, XXIII, pp. 483–96.

HAMMOND, K.R., HURSCH, C.J. and TODD, F.J. (1964), 'Analyzing the components of clinical inferences', *Psychological Review*, LXXI, pp. 438–56.

HEIDER, F. (1946), 'Attitudes and cognitive organization', *Journal of Psychology*, XXI, pp. 107–12.

HEIDER, F. (1958), *The Psychology of Interpersonal Relations*, New York.

HELMREICH, R. and COLLINS, B.E. (1968), 'Studies in forced compliance: commitment and magnitude of inducement to comply as determinants of opinion change', *Journal of Personality and Social Psychology*, X, pp. 75–81.

JANIS, I.L. (1972), *Victims of Groupthink: A Psychological Study of Foreign-Policy Decisions and Fiascoes*, Boston.

JANIS, I.L. and MANN, L. (1976), *Decision Making: A Social-Psychological Approach*, New York.

JERVIS, R. (1976), 'How decision-makers learn from history', in Jervis, R., *Perception and Misperception in International Relations*, Princeton.

JONES, E.E. et al. (1971), *Attribution: Perceiving the Causes of Behavior*, Morristown, New Jersey.

JONES, E.E. and NISBETT, R.E. (1971), 'The actor and the observer: divergent perceptions of the causes of behavior', in Jones, E.E. et al. (1971).

JONES, E.E. et al. (1968), 'Pattern of performance and ability attribution: an unexpected primary effect', *Journal of Personality and Social Psychology*, X, pp. 317–40.

KELLEY, H.H. (1967), 'Attribution theory in social psychology', in Levine, D. (ed.), *Nebraska Symposium on Motivation*, Lincoln, Nebraska.

LANE, R.E. (1962), *Political Ideology: Why the American Common Man Believes What He Does*, New York.

LANGFORD, G. (1971), *Human Action*, Garden City, New York.

LERNER, M.J. (1970), 'The desire for justice and reactions to victims', in Macaulay, J.R. and Berkowitz, L. (eds), *Altruism and Helping Behavior*, New York.

LEWIN, K. (1951), *Field Theory in Social Science*, New York.

R.P. Abelson

MCARTHUR, L.A. (1970), 'The how and the what of why: some determinants and consequences of causal attribution', Ph.D. thesis, Yale University.

MEEHL, P.E. (1954), *Clinical vs. Statistical Prediction: A Theoretical Analysis and Review of the Literature*, Minneapolis.

MILGRAM, S. (1970), 'The experience of living in cities', *Science*, CLXVII, pp. 1461–8.

MILGRAM, S. (1973), *Obedience to Authority*, New York.

MILLER, G.A. (1956), 'The magical number seven plus or minus two: some limits on our capacity for processing information', *Psychological Review*, LXIII, pp. 81–97.

NEL, E., HELMREICH, R. and ARONSON, E. (1969), 'Opinion change in the advocate as a function of the persuasibility of his audience: a clarification of the meaning of dissonance', *Journal of Personality and Social Psychology*, XII, pp. 117–24.

NEWCOMB, T.N. (1968), 'Interpersonal balance', in Abelson, R.P. *et al.* (1968), *Theories of Cognitive Consistency: A Sourcebook*, Chicago.

OSGOOD, C.E. and TANNENBAUM, P.H. (1955), 'The principle of congruity in the prediction of attitude change', *Psychological Review*, LXII, pp. 42–55.

PETERS, R.S. (1969), 'Motivation, emotion, and schemes of common sense', in Mischel, T. (ed.), *Human Action*, New York and London.

POITON, J.-P. (1974), *La Dissonance Cognitive*, Paris.

ROSENBERG, M.J. and ABELSON, R.P. (1960), 'An analysis of cognitive balancing', in Hovland, C.I. and Rosenberg, M.J. (eds), *Attitude Organization and Change*, New Haven.

ROSS, L.D., RODIN, J. and ZIMBARDO, P. (1969), 'Toward an attribution therapy: the reduction of fear through induced cognitive-emotional misattribution', *Journal of Personality and Social Psychology*, XII, pp. 279–88.

SMITH, M.B., BRUNER, J.S. and WHITE, R.W. (1956), *Opinions and Personality*, New York.

SPETZLER, C.S. and STÄEL VON HOLSTEIN, C.S. (1972), 'Probability encoding in decision analysis', Stanford Research Institute Memorandum.

STORMS, M.D. and NISBETT, R.E. (1970), 'Insomnia and the attribution process', *Journal of Personality and Social Psychology*, XVI, pp. 319–28.

TANNENBAUM, P.H. (1967), 'The congruity principle revisited: studies in the reduction, induction and generalization of persuasion', in Berkowitz, L. (ed.), *Advances in Experimental Social Psychology*, vol. III, New York.

TVERSKY, A. and KAHNEMAN, D. (1971), 'The belief in the law of small numbers', *Psychological Bulletin*, LXXVI, pp. 105–10.

TVERSKY, A. and KAHNEMAN, D. (1973), 'Availability: a heuristic for judging frequency and probability', *Cognitive Psychology*, V, pp. 207–32.

TVERSKY, A. and KAHNEMAN, D. (1974), 'Judgment under uncertainty: heuristics and biases', *Science*, CLXXXV, pp. 1124–31.

VALINS, S. (1966), 'Cognitive effects of false heart-rate feedback', *Journal of Personality and Social Psychology*, IV, pp. 400–8.

VALINS, S. and NISBETT, R.E. (1971), 'Attribution processes in the development and treatment of emotional disorders', in Jones, E.E. *et al.* (1971).

VALINS, S. and RAY, A.A. (1967), 'Effects of cognitive desensitization on avoidance behavior', *Journal of Personality and Social Psychology*, VII, pp. 345–50.

WIGGINS, N. and KOHEN, E.S. (1971), 'Man vs. model of man revisited: the forecasting of graduate school success', *Journal of Personality and Social Psychology*, XIX, pp. 100–6.

ZAJONC, R.B. (1968), 'Cognitive theories in social psychology', in Lindzey, G. and Aronson, E. (eds), *Handbook of Social Psychology*, vol. 1, Reading, Mass.

Part Two

Rationality in action

(a) Strong and weak criteria of rational action

4

Rational action

G.W. Mortimore

A Introduction

The aim of this essay is to give an account of the ordinary notions of rationality in action and of the rational agent. I use 'ordinary' here to contrast with the variety of technical notions, common in economics, decision theory and other disciplines. The technical notions (to be discussed in Chapters 7–10 of this collection) can, in one way or another, be understood as the outcome of simplifying, supplementing or making precise the criteria employed in ordinary assessments of rationality, and of simplifying or tightening the logical connections with such cognate concepts as choice, action and preference. The ordinary notion is used in two ways in many areas of the social sciences: first, as a conceptual tool for picking out and characterizing a phenomenon to be explained and understood, as a developmental psychologist attempts to understand the growth of rationality in the child[1] or as a sociologist attempts to understand the varying types and incidence of rationality in the sub-cultures of a society;[2] and, second, in explaining and predicting the acts and practices of agents to whom some degree of rationality in action can be imputed.[3]

1 Rationality and ends

It is common to identify rationality in action with choosing the appropriate means to attain one's ends. But there is some controversy over the proper interpretation of 'end' in this account. 'End' is sometimes used in the very broad sense in which '*A*'s end in doing x' means 'that for the sake of which A did x'. In this sense, an end-directed action is to be understood as aimed at either bringing about, maintaining, averting or bringing to an end a state of affairs. 'State of affairs' here embraces such causal consequences of one's actions as being despised by one's colleagues or possessing great wealth. It is also to be understood as embracing such ends as keeping one's promise or doing one's duty; when a man helps someone for the sake of keeping a promise, he cannot, of course, be conceived as trying to bring about a causally consequential state of affairs. This broad account of the notion of an end thus accords with the commonly held view that rational men act on a wide range of considerations besides those concerning the causal consequences or outcomes of their actions, and exhibit their rationality in acting according to principles or rules, and on normative considerations of obligation and duty.

On the other hand, it might be suggested that this very broad definition of 'end' obscures two very different and contrasting ways in which rationality might be exercised, i.e. in pursuing goals, and in acting consistently with rules and principles.[4] A third, historically influential view, favouring a narrower definition of 'end', holds that action in conformity to rules and norms, so far from being one form of rational action, does not manifest rationality at all, since norms and rules are non-rational influences and constraints on choice.[5]

For the moment I shall not attempt to decide between these three views, and—to avoid prejudging the question—I will initially confine myself to cases where the agent is not acting for the sake of meeting the requirements of some norm, or because he values the action for its own sake. The place of these other reasons for action in the account of rationality will be considered towards the end of the paper.

2 Ends, attitudes and reasons

So far we have only developed an account of the notion of an agent's ends *in acting*. But the means/end account of rationality in action holds that the rationality of a man's action depends on the relationship between his action and not just the ends for which he acted, but all the ends for which he might have acted if he had chosen differently. How, then, are we to understand statements about the ends a man has prior to choice, when it is an open question which, if any of them, he will pursue?

There are, I suggest, two conditions which have to be satisfied before we can say that the coming about of state of affairs S is one of a man's ends.

(i) He has a pro-attitude towards *S*. I use 'pro-attitude' very broadly here to embrace desires and preferences, as well as attitudes like approval. So a man who fervently desires God's rule over the earth is pro (in favour of) the state of affairs 'God's ruling the earth', and the man who approves of uninhibited behaviour is pro (in favour of) the state of affairs 'everyone behaving uninhibitedly'.

(ii) *S* is a state of affairs which he is in principle prepared to allow to weigh as a reason for or against certain choices. That is to say, his ends do not include states of affairs which are only objects of impulses or wishes to which he is not prepared to give reflective weight in his choices. If I happen to wish enviously that a friend's run of successes come to an abrupt end, that does not figure among my ends as long as I am not prepared to consider reflectively that state of affairs as a reason weighing for or against various choices I might make.

This account of the notion of an end has a number of important implications. First, it follows that we can talk of rationality either in terms of the relation of the rational man's actions to his ends, or of their relation to his attitudes. If we are comparing how much he wants various states of affairs, or considering how he ranks the objects of his wants, the notion of preference is a convenient catch-all for the attitudes to which we relate his actions. Second, we can translate a means/end account of rationality into one that relates the rational man's choice to the considerations he regarded as reasons for or against it, and to the alternative choices he might have made. Both sets of terminology have advantages over the terminology of ends. For talk of a man's ends suggests that what we have in mind are goals or aims like mastery of Europe, receiving critical acclaim as a great novelist, or making a decisive contribution to a scientific discipline. Whereas to serve in a general account of rationality, 'end' has to cover a man's liking for privacy, good food and beautiful women. To ascribe any of these latter 'ends' is not to attribute to the individual the pursuit of a single state of affairs, but the disposition to treat states of affairs of certain *kinds* as reasons in favour of certain choices. The formulation of particular purposes comes only after the process of weighing these considerations against competing factors (e.g. the costs of having *this* particular good meal, the disadvantages of buying *this* secluded house, the repercussions of *this* affair).

Nevertheless, I propose to discuss rationality of action in terms of ends, for this is both a simpler and more economical way of doing it. I hope it is clear, however, that one can switch easily from talk of the agent's ends to talk of his attitudes and preferences, and to talk of what he is prepared to treat as reasons for action.

3   A paradigm of rational action

The strategy of the paper is to look first at a case of a rational action in which a man does what he does because he believes it to be the best of the alternatives open to him. I do not suggest that it is a necessary condition for rationality in action that a man acts on such a belief. But it will be helpful to begin by asking how rationality is exhibited in such an action, and then consider cases where we assess the action as fully rational even though the agent does not believe that what he is doing is best. In later sections, I discuss the variety of ways in which a man may exhibit less than full rationality in his action—without his actions counting as totally irrational or non-rational.

Consider then a paradigm of a rational action: an action performed for the sake of an end which it is rational to pursue, and based on a rational belief that the action is the best (in terms of the agent's ends) of the alternatives open to him. To constitute such a paradigm an action thus has to meet three requirements:

1   The beliefs on which the agent acts are rational ones. It is plainly true that one way in which a man can fall short of rationality in action is by acting on irrationally held beliefs. Rationality in belief has been discussed in Chapter 1, and this paper will not explore the topic further. Quentin Gibson explores the contribution of the assumption of rationality in belief to explanations of action in Chapter 5.

2   The end for the sake of which the agent acts is one which it is rational to pursue. Because this relates to the content of a man's ends, I shall speak of it as a requirement of *substantive practical* rationality. Many deny, however, that any requirement about the content of a man's ends can be properly advanced as a requirement of rationality. This issue will be discussed in Chapter 11.

3   Finally, the agent believes that his action is better than any of the alternatives open to him, *given* his ends. Since the rationality exhibited in acting on such a belief is exhibited *irrespective* of the content of the agent's ends, I will speak of this aspect as his *formal practical rationality*. This notion will be the central topic of this paper.

B   Full formal practical rationality

1   The epistemic background

An account of formal practical rationality requires a schematic account of the background to the individual's belief that what he does is the best of the available options. How, first, are we to interpret his belief? We could, it seems, take it to be either of the following:

I 'This choice will have the best outcome in terms of my ends.'

II 'There are good and sufficient reasons, in terms of my ends, for making this choice.'

Clearly I, in the absence of countervailing considerations, entails II, but it remains to be seen whether I is the only basis for believing II.

Consider first, however, an agent who, believing his choice will have the best outcome (i.e. best in sense I), believes on that account that there are good and sufficient reasons for it (that it is best in sense II). I shall say that proposition I states a *practical* reason for choice since it is a statement about the relationship between an option and the agent's ends. I shall refer to proposition II as the agent's *practical conclusion*, since it states specifically what is to be chosen, i.e. which choice is supported by good and sufficient practical reasons.

Let us also begin with a case where the individual believes I and II having compared the options in relation to his various ends. To explain his beliefs we must, first, identify the considerations about ends and options which generated his beliefs. Here we might ask three questions:

(i) What were his beliefs about the range of options open to him?

(ii) What types of consideration did he entertain concerning the relationships between options and ends?

Thus he might have entertained non-comparative propositions like 'x will attain E with cost C', or comparative propositions like 'x is the only way to attain E'. He might have been prepared to predict outcomes as certain or only to assign probabilities to them.

(iii) How many options and how many ends did he consider? I shall follow Watkins[6] in calling the full set of considerations which influenced his choice his decision-scheme.

Then we need to consider how far the agent built up a comprehensive *summary* of the relationship of options to ends—for example, grasping that only x of the options would attain all of his ends, or that y was the least costly way of attaining the end to which he gave top priority. Finally, we need to identify the conceptions of optimality (in sense II) with which the agent was operating. Straightforward criteria in ordinary use (implicitly if not explicitly) include:

If $E_1 \ldots E_n$ are the relevant ends and x is the only course which achieves all of them, x is best.

If E is the only relevant end, and x is the option which attains E using least resources, x is best.[7]

Given a summary-belief about his choice-situation and the appropriate optimality criterion, the agent can then derive the conclusion that one of the available options is best in sense II. What the agent takes to be the good and sufficient practical reason for choice is, of course, his summary-belief about the options.

In the sorts of case we have been considering the agent comparatively assesses the options in terms of his ends before arriving at a conclusion about what is best. If the formal notion of practical rationality applies, it is because:

(i) the agent's choice results from a decision-scheme of the broad type sketched above, and a summary-belief derived from it;

(ii) his choice bears a certain relationship to the scheme—a relationship I have sought to capture by saying that the summary-belief provides a good and sufficient practical reason for the choice;[8]

(iii) the agent in some way sees or grasps the relationship under (ii).

To do justice to the varieties of choice-situation, of course, we would need to elaborate this account, distinguishing, for example, the case in which a man begins with an end he wishes to attain and looks around for ways of achieving it; the case in which he has a rough idea of ends and means and, like a man purchasing a car, has now to get down to clarifying his ends in considering the options; and the case in which a man is faced in the first instance with the options (e.g. a career choice) and has to consider, perhaps *ab initio*, which of his ends are relevant to this choice. We would also need to distinguish between two categories of choice: where the options are single, contemporaneous alternatives (as in the choice of a car); and where the choice is essentially between plans, i.e. between sets of actions phased over time.

2 Practical rationality without choosing what is best

Could an agent exhibit full formal practical rationality in choosing an option he does not believe to be best? As we shall see in Chapter 7, when outcomes are risky (i.e. the agent assigns a determinate probability of less than 1 to the possible outcomes of each option) it is arguably rational for the agent to discount the value to him of each possible outcome by its probability.[9] The agent does not then choose on the basis of a proposition of the form 'x will have the best outcome'. If we are to identify rationality with choosing what is best, then, we need to interpret 'what is best' in sense II:

'what is supported by a good and sufficient reason for choice'. The proposition that x will have the best outcome is only one type of consideration which can figure as a good and sufficient reason for choice.

But could not an agent be fully rational in choosing x, when he believes only that it is *a way* to achieve his ends? By our ordinary criteria we would, I think, take this belief to be a basis for fully rational choice only if he also believed that it was unlikely that any other option would achieve his ends to a greater degree or with less cost, or that it would be too costly to find out. A similar account could be given of an agent's rationality in cases where he compares a few options in terms of a few ends, or simply sees that this action is a way of achieving a single end with a modest absolute cost.[10] Such choices can be, and frequently are, practically rational when they are made against the background of two kinds of belief:

(i) beliefs about whether, in his choice-situation, further reflection would be likely to turn up further relevant ends or options superior to the ones he has considered;

(ii) beliefs about the accessibility of further information about relevant options and ends, and about the costs of acquiring and processing it.

The agent may then choose rationally despite the fact that the belief on which he acts is of the form 'x is the best of the alternatives I have considered'. We explain his act as fully rational by displaying his practical rationality in cutting short or refraining altogether from any exploration of the relationships between the full range of options and ends.[11]

We might still insist in either of two ways, however, that in such cases the rational agent believes that what he is doing is the best of the available options. For first, we can also understand his choice as being between the options 'choosing the best of the alternatives I have considered' and 'continuing to deliberate'. If he believes that further deliberation involves costs which outweigh any increased chance of choosing the option with the best outcome, the agent is in a position to identify the first of these two options as the best in sense II. Second, the agent might also be in a position to infer from his beliefs about the way the world is that the policy of choosing on the basis of 'x is the best of the options that cursory investigation has turned up' might be the best decision-policy in sense II.

We have so far concentrated on formal practical rationality as it is exhibited in cases where the individual considers the relationships of particular options to his ends. But rationality can be exhibited in choices not preceded by this kind of decision-procedure.

Indeed, such a decision-procedure may be practically irrational, because of the costs involved. One is inclined to say that choices based on rules of thumb are rational if made *because* the agent believes that choosing on the basis of the rules rather than relating options to ends more than compensates, by reducing decision-making costs, for any reduced chance of choosing the option with the best outcome. In this case, he regards the fact that the choice satisfies the conditions laid down in the rule of thumb as a good and sufficient practical reason.

Such cases are familiar and I shall not dwell on them. However, it is worth emphasizing that their prevalence does mean that those discussions of explanation in terms of rationality which concentrate on situational logic—on the agent's appraisal of the situation and its relation to his ends—miss out a whole range of cases where what needs to be explained as rational is the agent's operating with a decision-procedure which does not require his assessing the relationships of options to his ends.

3   Practical rationality as a trait

It appears obvious that formal practical rationality as a trait amounts to a disposition to be practically rational in action. But which of the following does this mean?

(i) A disposition to do x whenever it is rational to do x.

(ii) A disposition to act rationally rather than irrationally or non-rationally.

Account (i) is surely too weak. For an individual's decision-scheme may usually be too exiguous for any action on the basis of that scheme to count as rational, though he acts rationally whenever his scheme is such as to make one at least of the options a rational choice. On account (i) we would have to say that he is not deficient in practical rationality as a trait; whereas he would surely say the reverse.

For constitutive of formal practical rationality as a trait are two higher-order ends,[12] superimposed on the variety of wants and preferences which a man has simply by virtue of being a human agent:

(i) to do what has the best outcome, in terms of the agent's ends;

(ii) to act on the basis of considerations which provide good and sufficient practical reasons for choice.

The second end issues in two dispositions: to develop his decision-scheme (and the summary-belief derived from it) to the point where the agent is satisfied that it provides him with good and sufficient reasons for choice; and to choose x wherever his decision-scheme is seen to provide good and sufficient reasons for choosing x.

On some accounts, an explanation of an action as rational need not require attributing rationality as a trait to the agent. In Chapter 5, Quentin Gibson concentrates on explanations which are limited to the assertion that the agent acted because of certain beliefs about the relationship between his choice and his ends; and he does not feel it is necessary to discuss the trait of rationality (see p. 130, n. 8). But, in the case of a choice made by someone who has comparatively assessed his options in terms of his ends, we may need to introduce a trait of practical rationality at two points: in explaining his having a decision-scheme and summary-belief full enough for his choice to be practically rational, and in explaining why he acted on them. His practical rationality will be correspondingly displayed (i) in his actively exploring the relationship between his options and his ends, extending his decision-scheme, and in deriving a summary belief, and a belief about what is best; (ii) in not acting until he has done these things; and (iii) in acting on the belief once formed. To attribute formal practical rationality, whether as a short-term disposition or as a permanent trait, is to attribute a propensity to behave in these three ways. To explain someone's action by reference to such a disposition is to do more than assert that the agent acted because of certain beliefs: it is to explain why the agent came to act on such beliefs, by reference to this complex disposition.

In the process of extending his decision-scheme and summary-belief the rational agent accumulates more information about relevant options and ends, and about their interrelations. He also reflects on and weighs this information as he constructs his summary-belief or (in the cases where there is no explicit process of inference) arrives at his summary-impression. It may be suggested that these activities preceding choice are the consequence of the agent's *epistemic* rationality in forming a belief about what is the best thing to do.[13] Now since the practically rational man is concerned to identify considerations which are good and sufficient reasons for choice, his research and deliberative activities will no doubt conform to the requirements of epistemic rationality. However, they are performed *because* he is practically rational, i.e. because he has a conception of what count as good and sufficient practical reasons and cares about identifying and acting on such reasons.

I have identified the trait of practical rationality with a complex disposition to activities which include investigation and deliberation. This now needs to be qualified by the observation that a rational man may often see at a glance what is to be done, and that rational choice may often not require any reflection or deliberation, much less an elaborate process of investigation. For the rational man will have a view of the considerations which are relevant to choice in many of the choice-situations which are likely to arise, and may exhibit his rationality in using this 'know-how' unreflectively. All that may be required for us to be able to say that he chose rationally is that he made what was for him the rational choice, in a choice-situation where it is plausible to suppose that he noticed the features which, given his ends, were reasons for choice. Certainly, it will often be sufficient that he can afterwards explain his choice in terms of such considerations, even though it was a split-second decision which left no time for reflection.

C Partial practical rationality

In talking about full rationality in action I have been considering what I take to be the ordinary notion of a fully rational act and agent. No doubt full rationality in the ordinary sense is a comparatively rare phenomenon. However, the type of case we have considered is only one end of a continuum of degrees of rationality which may be manifested by agents.[14] The question arises, therefore, whether a concept of partial practical rationality might be more useful both as a taxonomical tool, and as an explanatory postulate. In this section I shall consider what might be meant by talk of partial practical rationality. Partial practical rationality presumably consists in acting for considerations which the agent regards as reasons, but not as good and sufficient reasons for choice. The man who sees that an option will promote one of his ends sees a reason for choosing that option; but the consideration is not in itself a sufficient reason for choice. Partial practical rationality *as a trait* consists in a disposition to explore the relationships between options and ends to an extent which allows a degree of rationality in action which falls short of full rationality.

My view of partial practical rationality can be usefully contrasted with the recent attempt by J.W.N. Watkins, to state what he calls 'a postulate of imperfect rationality'.[15] Watkins first formulates a rationality principle in general terms (p. 172):

> An individual... has certain aims (wants, preferences) or
> perhaps a single aim, and makes a factual appraisal (which
> may be a misappraisal) of his problem-situation. The rationality
> principle says that he will act in a way that is 'appropriate' to
> his aim(s) and situational appraisal.

Watkins is looking for a principle of appropriateness which we can apply in explaining a wide range of human actions. He examines and rejects the idea that the appropriate decision is the 'decision that could not be bettered, given one's present situational information' and ultimately formulates his principle of imperfect rationality as follows: 'a (rational) man who has a decision-scheme issuing in a practical conclusion will try to act in accordance with that practical conclusion' (p. 209).

I have four objections to Watkins's treatment. The first is that the principle of imperfect rationality is primarily contrasted with the technical notions of practical rationality to be found in economics and decision theory. This obscures two contrasts which are important for an understanding of the concepts of rationality which are or might be put to work in the social sciences. The first contrast is between the technical concepts and the ordinary concept of full rationality. (This will be explored in Chapter 7.) The second is that between full rationality and less than full rationality, both in the ordinary sense. The confusion is well illustrated by Watkins's account of the imperfectly rational man. He defines 'decision-scheme' as 'the set of all those considerations that enter into a piece of decision-making' and points out that we commonly simplify our decision-scheme in the course of decision-making, seizing any opportunity to narrow the range of options. Now it is clearly often fully rational, in the ordinary sense, to knock out a great many obvious non-starters and concentrate one's attention on a narrow range of feasible alternatives with obvious and direct relationships to one's ends and preferences. The costs of decision-making will usually make it fully rational to limit one's consideration to a narrow range of alternatives, and there will usually be some non-random method of imposing these limitations. On the other hand, it is quite common for individuals to limit the range of alternatives they will consider without any reflective belief about the costs and benefits of a more extended consideration; choosing by identifying the best of a range thus limited will be less than fully rational. This distinction is obscured by Watkins's failure to make it clear whether his imperfect rationality is imperfect in relationship to the technical models, or in relation to the ordinary notion of full rationality.

My second objection is that as an account of less than full rationality, in the ordinary sense, Watkins's account is incomplete. Watkins portrays the partially rational man as simplifying his decision-scheme in the course of making his choice, by restricting the range of alternatives considered. But there may be a failure of rationality even where such a process of simplification does not take place, by virtue of the fact that the agent does not attempt to *extend* his decision-scheme—considering further options, collecting further considerations about them, and making full use of the information and arguments already in his possession. There are, therefore, a variety of ways in which the partially rational man's consideration of options and ends may be too limited to generate a summary belief which provides adequate grounds for choice.

My third objection concerns Watkins's final statement of his principle of imperfect rationality. Watkins initially sets up his problem as a question about the account we are to give of the relation between the imperfectly rational man's aims and situational appraisal on the one hand, and his actions on the other. Watkins's strategy, which is surely correct, is to give an account of the various limitations on the partially rational man's decision-scheme. Yet in his final statement of the principle, imperfect rationality is identified with action in conformity with the practical conclusion issuing from the decision-scheme. On the view I have been developing in this paper, a trait of imperfect or partial practical rationality may consist in:

    (i) the disposition to extend one's decision-scheme—by information collection and processing—until it provides at least some grounds, but not good and sufficient grounds for choice;

   (ii) the disposition not to act unless one has a decision-scheme of some kind;

  (iii) the capacity and disposition to appreciate which of the options the decision-scheme 'supports' (or, in Watkins's terminology, to derive a practical conclusion from the decision-scheme);

  (iv) the disposition to choose that option.

Only (iii) and (iv) are covered by Watkins's principle.

My fourth and final objection is that Watkins is too eager to dispense with the notion of optimality. It may still be crucial in accounting for the partially rational agent's choice. For his degree of rationality in a choice may depend on the extent to which his choice derives from a comparison of options, however incomplete. And partial rationality, given an incomplete comparison of options in terms of an incomplete range of considerations, requires that the option chosen be the best of the options considered, at least with respect to the considerations the agent has taken into account. Thus canons of optimality, even if rather unsophisticated ones, can and need to be brought to bear on cases of partial rationality.

D The ubiquity of rationality

There are at least three ways in which writers have been tempted to regard a postulate of practical rationality as universally applicable to all agents.

First, some writers maintain that, at the time of choice, every chooser believes that he has chosen the best of the options. It may be, they contend, that his decision-scheme is too exiguous to make this a *rational belief* but, given that he has the belief, he is practically rational to act on it. Quentin Gibson takes up something very like this position in Chapter 5 (see his note 15). I have suggested the very different view that:

    (i) a man cannot be fully rational unless he believes that there is a good and sufficient practical reason for what he chooses, i.e. it 'is best' in that sense;

  (ii) a man can be fully rational without acting on the proposition 'my choice will have the best outcome', since this is not the only form a good and sufficient practical reason can take;

 (iii) a man can exhibit partial rationality in acting on considerations which he does not believe to be good and sufficient practical reasons for action.

To this I now add:

 (iv) a man's reasons for the action he performs may, in his view, be outweighed by much more powerful reasons for some alternative choice; he then exhibits practical irrationality. The actions of impatient, impulsive or procrastinating individuals are amongst the more obvious examples.

Second, there is a recurrent tendency to hold that it is a necessary truth that if a man believes an action to be optimal, he will choose it if he can.[16] This second position is also one I reject. There are cases, I believe, in which an individual chooses x but either satisfies criterial conditions for saying that he believes y is optimal, or at least fails to satisfy those for saying he believes x to be so. A procrastinator gives every sign of believing y is best, but puts off doing it; an impulsive man may have exhibited none of the usual signs, prior to doing x, of believing x to be the best thing to do. This is another point on which Quentin Gibson disagrees with me (see Chapter 5, p. 124 and note 15). I regret that there is insufficient space to develop the controversy further in this paper.

There is, third, the view that any end-directed action exhibits rationality, simply in so far as it is chosen as a means to an end: this is to identify teleological explanation in terms of beliefs and ends with explanation involving the ascription of rationality. This raises the question of what we are prepared to regard as the weakest degree of rationality exhibited in an action. Is it correct or useful to think that impulsive end-directed actions or unconsciously motivated actions manifest a degree of rationality?

There are in fact a variety of points at which one might draw the line distinguishing minimally rational behaviour from the wholly non-rational.[17] On the least restrictive view, an agent exhibits some degree of rationality as long as he acts for reasons: this would then bring impulsive and unconsciously motivated actions within the rational sphere. There are clearly some methodological purposes which would be served by identifying the class of actions exhibiting some degree of rationality with the class of actions which can be explained as performed *for a reason*. Alternatively, we might limit the ascription of rationality to actions performed for reasons which are the *agent's reasons*, in a sense which requires that he be conscious of his reasons. Or we might further require that the agent act for a reason which he *reflectively* regards as *a reason* for action: this might then rule out some impulsive actions as non-rational where the impulsive agent is acting on a consideration to which reflectively he would not be prepared to give weight. An even stronger requirement would hold that rationality is not exhibited in an action unless the agent possesses, and the action reflects, the trait of practical rationality—understood in terms of the higher-order concerns to do what has the best outcome, and to act on good practical reasons. There seems little point in arguing for or against any of these taxonomical proposals on grounds that they are more or less true to the ordinary notion of rationality. Their merits for the individual social scientist must surely depend on his particular theoretical purposes and preoccupations.

When we turn to rationality as a trait, however, there is surely a good case to be made for treating rationality as a complex trait *superimposed* on a person's basic status as an end-pursuing agent. On my account, we cannot attribute formal practical rationality to a man until his choices can be traced to his recognition that certain considerations are reasons for action, or—to put it another way—to his acceptance of certain norms of practical rationality. The most elementary norm is, of course:

If you have end E and x is a way of achieving E, then—*ceteris paribus*—do E.

But elementary as this is, the young child, acting purely out of impulse, may not be said to have grasped it. For grasping and accepting even this elementary practical norm involves a complex normative attitude, which issues in such activities as advice and criticism, and which consists in a concern to do any action falling under the norm *because* it falls under it. We cannot attribute rationality until we can attribute a conception of a prescriptive practical reason for action, and a concern to act on reasons.

Second, assessments in terms of all but the most basic norms of reason are, as we have seen, essentially comparative. So a crucial development in practical rationality takes place at the point at which an agent learns to *comparatively assess options* in terms of his ends, and to act on his assessments. The impulsive man does x because he sees that it is a way of achieving E. He does not exhibit rationality as a trait until he is disposed before acting to establish the relationship of x to alternative actions, e.g. that x is a necessary condition for attaining E, or that x is a better way of achieving E than y; and his grasp of this relationship makes some difference to what he does. On the view of rationality which I am advancing, unconsciously motivated acts will not exhibit the trait of rationality. For we cannot conceive of the agent in most cases as acting on anything stronger than the belief than x *is a way* of achieving E, and we cannot see in his act the working of any higher-order concern to perform an action with a certain relationship to his ends.

A further factor in the development of a man's rationality is his learning to assess comparatively his ends in choosing what to do. This requires more than the capacity to order the objects of his inclinations in terms of the felt strength of inclination at the moment of choice. Rationality requires the development of a hierarchy of ends independent of the individual's immediate inclinations. There are other things that the rational man knows he wants, even though he may feel no immediate inclination towards them. And he can distinguish his reflective ranking of these things from the comparative strength of the inclinations he may momentarily feel towards them. This is connected with the historically influential view that rationality consists in a disposition and a capacity to say 'No' to oneself—something which the man of impulse may not possess.

For these and other reasons, then, to identify the trait of practical rationality with the disposition to act for reasons would be to lose a valuable taxonomical distinction. The impulsive man and the young child continually act because they believe that what they do is a way of bringing about what—at the moment of choice—they want. There are surely taxonomical advantages in keeping 'rationality' as a trait-term for the complex of dispositions, outlined above, which each can acquire through a particular kind of socialization.

E   Rationality and norms

Should acting or being disposed to act under the influence of rules, norms, principles and standards be regarded as falling short of rationality? Is there any significant difference between the way rules enter an agent's choice, and the way considerations about the consequences of his actions influence his choice? As we have seen, having something like mastery of Europe as an end is to be identified with treating the consideration that an act will promote European mastery as a reason for action. If rationality consists in taking proper account of the considerations one regards as reasons, does it not also require and consist in taking proper account of one's rules and standards? For in accepting a rule an agent certainly accepts some consideration as a reason for action. In what follows I shall consider briefly a number of reasons which might be advanced for saying that norms are a non-rational constraint on rational choice.

(i) *The application of rules to choice is so direct that there is no room for the exercise of a mediating faculty of reason. If the choice is whether to keep a promise, no rationality is needed to see what action is called for by the rule 'one ought to keep one's promises'.* However, the 'application' of ends to choice may be equally direct: one might as readily argue that no rationality is needed to see what I must do if I desire the respect of my peers and the choice is between x which will enhance that respect and y which will destroy it. Establishing that y will destroy their respect is parallel to establishing that in doing b rather than a I shall be breaking a promise.

(ii) *There is no analogue in the normative realm to the comparative assessment of a number of alternative means to an end.* This is, however, not true. There may be a number of alternative ways of meeting a moral commitment which can be comparatively assessed by the agent both with a view to their costs and with a view to the differing degrees to which they meet the commitment.

(iii) *Normative considerations are overriding and absolute, so that there is no room for either considering options or for weighing different considerations against each other.* This is, of course, not always or even frequently true. Several normative considerations may conflict and it not be easy to decide what ought to be done and how the considerations are to be ordered or qualified. Normative considerations can be given lower priority than some high priority consequential ends. Consequential ends may even be assigned absolute and overriding priority.

However, there are certainly ways in which normative considerations *can* inject a non-rational element into a choice. If someone plants his maize in a certain way because the traditional rule demands it—not considering alternative options, not weighing competing considerations, not thinking of the rule's existence as *a* powerful consideration in favour of *one* possible planting method, not having to consider different ways in which he might conform to the rule—then none of the distinctive features of practical rationality is present in his act. To the extent, then, that normative considerations act as rigid barriers to reflection about other considerations and other options, they are non-rational influences. If, however, they are treated by the agent as simply some amongst his range of relevant considerations to be taken into account in comparatively assessing options, to be weighed against each other in such assessments, rationality is unimpaired by the influence of normative considerations.

Notes

1 Cf. Piaget's developmental theory discussed in Chapter 13.
2 Cf. index references to rationality in Klein, J. (1965).
3 The use of the notion of rationality in sociological explanation is discussed in Rex, J. (1961).
4 Cf. Max Weber's distinction between instrumental and value-rationality. This is discussed in Chapter 6, section B2.
5 See Chapter 6, section C1(a).
6 Watkins, J.W.N. (1970).
7 It has been one of the major objectives and achievements of decision theorists to extend and elaborate canons of optimality for highly complex choice-situations. These are discussed in Chapter 7.
8 Other notions which have sometimes been used to capture the relationship include the idea that the agent's choice is *appropriate*, given his summary-belief, or that his belief about his choice-situation *commits* him to that choice.
9 See the discussion of the rationality of maximizing expected utility in Chapter 7, pp. 172–4. It remains to be seen whether other propositions only count as good and sufficient reasons for choice if the policy of acting on them can be shown to have the best outcome over a series of choices.
10 In Chapter 8, Clem Tisdell explores the possibility of an agent's identifying the optimal option despite incompleteness in his knowledge of, or deliberations about, his choice-situation.
11 For accounts of the ways actual decision-making falls short of the paradigm of the rational agent who considers all the options and all the relevant considerations, see Simon, H.A. (1957), Lindblom, C. (1964), and Cyert, R.M. and Welsch, L.A. (1970).
12 For another account of the trait of practical rationality as a higher-order disposition, see Hempel, C.G. (1961–2).
13 Quentin Gibson suggests this in Chapter 5, p. 120.
14 The contrast between the strong and weak notions of rationality in action is further explored in Chapter 5 and Chapter 6.
15 Watkins, J.W.N. (1970).

16 Cf. Mortimore, G.W. (1971).
17 The location of this dividing line is discussed by Percy Cohen in Chapter 6, section C2.

Bibliography

ALEXANDER, P. (1962), 'Rationality and psychoanalytic explanation', *Mind*, LXXI, pp. 326–41.
BARBU, Z. (1960), *Problems in Historical Psychology*, London.
CYERT, R.M. and WELSCH, L.A. (eds) (1970), *Management Decision Making*, London.
DRAY, W. (ed.) (1966), *Philosophical Analysis and History*, New York.
EDGLEY, R. (1969), *Reason in Theory and Practice*, London.
HEMPEL, C.G. (1961–2), 'Rational action', *Proceedings of the American Philosophical Association*, pp. 5–23.
KLEIN, J. (1965), *Samples from English Cultures* (2 vols), London.
LINDBLOM, C. (1964), 'On muddling through', in Gore, W.J. (ed.), *The Making of Decisions*, London.
MORTIMORE, G.W. (ed.) (1971), *Weakness of Will*, London.
PARSONS, T. and SHILS, E.A. (eds) (1951), *Towards a General Theory of Action*, Cambridge, Mass.
REX, J. (1961), *Key Problems of Sociological Theory*, London.
RICHARDS, D.A.J. (1971), *A Theory of Reasons for Action*, Oxford.
RYAN, A. (1973), 'Deductive explanation in the social sciences', *Aristotelian Society*, supplementary volume XLVII.
SIMON, H.A. (1957), *Models of Man*, New York.
WATKINS, J.W.N. (1970), 'Imperfect rationality', in Borger, R. and Cioffi, F. (eds), *Explanation in the Behavioural Sciences*, Cambridge.

5

Arguing from rationality

Q. Gibson

In this paper, I wish to exhibit the form of an argument which takes the rationality of human beings as a premise, and has assertions about their actions as its conclusion. It is an argument of a kind which is extremely common in the social sciences, and without it our knowledge of human affairs would be very much more limited than it is. It has, however, not often been set out explicitly enough for its effectiveness to be properly examined.

In Chapter 4 Geoffrey Mortimore was concerned with the *concept* of rationality in action. We are now turning to the question of the *application* of this concept to the study of behaviour. These questions are obviously closely related. The effectiveness of the application depends on what it is that is being applied. And Mortimore has made it clear in his analysis that there is not one concept of rationality but several related concepts. It follows that in examining the effectiveness of the argument we have to consider for which of these concepts it is effective.

In other words, if we take as a premise the proposition that the people we are concerned with are acting rationally, we must be careful to notice what kind of a premise this is. Mortimore has pointed out (Chapter 4, p. 102) that postulates of rationality may vary from very strong to very weak. The trouble is that we seem inevitably led to make our postulate so strong that it becomes inapplicable. If we withdraw, we may well make it so weak that, though undoubtedly applicable, it remains useless as a source of any interesting conclusions. In view of these opposed dangers, we must try to understand why the argument is so effective.

A The argument

1 Its structure

The argument I have in mind is used in the context of various kinds of enquiry. It can be used for explanation, for the making of historical inferences, and for prediction.

Consider, for example, how you might go about explaining the fact that the government of Rhodesia is encouraging European immigration.

Clearly Mr Smith and his colleagues want to maintain the way of life to which the white community has become accustomed. And obviously it will help towards this end if the size of the white population is increased to compete with the growth of the black. Any reasonable man will recognize the evidence in favour of the propositions, first, that increase in supporting numbers contributes to some degree to the maintenance of power, and second, that the maintenance of power is a condition of the maintenance of an élite way of life. You assume that Mr Smith is such a reasonable man. You need only put yourself in his place; if you had his aims, this is the kind of thing that you yourself would do.

Or again, consider what happens when you dig up an artefact and infer from it something about the way of life of people in the past. You look at the ruins of a building, for example, its shape, its size, its materials, and ask yourself what it could have been used for. You assume that the people who built it had some end in view, and were rational enough to build something that was suited to this end. You conclude, perhaps, that it was a place of public assembly. If you had been in their situation and had built a place like this, you say, it would have been for just such a purpose.

Finally, you may argue to the future. You observe that someone has acquired a monopoly in the production of razor-blades. You ask—what is their price going to be? Knowing that above all else he is concerned to maximize his profit, you consider the elasticities of demand and the cost of production curves for razor-blades, and conclude that the price will be so-and-so. You are assuming, of course, that the monopolist is a rational man, and will calculate correctly the point at which the different curves will intersect. You say that if you, the economist, were in his place, this is the price that you would fix.

These illustrations, it should be noticed, do not come from any specialized pocket in the social sciences. They come respectively from the fields of politics, history and economics. And they could easily be followed up with others from other fields.

In each case the result is obtained by relying on the assumption that the people being considered are acting in a rational way. If the beliefs which they held about the causal relation between means and ends were based on miscalculations, or affected by prejudices, we would find it much more difficult to explain why they did what they did, or to tell what they did, or foretell what they will do.

The point of the argument, in these cases, is obvious enough. Its structure, however, has a certain special complexity which it is worth paying some attention to. There are in fact here two arguments, one incapsulated in the other.

First, there is the argument which we attribute to the person whose action is being explained or predicted, or whose intention, given his action, is being retrodicted. This person—the agent—has something he wants to do, some end in view. What he does will obviously depend on what he believes about ways of achieving this end, and our procedure depends on the assumption that he arrives at that belief by way of an argument.

Thus the Rhodesian government may be pictured as involved in an argument, the conclusion of which is the proposition that the building up of the white population contributes to the maintenance of an élite way of life. The argument is not a tidy mathematical one but an untidy empirical one depending in the last resort on evidence for generalizations about social origins, ethnic grouping and ways of maintaining power, together no doubt with direct analogical evidence from closely related colonial situations.

Similarly we think of the ancient builders as drawing the conclusion that their proposed building is suited to its purpose, the difference in this case being only that the grounds are much simpler, consisting mainly of truisms about the numbers of people who can fit into a given space. And again, the monopolist is seen as arguing to the best price from general economic principles combined with the results of market and production research on his product.

We need not of course envisage these arguments as having been worked out on the spot. It may well be that the monopolist has made systematic calculations, or called in his economic advisers to do it for him. But the prime minister of Rhodesia may be doing no more than using his political intuition or carrying out a policy formulated long before. When we attribute an argument to him, or say that he has drawn a conclusion, we need only mean that he could state his reasons explicitly if required, or at least at some time in the past has seen the force of the evidence and fixed a policy accordingly.

The point about such arguments is that, considered in themselves, they need not be attributed to anybody in particular. We can consider them hypothetically, simply as arguments. And if we so consider them, we as social scientists will recognize that they are *good* arguments, that the evidence mentioned does in fact support the conclusion. In Mortimore's terms, the conclusion is something that it is rational to believe, quite apart from anyone's actually believing it. Given the information available, we claim, it is the correct conclusion about how the end in question is to be achieved in the circumstances. We contrast it with other conclusions which would have been incorrect. In circumstances such as those of Mr Smith, for example, it would be incorrect to conclude that his end could be achieved by establishing a universal suffrage.

The conclusions in such arguments can of course never be drawn with certainty, and the borderline between correctness and incorrectness is not fixed and final, as in the case of a deductive argument. The policy of European immigration may always backfire. The monopolist's advisers may have neglected relevant data. The degree of conclusiveness of the argument, therefore, must be taken into account, and there will be some point below which the conclusion is so risky that it would be rational not to accept it and act on it but to withhold judgment.

We may now turn to the second argument. This is that in which we attribute the first argument to the agent and conclude that he will act accordingly. It is on this that, as social scientists, our explanation, retrodiction or prediction depends. Though it *refers* to the first argument, it is not to be identified with it. Its premises may be set out as follows:

(a) The person concerned is acting rationally; that is to say, his doing what he does is the result of his having a belief, based on the correct assessment of the available evidence, that his doing it will lead to an end he desires.[1]

(b) The correct assessment of the available evidence leads to the conclusion that the way to achieve such an end is to do so-and-so; for example, to promote white immigration, to build large rooms, to fix the price at 65c. for five.

From these two premises we draw the conclusion that he does, did, or will do, so-and-so.[2]

It is the second of these premises, it should be noticed, which incorporates the agent's argument. It tells us that a certain conclusion will be drawn by anyone in the agent's circumstances if he argues correctly. The first premise states that the agent in question does argue correctly. Thus, it is the second premise which is the general one. The first premise is the application of it to the particular action.

No evidence whatsoever is produced for the first premise in this argument. Thus our conclusion, as social scientists, may be said to be based on the *assumption* that the action is a rational one.

But if our argument is to be a good one, there must be some reason for our holding this assumption. The most general reason we can give is that we have discovered from experience that *people in general* do act for the most part rationally. We may defend this broad approximate generalization by arguing that it *pays* to be rational—that it is the use of reason which has enabled the human species to survive and to gain power over all other creatures. And it seems to me that this is a pretty good argument.

This generalization, however, is only approximate. People vary in the extent to which they perform rational actions, and whether people act rationally varies also with the kinds of situation with which they are coping. Hence in any given case, we may protect ourselves by limiting the generalization to the *individual* (Mr Smith is a very rational person) or to some given *subject matter* (people in general are rational in economic matters even if not in religious ones).

How we establish the rationality of an action is certainly something we might go on to discuss with greater care. But what I have said is surely enough to make it clear that we establish it *empirically*, and without reference to *any other* character of the action we are concerned to explain. Once we have accepted it as an empirical truth, we go on to argue *from* it in the manner which I have tried to set out.

2 Some comments on the argument

Before we can consider the effectiveness of this argument, we need to enlarge on some of its features.

(a) In the argument as I have presented it, no attention whatsoever is paid to the rationality of ends as such. This is quite deliberate. It may be that some use can be found for the idea that there are degrees of what Mortimore called substantive practical rationality.[3] I do not intend to discuss this question. It is sufficient for me to point out that the argument we are considering can make no use of an appeal to a rationality of this kind. For the plain fact is that such rationality cannot be assumed to be common to all men. All we can do is take actual ends as given. Where ends are very widespread, like the pursuit of money and power, we can of course make good use of this fact. We may come to rely on the assumption that people seek to maximize their money gains, just as we come to rely on the assumption that they go the right way about it. But to say this is not to say that the maximizing of money gains is either rational or irrational. And conversely, though you may claim that it is rational, say, to promote the maximum freedom for individuals, you cannot rely on people, in general, pursuing this end because of their perception of its rationality.

(b) It is the kind of argument for which the talk of sympathetic understanding makes good sense. The second premise of the argument is in effect an answer to the question, what you yourself as a rational person would do, if you were in another person's circumstances and had his aims. This of course would make no sense unless you assumed that you yourself were rational as well as the person whose action you were considering. But if you did not assume this, you would presumably stop trying to give explanations or make discoveries. Social scientists are no doubt on occasions inclined to be modest about their powers of reasoning. But if they were so modest as to claim that others could see the point of an argument when they could not, they would have to forgo the use of the method. One thinks of Edmund Burke, who claimed that the British constitution was fashioned by the wisdom of the ages for the benefit of the British people, even though he and his contemporaries could not see it. Clearly he could not use the method, since he had, on his own admission, no independent way of establishing the second premise.

In fact, when we are modest, it is not usually about our own powers of argument, but about the information we have concerning the agent's circumstances, and particularly his ends. When we do not understand what he is doing, we assume very reasonably, that it is neither because we are irrational, nor because he is, but because he is pursuing other ends than those we originally thought him to be pursuing. And this of course is another matter altogether.

Anyway, if we are to use the argument, we must assume a common rationality, and argue from what we would do to what others would do. If we are considering the explanation of past actions, this might aptly be described, in R.G. Collingwood's terms, as 'rethinking people's thoughts'. It is because rationality is common to people in different periods that the procedure applies so much better to thoughts than to emotions or desires. It is when one starts querying the commonness of standards of rationality that one begins to run into serious trouble.[4]

(c) The argument, as I have stated it, is of course applicable only to individuals, and not to groups, institutions or social structures. For many, this will suggest a severe limitation on its usefulness. It must be remembered, however, that there are many facts about aggregates which come within its scope. Whenever we explain such facts in terms of the actions of numbers of similarly situated individuals, the door is left open for its use. I have in mind things like a swing in votes from one party to another. Suppose there is a swing away from the government in middle-class electorates. This might be explained by pointing to the government's taxation policy which had ignored the interests of the middle-income group and to indications that the opposition would not ignore them. In these circumstances, it might be argued, it is reasonable to suppose that voting against the government party would promote these interests. Given that sufficient numbers are motivated by these interests, then all we need is the assumption of their rationality to provide the explanation.

(d) The rationality of the action, which is asserted in the first premise, has two facets which we should distinguish. First, there is the rationality of the belief about means to an end, which consists in the recognition of the correctness of the belief, given the available evidence for it. And second there is the rationality of the action which consists simply in the recognition of the correctness of the action, given the belief. Mortimore has distinguished these as epistemic rationality and formal practical rationality.[5] Our monopolist would exhibit practical rationality in this sense if he fixed his price at 65c. because he believed this was the required price; it would not matter in this context if this belief were put into his mind by his remembering the first two digits of his telephone number. Whereas he would be exhibiting epistemic rationality only if he came to form this belief as a result of making well-founded estimates of marginal costs and elasticities of demand.

In the account which I have given of the argument, it is clearly presupposed that both these forms of rationality have to be attributed to the agent. The monopolist, for example, must be practically rational, since we could not predict his price-fixing, given his belief that 65c. was the required price, unless we were assured that he would act in conformity with his belief. And he must also be epistemically rational since we could not predict his arriving at this belief, given evidence of cost and demand trends, unless we were assured that his belief would be based on the evidence.

This requirement of a two-fold rationality has, however, been challenged, doubt being thrown on the need to insist on the epistemic component in the rationality of an action. This raises a crucial question about the effectiveness of the argument, which I will be considering in the second part of this paper.

(e) The belief about means, which we attribute to the agent, may take various forms. It may take the relatively weak form of believing that performing the action will *contribute* to the end,

117

without being sufficient to produce it. This presumably is the case with Ian Smith's belief about white immigration. It would be unreasonable to suppose that such immigration would by itself ensure white supremacy, but it could take its place alongside the operation of other factors. It would of course be irrational to implement the policy if there were reason to suppose that the other factors would not be operating. There would be no point, that is to say, in encouraging immigration if the other conditions for maintaining white supremacy were absent. It should be noted that it is considerations of this kind which lead to doubts about the rationality of voting for a minority candidate when there is overwhelming evidence that he cannot win. What we have to do here, to retain the rationality of voting, is to modify the statement of the end, taking it not as the defeat of the safe seat-holder but as the weakening of his support.

Second, the belief that we attribute to the agent may be to the effect that the action is *sufficient* to bring about his end though not necessary. We may point to the fact that it is *a* way, but not the *only* way of doing it. Thus we may explain a reduction in petrol tax as a sound pre-election popularity move, but a knowledge of the government's desire to win election support will not tell us whether it will make this move or some other. To tighten this up, we would have to move on to showing that the action was also *necessary*— that it was in fact the *only* way of achieving the end. To do this we would have to consider and exclude any possible alternatives. And this could be a much more extended undertaking. Within certain frames of reference, however, it can be straightforward enough. The razor-blade monopolist is a case in point. In his circumstances, there is no obvious way in which he can make more money than by fixing the optimum price, and so we can predict that that is what he will do.

Finally, we may suggest, as a form for the agent's belief, that it concerns the *best* way for him to achieve his end. Since there is by definition only one best way, any possibility of attributing a rational belief of this kind to the agent would be very useful indeed. In speaking of the 'best way' of achieving an end, however, I think we may have two rather different things in mind. One thing we may mean is the way in which we can achieve most of it. And this only applies where it is something which varies in quantity, and of which we can never have enough. Obvious candidates are money and power. In such cases we can present the end as that of obtaining the maximum quantity possible, and the best means as those which ensure that maximum. Ensuring the maximum, we assume, is what our razor-blade monopolist is trying to do in respect of his profits.

Talk of the 'best way', however, may also have other implications. It may mean the way to achieve the end at least *cost*. In
mentioning cost we immediately introduce a whole new dimension
into the picture. We introduce the obvious fact that a person
normally has a variety of ends, and in achieving one may have to
sacrifice another. We have to ask how we can apply the principle
of rational action in this case. But first one other comment.

(f) Nothing has been said so far about the need to choose between
alternatives. And yet there is a sense of 'rational' in which it requires
such choice. To be rational, it is sometimes said, the agent must
have reflected on the matter, considering other possibilities, and
not just have seized on the first way of achieving his end which
happens to present itself.[6]

It should be clear, however, that such consideration of alternatives
is not essential for the use of the argument. If all the agent is concerned with is doing something which contributes to the end, or is
sufficient for achieving it, it does not matter whether there are
other things which contribute to it or other ways of achieving it.
Mr Smith's reason for encouraging white immigration remains a
good reason even if there are other things he is doing or might be
doing with the same end in view. And if it is simply some electoral
support that the government is after, the effectiveness of the petrol
tax reduction is unaffected by whether the support could have been
gained in other ways.

The need for considering alternatives thus only arises if the
belief about means to an end is concerned with necessary conditions or with the best way of achieving the end. If it is a question of
what moves are essential for gaining electoral support, or of how to
maximize it, or of the cost of gaining it, one has to start immediately
setting out the different ways of gaining it and comparing them.
This, as I have pointed out, complicates the argument from rationality considerably. But the complication is by no means always
called for.

I have said that the argument can be used both for explanation
and prediction of people's actions, and have implied that the
very same argument could be used in both contexts. But it will
now be clear that where an agent adopts means which are contributory or sufficient we can explain his action in terms of his having
good reasons for his belief, but cannot predict it. Assuming we
know the end, we can still only predict the action if we know what is
necessary for the achievement of that end, or *a fortiori* what is the
best way of achieving it. And correspondingly we must for such
prediction assume that the agent is rational in the sense of having
good reason for a belief of this stronger kind.

(g) We may now return to the question of cost. The argument, as I have stated it so far, is concerned with a person's adoption of means to some given end. Where he has a variety of ends and they compete, it is clear that anyone who uses the argument should take them all into account. The rationality of an action is relative to the end the action is being performed to bring about. Given some end, say, arriving at one's destination on time, it might indeed be rational relative to that end to drive at 90 mph. But if this is not the person's only end and he has some concern for human life, driving at this speed would not be a rational thing to do. What we have to do therefore is find out the order of priorities among a person's ends. In other words, we need not merely an end but a preference scale, before we can use the argument.[7]

This at once opens up a whole new dimension for rational calculation on the part of the agent. It has been recognized, from the time of Plato onwards, that it is the function of reason not merely to devise means but to reconcile or harmonize ends. To achieve this, the agent must keep all his relevant ends in mind, he must ensure that his scale of preferences is internally consistent, and then he must work out which ends are in his circumstances capable of joint achievement and which have to be sacrificed. What he has to achieve in fact is not so much an end as an optimum position, given his scale of preferences. Though he may fall short of this in varying degrees, it is what is required for his full rationality.

It should be noted that this new dimension involves us in an expansion of the epistemic component of a rational action, not the practical one, in the sense of 'practical' introduced in comment (d). The calculation of the agent ends in a belief about what is the best thing to do. The practical component consists in seeing that this belief justifies his doing it. It is true that the calculation requires his taking into account a new kind of data, namely the full range of his own ends. A kind of self-knowledge, in short, must be added to knowledge of the environment before a person can estimate what is the best thing to do. But it is knowledge for all that. And as social scientists we must take account of it as part of the data when we reconstruct the argument which leads to his belief.[8]

As a result of this expansion, we end up with a somewhat rarified ideal picture of what it is to act rationally. Instead of thinking in terms of a variety of ends, we come to think of the optimum in terms of one grand consolidated end of maximizing satisfaction on the whole. And rational action comes to consist in making a survey of all possible courses of action open to one, calculating the gains and losses involved in each such course and setting out on the course which provides the biggest favourable balance.

Since the reasoning involved in the assessment of outcomes is inductive in character, and the conclusions subject to error, since based, however correctly, only on available evidence, the agent must also take into account in each case the degree of risk he runs in committing himself to them.

All this is the familiar stock-in-trade of decision theory. But though we seem to be led into it inevitably by considerations about cost, it is a far cry from the simple account of rational action with which we started. In the light of it, we may begin to doubt the usefulness of arguing from a person's rationality when we are trying, as social scientists, to gain an understanding of his actions.

It is to the question of the usefulness of the argument that I now turn.

B The usefulness of the argument

1 The problem of complexity

If we have to take account of a full range of the person's ends, and consider the outcomes of all possible actions to see which provides an optimum, it would seem that the incapsulated argument will become so complex that we will not be able to make use of it at all in arguing to what the person will do. Problems about the estimation of this optimum will be discussed in detail in later papers in this volume. But certain major difficulties can be indicated briefly here in an informal way.

In the first place there is difficulty about the assumption that the people we are concerned with are acting rationally. For the more complex a problem is, the less likely is it that people will cope with it adequately. Where they are faced with various alternatives the outcomes of none of which are certain, they will need, for one thing, to compare the probabilities of these outcomes on the available evidence, and such comparison is difficult. A person in Ian Smith's position, for example, might well have to answer questions like the following: Is it more likely that encouraging white immigration will assist in maintaining supremacy than that modifying the suffrage laws in a certain way will bring about reconciliation with the British government? Though in principle there is presumably a right answer, we can well imagine quite reasonable people differing about it. Such considerations tend to be overlooked by decision theorists because of their concentration on what they call risks—that is, numerically calculable probabilities.[9] But such calculable risks are rarely found in real social situations.[10] And in their absence, departures from the right answer become progressively more likely with the number and diversity of the hypotheses compared.

Similarly, departures from epistemic rationality are also likely to increase with the number and diversity of the person's ends. In concentrating on a project in hand, we may all easily overlook certain items in the cost. We may fail, that is to say, to keep in mind everything that is relevant in our scale of preferences.

It is true of course that rationality is a matter of degree, and that we can afford to allow for some deviations from the perfect optimum course. But for every deviation, an argument which depends on a person's rationality necessarily loses some of its power, and may in the end become not worth troubling about at all.

Further, even if the people we are considering were all to act in a perfectly rational manner, there would still remain a difficulty about our capacity, as social scientists, to reconstruct their reasoning. If they find comparisons of evidence difficult, so do we. And when it comes to their scales of preferences, we are in a considerably worse position, since we may assume that they know more about their own wants than we do. It must be remembered that, under the heading of 'wants', we must here include not only explicit desires for ends but also various temperamental tendencies such as the store set on adventure or on security. We would also have to add in, what is often ignored, the store set on immediacy of satisfaction as against long-range achievement. Such an all-embracing survey of a person's relevant desires and inclinations may be thought to be hardly a realistic undertaking.

In view of difficulties of this kind it may well be asked how the argument we are considering can possibly be effective. The answer, I suggest, is not in any way to deny the difficulties but simply to point out that in most situations in which people have to act, the complexities which give rise to the difficulties are in fact not present. In the case of difficult decisions, where there are many ends to be reconciled and many ways of doing it, the reconstruction of a person's reasons will hardly ever be determinate, and certainly not determinate enough for us to predict what he will do. To that extent the use of the argument is limited. But difficult decisions are fortunately rare.

It may be pointed out, also, that decisions of medium complexity are often made to look more difficult than they are. This is because in talking about alternatives and ends we are inclined to represent a person's reasoning as if it started from scratch. Yet most people are already in possession of a general fund of knowledge about how to achieve at least their short-term goals, and that fund of knowledge is shared by the social scientist who seeks to understand their behaviour. This may enable them to pass judgment at once on what is the best thing to do in a given type of familiar situation. Similarly, the kinds of sacrifices that have to be made when they act are generally well known and roughly assessable. The sacrifice of time, for example, which might be used for doing other things, is an important item of this kind.

The idea of a widespread consolidation of all our ends into a total goal has its primary application in economics. But surely it is clear that economists do not have to face the difficulties which such a consolidation must encounter. The consolidation is automatically done for them by the device of money, which is simply power to achieve a great variety of alternative ends. They are therefore in the enviable position of being able to treat human beings as having a single predominant end, the maximizing of their money gains. Once they broaden their concept of utility to include, say, leisure, they begin to get into trouble. How could we tell what the price of razor-blades was going to be if the monopolist was more interested in playing golf than in making profits?

All this applies, whether the argument is being used for prediction or for explanation. But finally we should keep in mind that where we are using the argument solely for purposes of explanation, its scope is even wider.[11] Where an action has already been performed, and we know what the agent's ends are, we can quickly make the action intelligible to ourselves by seeing that it is sufficient for bringing about one of the ends or at least contributes to bringing it about. In other words, we introduce the hypothesis that the agent has a correct belief about there being a sufficient or contributory connection between an action of this kind and that particular end. We may of course be wrong, but in order to find out whether we are wrong we do not have to consider all the alternative courses of action open to the person, or check whether there were alternative or better ways of achieving the end. It may be, for example, that before formulating its immigration policy the Rhodesian government was faced with a difficult political decision between various things it might do, and it would have taken a most astute political forecaster to predict the outcome. But given the outcome, we can immediately present a plausible explanation, even if only a partial one.

It is a commonplace that prediction is difficult in the social sciences, and this for reasons which have nothing to do with the rationality or irrationality of human beings. Working with the hypothesis of their rationality, therefore, can provide no panacea. But even for prediction, let alone explanation, it can still provide a powerful guiding thread where conflicting ends are manageably small in number and the evidence for beliefs is relatively simple and cogent.

2 The need for epistemic rationality

Unfortunately, fear of the difficulties I have discussed has led some not so much to admit a limitation on the application of the argument as to reinterpret the argument itself in a way which would rob it of its fundamental point.

What they have done is to devise an accommodating criterion of rationality which takes no account of whether a person's beliefs are well-grounded or not. Beliefs about means are, like ends, to be taken as given, and rationality is to consist in acting in accordance with them. Epistemic rationality, in other words, is abandoned, and practical rationality, in Mortimore's minimal formal sense, is accepted as sufficient.

Thus, Hempel says in one place that 'in order to explain an action in terms of the agent's reasons, we need to know what the agent believed, but not necessarily on what grounds'.[12] The same idea is to be found in the account of 'rational explanation' given by William Dray. In reconstructing the agent's calculation of means, he says, we must look at the situation as the agent envisaged it, even though his beliefs are erroneous.[13] And recently John Watkins has argued explicitly in favour of what he calls the 'imperfect rationality principle'—the principle that a person will act in a way appropriate to his aims and situational appraisal, whether or not this is a mis-appraisal.[14]

There is no doubt that if we weaken in this way the assumption from which we argue, we automatically make it true of virtually everybody. For any departure from rationality in the sense of conformity of one's actions to one's actual wants and beliefs is surely extremely rare. I would accept it as a very general truth about human nature that if anyone wants something and believes that performing some action is a way of getting it, he will perform that action. It makes no difference to this generalization whether the ends are one or many. Where they are many and they conflict, it is still safe to say that a person will do what he *believes* will achieve the optimum.[15] Cases of unanticipated paralysis or sheer weakness of will might be suggested as providing the occasional exception. But there are even many philosophers who would rule these out *a priori* by claiming that the connection between wants and beliefs on the one hand and actions on the other is a conceptual rather than an empirical one.

This being so, Watkins's 'imperfect rationality principle' has this to be said for it—that it could be applied to almost any human action, however crazy. He himself accepts this as one of its virtues and proceeds to show how it explains bungled actions which are seemingly irrational, as well as others which are successful and seemingly rational. In a similar vein, Hempel claims that for a person who believes that walking under ladders brings him bad luck, walking around a ladder is a rational thing to do, and we can explain his action by reference to this rationality.

That the first premise of the argument should be true of every-body is of course in itself no disadvantage. For one thing it elimi-nates the need to establish that it holds for any given person or for any given subject matter. The trouble is rather that this advantage is gained only at very great cost. For with the weakening of the criterion of rationality, we no longer have any incapsulated argu-ment referred to in the second premise and attributed to the agent. And as we have seen it is our capacity as social scientists to recon-struct this argument from the evidence available to the agent which gives its whole point to the procedure.

In their new form the premises of the argument may be expressed as follows:

(a) The person concerned is acting rationally; that is to say, his doing what he does is the result of his having a belief that his doing it will lead to an end he desires.
(b) He believes that doing so-and-so will lead to an end he desires.

From these premises, we draw the conclusion that he does, did or will do, so-and-so.

There is no doubt that arguments of this form are sound, and if we are explaining or predicting an action or making historical inferences from one, they tell us something which it is minimally useful to know, namely, that for any action there is a belief with which it is in accord. Thus we are enabled to explain Rhodesian immigration policy by claiming it to be a belief of the government that the policy will assist in maintaining white supremacy. We are enabled to discover the intentions of the ancient builders if we accept as a belief of theirs that buildings so constructed are suitable for public meetings. And, correspondingly, if we happen to know that the monopolist believes that a price of 65c. is the profit-maxi-mizing one, we are enabled reliably to predict that he will fix that price.

We are also enabled, we should add, to explain a refusal to employ non-Aryans in terms of a belief that they are intellectually inferior, to infer that Agamemnon wanted a victory over Troy from his belief that sacrificing his daughter would promote it, or to predict that someone will lie down on the pavement from his belief that this is essential to his catching the bus. For the baselessness or absurdity of the belief is irrelevant for arguments of this form.

It should be clear, however, that such arguments, though appealing to rationality of a kind, completely fail to provide us with the special advantage which I have been pointing out. We commonly suppose that there is a difference between the case where someone is refused employment because of his ethnic origin and the case where he is refused employment because of his qualifications and experience. In each case there is an appeal to certain beliefs of the employer. But in the second case we have an explanatory and predictive advantage which is absent in the former. And this for two interconnected reasons.

In the first place, while explaining an action by reference to a belief has some point, it is evidently more satisfactory if we can say how the agent came to have the belief. Merely to point to the practical rationality of the action does not help us here in any way. Whereas to point to its epistemic rationality is to give us the argument by which the agent arrived at it. We assume there is good evidence for the belief that a person with more qualifications and experience does a better job, and we assume that the employer is aware of this. We therefore have an explanation ready to hand. But we have no such explanation for the belief that an Aryan does a better job. We have to look for a sociological explanation for such a belief in the same way as we do for any other social fact, by delving into the employer's attitudes and background.

It should be noticed that we are here taking it for granted that we know what the beliefs are. But we must now point out, second and more importantly, that with the argument in its weakened form we are deprived of our special independent way of finding out what the beliefs are. The fact is that what a person believes is often hard to discover directly. This remains true even if he happens to make autobiographical statements about his beliefs. Our ability to infer the belief from the information he has at his disposal, on the assumption that he is epistemically rational, is therefore almost indispensable.

It is true that in the special case where we already know what action is performed, and know that the agent is unambiguously in pursuit of a single goal, we may immediately infer what his belief must have been, without assuming anything more than his practical rationality. In other words, if we have the first premise and the conclusion of the argument in its new form we can automatically fill in the second premise provided there is only one such premise which will make it into a sound argument. For example, if we know of the Rhodesian immigration policy and know that the Rhodesian government has the maintenance of European supremacy as its overriding goal, we can automatically fill in the gap in the explanation of the policy by saying that the government believes the policy will promote that goal.

This way of inferring the belief might seem at first sight to be adequate for explanation of the action, though not of course for its prediction nor for the retrodictive inference of the goal from the action. Yet even for explanation, it will not do. For a proper explanation requires that there be some reason for accepting the explaining facts which is independent of the fact to be explained. If the only reason for accepting that a person has a certain belief is that without it, given his ends, he would not have done what he did, it is hardly illuminating to mention the belief as part of the explanation of what he did. To do so would be to invite the comment that we know all that already, and have not increased our understanding of why the action was performed.

In the case of retrodiction and prediction, moreover, we have to rule out even this unilluminating way of establishing the existence of the belief. Hence the importance of the invaluable device of inferring it from the situation the agent is in and the availability of the evidence.

There are of course other ways of inferring beliefs. Otherwise we would never find out about people's prejudices, superstitions and miscalculations. But to find out about these things is notoriously difficult and requires a great deal of enquiry into the complex conditions of the special case. All this is by-passed if we assume that the agent is arguing from evidence which is available to all, including the social scientist.

Consider for example the person approaching the ladder. If you see a pot of paint balanced precariously on it you may infer that he will walk around it, on the ground that this is the rational thing to do. But to know about his superstitions, you have to know quite a lot about his social background, his upbringing and so on.

Or again, take the monopolist. His conservatism may affect his judgment about what is the best price. Or sheer inattention to economic reasoning may make him believe that the higher the price the higher the profit. In such cases, it is quite safe to assume that his price will correspond to his beliefs, if we know what they are. But to find out what they are, we would have to enquire into a lot of details of his character, intelligence and social affiliations, to say nothing of all those transient and accidental causes which might make him decide on 45c. or 80c. Whereas, if we could attribute to him a capacity to assess economic evidence, we could at once infer his belief and his price.

What is true of predictions is true *a fortiori* of historical inferences about people's goals. Baseless beliefs held by people in past periods are hard to disinter. If our ancient builders miscalculated and what they really built was a dwelling which came out too large by mistake, it is doubtful whether we would ever know about it. Whereas if we assume that it was effectively designed to fulfil their purpose, we can immediately detect the purpose.

In conclusion, let me return to the case of explanation, and consider an illustration given by Watkins of the explanation of a bungled action. For this, it seems to me, will help to illustrate my point.[16]

In 1893, Admiral Tryon, with thirteen ships of the British Mediterranean Fleet under his command, gave an order which led to a collision in which his flagship was sunk and 356 people were drowned, including himself. Why did he do it? An autobiographical statement of what he had in mind was not available; all he was heard to say as he went under was: 'It was all my fault.'

Watkins rightly wishes to rule out something which might be suggested—a failure in practical rationality. We must not let ourselves accept that his actions were at odds with his intentions and beliefs. But what then were his intentions and beliefs?

There is, of course, one possible explanation, not mentioned by Watkins, which would make his action rational in our sense as well as in his. This is that he had undergone a conversion and wanted to destroy the flagship of the British navy. If that was his goal, a belief that his actions would lead to it would not only have fitted in with his action, but would have been a completely rational one to hold. Unfortunately, however, there is no evidence whatsoever of such an upturning of his preference scale. We are left to assume that his intention was to execute a naval manoeuvre, and that there was something wrong with his idea of how to go about it.

What then did he have in mind? Watkins presents the following hypothesis taken from Richard Hough's *Admirals in Collision*. The ships were two abreast, six cables apart. The turning circle of each was four cables. He had two complementary ends in view, to change course into deeper water and at the same time to test out his officers with an unusual manoeuvre. To carry out these ends, he conceived the idea that they should change course by turning inwards, pass each other, and steam off in line in the opposite direction. He gave an order for them to turn inwards, but made no explicit mention of their passing each other, or on which side. Like two people swerving the same way to avoid each other, the leading ships collided.

This account of the matter looks very plausible. But why is it so plausible? I suggest it is because Watkins is construing Tryon's beliefs about how to achieve his ends as almost entirely rational, though not quite. What Watkins is doing is putting himself in Tryon's place and considering what a naval man would do if he had those ends in view. Within the framework of such a rationally worked out plan, it is not so hard to detect where things went wrong. The suggested trouble was that the signals were not explicit enough to avoid misunderstanding. Tryon presumably believed that they were. The one thing, it should be noted, that Watkins does not explain, is how he came to make this mistake. This brings out the point that it is precisely when beliefs are mistaken that they become difficult to explain.

It seems to me then that Hough's account of the Tryon catastrophe is a good illustration of the method as I have described it, but not as Watkins has described it. Given the end, we have to try to reconstruct the thought processes which led to the action. Merely saying that Tryon believed that giving the orders he did would lead to a successful naval manoeuvre does not get us anywhere. With the end and the actions as described this should be obvious to anybody. What we have to do is understand why this belief was held in the circumstances. Watkins's hypothesis does in fact give us this understanding only in so far as he presents it as being close to a rational one. He wisely shies off the problem of accounting for the error.

My conclusion, then, is that in order to use the method effectively we must attribute some epistemic rationality to the agent. It remains true, however, that it becomes progressively less safe to use it, the more complex and controversial the grounds for the agent's beliefs become, and the more varied and competing his ends. My suggestion is that this leaves a large number of cases in which it can be used to great effect.

Notes

1 To this, in strictness, we should add: 'together with a realization that, given this belief, he has good reason for so doing.' This element of 'practical rationality' is omitted at this stage to avoid prolixity. See note 5.

2 For a previous formulation of this argument, see Hempel, C.G. (1965), p. 471. Hempel has three premises: (1) A was in a situation of type C; (2) A was a rational agent; (3) in a situation of type C, any rational agent will do X. My (a) and (b) correspond roughly to his (2) and (3), differing principally in referring only to the rationality of the action and avoiding the further references to the rationality of the agent. What is

required from (1) is covered by the reference to the available evidence and the ends, which are relevant parts of the situation at the time of the action.

3 See Chapter 4, p. 96.

4 This remark applies to those 'cultural relativists' who refuse to pass judgment on the thought processes of people in other cultures on the ground that standards of reasoning are not commensurable. See Chapter 2 in this volume for a discussion of this idea. Karl Mannheim's sociology of knowledge is often thought to imply the thesis, as are also the statements made by Winch, P. (1964), pp. 78–111.

5 See Chapter 1, p. 12, and Chapter 4, p. 96. Mortimore points out that for formal practical rationality, it is not enough that the action results from the belief, it must result from a grasping of the point that, given the end the belief justifies the action. For the action to be performed, that is to say, the agent must be sufficiently rational to grasp this point. The belief by itself will not do the trick. I claim (section B2) that it is safe to attribute this element of rationality to virtually everybody.

6 See Chapter 4, pp. 96–100.

7 Mortimore's 'assumption of minimal rationality' has to do with the case where there is only one end. It must be remembered, however, that where a person has a variety of competing ends, or (which is a species of this) has a need to conserve resources, the assumption is not to be regarded as a convenient simplification, but as false. If one has more important concerns than arriving on time, driving at 90 mph is not even minimally rational, it is irrational. Strengthening the assumption is not a matter of choice.

8 Mortimore claims that practical rationality as a *trait* may also require the person to have the aim of improving the epistemic basis of his belief by exploring alternatives and considering costs. I am not discussing traits here, being concerned with the rationality of actions rather than of agents. But if I were to do so, it would still seem to me advisable to restrict the use of the term 'practical rationality' to its stipulated sense— that of acting in accordance with one's actual beliefs, whether or not one has striven to find good reasons for them.

9 Decision theorists are also inclined not to consider this epistemic problem about probability estimates at all. They are often concerned more with the practical rationality of a person's actions, given his *beliefs* about probabilities, however arrived at. I am not raising this question here.

10 See Watkins, J.W.N. (1970), p. 193: 'We no longer meet with [conditions of risk] when we venture out of the casino on to the race-course; still less do we meet with them in the worlds of business, politics and war.'

11 See my comment (f) in section A2 of this paper.

12 Hempel, C.G. (1965), pp. 464–5.

13 Dray, W. (1964), pp. 125–6.

14 Watkins, J.W.N. (1970), p. 172.

15 Mortimore appears to doubt this, mentioning people who act

impulsively, procrastinate, or are impatient with deliberation, as counter-instances (see Chapter 4, p. 105). The reader must judge whether we are not at cross-purposes here. An impulsive action is one done without consideration of cost—perhaps also one done without consideration of its effectiveness in achieving its end. To that extent it fails in epistemic rationality. But surely someone who buys the latest gadget on impulse, for example, believes at the time that he is achieving what he wants—and wants most. Similarly, the procrastinator believes either that tomorrow will do as well, or that the delights of inaction outweigh any positive ends he might achieve. And so on. I am not sure whether Mortimore is denying this, but if he is, our difference of view should be noted.

16 Watkins, J.W.N. (1970), pp. 211–16.

Bibliography

DRAY, W. (1964), *Laws and Explanation in History*, Oxford.

HEMPEL, C.G. (1965), *Aspects of Scientific Explanation*, New York.

MORTIMORE, G., 'Rationality in action', this volume, Chapter 4.

WATKINS, J.W.N. (1970), 'Imperfect rationality', in Borger, R. and Cioffi, F. (eds), *Explanation in the Behavioural Sciences*, Cambridge.

WINCH, P. (1964), 'Understanding a primitive society', *American Philosophical Quarterly*, reprinted (1970) in Wilson, B.R. (ed.), *Rationality*, London, pp. 78–111.

6

Rational conduct and social life[1]

P.S. Cohen

A Introduction

Most writers on the subject of rational or non-rational conduct
have tended to take one of the following positions: both rational
and non-rational conduct occur in social life and the one can be
distinguished from the other; social conduct is, on the whole, non-
rational, even though it is made to appear rational; social conduct
is on the whole, rational, even though some of it may appear to be
non-rational; an assumption of minimal rationality is necessary
to the study of social life whether or not rational conduct does occur.

I propose to show that each of these positions is in some senses
and for some purposes, correct; but I shall try to go further, and
argue that all of them have outlived their usefulness in sociology.
In doing this I hope to demonstrate: that the existing characterizations of rational and non-rational conduct are inadequate; that,
in real social life, pure forms of rational and non-rational conduct
are rarely, if ever, found; that these pure forms contain a number
of different components which are often assumed to occur together,
though they commonly do not; that all forms of social life lie
somewhere between the purely rational and the irrational; that
different forms of conduct comprise different combinations of the
elements which constitute the polar forms.

The solution which I propose arises out of a critical appraisal
of the ideas of certain 'classical' authors. I start with the ideas of
Max Weber, which represent the first position; next, those of Pareto,
which best represent the second; then I refer to those of Parsons,

an attempted compromise between the first and second; finally I consider those of Schutz and of other writers who represent the third and fourth views. Only then do I confront a number of key problems which arise out of a consideration of these positions and suggest how they might be dealt with.

B Theories of rational conduct

1 Max Weber[2]

According to Weber, conduct should be distinguished, at the outset, from behaviour which is purely reflexive and which can be described and explained without any reference to a meaning which is attached to it by the behaving individual. To explain why someone bats an eye-lid to avoid a dust particle, one does not have to assume that he attaches a meaning to his eye, to its lid or to the particle of dust. To explain, however, someone's batting of an eye-lid in response to a physical attempt to punch him in the eye, one would have to assume that a meaning is attached to the gesture, though the response itself is reflexive and not therefore to be classed as conduct. If the response occurs to a mere verbal threat, it comes even nearer to being meaningful conduct. However, to explain why someone avoids contact with a lower caste person, one must understand the meaning which he attaches to avoidance and also to the categories of social caste. In short, conduct is a form of behaviour which needs to be understood in terms of meanings which are attributed to it by those who act.

There are, according to Weber, four main types of conduct and of social conduct: two rational and two non-rational. Conduct is rational if it involves the choice of means to achieve an end. It is instrumentally rational (*zweckrational*) when it is determined by expectations of the behaviour of objects, including other humans, which are used as conditions or as means for the attainment of calculated ends. One example of everyday, instrumental rationality is that of travelling outside of one's neighbourhood to purchase goods which are cheaper there; yet another would be to pay higher prices in one's neighbourhood shops to save time and money otherwise spent in travelling. Men who are instrumentally rational will give up acting in any way that they believe will not achieve the ends desired. Often, or even usually, instrumental rationality requires that the choice of means and the pursuit of one particular end take account not only of whether the particular means achieves the particular end, but also of whether this will permit the achievement of other ends.

Instrumentally rational conduct must, according to Weber, be distinguished from that which is *value-rational* (*wertrational*). This last is governed by a belief, which is, at least in part, either aesthetic or moral, that what is done is valued in its own right, regardless of its prospects of success; what makes such conduct rational is that it is based on an assumption that there is a connection between means and ends. A clear example of value-rational conduct would be the giving of a gift to communicate loyalty, affection or friendship; there is here an assumption that the giving of the gift is a means to the end of communicating a sentiment, but there is also the assumption that this particular means is intrinsically joined to this particular end as part of its moral character. To give a gift in order to secure a favour, however, would count as instrumental rationality since the means would be discarded if they were found not to produce the desired result.

The two non-rational forms of conduct are, according to Weber, the *affectual* and the *traditional*. The former is determined by specific affects and feeling states, while the latter is determined by ingrained habituation. An example of affectual conduct would be that of striking someone in a state of rage; here one does not calculate whether the blow will have a specific, desired effect, nor does one attach a value to the act as such; but although one's behaviour is, or appears to be, almost a reflexive expression of rage, it can only be understood with reference to the meaning of that which aroused the state of rage.

An extreme example of traditional conduct would be one's everyday use of the rules of language: one is not prompted by an affective state; one does not consider a means/end connection between using language and being understood; nor does one really value the linguistic rules as a means of communication; one simply does what one has learned, more or less unquestioningly, to do, without necessarily recognizing that the language has rules.

Weber recognizes that the assumptions underlying this typology require qualification, that the types are ideal or extreme forms, that any given action might contain elements from different types and that many actions may fall on the borderlines between types: thus, some habitual or traditional actions are not easily distinguishable from those which are value-rational; some actions which are value-rational are not easily distinguished from those which are instrumentally rational; while some affectual actions might not be easily distinguishable from rational or habitual actions. Thus, one type of rational conduct may shade into another, just as non-rational conduct may shade into non-meaningful behaviour.

Why, one might now ask, does Weber consider affective and

traditional conduct as meaningful but not rational? And why does he consider value-rational conduct as different from instrumentally rational conduct, considering that the latter, too, is oriented towards valued ends?

There are two possible answers to the first question: one is that Weber considers traditional and affectual actions as not oriented towards ends, as not done for the sake of anything; the second is that he doubts that such actions involve the exercise of options. It is unlikely that he subscribed to the first view since it is fairly clear that Weber considered goal-orientation to be a necessary, though by no means sufficient, criterion of meaningfulness; so it is more likely that he subscribed to the second. For the only option available in value-rational conduct is whether or not to pursue the goal in question, since the decision to pursue it compels the use of particular means. Nor can the decision to pursue the goal be located in a broader strategy of goal-orientation, since it is assumed that the goal is valued in itself. This does suggest that Weber was only half sure that this type of action should be considered rational. It is rational in so far as the actor is conscious of the beliefs which 'cover' it, in so far as such beliefs state a connection between means and ends, and also in so far as the actor opts in favour of the action and is not compelled to perform it. But it is less than fully rational in so far as there is no choice of means and the goal may not be considered instrumental in achieving other ends. Finally, it may be less than fully rational because there are commonly no clear criteria for assessing degrees of success in attaining the goals characteristically pursued in value-rational conduct. All of this amounts to saying that value-oriented action may be a little more rational than much traditional conduct in that the agent can be understood as choosing means to ends, but it falls a good deal short of Weber's paradigm of instrumentally rational conduct.

2 Pareto: logical and non-logical conduct[3]

Whereas Weber considers that human conduct is at least as likely to be rational as not, Pareto holds that it is far more likely than not to be what he terms 'non-logical'. Behind Pareto's elaborate system of analytical categories, nice distinctions and elegant arguments, lies the fundamentally simple idea that the reasons men give for what they do are seldom to be taken at their face value and do not usually explain their conduct. For these reasons are the product of certain states of mind of which men are not usually aware, as are the forms of conduct with which they are correlated. For example, beliefs about witches no more explain the existence of witchcraft practices than beliefs in sovereignty explain the existence of sovereign states: in both cases the belief is the consequence either of the practice itself or of the mental state which produces that practice. In short, human conduct and social institutions do not come about because men have reasons for their existence; and these reasons are to be treated as pseudo-logical camouflage which conceals the real non-logical nature of most social conduct.

Although Pareto is ultimately concerned to demonstrate the pervasiveness of non-logical conduct, he can do this only by starting from the nature of logical conduct which, in its purest form, approximates to what he calls the logico-experimental method (of science). This method consists in the following procedures: observing a fact; discovering, or assuming to have discovered its relation to another fact; generalizing this discovery by stating it as a law; and deducing from this law certain facts other than those which have been originally observed. The principal ingredients of this method are: the observer's capacity to use his past experience to make observations and to link these observations one with another; the use of strict logic to make derivations from the propositions at hand; and the state of mind which permits pure objectivity and logic to dominate. Thus, logical *conduct* can be said to follow three stages: an objective state of mind, the use of this state of mind to make observations and to engage in reasoning and, finally, an action which follows logically from the theory which is based on observation and reasoning. If A is the state of mind, B the conduct and C the theory, then the sequence in logical conduct is: A → C → B. Logical conduct is rare, but is found in science and, to a certain extent, in the entrepreneurial activities of capitalist societies.

Pareto insists, then, that one of the necessary conditions for logical conduct is that the beliefs themselves be logical in nature—which means that they must be arrived at and held by logical mental processes. In addition, they must also give rise to conduct in such a way that it can be shown that the conduct truly follows, logically, from the beliefs. In logical conduct, then, there are three ingredients, a state of mind, a mental operation, and an action. The state of mind is a state of receptivity to objective truth and valid reasoning; from it flows a logical theory, which in turn generates the logical conduct. In non-logical conduct there are the same three ingredients but the order in which they occur is different; the state of mind produces both the action and the mental processes as direct consequences of itself. So if A is the state of mind, B the conduct and C the creation of a theory, the sequence is as shown in Figure 6.1.

Figure 6.1

A is a state of mind which Pareto calls a 'residue', and C he calls a 'derivation'. Residues propel men to act in certain ways and predispose them neither to objectivity nor to strict logical reasoning. The derivations—the theories which men give to explain or justify their conduct—are products of these residues. Unlike the theories which enter into logical conduct, the derivations make use of spurious rather than logical reasoning, and they link things together not on the basis of some scientific possibility of their connectedness, but rather on the basis of associations and other mental procedures foreign to scientific thought. It is not just the reasoning which is faulty, but also the content of the thought itself. Given this, conduct cannot be said to follow logically from the theories; hence the conduct cannot be said to be logical.

Pareto acknowledges that the difficulty with his theory lies in discovering the residues themselves: for unlike actions, they are not directly observable, and, unlike derivations, they are not clearly articulated. One cannot rely on introspection, since the study of one's own mind, however objective this may be, does not reveal the full range of possible residues. Nor can residues be studied in the raw: true, it is helpful to know something about the behaviour of animals and of children in order to understand adult human nature; but residues themselves are not found in the raw, for they are not natural states, like instincts, but are modifications of them which occur as a result of the interaction between man and his external environment, which latter includes not only the natural but also the social world.

One could, of course, try to infer the residues from conduct itself: but that is experimentally impossible, since conduct does not occur in simple forms as the product of a single residue. The only method available is to get at the residues by studying the derivations; and this can be done on the assumption that the derivations somehow reflect the residues. This is another way of saying that when men construct their pseudo-theories to account for or to justify their conduct, in the mistaken belief that their actions result from these theories, they leave on these theories the imprint of the true causes which prompt their conduct. And the task of extracting or abstracting the characteristics of the residues is made easier, paradoxical though it may seem at first sight, because the derivations associated with a particular form of conduct may themselves vary, at least in their superficial features, from one culture or society to another; so that it is by discerning the common element in these derivational variants that one can establish what the common residue is which has produced these seemingly different theories, and which has left its imprint upon them.

Thus, in one culture there is a ritual mass which is associated with a particular doctrine concerning a crucifixion and a last meal which precedes it; in another culture there is a ritual of eating a totemic object and a belief associated with its own nature and of its relation to the particular social groups to which it belongs. These seem like very different phenomena: but looking more closely one finds that they have a common element which emphasizes the importance of ritual commensality for creating binding ties between members of a cult; this last is the residue which produces the ritual conduct in both cases as well as the derivations which are used to justify and account for it. The common element is called a residue because it is that which remains when the peripheral elements are stripped away, leaving the essential core. The residue is, then, a vague feeling or notion which, in particular 'objective' circumstances, produces a particular form of conduct.

The first task of sociology, according to Pareto, is to discover the residues behind the facade of the derivations. The second, no less important, is to show that there is a limited number of these residues, thus providing a limited number of specific sociological laws to be subsumed under the general law that social conduct is the product of such residues. These residues are states of mind which are a mixture of subliminal notions and feelings which, when operating in particular 'objective' conditions, produce particular forms of conduct which, when repeated, become social institutions.

Residues are not to be confused with instincts, though *some* of them are modifications of instincts which occur as a result of cultural and other experiences: for example, the need for sex and food are instinctive, while the desire for stable marital sexual relations and for prepared meals consumed by groups of kinsmen are residues which derive from these instincts. Nor are residues to be equated with sentiments. The 'residue of combinations', which prompts men to combine things in new and different ways, contains little or no element of sentiment; while national loyalty, which does express a sentiment, is a modification and extension of familial sentiments. Nor are residues simply to be equated with interests; for though they may be based on interests as basic and universal as wealth, power and prestige, they emerge nevertheless transformed by social experience and interaction. This may result even in some men being willing to renounce their interests. In fact, most of the time men do not pursue all of their interests effectively, for to do so requires logical conduct, which is usually absent.

Pareto concedes that non-logical conduct is, in most of its forms, closer to logical conduct than to the instinctual behaviour that governs the conduct of social animals. Nevertheless, he insists that non-logical conduct is not to be treated as some unsuccessful form of logical conduct, for it is something quite different from the latter and in no way competes with it. For this reason, he sees as quite absurd the attempts to make religions and ideologies more scientific or more palatable to scientific minds; for it is, in his view, in the nature of religious beliefs and ideologies to be non-logical and to be associated with non-logical conduct which is prompted, in the one case, by residues relating to worship and, in the other, by interests and sentiments relating to political affiliation. Nothing that is done to 'rationalize' such beliefs and practices can make them other than they are.

Despite this, one is still left wondering whether Pareto is fully convinced by his arguments, or alternatively, whether they might not be given a somewhat different interpretation and emphasis from that which he gives them. He does, after all, refer to the 'vague notions' which are part of all residues; and he does abstract these from the derivations themselves—that is, from the more articulated sets of beliefs which others treat as 'covering' the conduct in question—and does not infer them from, say, free associations or from actions themselves. Can one, then, not treat these 'vague notions' as simple sets of half-consciously held assumptions—theoretical, factual and evaluative—which, however remote they may be from those of science, may be correctly said to be held and believed and to contribute to conduct, even if they do not fully account for it? Is Pareto, then, being intellectually honest with us when he denies that non-logical conduct follows from assumptions which cover it? Does his treatment of the *formulated* assumptions which are used to explain conduct—assuming that such explanations are often spurious, though often they are not—justify his assertion that *no* assumptions of the actor underlie meaningful acts? Surely Pareto's system could accommodate the idea that there are forms and degrees of rationality.

3 Talcott Parsons

The views of Talcott Parsons on the rationality of conduct have been greatly influenced by those of Weber and Pareto.[4] Accepting

Weber's distinction between rational and non-rational conduct, Parsons is content to distinguish the rational choice of means—which of course embraces also the choice of those ends which are themselves seen as means to yet further ends—from the non-rational commitment to ultimate values as well as to those norms which set limits to the choice of means. Most social conduct is far from being highly rational in so far as it involves prescriptions which are underpinned by notions of moral propriety and even a quality of sacredness. Rationality is almost identified with instrumentality and norms and values are seen as providing the bounds within which the choices of the actor are made.

Within those normative bounds some actions are truly rational, or approximate to the ideals of rationality, while other actions are, by their very nature, non-rational in that the goals pursued are not empirically observable states, while the means are chosen not in terms of some criteria of effectiveness but more for their symbolically expressive significance. Thus Parsons, following Pareto, incorporates a strong epistemic requirement in his conception of rationality: the beliefs and modes of thought covering rational conduct must satisfy the standards of experimental science or come near to doing so. For the attitude to ultimate values is more one of religious commitment than one of rational appraisal. In later writings Parsons is even more explicit in distinguishing the rational and practical manipulation of objects to achieve more or less clearly specifiable ends from activities, especially those of symbolic manipulation, which express aesthetic, moral or other values as ends in themselves.[5]

Parsons would, on the whole, agree with Weber that truly traditional conduct is not rational in that it does not provide for a choice of means according to criteria of effectiveness, while the values underlying tradition tend to inhibit the acquisition of knowledge and modes of thought which are necessary for rational calculation; though he would also agree with Malinowski that men in traditional societies do and must exercise options in most practical activities and thereby exhibit a degree of rationality based on technical 'rules-of-thumb'.

In later writings, Parsons also confronts the problem of affectivity, though in a manner far more sophisticated and satisfactory than Weber. Parsons follows psychoanalytic thinking in holding that the expression of affect usually demands immediate rather than deferred gratification, and that even when it does not, it commonly involves a regression to more infantile modes of behaviour so that the effective gratification may come to dominate a line of action at the expense of reality considerations. For both of these reasons affectivity is something of an obstacle to rationality. So an emphasis on affective neutrality is associated with increased rationalization, and a growth of universalism, specificity and achievement orientation in certain areas of social life,[6] just as Weber stressed the growth of impersonality as part of the process of judicial and other forms of substantive rationalization.

In his most recent work[7] Parsons adopts the view, to be found also in Tönnies, Spencer, Simmel, Weber and Hobhouse, that with increased social differentiation, individuals and groups enjoy greater freedom to apply autonomous criteria of instrumentality as well as of evaluation of ideas and procedures in a number of areas of social and cultural life, especially in the development of science itself. This shows Parsons still wedded to the idea that the growth of true rationality lies both in the growth of instrumentality as well as in the growth of an epistemic orientation based on logical and empirical procedures.

4 Weak rationality

Alfred Schutz has argued that the kind of rationality discussed by Parsons, and which one may call 'strong rationality', has little relevance for the ordinary, everyday, mundane, routine activities carried out by most individuals and groups in most societies.[8] Nevertheless, these routine activities can be seen as containing an inner rationality. For every individual acquires certain 'commonsense' theories and facts about the nature of the physical and social world which evolve also into 'typifications' of other individuals and groups, enabling him to deal with them in a fairly predictable manner. The individual can be said to be acting rationally in the sense that what he does follows from the theories and facts which he has at his disposal. We may refer to this usage of Schutz's as 'weak rationality'.

Now Schutz does not use the term casually. He implies in opposition to Pareto, but using a common criterion of rationality, that men's actions *do* follow from their assumptions. This does *not* mean that ordinary individuals are normally conscious of the inner rationality which characterizes their routine, mundane activities; in fact, Schutz would argue that most men can go about these routine activities almost semi-consciously because they habitually do take so much for granted. And their 'commonsense' beliefs may not satisfy the standards of scientific rationality. Consequently, their everyday conduct is not the rational conduct of Parsons or the logical conduct of Pareto. But neither is it the non-logical conduct of Pareto.

Schutz's position is influenced by phenomenology as well as by the subjectivist school of economics. According to the latter, all men have to have certain assumptions about the nature of the economic world to guide their conduct. If their conduct appears to conflict with the ideals of rationality, it is because their knowledge is inadequate, or even, inevitably, uncertain. One need not assume that all men go about making self-conscious, deliberate, complex rational calculations based on scientifically rational beliefs; rather, one assumes that they reveal a rationality in their actions within the constraints which their position in the world imposes on them.

Karl Popper argues for somewhat similar ideas; like Schutz's, they derive from the Austrian economists.[9,10] Against the view that explanation in the social sciences should be reducible to psychological propositions Popper proposes the counter-argument that most social scientific explanation could and should rest on the analysis of 'situational logic'; by which he means that one should explain men's actions by reference to the situations in which they occur, and to the ideas and information which men have about these situations. Popper's explanatory model includes no assumptions about the rationality of the agent's beliefs.[11] He contends that almost all social scientific theory should assume that man's conduct is, on the whole, more or less rational in this weaker sense; even non-rational conduct can be understood only against a norm of rationality, a point already made by Weber.

Ludwig von Mises goes even further and argues that psychoanalytic explanations exhibit the inner rationality of seemingly irrational acts. All that is necessary for rationality is that the action can be understood as one which the actor in some way apprehends as a means to an end.[12] Not only is it not necessary that the actor be *consciously* pursuing the ends for the sake of which he acts; but, the beliefs on which he acts may be deeply buried in his unconscious. Schutz does not go as far as von Mises; for him it is sufficient to show that at least most semi-consciously directed activity exhibits a 'weak' kind of rationality.

C   Varieties of rationality?

Several sets of questions arise out of the foregoing discussion: Does rationality of conduct presuppose rationality of belief? Does the influence of norms and values (other than those of rationality itself) weaken the rationality of action? How conscious and deliberate need the actor be to perform rational actions? And, finally, does the expression of affect involve an element of non-rationality, so that the greater the expression the lower the degree of rationality?

One way of resolving these questions is to recognize that one is dealing with varieties and degrees of rationality so that an action may be more or less rational with respect to one or more of the following criteria: the beliefs which cover it (assuming that they do); the relationship between beliefs and conduct; the constraining influence of norms (assuming that such constraint sets a limit on the exercise of rationality); the consciousness of empirical, normative and other assumptions; and, finally, the influence of affectivity.

But although this solution or resolution—which will be developed in greater detail in the last section of this paper—is necessary, it is not, of itself, sufficient for our purposes. For one is still left with the question: to what extent does a high (or low) degree of rationality with respect to any one factor contribute to a high (or low) degree of rationality with respect to another? Let us consider a number of problems in the light of these considerations, especially the following: the relationship between rationality and normative constraint; the nature of affectual conduct; and the importance of consciousness.

I shall not here develop a discussion of the rationality of belief nor of the relationship between belief and conduct. Suffice it to say, in brief, that I follow Agassi and Jarvie,[13] rather than Pareto, in holding that the question of the rationality of belief can be, for at least some purposes, separated from that of the rationality of conduct, though I would follow Pareto in holding that fully rational conduct requires rational beliefs. I take rational beliefs—other than the belief in rationality itself—to be those which can be and are subject to rational appraisal in the light of evidence or of other beliefs and which, when they are not empirically testable or logically provable, are recognized as necessary metaphysical assumptions which promote the use of testable and provable statements. I also follow Pareto in holding that fully rational conduct presupposes that statements describing such conduct do follow logically from the assumptions which an actor can explicate in advance of his conduct.

1 The non-rational

(a) Rationality, norms and values

According to Weber, traditional conduct is non-rational because, so he thinks, it is more or less habitual, so that no consideration is given to the efficacy of means to attain ends. One objection to Weber's view can be developed by looking briefly at the nature of marital choice in so-called traditional societies. (These last are societies which, on the whole, change imperceptibly from one generation to another.)

Even in the simplest societies, marital choice is not, and could not be, governed purely by prescriptive and prohibitive rules. Consider the extreme case of so-called systems of prescriptive marriage. In certain societies a man is expected not only to choose a wife outside a particular category of kinswomen, but is expected to choose a woman from within a very specific category; for example, he should marry a mother's brother's daughter, otherwise known as a matrilateral cross-cousin. Now the simple facts of demography alone make it impossible for every man to marry the actual daughter of his actual mother's actual brother. Tribesmen do not really expect every boy or girl to be married to a specific cross-cousin; rather, they expect every boy to marry a girl from the broader social category of which a mother's brother is or would be a member.[14] Thus, where marriage is at its most prescriptive, there is still room for choice; and, since marriage, because of its very nature, can be used for a variety of purposes, such as the formation of alliances or the consolidation of property, the creation of marital ties is compatible with a degree of rational calculation even where tradition is most restrictive. However, Weber might concede that conduct can be traditional in varying degrees. At the one extreme is highly habitual conduct, such as the use of particular facial expressions, gestures and other forms of 'body-language', to say nothing of the use of oral language itself; at the other extreme may lie such acts as marital choice or political alignment, where rational calculation may be possible within the limits imposed by normative constraints. The non-rational element in the latter types of conduct lies in the uncritical acceptance of the norms and in the limitations which the norms place on the range of options open to one, especially where a rejection or modification of the norms would permit one to maximize or optimize particular advantages. But could it not be argued that rule-governed conduct is rational regardless of whether it involves a subjective assessment of means effectiveness, that, as long as conduct can be shown to follow from a norm or rule, it is to that extent rational? For example, if a man pays tribute to a chief, then his conduct is rational in as much as it follows logically from the belief that he is obliged to do this; if a man makes payment in kind to his sister his conduct is rational because it is covered by a socially recognized obligation to do so; and so on.

One objection to this, however, is that such conduct often strikes us as rational, or weakly rational, not because it conforms to a norm, but because it uses certain means to attain a goal, so that the appearance of mere rule-following conceals a hidden rationale of a different sort. A man who pays tribute to a chief may do so either perhaps because he recognizes that the chief has the power to punish him if he fails to pay, or because the chief rewards only those who behave as loyal subjects should, or because he has some vague expectations that he may require the chief's protection.

Of course, our tribesman may pay tribute simply because he thinks it right or because doing so expresses a value of loyalty to the 'father of the people'; if these are the reasons, then a Weberian might classify such conduct as value-rational. However, value-rational conduct differs from the highly habitual forms of traditional conduct—like using the rules of language, or exhibiting particular body postures, where there is no value-orientation as such—only in so far as the actor is conscious of a value which he places on the act. It is rational only if one can discern behind the cultural practice a concealed instrumentality—of which the actor may not be fully conscious, but of which he can become conscious, perhaps as a result of being asked to explain his acceptance of the rule—and even then it is rational only in a partial and/or weak sense. If, however, one is convinced that the actor conforms to the rule for no other reason than that it is a rule, then one wonders at the value of considering it rational.

The view I am developing is that what makes rule-following rational is the existence of other reasons and motives for following the rules which may be such as to encourage deviance from or rejection of them in circumstances in which the pursuit of certain valued goals requires this. The greatest influences which norms can have are to demand forms of conduct for their own sake and to limit the options open to the actor to pursue certain goals or to choose the means to pursue these goals. In these extreme cases normative constraint reduces rationality to a very low level. It can be argued, of course, that the existence of some normative constraints provides most actors with guidance in the choice of means and by setting limits to their options provides them with ready-made modes of activity rather than demand of them that they flounder in a world of uncertainty seeking their own solutions to life's problems. Nevertheless, this limits the expression of complete instrumentality and, therefore, of total freedom for rational experimentation and problem-solving.

(b) Affectual conduct

Weber's treatment of affectual conduct is analogous to his treatment of traditional conduct: both forms are non-rational; and both forms shade into the category of reflexive non-meaningful behaviour, the one because of the power of impulse, the other because of the power of habit. This suggests, as I have already stated, that Weber considered some forms of the non-rational as close to the non-meaningful.

There are a number of difficulties with Weber's view of affectual conduct. The first and, for our purposes, the least important, is that Weber overlooked the possibility that even affectively expressive behaviour which is not oriented towards a goal can be meaningful.

If an anxious person bites his lip or his finger-nails he may do so not in order to communicate his anxiety, or for the sake of any other end, but simply to express it. But we can say that his conduct is meaningful to others.

The second difficulty is more serious: Weber overlooks the fact that much seemingly reflexive conduct is not only goal-oriented but exhibits an underlying ends/means rationale. For example, let us say that a man responds to a slighting remark with an insult. One might explain his conduct by merely showing that the remark angered him and that the anger produced an insult. But there may be more to it than that. The man who is slighted may feel that his honour requires that he give as good as he has received. Here one could say that the goal is that of protecting his honour and the means that of returning an insult. One cannot then treat the insult as an automatic, conventional response, for one recognizes that the response is dependent both on a state of anger and on a stratagem for expressing it and for correcting a situation. True, one does not usually construct such a rationale; one tends to explicate the elements which are normally contained or concealed in a condensed account of the act only when the act itself seems out of the ordinary.

Let us say that the response to a slighting remark is to challenge the other party to a duel; and let us assume that the challenger is not and never has been a member of a society in which duelling is now practised. According to Weber one might have to say that the challenger's conduct was probably insane and, at least, affectual. But von Mises would argue that if we were to psychoanalyse our would-be duellist we would be led to discover that his 'purely affectual' reaction contained an inner rationale or indeed, an unconscious strategy.[15] We might show that he had been constantly subject to verbal slights in early childhood, that his unquieted rage had led him to create fantasies of violent revenge—possibly patricidal or fratricidal—and that he had been influenced, in the creation of these fantasies at a formative period, by stories or pictures of duelling. We might then explain his adult and admittedly

pathological reaction to the merest verbal slight as part of an unconscious strategy to put down all those who wield such aggressive
verbal power. His 'acting out', though seemingly irrational, thus
becomes unconsciously rational.

This would not be the view taken by the psychoanalytic theorist,
Heinz Hartmann.[16] Hartmann's view is that such conduct is
irrational for two reasons. First, there is an overspilling of affect,
much of it deriving from unconscious sources relating to childhood
situations which are relived in later life, so that there is a strong
influence of irrational cognitive processes and fantasy thinking.
And second, there is a conflict between unconscious and conscious
motives, with the former being successful, and the agent defeating
his own conscious aims. Hartmann acknowledges that understanding the unconscious—as opposed to providing causal explanations of the mechanisms at work within it—involves treating
non-rational conduct *as if* it were rational in its own terms, but
asserts that that does not make it rational in the true sense.[17]

This view would not satisfy the psychoanalyst R.D. Laing[18]
who holds that the individual in the family who is subjected to the
emotional 'double-bind', and who is labelled and stigmatized as
'odd', is finally compelled, even from an early age, to retreat into
a world of beliefs, evaluations and symbolic devices, which enable
him to protect himself from that family. Laing does not deny, what
Hartmann would assert, that in pursuing his goals the psychotic
not only fails to pursue others which would give greater satisfaction,
but actually puts himself into a situation in which others are compelled to restrict his pursuit even of those goals which do give him
some satisfaction. He would argue only that the additional pain is
inflicted on the patient by others who cannot deal with his threat to
their psychic well-being, such as it is, and is not inflicted on himself;
so that his own conduct remains strategically rational in the circumstances. Thus, where Hartmann insists that a retreat into a
world of psychic pain cannot be considered rational, Laing contends that one sort of pain is used to 'defend' the agent against
others, as a rational choice of a lesser evil. Those sympathizing with
Hartmann's view could reply that by doing this a patient may
bring upon himself even greater evils which he could not bargain
for even in his unconscious fantasies.

I agree, for most purposes, with Hartmann's more conventional
view, though not on account of any motive to stigmatize the insane
or neurotic as irrational, nor because of any failure to recognize
that psychotics may penetrate the inner reality of the mind more
effectively than many so-called sane people, nor because of any
desire to deny Laing and others their great insight into the mental

process of madness. I do so because Hartmann's view avoids additional ambiguity in the use of the term 'rational'. The spilling over of affect interferes with the rational ordering of means in relation to ends by obtruding ends, which, on the whole, demand to be gratified regardless of the effect which this may have on a total strategy of action. Although much truly rational conduct operates with a substratum of affective impulse, of fantasy thinking and of unconscious motivation, it does so without permitting these to govern it. I would agree that it is not only permissible but necessary to seek out the unconscious or even conscious strategies of action which may underlie affectual impulse and to treat such actions *as if* they were rational. But in recognizing the 'as if' *qualification* I would emphasize that the conduct was less than fully rational or possibly, to a large extent, non-rational.

It seems useful, then, to accept that part of Weber's argument which suggests that strong affect tends to impair the capacity for rational decision-making. It is even more useful to accept that where the affect is not only strong but rooted in the unconscious, it is even more likely that rational thought and conduct will be impaired: for, when this is the case there is even less chance that the actor will be able to discipline his thought processes so as to order the relationships between means and ends.

2 Degrees of rationality

(a) Imputed and weak rationality

All conduct can be treated *as if* it were rational. Conduct which is purely rule-following can be made to look rational by showing: that it does conform to a rule; that the actor could, in certain circumstances, be made aware of his reasons for following it; and that the actor does not follow the rule purely and simply for the sake of doing so. Conduct which is seemingly irrational or highly affectual can be made to look rational by showing: that the action cannot be explained as purely reflexive and without reference to 'covering' assumptions and motives; and that the action is directed towards a goal and makes use of certain means to achieve it.

Conduct which is *treated as if* it were rational, because it is not *really* thought to be rational, must be distinguished from conduct which is rational in a very weak sense. This distinction turns on the ability of the actor to provide reasons for his conduct which are taken from the store of common-sense assumptions—theoretical, factual, and evaluative—of which he is more or less conscious, or of which he can be made conscious without subjecting him to psychoanalytic study.

There are also degrees of weakness of rationality. An act, such as catching the Clapham omnibus in order to reach Clapham, is one of moderately weak rationality because the assumption connecting the means to the end is not consciously considered and is not normally subject to review. The rationality of paying the price demanded in a retail store is even weaker: for the actor is hardly aware that he does make an assumption about what is proper and what the consequences might be of trying to bargain. Its rationality consists only in deciding whether it is worth paying the price rather than spending the money on something else or saving it. Such actions can be said to lie on the borderline between very weak rationality and imputed or 'as if' rationality; but consideration of such examples shows that this line cannot and should not be fixed too firmly, but should be allowed to 'float', this way and that, like a troublesome currency. For it does not matter very much for our purposes exactly where we draw the line as long as we recognize that we are moving away from situations in which the actor can be easily made aware of his assumptions, through those in which he can be made aware only with some difficulty, or in rather special circumstances, to those in which the actor can only be made aware of his 'covering' assumptions by promoting them from the unconscious proper to the conscious, assuming that this last can be done at all.

Of course, constructing another's rationality is easier where there is less chance that the 'covering' assumptions which are attributed to an actor can be challenged. This explains why it is always so much easier for historians and ethnographers to make the conduct studied by them appear rational: dead men can never answer back and ethnographers' informants used not to be able to do so.

I have argued up till now that where the actor is thought to be scarcely or not at all conscious of the 'covering' assumptions of his actions his conduct should be viewed as either non-rational or only partly or weakly rational. I now propose to question that very argument by considering the case of linguistic usage. Most men, it will readily be agreed, use language quite effectively without necessarily knowing the rule which guides their conduct, without its being likely that they will be made aware of the rules, and even without knowing that there are rules which govern linguistic usage. But is not the effective use of language as a means to communicate with others tantamount to the rational use of language? Our first, provisional reply must be in the affirmative. For if it is clearly irrational, or at least non-rational, to expect understanding from others if one does not bother to master the rules of their language, or if one uses private syntax and semantics which communicate no intelligible messages to others, does not this make the correct use of linguistic rules rational, regardless of whether the user consciously knows what the rules are or that they exist? One might add that the case of linguistic usage is paradigmatic for the study of many or most social institutions; for the everyday effectiveness of the language depends on the whole upon the unreflecting observance of its rules.

For, although rationality presupposes effectiveness and the capacity to learn by trial and error, it also presupposes the capacity to reflect consciously on the procedures which are involved in learning and in becoming effective.

(b) Strong rationality

The reason that one can make any act appear rational and that it is so difficult to concede that any act lacks at least a weak rationality, is that it is always possible, after the act, to supply it with a set of assumptions from which a description of it can be logically derived. It is in the nature of *ex post facto* constructions of a rationale that actions can be made to appear both perfectly rational and successful in their own terms. For assumptions can be readily chosen, with the benefit of hindsight, that would be completely appropriate to the action. To be fully rational, the conduct must derive from a set of assumptions which could have been stated in advance of it, and which could thereby have been put at risk. Of course, it is possible for an *ex post facto* explanation to treat an action as unsuccessful and to seek to explain its lack of success either by a failure of rationality or by weakness in the information or assumptions available to the actor who may be shown to have acted quite rationally in terms of what he thought he knew to be the case. However, any *ex post facto* account which presents an act, successful or not, as rational, must be suspect; while any such account which also presents the action as successful is suspect on that score as well.

For most purposes conduct can be said to be fully rational when all of the following conditions are met: when the assumptions and goals are stated unequivocally in advance of the action; when the assumptions, other than the evaluative, are empirically testable statements which are also treated as such, and when those which are neither empirically testable or evaluative are logical or methodological statements which can be assessed in terms of criteria of internal consistency, plausibility, suggestiveness, and so on; where there is a clear distinction made between the ends pursued and the possible variety of means to be considered in pursuing those ends and where the relationship between means and ends is stated unambiguously, so that the effectiveness of the action can be properly assessed; where a statement describing the action can be deduced, by correct logical procedures, from the assumptions of action.

The first condition has already been discussed and no further amplification is required for our purposes. One or two further comments on the second condition are called for. It is necessary to *stress* that the assumptions be not only empirically refutable; but that they be treated as such. An idea which links the symbolic manipulations of magic with practical results is, in itself, testable and empirically refutable; however, it is seldom treated as testable, being saved by resort to *ad hoc* qualifications. A further point implied by this condition is that the ends pursued be those which can be described by a statement which can be empirically checked to the best of anyone's ability: an end such as the attainment of salvation does not fall into this category, while an end such as the social recognition that one may have attained such a state may well do so.

The third condition is an important one; for where the distinction between means and ends is blurred there is less chance, at the outset, of putting the rational enterprise at risk. This condition is implied by the second but is stated separately because of the issues which arise out of Weber's discussion of value-rational conduct.

(c) Rationality in real-life situations

We have seen what criteria must be met for an action to be fully rational. We shall conclude by asking whether those criteria are ever met all at once and whether they are ever met in full.

In principle, almost anyone can, in ideal circumstances, construct a set of assumptions from which a directive to act follows logically. But in everyday life this rarely happens, since most actions are guided, at least in part, by a number of implicit normative theoretical and factual assumptions about the social world, and as Harold Garfinkel has shown, it requires some rather startling experiments to make most men, including some sociologists, aware of them.[19] There is a partly unconscious quality about much of social life which makes its rationality partial and weak in this respect.

Nor can all of the assumptions of action be either empirically testable or logically provable, even when the activity engaged in is natural science; for one can no more prove nor empirically test the

151

epistemological theories which underlie science than one can defend rationality by rational argument.[20] And what is true of science is, *a fortiori*, true of everyday social life in which all kinds of half-baked assumptions are taken out of the rag-bags of the mind and put to use in one implicit way or another.

Nor, in most real life situations, can actors resort to the kind of experimentation—even mental—which would enable them to choose the most effective means for attaining a given end or to locate their actions in a wider strategy so as to optimize their goal attainments. Of course, it is easier to do this where there is time to plan, and where there are some ways of measuring effectiveness: companies do not employ cost-accountants simply to adorn their executive suites. But most of life is not lived by amateur cost-accountants; nor can most of life's activities be dealt with by their practices.

We have insisted that the criterion of strong rationality be that the actor put his assumptions at risk by making the action literally and strictly follow from them. However, in most real-life situations this can hardly be done. In fact, most of social life would be almost unworkable if not unbearable if action were to be consequent on the deliberate and self-conscious formulation of assumptions. Despite the impression that social institutions sometimes give of having been almost rationally designed, most are effective only on account of the fairly weak rationality of the conduct of which they are constituted.

It is clear from the foregoing that the criteria of fully rational conduct are such as to make it an ideal type in the true sense of that term. Real forms of rational and non-rational conduct can be characterized in terms of the presence or absence of those elements which constitute the ideal type. Though there is little point in trying to list every type imaginable or even known to occur, we can give some idea of the range. First, there are those forms which approximate to the ideal type of pure rationality, the most obvious of which is science. Second, there are those types, such as various forms of business administration and even government planning, which approximate to the pure form in all but one or two of the epistemic conditions. The third type is the everyday technical in which few of the epistemic conditions are met but in which there is a self-conscious attempt at instrumental effectiveness or even at goal optimization. The fourth type is the everyday, common-sense rational, in which none of the epistemic conditions is met in any self-conscious sense and in which the actor opts for a goal-attainment which is taken for granted as being optimal, but without attempting to achieve a calculable optimization. The fifth type is the everyday weakly rational action in which the actor is barely aware of engaging in an activity which requires the relating of ends to means. The sixth type is that in which the actor consciously makes use of assumptions which are treated in such a way as to be untestable, so that, while the action may have a semblance of rationality to it, it also has a distinct quality of non-rationality. The seventh type is that in which the actor is unaware either of the nature of his non-rational assumptions or of the ends/means relationships involved in his actions. The eighth type is that in which the actor's assumptions, though non-testable and in no way contributing to testability, are recognized as acts of faith relating to events which are not strictly of this world. The ninth type is that in which the actor uses such articles of faith implicitly. The tenth type is that in which the actor loses in varying degrees the capacity for rational control in one area or another, because of his commitment to a value which is rooted in strong affectual states or because he is otherwise affectually 'involved' in a situation. The penultimate type is that in which the actor's unconscious 'rationale' leads to the total defeat of those goals which he might consciously wish to pursue using means rather different from those which he does use while in the grip of unconscious motives and fantasy thinking. The final type is that in which the actor retreats almost totally into the inner world of fantasy so that all of his actions have the appearance to the untutored of having neither meaning nor rationale. One might say of the final type that it, too, is ideal-typically irrational and that, at the unconscious level it mirrors the characteristics of ideal-typical rationality, while distorting them in the process.

Notes

1 This essay was written while I was privileged to be a Fellow at the Center for Advanced Study in the Behavioral Sciences at Stanford, California. I am indebted to a number of my colleagues at the Center with whom I have discussed one or another aspect of this topic. I am also greatly indebted to Stanley Benn and Geoffrey Mortimore for most valuable editorial assistance in the writing of the final version of this essay. My greatest debt is to my wife, Ruth Cohen, without whose help I would write even less clearly than I do.

　　An earlier discussion of this subject is to be found in the fourth chapter of Cohen, P.S. (1968). The present essay re-states some of the arguments contained there but also purports to go beyond them.

2 As a source for my presentation of Weber's views I have used the three-volume English translation of *Wirtschaft und Gesellschaft*. Almost everything which Weber has to say about the types of rational and non-rational conduct is contained in Weber, M. (1968), pp. 22–6.

3 As a source for Pareto I have used the four-volume English translation

of his *Trattato di Sociologia generale*. I have tried to give a concise and, perhaps, rather personal summary of his main views and have needed to conflate different sources in order to do this; for this reason I have not given page references.

4 See Parsons, T. (1949), especially pp. 58, 162–4, 170, 187, 265, 588, 606, 616, 698–9. (This work was originally published in 1937.)
5 Parsons, T. (1951), p. 49.
6 Ibid., pp. 86–8 and 157–8.
7 Parsons, T. (1966), pp. 21–4.
8 See Schutz, A. (1964), pp. 64–88.
9 See Popper, K.R. (1950), pp. 289–90.
10 See Jarvie, I.C. (1964), pp. 131–43.
11 But on this, see Jarvie, I.C. and Agassi, J. (1967).
12 See Mises, L. von (1966), p. 12.
13 Op. cit.
14 See Leach, E.R. (1963), pp. 54–104.
15 Op. cit.
16 See Hartmann, H. (1964), pp. 37–68.
17 Ibid., pp. 369–403.
18 See Laing, R.D. (1967).
19 See Garfinkel, H. (1967).
20 See Popper, K.R. (1950), pp. 415–47.

Bibliography

COHEN, P.S. (1968), *Modern Social Theory*, London.
GARFINKEL, H. (1967), *Studies in Ethnomethodology*, Englewood Cliffs, New Jersey.
HARTMANN, H. (1964), 'On rational and irrational action', and 'Understanding and explanation', in *Essays in Ego Psychology*, New York.
JARVIE, I.C. (1964), *The Revolution in Anthropology*, London.
JARVIE, I.C. and AGASSI, J. (1967), 'The problem of the rationality of magic', *British Journal of Sociology*, XVIII, pp. 55–74.
LAING, R.D. (1967), *The Divided Self*, Harmondsworth.
LEACH, E.R. (1963), 'The structural implications of cross-cousin marriage', in *Rethinking Anthropology*, London.
MISES, L. VON (1966), *Human Action*, Chicago.
PARETO, V. (1935), *The Mind and Society*, ed. Livingston, A., New York.
PARSONS, T. (1949), *The Structure of Social Action*, Chicago.
PARSONS, T. (1951), *The Social System*, Chicago.
PARSONS, T. (1966), *Societies: Evolutionary and Comparative Perspectives*, Englewood Cliffs, New Jersey.
POPPER, K.R. (1950), *The Open Society and Its Enemies*, Princeton, New Jersey.
SCHUTZ, A. (1964), 'The problem of rationality in the social world', in *Collected Papers II*, ed. Brodersen, A., The Hague.
WEBER, M. (1968), *Economy and Society* (3 vols), ed. Roth, G. and Wittich, C., New York.

Part Two

Rationality in action

(b) Technical notions of rational action

7

Technical models of rational choice

S.I. Benn and G.W. Mortimore

A   Technical models and the ordinary notion of rational action

The subject of the present paper is a broad class of theories, developed first in economics, but extending now to a variety of studies concerned with competitive situations in economic markets, politics, labour relations, and international relations.[1] Such theories are variously known as 'preference theories', 'decision theories', or 'theories of conflict resolution'. The specific ways in which rationality concepts are used to formulate such theories in certain particular fields will be looked at in later papers. Here we shall be concerned with the content of the technical models deployed in these fields, and with some of the general conditions for their theoretical usefulness.[2]

The distinctive features of the concept of rationality employed in these technical models can best be understood by comparing them with the features of the ordinary notion of rational action, analysed in Chapter 4.

(i)   Common to both notions is the condition that the agent may choose one and only one option from an available set. This is the basic constraint built into the notion of choice.

(ii)   The ordinary notion includes a requirement that the agent believes his choice to have a specified relationship to his ends. This may be, for instance, that his choice is the only means to his ends, or that it is the most economical. In the technical models, the notion of the agent's ends is narrowed down to a set of preferences, and the key relationship is that between his preferences and his choice. The notion of preference may itself be given a technical definition, tying it in an especially close logical relationship to choice; and certain technical requirements are specified that an agent's set of preferences must satisfy to be rational. These matters are discussed in section B.

A further condition of the technical notion is that the relation between choice and preference must be that of *optimality*, i.e. the option must be the best, given the agent's preferences. The ordinary canons of optimality are then extended and supplemented to apply to more complex choice-situations, including, for instance, situations where outcomes are risky or uncertain, or depend on strategic interaction between the decisions of competing agents. Such situations are specified in a technically precise way, and in terms of simplified paradigms. The technical canons of optimality devised for such situations (discussed in section C) thus constitute technical elaborations of the notion of formal practical rationality discussed in Chapter 4.

(iii) The ordinary notion requires that the agent act because he rationally believes his choice to have the specified relation to his ends, and that this relation provides a good and sufficient reason for his choice. Technical models, by contrast, sometimes neglect the epistemic state of the agent altogether, or assume that he has complete knowledge of his choice-situation. In either case, the focus is on the actual relationship between the options and the agent's preferences, rather than on what he *believes* the relationship to be; the condition of rationality in belief is then dropped, leaving an analysis purely in terms of practical rationality. Epistemic assumptions employed in technical models are discussed in section D.

(iv) The ordinary notion of rational action commonly includes the condition that the agent's ends are ones it is rational to pursue. Technical notions commonly impose corresponding restrictions; but now they confine the agent's ends to his preferences between the outcomes of his options, i.e. the objects of his preferences are supposed to be states of affairs which would be the consequences of the choices open to him. This and other restrictions on the content of the rational agent's preferences, supplementing the formal conditions for practical rationality with substantive conditions, will be discussed in section E.

The technical theories with which we are concerned envisage, therefore, a rational agent equipped with an optimality canon making a choice under a set of postulated conditions which together comprise his choice-situation. These conditions include, for instance, his knowledge of the outcomes, their degree of certainty, the range of options, and so on. The aim is to infer from such elements a determinate decision that a rational agent would make.

First developed in economics, this mode of theorizing achieved a high level of sophistication with the marginal utility theories of Jevons, Wicksell, and Marshall. It has since been freed of its special economic application to become a general theory of action, explicating canons of rational decision and, through subtle chains of mathematical inference, deriving formal characterization of the choices a rational agent would make in a variety of decision-situations. This study has been called 'praxeology' by von Mises and other continental scholars.[3] We shall adopt the term in this essay.

Praxeology is distinguished from economics and analogous studies by the greater level of generality and abstraction of its theories.[4] The economist's aim is to explain and predict the behaviour of agents acting under specifically economic constraints, like those of the competitive market, or monopolistic production, or those of investment under conditions of uncertainty, and so on. The praxeologist, by contrast, sets out to derive from a few limited very general postulated canons and formally defined choice-situations the forms of rational decisions. Because the content of his postulates is so general his conclusions may apply just as much (or as little) to politics, economics, military strategy, or industrial bargaining. The constraining conditions characteristic of decision-making in each field are added to the praxeological model, generating theories and hypotheses capable of empirical testing.

The usefulness of praxeology depends, of course, on the extent to which its postulated choice-situations are found in real life, and on the degree to which agents' choices conform to the canons it stipulates. Experimental psychologists have contrived laboratory situations designed to test directly whether decisions do in fact reflect these canons, isolating their subjects' decision-making processes so far as possible from the special complications of the world of economics and political science.[5]

In both experimental and non-experimental social sciences, the praxeological model has something to offer. The researcher's interest may be excited in the first place when he encounters behaviour deviating from the expectations the model has led him to form. In this way the model generates problems for research. But it may furnish the researcher, too, with hypotheses to be tested, whether by experiment or by observation of outcomes in noncontrived situations. Should such tests falsify the hypotheses, the theorist may be led to complicate the praxeological model, to derive from it revised inferences to accommodate the discrepancies.

Such deviations may lead the social scientist in a different direction, however, away from further elaboration of the model of rational action towards a search for interfering factors that account in a regular way for the departures from rationality. If deviation from the model is very great, the investigator may abandon it altogether, substituting for it, perhaps, some causal model instead, looking rather to emotional states or anxiety factors as determinants of behaviour.

This paper and the three that follow are concerned with praxeology and its applications in economics, and in other disciplines in which specific economic models have been used as conscious analogues in theory-construction.

B Preference, choice and utility

1 Conditions for rational preferences

(a) The ordinary notion of preference and technical notions

Rational actions are fully explicable and predictable in so far as they proceed from decisions governed by considerations, and are not the consequence of random picking, as an inexpert punter picks winners. A man who is indifferent between alternatives may *have* to pick one—but his selection is, praxeologically speaking, a random event, neither explicable nor predictable in terms of his rationality, because it expresses no preference.

'The relation between preference and choice is therefore a crucial one for praxeological theories. Like the concept of rationality, the technical concept of preference, while clearly related to, and deriving from, the ordinary notion, acquires certain special conditions and drops others. In ordinary speech, I *can* decide (or choose) to do something different from what I should prefer to do, as for instance when I do something reluctantly from a sense of duty. 'To prefer', in that case, is roughly speaking to 'like better'; and when we act dutifully we often do what we like least. Yet with due deliberation we may decide to do it all the same. The praxeologist seeks to explain decisions, however, by exhibiting what a rational man in a certain choice-situation would do, given his preferences and nothing else. All considerations that can function as ends must then be subsumed under the notion of 'preference', so that any rational person choosing to do x must do so because he prefers x to any alternative either for itself or for what he believes will be its consequences. For the praxeologist, it is a logically necessary truth that if a man chooses x out of the set $\{x, y\}$, then he prefers x to y.

Economists like Paul Samuelson and I.M.D. Little[6] have postulated an even closer connection between 'preference' and 'choice'. According to what is known as the 'revealed preference' account of choice, a person's preferences are to be inferred only from his behaviour. A preference for x, therefore, is not merely a disposition to choose x—so much is true of the ordinary notion, too; it is a disposition that can be ascribed if and only if the agent chooses x whenever opportunity offers. Should he sometimes choose y one would have to say that on those occasions his preference has changed. (Another possibility, probably not open to the revealed preference theorist, is to say that the agent is indifferent as between x and y. We shall consider the status of indifference later.) It is logically impossible, under revealed preference theory, not only that the agent choose y though preferring x, but that he could be said to prefer x without his actually having chosen x.

(b) The conditions for rational preferences stated

For a model to yield a determinate prediction of an agent's choice between a given set of alternatives, it must assume that his preferences satisfy the technical conditions of connectedness, asymmetry, and transitivity, necessary to constitute them an *ordering*.

(i) *Connectedness* This condition (also known as connexity, or completeness) requires that for any pair of different alternatives x and y, one of the pair is preferred to the other (either xPy or yPx). Over the relevant range, therefore, the agent's preferences form an unbroken ordering.

(ii) *Asymmetry* This condition requires that for any pair of alternatives x and y, the agent shall not prefer both x to y, and y to x (not both xPy and yPx).

(iii) *Transitivity* This condition requires that for any x, y, and z, if xPy, and yPz, then xPz.

The above are requirements for a *strong* ordering. Conditions for a weak ordering extend also to cases of indifference. Thus:

(i) *Connectedness* For any x and y, either xPy, or yPx, or xIy (where xIy means 'The agent is indifferent as between x and y'). The weak condition, which embraces both preference and indifference as disjuncts, is generally symbolized as R. So the weak condition of connectedness is: xRy or yRx.

(ii) *Asymmetry of preference, symmetry of indifference* Whereas preferences are asymmetrical, indifference relations are symmetrical. So, for a weak ordering, either [xPy or yPx but not both] or [xIy and yIx].

(iii) *Transitivity* The conditions for a weak ordering are: if xRy and yRz, then xRz.

Whereas a strong ordering is necessary for a determinate prediction of the agent's choice between a given limited set of options, there are heuristic advantages, as we shall see, in treating the strongly ordered preferences as part of a more extended preference field, which includes both preference and indifference relations. A model which left no room for indifference would, in any case, have only a very limited application to real choice-situations. The remainder of this section (B1) will therefore be concerned with the weak conditions of rational preference.

(c) Do all preferences necessarily satisfy the conditions for an ordering?

It is sometimes suggested that it is a logically necessary truth that any set of preferences must satisfy the conditions for an ordered set. Our own view is that, so far as concerns the ordinary notion of preference, this may be true of the asymmetry of preference, but it is not true of the other two.

(i) Connectedness One can readily envisage cases in which this condition is not satisfied: an agent may be unable to make up his mind about his preferences, but may not be indifferent as between the alternatives. A man choosing a new car may produce a short list of, say, four between which to choose, and he may order these differently in respect of performance, design, reliability, and durability, without being able to settle his trade-off rate between these desirable qualities. He does not know which car he prefers, yet he cannot be said to be indifferent to which he takes, since reaching the right decision is a matter of considerable anxiety to him; he would not dream of settling the matter by a toss of a coin.

A revealed preference account would presumably sidestep such cases, since, the agent being unable to choose, there would be no preference to take account of. Still, the case highlights the difficulty of deriving a composite ordering of items which an agent orders differently in respect of different and non-convertible desiderata. Attempts have been made by some economists to extend the technical notion of rational preference at least to a sub-class of these problem instances. An agent might be able to order his preferences for $P, Q, R, \ldots, Z$ provided that for any set of desiderata $a, b, c, \ldots, n$, variously attributable to these options, he could say that he preferred any that satisfied *a* to any that did not, whatever its other attributes; and similarly, thereafter, in some appropriate order, for *b*, *c*, . . ., *n*. This is known as a lexicographical ordering. Because it would not permit the ordering of a set of items all of which satisfied the same desiderata but in different degrees, its applicability to real-world choice-situations is probably limited.

(ii) Asymmetry of preference, symmetry of indifference It is doubtful whether one could make sense of a claim to have preferences, in the ordinary sense, if they did not satisfy this condition. If someone seriously said that he preferred both *x* to *y* and *y* to *x*, or was indifferent as between *x* and *y*, but had a preference for *y* over *x*, we should think he had not understood the meaning of 'preference' and 'indifference'. Asymmetry is not then a separate condition, independent of the notion of preference. If one adopts the conceptual requirements of revealed preference theory, however, symmetrical preferences would not be logically impossible. Consequently if a subject does in fact choose *x* from $\{x, y\}$ at one moment, and *y* at the next, it would be open to the theorist to say that his choices reveal symmetrical preferences. This would be theoretically very awkward. One solution would be to weaken the notion of revealed preference to include a condition for indifference, such that a disposition to make wholly random choices could reveal indifference. Alternatively, the theorist might claim that what is revealed is a change in the agent's preferences whenever the choice changes.

(iii) Transitivity Some writers have claimed that transitivity is logically required by the ordinary notion of preference. Yet one can envisage what certainly seems to be a counter-instance. Imagine a serving hatch, at which a subject, Smith, may obtain cups of tea, coffee, and cocoa. These drinks are presented to him in pairs on a revolving table; each time the table stops, Smith is confronted with a pair, and invited to choose, which he does quite successfully. But he is told not to drink the beverage he has chosen yet awhile, for the table will turn again, and if he wishes, he may substitute a different one for his present choice. Offered first a choice of tea or coffee he chooses coffee; offered, at the second turn, coffee or cocoa, he replaces the coffee and takes the cocoa. At the third round, he replaces the cocoa and takes tea.

Round 1: coffee P tea
Round 2: cocoa P coffee
Round 3: tea P cocoa

His preference ordering is therefore:
tea P cocoa P coffee P tea.

At each stage, he is quite clear about his preferences and supports it by actually choosing. The carousel may continue to revolve, and he may be able to predict correctly what he will do at each turn, so one need not accuse him of shifting his preferences. If the turntable stops, then presumably he will stick with the last choice, whatever it happens to be, since of *that* pair he certainly took the one he preferred.

Granted the possibility of preferences so ordered, one cannot say that transitivity of preference is *logically* necessary, given the ordinary notion of preference. So unlike the case of symmetrical preference, one does not have to treat a claim to have such a preference as a failure to grasp what is logically implied in claiming to have a preference at all, and therefore as a failure in epistemic rationality. We shall consider a little later whether it should be deemed a failure in practical rationality.

Gordon Tullock has argued[7] that apparent intransitivity arises only because the options are presented in pairs. He takes it to be 'a basic statement about the world' that (ruling out indifference) 'a man confronted with a small...collection of alternatives' will prefer one of them. Suppose the subject were presented with all the options simultaneously, and told to choose:

> If the individual is alleged to prefer A to B, B to C and C to A, we can inquire which he would prefer from the collection, A, B, and C. *Ex hypothesi* he must prefer one, say he prefers A to B or C. This, however, contradicts the statement that he prefers C to A, and hence the alleged intransitivity must be false.

Tullock claims that alleged cases of intransitivity found in experimental situations must be explained as cases, for instance, where the subject changes his mind in the course of the experiment, was really indifferent but was not allowed by the restrictions of the experiment to say so, or by some similar *ad hoc* condition. But one does not show that a truly intransitive ordering of pairs is impossible by insisting that all the alternatives be ordered simultaneously. For this serves only to point up the paradox, that a man capable of choosing between three alternatives presented simultaneously might nevertheless produce an intransitive ordering when the options are paired.

It seems likely, however, that Tullock has his eye not so much on the possible implications of the ordinary notion of preference, but on the heuristic convenience for praxeological theories of a concept of preference that would exclude intransitive preferences as logically impossible. If such theories are to have wide practical application, there must be some way in which they can describe the apparently deviant cases. Tullock offers various suggestions, such as that the subject be deemed to have changed his mind. One might object that, in the case of Smith at the serving hatch, this is evidently not the case, since he can (*ex hypothesi*) predict in advance the intransitive sequence of choices he will make. However, the more strictly behavioural theorists—like the economists who adopt the revealed preference theory of consumer's choice—would simply refuse to count what he says as relevant; since the choices are made sequentially it remains open to them to maintain that his tastes do change, whatever he says. This guarantees that apparently deviant behaviour can be described in the theory's terms without contradiction; it merely places it outside the explanatory scope of the theory, since the theory is admittedly concerned only with cases where tastes remain constant throughout the experimental period, and, like all praxeologically-based theories, makes no predictions about changes in tastes. On the other hand, an economist using a weaker notion of preference allowing for indifference relations in a subject's ordering, might interpret intransitive choices to indicate that the subject had no preference, but in the sense that, being indifferent as between the options, he chose at random. That would not be grounds, of course, for saying he was irrational; where one is indifferent, and has to choose, choosing at random is the rational way.[8]

(d) Why should connectedness, asymmetry, and transitivity be considered conditions for rational *preferences?*

If we are right in saying that asymmetry is a logically necessary condition for any preference, it would clearly be epistemically irrational to claim that one's preferences were symmetrical. We have argued that this is not the case, however, with connectedness or transitivity; so why should these be considered conditions of *rational* preference, and not treated simply as further postulated restrictions on preference, justified by common experience, but having no special standing as conditions of *rationality*?

(i) Connectedness An agent having preferences relevant to a given choice-situation which nevertheless could not be arranged in an unbroken ordering might properly be considered irrational in a practical sense; for he would be incapable of choosing for a good and sufficient reason. The inability of the man in our earlier example

to arrange cars in an order of preference would have left him making either an arbitrary choice or no choice at all. Nevertheless, a complete preference ordering of all conceivable alternatives is not a necessary condition for rational choice; an agent may function satisfactorily as a chooser so long as the gaps are in parts of the preference field remote from any likely point of decision. If one does not know how one would optimally dispose of the entire gross national product, one is not irrational on that account—for one is unlikely ever to have to do it.

(ii) Transitivity Like connectedness, transitivity of preference is a condition for efficiency as a chooser. Smith, choosing between drinks, could choose optimally between any *two*, but cannot terminate the period of non-decision if he knows that the options will be presented to him successively and indefinitely. As a chooser, then, he too is a failure. If a test of the rationality of an action is the degree to which it is appropriate for putting the agent in his most preferred position, an agent with a preference set with no optimum, providing no criterion of successful achievement, would simply not be equipped to act in any way that could satisfy such a test.

(e) The heuristic role of the ordered preference postulates

(i) Equilibrium Economic theory makes extensive use of the notion of equilibrium. A state of affairs constitutes an equilibrium if, given only the forces (or motives) operating within the defined situation, there is no tendency in it towards change. In terms of action, an equilibrium situation is one that, supposing no change in the constraining conditions, a rational agent would have no good reason for seeking to change. So one can predict where a rational agent will finish up if there is reason to believe that such an equilibrium position is among his options. Similarly one can use the notion of equilibrium predictively for the outcome of a set of interacting decisions taken separately by a number of rational agents; if such individuals can be expected to arrive at a state of affairs that no one of them would have reason to change, this state will be the predictable outcome of their decisions. The theory of a competitive market, in which buyers and sellers arrive at a price which just clears available supplies, offering sellers and buyers alike the best they can reasonably hope for, is a familiar enough example of equilibrium theory. The heuristic merit, then, of the assumption that choosers whose decisions affect one another all have preferences satisfying the connectedness and transitivity requirement, is that a period of indeterminacy of interaction (e.g.

of fluctuating prices) can be thought of as terminating in a predictable outcome, namely, an equilibrium in which each, having attained his optimum for that situation, has no reason to disturb the situation by further varying his arrangements.

(ii) Ordinal ranking and indifference Neo-classical economic theory requires at least the notion of an ordinal scale, in which items are ranked in order of preference. Such a scale gives no indication, however, of the degree to which one thing is preferred to another. We shall discuss later its consequent theoretical limitations, and the possibility of extending the range of praxeology by giving some content to the notion of quantitative measurement of preferences.

The explanatory and predictive role of ordinal preference is illustrated by the classical theory of consumer's choice. A preference field is represented by a set of contour lines (indifference curves) each linking combinations of valued objects between which the subject would be indifferent (see Figure 7.1). Moving from one contour to another would always mean moving to a more or a less preferred position: but the intervals *between* contours can be assigned no significant numerical value, nor can one say that contour C_1 is as much above C_2 as C_2 is above C_3. Nevertheless, if the subject's income is represented by OB_1, and the exchange rate between A and B by the slope of the price line A_1B_1, one can predict that a rational chooser would select that combination of A and B that corresponded to P, the point of tangency of AB to C_n. This is because, given the constraining conditions OB_1 and the slope of A_1B_1, P lies on the highest attainable indifference curve. Given the convexity of indifference curves to the origin (an independent postulate), once the subject has parted with B_2B_1 out of his initial income OB_1, and received in exchange OA_2, he has made an optimal choice, and could not be induced under the given constraints, to alter his position by further exchange. The equilibrium analysis thus enables one to predict how a rational chooser will dispose of his available income, assuming knowledge of his preference ordering and of the prevailing market prices.

Although the notion of indifference is convenient for the exposition of this analysis, it is not strictly necessary to it. Revealed preference theory, indeed, has some difficulty in giving a coherent account of indifference as such, since it admits only choice as evidence of preference; and to choose is to prefer, not to be indifferent. One might plausibly say, perhaps, that a person whose choices are inconsistent is choosing at random, and is therefore to be held to have no preference. But, as we saw earlier, some revealed

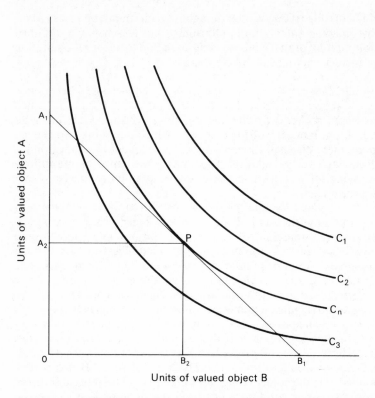

Figure 7.1 Indifference curve C_n links points representing combinations of A and B between which the subject has no preference. (Alternatively, C_n is the boundary between all combinations of A and B preferred to P, and all combinations to which P is preferred.) Note that though all points on C_1 are preferred to points on C_2, and all on C_2 to C_3, the intervals between the curves are, in a purely ordinal scaling, not significant.

preference theorists at least would prefer to treat such a case as one of changing preferences. In practice, the point is not all that important. For the indifference curve is significant not for the points it connects but for the points it separates. It is true that where a person is indifferent between certain options his choice is indeterminate, because he can only choose randomly. But in the analysis of consumer's choice, the important points are the one on the price line tangential to the indifference curve, C_n, and the points on the price line adjacent to it, each of which represents a less preferred position. Points on the same indifference curve as P get into the analysis only incidentally, as ways of defining the location of P.

The revealed preference theorists, therefore, tend to jettison the concept of indifference, to treat the curve C_n simply as a boundary between combinations of A and B that would be preferred to P and those that would not. The preference field can be defined, therefore, by a strong ordering, that excludes indifference altogether.

2 Preference and utility

So long as one is dealing with choice between *certain* outcomes, an ordinal analysis will go a long way. It could not account, however, for choices under conditions of risk, with outcomes of different probabilities. For this purpose one needs (as we shall explain in a moment) some way of expressing degrees of preference, such that they can be combined with probabilities in arithmetical expressions with determinate values. There are advantages, then, in thinking of different options as ordered in terms of the quantity of utility they yield, and as preferred or not preferred on that account.[9] This represents a reversion to the terminology of Jevons and Marshall, who couched the marginal analysis that resolved so many of the perplexities of the classical economists in terms, not of optimizing in relation to preferences, but of utility, a concept suggesting a quantity to be maximized in a kind of Benthamite hedonic calculus. No doubt for modern economists these terms are interchangeable, an indication of the extent to which quantifying preferences is now taken for granted, at least as something that could be done in principle, even if operationally difficult.

Replacing 'preference' with 'utility' would be misleading, however, if it were taken to suggest that the utility to an individual of the items on his preference schedule could be assigned absolute quantities, i.e. could be ranked *cardinally*, or if it seemed to provide a solution to the problem of choosing with multiple desiderata, by reducing them to a common measure of utility. Utility is not, of course, directly quantifiable in the way in which, for example, we measure a person's height, nor did Jevons suppose that it was. So it cannot serve as a *numeraire* for other values. The only criteria for talking about the utility an individual assigns to outcomes are his preferences and his choices; i.e.

$$x\mathrm{P}y \equiv \mathrm{U}(x) > \mathrm{U}(y)$$

where $\mathrm{U}(x)$ and $\mathrm{U}(y)$ represent the utilities of x and y respectively. So talk of maximizing utility can always be exhaustively translated into talk of optimizing in relation to a preference ranking. Thus the introduction of 'utility'-talk makes it no easier to explain how a man ranks complex outcomes. And it leaves it an open question whether we can ever express an agent's preference ranking in cardinal terms. Nonetheless, characterizing choice situations in terms of utility rather than preference has undoubted advantages for simplicity of expression and is standardly used for that reason by decision theorists.

3 Constructing an interval scale of utility from a preference ordering

We said earlier that for analysing choice-situations in which out-comes are not certain, an ordinal scale of preference is inadequate.[10] For some purposes, of course, money may serve as a cardinal index of utility. If a firm is indifferent to everything except the size of its profits, its production strategies can be ordered on a cardinal money scale, a strategy being preferred to others in exact proportion to the expected net profits. But because money is generally valued instrumentally for what it can buy, the marginal utility of money generally diminishes as one's stock of it increases. So one is pre-pared to pay more for a given car—or to risk wagering more for a prize—if one has a large income rather than a small one. Conse-quently though someone could readily arrange a given set of items in order of their utility to him, he could not say how much money he would be prepared to pay for each without knowing the size of his total stock of money. Paying for one item reduces his capacity to pay for others, so he needs to know how much he will have left for other things before he can say what he can afford for anything.

If money is not an invariant measure, is there any other way in which utility might be measured? We shall sketch the solution to this problem proposed by von Neumann and Morgenstern,[11] because it opens the way to extending the scope of the praxeological models to choices under risk.

Given xPy and yPz, the problem is to be able to set out x, y and z on a preference scale such that one can say that the agent A's preference for x over y is n times as great as his preference for y over z. The von Neumann-Morgenstern solution, commonly known as the standard gamble method, is to suppose that A is offered a lottery ticket, inviting him to exchange the certainty of y for a gamble between receiving x or z, each with an assigned probability (summing to 1), say, $(\frac{3}{4}x, \frac{1}{4}z)$. Call this lottery L. Let the probability of x be p, and the probability of z be $1-p$. There will be some value of p at which A will be indifferent whether he accepts the certainty of y or takes the lottery L. Using utility terminology,

$$U(y) = U(L) = pU(x) + (1-p)U(z).$$

Put the utility of x, as the most preferred outcome, at 1, and z, the least preferred at 0; and suppose, at $p = 3/4$, A is indifferent between the lottery and the certainty of y. Then

$$U(y) = U(L) = \tfrac{3}{4}(1) + \tfrac{1}{4}(0) = \tfrac{3}{4};$$

that is, the interval on A's scale of preferences between the certainty of y and the certainty of z is three times that between the certainty of x and the certainty of y, since he is indifferent as between the certainty of y and a lottery in which $1/4$ chance of z will just compensate for a $3/4$ chance of x. So the arithmetical relations of probability would be translated into measures of preference or of relative utilities. The *numeraire* is now provided by the odds in a presumptive lottery. The resulting scale is an interval scale not a cardinal scale; like temperature scales, and unlike measurements of height, it does not specify a non-arbitrary zero point but only compares the intervals between the points on the scale. It is adequate, nevertheless, to provide measurements of preference that can be manipulated arithmetically.

Despite these complications, however, the von Neumann-Morgenstern calculus of preference does suggest that a vastly heterogeneous collection of potential outcomes can in principle be arranged not only in order of preference, but in a way that can indicate how much one is preferred to another. Diversity of ends and values need not rule out, therefore, the praxeological analysis of choice-situations, provided the subjects can choose between the hypothetical certainties and lotteries indicated.

C   Canons of optimal choice

In this section we shall consider the ways in which the canon of optimality applicable to outcomes that are certain—'maximize the utility of the option'—has been extended and modified for a variety of choice-situations in which outcomes are not certain, thus generalizing the idea of formal practical rationality.

There are two senses in which a rational agent might be said to choose optimally. The individual with complete and certain knowledge of the outcomes chooses rationally if he chooses the option with optimal consequences (call this the 'outcome-optimal option'). He also chooses optimally in the sense that, given his knowledge about his choice-situation, he chooses the option which as a rational agent he has good reason to choose (call this the 'choice-optimal option'). Where, however, the agent does not have certain knowledge of the outcomes, he is in a position only to assign various probabilities to them; the fact that an outcome ranks highest on his preference schedule of outcomes would then be commonly thought to be an inadequate reason for choosing it. Whatever the criterion of choice-optimality in such choice-situations, the choice-optimal option may in the event turn out not to have been the outcome-optimal one.

Discussions of criteria of choice-optimality have usually been conducted in maximizing terms. That is to say, theorists interested in what consideration provides a good reason for choice have stated their criterial condition for a choice-optimal option in the form that it maximizes some property or function f. Where outcomes are not certain, what content should be assigned to f?

1 Canons of optimality for decisions under conditions of risk

(a) Maximizing expected utility

We explained in the previous section that relative money values cannot be taken as safe indications of relative utilities, since the marginal utility of money need not be assumed to be constant. For the sake of simplicity in exposition, however, we shall assume it to be so, in order to be able to express utilities in terms of dollars.

Consider a gambler about to enter a game in which he will stake $10 on a throw of pair of dice; he can choose to play either for a large prize, say $1000 if two sixes come up (a 1/36 chance), otherwise nothing, or for a smaller prize, say $50 if the dice sum to an even number (a 1/2 chance), otherwise nothing. Call these two games A and B respectively. A maximax policy (maximizing the maximum prospective gain offered by the available alternatives) is a strategy for only the most optimistic, just as a maximin policy (maximizing the minimum prospective gain) is for only the most pessimistic.

To predict—or to instruct—the choice of a rational gambler, we need a way of expressing the utilities of the options taking account both of the difference between the *possible* gains and of the difference in the probabilities of making them. One possibility is to evaluate each of the options by adding together the values of all its possible outcomes, each discounted, however, by the probability of its actually occurring, i.e. the utility of each game would be the sum of the 'expected utilities' (EU) of its outcomes.

In the example given above, the expected utility of game A can be calculated thus (supposing the gambler to lose his $10 stake if he does not throw a winning combination):

$$EU(A) = \tfrac{1}{36}(\$1000) + \tfrac{35}{36}(-\$10) = \$27{\cdot}78 - \$9{\cdot}73 = \$18{\cdot}05;$$

and of game B:

$EU(B) = \frac{1}{2} (\$50) + \frac{1}{2} (-\$10) = \$25 - \$5 = \$20.$

Supposing, then, that it is rational to maximize the expected utility of his gambling options, the rational gambler will choose game **B**.

(b) The rationality of maximizing expected utility

In place then of the classical economist's maximization of utility, the criterion of rational decision under conditions of risk, according to this account, is the maximization of the expected utility of the chosen strategy. But why should someone who has as his aim to achieve the most preferred situation, be rationally committed, under conditions of risk, to this canon? Why is it irrational, for instance, to disregard probabilities, and go for the big prize? Consider, for instance, the man who takes a lottery ticket in the New South Wales Opera House Lottery, knowing that the odds against his winning a big prize are so great that the expected utility of his ticket is far less than its cost. Leave aside any question of an interest in the excitement of gambling for its own sake, or of his being so urgently in need of a large sum that one can attribute to him increasing marginal utility of money. His interest is solely an investment-type interest. Taking his situation as wholly standard, then, one says that he is irrational to buy the ticket. He replies: 'But this is the investment that pays the winner the biggest return, and someone has to win—why shouldn't it be me?' Whatever discouraging reply one thinks appropriate, one cannot deny that one may be making it to the future lottery winner.

According to one account—the 'relative frequency' account, as exemplified in the work of Richard von Mises and Hans Reichenbach—the probability of an event is the limit of the relative frequency, given a standard set of conditions, of the occurrence of events of that type, within a given infinite sequence.[12] On this account, for an infinite run of experiments, the expected utility of a course of action would, in fact, equal the limit of its realized utility. So, with an infinitely reiterated experiment, maximizing the expected utility is rational because it is precisely the same as maximizing the limit of utility attainable. But we cannot deduce from that that the probability distribution will *hold* for any finite number of trials, however long the run. Nor can one infer it from the proposition that the longer the run the greater the probability that the probability distribution will be actualized; for that probability, too, would amount to a limit of relative frequency given an infinite number of runs of different lengths, and could yield no sure inference about any particular run. It is something of a puzzle, then, to know why it should be thought rational to base one's strategy for a finite number of trials on the distribution expected for an infinite number.

It might be argued that it is simply a contingent truth that in any long run of trials the proportional distribution of results clusters around the point indicated by the mathematical theory of probability, that the longer the run the denser the clustering around the point. According to this view, it is rational to take account of probability because experience shows that in the long run it pays to do so. The problem then merges into the broader philosophical question of the rationality of inductive inference.

Allow, however, that it is rational to act on a probability distribution when the trials are reiterated in a finite series; allow that in 6,000 throws one could be reasonably certain that there would be 1,000 sixes; it would be a rational policy then to accept gambles on the six only if the odds offered on each throw were at least 6 to 1, for should one bet on odds poorer than that for any given throw (even should one win), the 1,000 wins would not balance the 5,000 losses.

To exhibit the rationality of the expected utility criterion for a series of reiterated trials, and for each trial in that series, may still seem to leave undetermined the rationality criterion of the never-to-be-repeated, strictly one-shot case, where relative frequency distribution could not actually apply. But to state the problem in this way is to suppose that some experiments are by nature 'one-shot cases', incapable of being included in any series, whereas in truth a relative frequency distribution can be assigned to any collection of sequences of decisions and outcomes, provided some property common to them all can be specified. All one's decisions, no matter how varied, could be regarded, then, as members of the single series consisting of trials in which the decision always took due account of the probability distribution of the outcomes, even though these varied with each trial. If, in such a series, the gains exceeded the losses, that would be a reason for acting on probabilities in any chance set-up, and for betting, even in cases that might otherwise be classed as 'one-shot', on nothing less than fair odds. If one regularly accepts odds poorer than the relative probabilities, no matter how varied the games, one will be out of pocket in time, even if one makes it a rule to play any particular game once only. The reason, then, for deciding in accordance with probability conditions in the never-to-be-repeated trial would be that decisions reached in that way will maximize utility in the long run.

(c) Expected utility and expected value

We suggested, in section B3, that monetary values could not be treated as an invariant index of utility. It was for this reason that we explored the von Neumann-Morgenstern notion of the standard gamble. Nevertheless we have chosen, for the sake of convenience, to identify the expected utility of an option with its expected value. We now have to take note of certain other qualifying conditions, besides changes in the marginal utility of money.[13]

A gambler who derives positive satisfaction from the excitement of gambling may rationally choose a gamble for a big prize, even if its expected value is less than that of the sum he stands to lose; the utility of gambling must then be added to the expected value of the gamble, to determine its expected utility to him. Conversely, one may be reluctant, whatever the expected value, to accept a gamble in which one stands to gain a lot, but also to lose everything. Beyond a certain point, risk-taking as such may be assigned a negative utility. A prudent householder is not necessarily irrational, then, to insure against loss by fire, even though the expected value of the loss he would sustain is less than the value of the premiums he pays (as it must be, given that fire insurance companies make profits).

Considerations of this kind pose problems for those who rely on the standard gamble as a way of converting preferences for risky outcome-values into expected utilities. For in the case of the prudent householder, the fact that his preferences do not correspond with the expected values of his options may be due, not to the diminishing marginal utility of money, as hypothesized, but to the negative utility of taking risks beyond a certain point. Or it may be due to a bit of both. The method offers no way of distinguishing between these two effects.[14]

Some economists concerned primarily with investors' decisions, where outcomes are most naturally expressed monetarily in terms of expected net profits, have been reluctant to substitute expected utilities, which they cannot measure in practice, for expected values of profits, which they can. But investors, like householders, may reasonably prefer 'safety-first' policies, that promise moderate profits at the risk of moderate losses, rather than policies with a greater expected value, but which balance the expectation of far bigger profits with the threat of bankruptcy. Attempts have been made, accordingly, to specify 'safety-first' criteria of optimality, prescribing the choice of an option that maximizes expected net returns, subject, however, to the condition that should the worst happen, returns will not fall below a stipulated minimum.[15] What that would be is, of course, a matter of individual preference.

2 Canons of optimality for decisions under uncertainty

We have made no distinction hitherto between risk and uncertainty.

Statisticians and decision theorists do distinguish these, however. In decisions under risk, calculable mathematical probabilities can be assigned to outcomes. In decisions under uncertainty, no determinate probabilities can be assigned.[16] Under conditions of certainty, the rational agent maximizes gain (or utility), and under conditions of risk expected gain (or utility). If, through ignorance, one has no more reason for expecting one outcome rather than another, a moderately prudent man may choose to act on Laplace's principle, that under those conditions the alternatives should be treated as equally probable. This would assimilate conditions of uncertainty to conditions of risk, and so place one in a position to maximize expected gain (or utility). Though intuitively plausible, Laplace's principle is not, some think, rationally compelling. If they are right, we need some alternative criterion for rational action in conditions of uncertainty. An optimist may maximax, i.e. adopt the strategy which includes among its possible outcomes the one most profitable to him, irrespective of the dangers to him should it fail. A pessimist may minimize his maximum losses (minimax) or (what comes to the same thing) maximize his minimum gains (Wald's maximin criterion). Another may weight the best and worst payoffs for each strategy by a personal coefficient of optimism, and then go for the weighted maximum payoff (Hurwicz's variant of the maximax criterion), introducing subjective probability to supply the lack of objective probability coefficients; or with L.J. Savage, he may choose to minimize the maximum regret he will experience should the chosen strategy turn out badly.

Attempts have been made to derive one or other of these criteria from various basic axioms of rational choice, but none has gained general acceptance. It may be that praxeology can offer no such derivation. If that is so, though such proposals might be referred to loosely as 'alternative criteria of rationality', because they specify some function to be maximized, and are therefore analogous to standard criteria such as maximizing utility or maximizing expected utility, deciding between them would be, strictly speaking, an arbitrary matter of temperament and taste, the cautious opting for a maximin, the adventurous for a maximax. To that extent, no such criterion would be a criterion of rational action.

For all that, such criteria might provide a social scientist with hypotheses for explaining and predicting social phenomena, using the inferential methods of praxeology. But he will need to determine experimentally which of these functions his subjects actually maximize. A certain amount of experimental work has been done, albeit in very limited and contrived laboratory conditions. We are a long way, however, from being able to apply such findings to the study of the complex and uncertain decision-situations of real-life politics, military strategy, or diplomacy. And there are plenty of sceptics who doubt whether decision-makers in these fields satisfy any formal rationality conditions with sufficient uniformity to make axiomatic theory profitable. According to the sceptics, we must simply go out and examine people's propensities to respond to situations, without expecting them to be optimizing or maximizing any function whatsoever.

3   Canons of optimality for conflict-situations

(a)   The theory of games—maximizing the value of the game

We shall now turn to a class of decision-situations, explored by von Neumann and Morgenstern in their pioneering work on game theory,[17] where the outcome distribution of an action by A depends on the decisions of another intelligent agent B for whom there is also a variable payoff, and whose strategy may therefore be expected to take A's strategy, actual or expected, into account.

Under these conditions neither can adopt the policy of maximizing expected utility, for neither can rationally assign independent probabilities to the outcomes. In a competitive situation, if A has some reason to suppose that B has a reason for adopting a particular strategy, A's reason may be a reason for B to avoid that strategy, to frustrate an attempt by A to profit from his foresight. Acknowledging that under such conditions one cannot maximize expected utility, game theorists have turned instead to explore an alternative criterion of practical rationality, the maximizing of minimum gain (maximin) or, what is equivalent, the minimizing of maximum loss (minimax).

Game theorists classify such strategic interactions as zero-sum/non-zero-sum, and two-person/n-person. In a zero-sum game, any player's losses are some other players' gains, the sum of the outcomes for any given combination of strategies being zero. In a non-zero-sum game, the sum of the payoffs accruing to different players is itself variable according to the strategies adopted, so that, under some conditions, every player might have something to gain if one combination of strategies were chosen rather than another.

Consider an outcome matrix of a two-person zero-sum game, three strategies being available to each player (Figure 7.2). The sum shown in each cell is the payoff P to X from that combination of strategies. Y's payoff is −P.

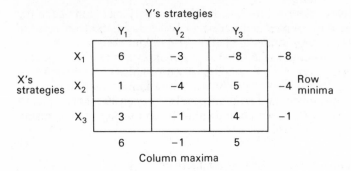

Figure 7.2

The best of the worst results that X can get from any of his three strategies is -1, shown on the right as the minimum for Row X_3. Choosing X_3, X would be sure to maximize his minimum payoff from the game—he could not do worse than lose 1, whatever Y did. Similarly, Y can minimize X's maximum gain, and therefore his own maximum loss, by selecting Y_2. The strategies selected, X_3 and Y_2, will be an equilibrium point since, even knowing in advance what the other proposed to do, neither could better his situation by substituting a different strategy. A game having a point at which the least X can succeed in winning, whatever strategy Y adopts, equals the most Y may be forced to part with, whatever strategy X adopts, is said to have a 'saddle-point',[18] and to be 'strictly-determined'.

Not all games, even two-person zero-sum games, have a saddle-point. In the game indicated by the outcome matrix in Figure 7.3, if X maximized his minimum payoff by playing X_1, Y could do better than lose 3 (the outcome of strategies X_1, Y_2) which is his minimum maximum loss; for if he foresaw X's strategy, he could settle for a loss of only 1 by playing Y_1. On the other hand, foreseeing this reasoning, X could gain 5 by playing X_2. Because for a single play of this game there is no equilibrium point, it has no strictly determinate solution.

Suppose, however, the game were frequently repeated. If X chose his pure maximin strategy X_1 and stuck to it, he would certainly do less well than if Y had no idea what to expect of him. For then Y need never lose more than 1, whereas if X sometimes played X_2 he could pick up 5. Of course, if Y knew when to expect this move, he would counter with Y_2 and X would get nothing. So X must mix his strategies randomly. Equally, it will pay Y to do the same. The best strategy, therefore, will be a random mix, in a mathe-

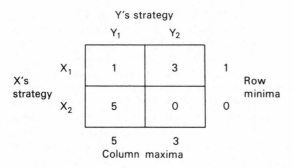

Figure 7.3

matically calculable proportion governed by the number of strategies and the difference in the sizes of the payoffs. Notice, this does not convert the game into a game of pure chance, like 'snakes and ladders', in which rational decisions have no place. The player is selecting a rational strategy, one constituent of which is a randomizing element designed to make his choice of strategy for any particular play unpredictable. A correctly mixed randomized strategy is still a rational maximizing strategy, but in the special case that the conditions determining the outcomes include the decisions of another player capable of responding to clues to one's own.

Von Neumann and Morgenstern have shown that every zero-sum two-person game, if repeatable, and allowing mixed strategies, has a saddle-point and therefore has a determinate solution. The average payoff which a player can expect from playing his best strategy (mixed when and as appropriate) is known as *the value of the game*. This, then, is the function to be maximized according to the game-theoretical rationality analysis. It corresponds to the use of a pure minimax strategy when there is a saddle-point, and a mixed minimax when there is not.

Solutions for n-person games and non-zero-sum games are not so readily found, not, at least, using the rationality postulates offered so far. However, n-person zero-sum games can be assimilated to the two-person model if the players are permitted to form coalitions; the game can then be analysed as a game between two coalitions—a two-person game. Coalition formation then becomes itself a subject for a game analysis, the players having a choice between possible partners, each negotiating an optimal division of the spoils accruing from a joint strategy. Bargaining games may then precede the playing of the principal game, determining its outcome. Applications of this type of analysis to problems in economic theory are dealt with by Clem Tisdell in Chapter 8; its application to coalition formation in international politics is discussed by Oran Young in Chapter 9.

Despite the elegance of zero-sum game solutions, so much admired by mathematicians, this part of game theory has only limited usefulness in the social sciences. In the first place, most of the practical problems in economics and politics, problems of bargaining, duopolistic and oligopolistic trading alliance, cartel or party-coalition formation, the use of strategic threat deterrence, and so on, must be formalized as non-zero-sum games. But even were this not the case, determining whether a particular game is zero-sum or not is a problem in itself that the pure theory of games sets on one side.[19] The matrix of a zero-sum game includes utility values confidently written in, and common to both parties—one's losses are the other's gains. But in practice opponents do not always assign equivalent utilities to a given objective payoff. Suppose, for instance, one's opponent cared very little about losing to you something you cared greatly about winning, and conversely. The same 'objective' outcome conditions in an apparently zero-sum matrix would have to be replaced by a matrix in which gains and losses did not sum to zero. Game theorists have not given much attention to the epistemic problem of how one forms beliefs about one's opponent's value-structure: they take for granted that one knows whether the game one is playing is or is not zero-sum.

(b)   The problem of a canon for non-zero-sum games

If determinate solutions were easily available for non-zero-sum games, this would represent a considerable theoretical advance, even given the epistemic difficulty. Classical economics has so far failed, for instance, to provide a solution for a two-person bargaining game between a monopolist and a monopsonist (between, say, a trade union and an employer's organization); the best it can do is to define limits within which the outcome must fall—limits set by the fact that for both sides some agreement is better than no agreement; but the precise point remains indeterminate.

A general solution to non-zero-sum games would require some strengthening of the stipulated rationality postulates. John Harsanyi has sketched a programme for arriving at determinate solutions for all classes of games by adding to the standard conditions of practical rationality a set of 'postulates of rational expectation', characterizing the strategies that a rational player would expect his opponent to adopt, *supposing him to be a rational player too*.[20] 'In the same way as you will yourself follow the present postulates if you are rational, you must expect, and act on the expectation, that *other* rational players will likewise follow these rationality postulates.' Such a postulate is an innovation in game theory. The standard maximin strategy for a zero-sum game is not restricted, for instance, to cases in which one can suppose one's opponent rational; if he turns out not to be, one simply does better than minimize one's maximum loss. Harsanyi's postulates are aimed to provide strategies in which rational players could do better than that, by relying on one another to co-operate where, for example, co-operative strategies offer each player better results than strategies aimed only at minimizing losses should the other player prove hostile. Whatever the validity of Harsanyi's proposal, its application is necessarily restricted to conditions in which it is rational to suppose one's opponent rational—an epistemic condition novel in praxeological analysis.

D   Epistemic assumptions

We saw, in the previous section, that the canons of practical rationality vary with the state of an agent's knowledge of the outcomes of his different options. One would expect, therefore, that some attention would be paid in praxeological theories to the rational agent's attempts to increase his knowledge about his choice-situation. Some economists have indeed been turning their attention in recent years to such activities as information-search, but the integration of such inquiries into the general body of economic theory has not gone very far as yet. This is due in large part to the wealth of theoretical opportunities that could be expected if such questions were put on one side.

In the classical economic model, the rational agent has perfect knowledge of the certain outcomes of the alternatives open to him, can identify the best of them, and chooses it on that account. The advantages of operating with this assumption are clear: to predict what such an agent will do, we need to examine his situation and determine the option that *will in fact* maximize utility. By contrast, to explain or predict using the ordinary postulates of rationality, we should have to identify the agent's actual belief about his situation, which, though rational, may be mistaken. In the absence of more direct evidence (like avowals) we might have to infer it from what in that situation it would be rational for him to believe. It is not surprising, therefore, that theorists have been content to use a technical postulate which allows a prediction about the agent's choice to be inferred directly from the facts about his choice-situation.

In its most complex form, this postulate holds that:
  (i) the agent chooses what is the best;
  (ii) he acts on the true belief that his choice is certain to issue in an outcome higher on his preference schedule than the outcome of any other option, and is therefore best;
  (iii) the latter belief derives from complete knowledge of the certain outcomes of all the options.

Any theory that extended from certain to uncertain or risky outcomes could not, of course, embody requirement (iii) in that form. But the postulate can be adapted to require only that a rational agent choose on the basis of a rational belief about the probabilities of the outcomes; his choices can then be predicted by assuming that he employs the optimality criterion appropriate to the degree of expectation that his epistemic situation would reasonably warrant, e.g. he may act to maximize expected utility rather than to maximize the utility of any possible outcome (the criterion appropriate to certainty).

Requirement (i) is the one responsible for the predictive advantages of the technical postulate. Given the assumption that the agent will choose what is in fact the best of the options, we can read off what he will do from the facts of his decision-situation. From the point of view of someone concerned with prediction, therefore, items (ii) and (iii) could be dropped from the postulate; and what we in fact find in a good deal of theorizing, particularly in economics, is a tendency to reduce the postulate to (i) alone. Thus in Chapter 8, Clem Tisdell explores the possibility of an economic agent's correctly identifying the optimal option *without* possessing complete knowledge of the options open to him. This would allow the theorist to drop (iii). Later in his essay, Tisdell considers the theoretical use of an 'as if' notion of rationality, in which the agent's correct choice of the optimum is not even assumed to derive from the application of one of the canons of rational choice (i.e. (ii) is dropped as well). A postulate confined to (i) could then, for example, be used to predict the choices of businessmen operating with rules of thumb in fixing their prices. It should be noted, however, that the 'as if' postulate is taken to have not merely predictive force, but some sort of explanatory force, too, since it shows that economic agents behave 'as if they were rational'. Of course, A's behaving *as if* he made rational decisions could not be an explanation of what he does. It may simply be an odd coincidence. But economists are generally interested in explaining not the actions of particular individuals, but in explaining aggregate societal facts, like price rises, monetary crises, or increases in unemployment. And a theory capable of showing that individuals trying to optimize under the given existing conditions would bring about the phenomenon to be explained, would indeed appear to explain it; for the explanation would then be accounted for in terms of the regular behaviour of 'particular' theoretical entities, much as the behaviour of material objects may be explained by inference from the postulated properties of unobservable physical particles. For explanations at this level, the epistemic antecedents of action may be quite unimportant.

The development of theoretical accounts of choice could move, however, in several quite different directions from the one discussed above. One move is to reject the optimizing model altogether. Simon's major contribution in this area, for example, has been to suggest that in complex decision-situations the agent does not seek to identify the optimum, but to find an option which meets a predetermined level of satisfactoriness.[21] There are, however, several ways of treating such cases as cases of rational choice. The theorist might, as we have seen, insist that they can be subsumed under an 'as if' rationality postulate. Or, if we suppose that the agent uses this criterion after assessing the consequences of operating with alternatives, we might judge that, taking account of the costs of gathering and processing the information necessary to operate with a full optimizing criterion, he has in fact adopted the optimal decision-criterion for that type of decision-situation.

Another possible development is to work with an optimizing model which attributes the agent's choices to his comparative assessment of options, but to build into the model a series of constraints on:

(i) the range of options considered;
(ii) the rationality with which beliefs are formed about the options;
(iii) the amounts of information gathered, up to the moment of choice;
(iv) the quantities of information processed;
(v) the rationality with which the assessment of options is derived from the available information.

Under (i), (iii) and (iv), the model might employ technical postulates of practical rationality, given the costs to the agent of widening his consideration of options, gathering more information and engaging in more elaborate or extensive processing procedures. Under (ii), it might assume some level short of complete epistemic rationality; thus firms might be assumed to infer price predictions in a highly simplistic way from the most recent price levels. Under (v), the level of rationality displayed might be qualified by such factors as the conspicuousness of certain alternatives or the predisposition of the agent to choose a favoured option.

Such a highly complex model retains the general form of the optimizing account, while allowing us both to explain choice in terms of belief, and belief in terms of antecedent information-gathering and information-processing activities. While it sacrifices the simplicity of the classical epistemic postulates, it promises better explanations of individual cases of complex decision-making.

E Postulated ends and rationality criteria

To move from the logical calculus of choice to behavioural theories, the formal conditions of rationality need supplementing with specifications of the agents' goals. In this section, therefore, we shall examine the relation between such supplementary postulates and rationality criteria.

1 The concentration on outcomes

The usual mode of presenting rational decision models seems to suggest that they depend on a clearly defined distinction between means and ends, an end being some valued condition to be realized in the future by some present action, the means. Decisions must be taken about what to do now, for the sake of a valuable situation later. Consider this passage from von Mises:[22]

> Action is always...a planning and acting for a better future.
> Its aim is always to render future conditions more satisfactory
> than they would be without the interference of action...action
> can influence only the future, never the present. ...

The terminology of game theory and decision theory, of 'strategies', 'outcomes', and 'payoffs', reinforces this impression.

How far does praxeological rationality require that the value of an action derive wholly from some expected valued outcome distinct from it? Can non-consequentialist ends be assimilated into the praxeological model?[23] After all, a strategy promising a very big return might fill the agent with such disgust that he would much prefer a less promising one. Is this necessarily irrational? A possible response would be to put as the future end of a strategy the enjoyment of feelings like self-approval, or the avoidance of the pangs of remorse. But this is implausible. Someone who would be disgusted with himself were he to do something he abhors, avoids the act because he abhors it, not in order to avoid the unpleasantness of a future state of self-disgust. Were that really his reason for avoiding the act, he might have reason now for self-disgust, for being the sort of person who avoids an act not because it is abhorrent but for the sake only of his own peace of mind.

This somewhat naive trick of converting non-consequentialist ends into expected inner rewards and penalties would be unnecessary but for the mistaken belief that if strategy and outcome are to be distinguished they must be *temporally* distinct. One can lay out a matrix, however, in which the agent's principled attitudes to the options (as distinct from his self-satisfaction in acting like a man of principle) are written into the payoff cells to be preferentially assessed along with consequential outcomes. After all, a politician who has to choose between the chance of preserving his integrity and losing an election, and of telling lies and winning it, must see these as competitive bundles, even though dishonesty and integrity are not outcomes but evaluative descriptions of the competing strategies of telling the truth and telling a lie.

Call the utility of winning honestly $U(W+H)$, of winning dishonestly $U(W+D)$, of losing honestly $U(L+H)$, and of losing dishonestly $U(L+D)$, and call the strategies of telling the truth and telling falsehoods S_t and S_f respectively; then, assigning a probability of p_1 to $(W+H)$ and of p_2 to $(W+D)$, the expected utilities of the payoffs might be represented as shown in Figure 7.4.

	Outcomes	
S_t	$U(W+H)p_1$	$U(L+H)(1-p_1)$
S_f	$U(W+D)p_2$	$U(L+D)(1-p_2)$

Figure 7.4

Whether it would be rational for him to decide on S_t or S_f will then depend on the relations between the values assigned to the utilities and to the probabilities.

It may be objected, however, that unless these heterogeneous utilities can be expressed in terms of a common *numeraire*, or (what amounts to the same thing) can be assigned some determinate rankings on an interval preference scale, bundling them into lots in outcome cells is just another way of setting out the alternatives, and represents no progress towards inferring a rational decision from the data. For we need to know how the agent weighs the utility of electoral success against dishonesty, and whether some lies would count against it more heavily with him than others. If we are to predict his decisions we must be able to assign values, both to the mixed utilities and to the probabilities, to yield determinate values for expected utilities.

Our sketch of a standard gamble recipe for making an interval scale of preferences (see B3 above) suggests that this may not be an utterly absurd requirement, at least in principle. One can envisage offering the subject the choice of the appropriate lotteries, between the certainty of losing honestly and some disjunctive probabilities of winning by telling a given lie and losing despite it. One would then ask him what values would have to be assigned to these probabilities for him to be indifferent as between remaining honest and losing for sure, and the chance of winning dishonestly. And the probabilities assigned would count as indices of his relative preference for winning and for avoiding *that* lie. And the same could be done in respect of more and less serious lies. So an interval scale could be constructed, showing what degree of certainty of winning he was prepared to surrender for the sake of the truth.

This analysis has the interesting consequence of bringing together Max Weber's two ideal types of rationality, instrumental and value-rationality, as the polar limiting cases on a continuum.[24] For someone just short of the uncompromisingly honest pole, exemplifying value-rationality, only certain victory would compensate for the loss of integrity involved in the tiniest lie. At the opposite pole, preserving one's integrity would not be valued as a prize, and only the consequential value of winning would count. Weber regarded value-rationality as a rather inferior kind of rationality.[25] If we are right in thinking that principles can be rationally traded off against valued consequences, however, value-rationality can be accommodated within the praxeological scheme without involving any discontinuity with other means/ends rationality conditions; consequently, the substantive postulates with which action models supplement the formal requirements of rationality need not be limited to ones embodying consequentialist values.

2   Substantive value-postulates and 'role-rationality'

In so far as the social sciences are concerned with the prediction and explanation of the behaviour of agents—especially aggregates of agents—whose actual preferences are virtually impossible to explore in detail, they proceed by setting up models of what can be expected of a rational agent in defined situations. The conditions postulated include certain substantive restricting goals or interests which are often represented as 'rationality conditions'.

These restrictions are generally suggested by the nature of the relations being studied. Consider, for instance, Wicksteed's concept of 'non-tuism', which he substitutes in the theory of market exchange for the classical *homo economicus*. Non-tuism is not the same as selfishness or egoism, for my motive in driving a hard bargain with you may be a profound concern for the widows and orphans for whom I am a trustee. Still,[26]

> if you and I are conducting a transaction which on my side is purely economic, I am furthering your purposes, partly or wholly perhaps for my own sake, perhaps entirely for the sake of others, but certainly not for your sake. . . . The economic relation does not exclude from my mind everyone but me, it potentially includes everyone but you.

This limitation is required, however, not by the concept of rationality as such, but by the concept of exchange or, more generally, for any theory of collective decision where individual interests conflict. If in transferring an article to you, I have primarily in mind the advantage to you, and there is no attendant condition or intention that you shall transfer a corresponding article to me, I shall not be engaging in exchange, even if you do transfer an article to me at the same time. For my action is not then influenced by yours. We shall simply be giving each other presents. And if we are indeed exchanging, but out of benevolence I knowingly give you more than the market price, more than I need to pay for your commodity, the payment clearly includes a gift component. Now, one *can* have an economic theory even of gifts, calculating how much income to assign to essentials and how much to give away, equating utility at the margin, i.e. indicating that allocation at which the marginal increment devoted to each purpose is of equal importance.[27] This would be an account of an economic decision satisfying rationality conditions—but of resource allocation, not of an exchange transaction.

A particularly explicit stipulation of substantive rationality conditions is provided by W.H. Riker.[28]

> What the rational political man wants, I believe, is to win. . . .
> Unquestionably there are guilt-ridden and shame-conscious
> men who do not desire to win, who in fact desire to lose.
> These are the irrational ones of politics. . . . Politically rational
> man is the man who would rather win than lose, regardless of
> the particular stakes.

'Winning', for Riker, evidently means gaining the control of human resources, succeeding in mobilizing the efforts of other men, and thwarting the attempts of rivals to do so, for purposes unspecified. If *homo politicus* is taken to manifest 'a restless desire for power after power', as if no other end could count as rational, this is because politics, as Riker understands it, is characteristically

187

such a mobilizing activity. The *ultimate* objectives of politicians are no doubt diverse; the activity required in pursuing them *politically* has this common feature. Accordingly, Riker sets up a kind of ideal type, building this feature into it as an axiomatic condition, together with the postulates of formal practical rationality, in order to convert a purely formal calculus into a theory of political coalitions, from which non-formal, testable hypotheses can be derived.

Similar postulates appear in economic theory. Scitovsky, for instance, stipulates[29] as a condition for a theory of the firm that the 'entrepreneur's choice between more and less activity or between income and more leisure—must be independent of his income', an assumption equivalent to Marshall's assumption of constant marginal utility of money. If the 'income elasticity of supply of entrepreneurship' were zero, then it will be correct to ascribe to the entrepreneur the desire to maximize his profits.

> To say that the individual maximizes his satisfaction is a perfectly general statement. It says nothing about the individual's psychology or behaviour, is, therefore, devoid of empirical content, and is true by definition. As against this, the assumption that the entrepreneur maximizes his profits is based on observation and implies a special hypothesis concerning the business man's psychology. It is therefore an empirical law, which need not apply to every businessman...[30]

Scitovsky does not expressly call profit maximization a rationality condition; other writers, however, do use this term when making corresponding stipulations. Frohlich, Oppenheimer and Young,[31] for instance, have a concept of 'role-rationality', involving a 'role premise' defined as 'a particular set of aspects of the alternatives in terms of which an individual evaluates his utility', the set being characteristically linked with the role in question; for instance, 'the role premise of economic entrepreneurs is profit maximization'. The formal theory specifies, then, that a role-bearer be taken to maximize in accordance with the role premise; and the authors suggest that under certain given conditions (roughly, that the agent values his performances in this role more than in any other), the postulate will be realistic. Anthony Downs uses a notion similar to that of 'role-rationality' in developing a theory of democratic party programmes and voter's choice, in *An Economic Theory of Democracy*. In Chapter 10, Stanley Benn examines the use Downs makes of substantive requirements for voter rationality, a special case of what Downs calls 'political rationality' to distinguish it from a more general 'personal rationality'.

3   The theoretical role of substantive value-postulates, and the canons of rationality

Theoretical economists, and their equivalents in other fields, have been much criticized precisely on the grounds that they rely on allegedly 'unrealistic' postulates of this kind. We cannot take it for granted, it is said, that firms seek to maximize expected profits. Over what time span? What if the managing director cares more about prestige and power? Still, in the central areas with which economics has been traditionally concerned, it seems none too bad a first approximation to assume that economic agents are interested in maximizing their incomes of goods and services; that hours spent in working count as cost items, for which compensatory advantages in incomes are sought, and so on.[32] By specifying these as 'pure cases', as Weberian 'ideal types', the economic theorist can arrive at a set of relations that *would* obtain, but for certain intrusive or complicating factors. The latter are taken to account for divergences between the conditions theoretically derived and those observed.

Theoretical interest then shifts to the complications, which have to be assimilated to the theory as special cases. An economic theorist who *began* by assuming no kind of uniformity in utility functions, who assumed nothing, for instance, regarding relative preferences for more working hours and more leisure, and made no inferences until he had assembled a complete preference map of the economy, might well be turning his back on a fruitful source of testable hypotheses, and a useful selection for empirical research projects.[33] If the observations came reasonably close to the theoretically derived conditions this would surely be a reason for thinking that the actual utility functions were not totally unlike those of the theory; and the direction of the divergences might well suggest what to look for in the way of complicating conditions.

The method is the more practical in economics because economists are very often concerned with the aggregate outcome of unco-ordinated acts, like shifts in market prices, rates of investment, and so on. 'Role premises', though unreliable as guides to the actions of specific individuals, could nevertheless reliably explain such outcomes provided the random variations (i.e. variations not systematically related to roles in the fields of action under direct study) tended to cancel out. It has been suggested, too, that in a competitive activity, in politics as well as in business, those who do not accept their role-premises as conclusive grounds for decision may be eliminated by their more single-minded rivals. Riker claims that the 'fiduciary' role of major actors in political and economic life, as company directors, public servants, or ministers, ensures that in performing these roles they optimize in terms of their role premises.

Granted the theoretical usefulness of these substantive action postulates, however, it is not evident that they should properly be called criteria of *rationality*. A politician who cares more for telling the truth than for winning votes would be irrational on Riker's criteria—yet it is difficult to see why one should say so. Consider the entrepreneur who cares more for leisure than for profit. He is not being irrational as a man; indeed, there is nothing irrational about a man's rejecting the role of entrepreneur altogether, together with its corresponding ends. Is the irrationality due, then, to a conceptual incoherence, like that of a square circle, in the concept of a non-profit-maximizing entrepreneur? Since we can envisage such a person existing, for a time at least before going bankrupt, this surely cannot be the case.

We are forced to conclude that, while such role premises are necessary for theory construction, there is no particular reason for calling them rationality conditions. But equally, for the explanatory and predictive purposes of these studies, it is of no importance whether the postulated substantive ends are in any sense rational or not, provided they approximate to the actual ends of the agents studied. The notion of rational ends is important, not in praxeologically-based studies which are concerned with the rationality of actions *given* ends, but in studies that use the idea of a rational man, or of a rational society. The last two sections of this collection will be concerned with these.

Conclusion

We said in section A1 that a key step in the elaboration of theories of the kinds discussed in this paper is the explication of the concept of rational choice, and that applying such theories to complex choice-situations required a high degree of logical or mathematical sophistication. For all that, the practical payoff in explanation and prediction of such theoretical ingenuity is frequently disappointing. An elaborate symbolic function takes one but a very little way towards understanding unless one knows how to go about putting values to the variables and functional constants. Not every social scientist is in a position to emulate his economic colleagues, some at least of whose data can be quantified. Others are deluded if they think they have made progress *in explanation* when they have translated a qualitative relationship from English prose into a symbolic formula. There are people for whom such translations are useful aids for checking faulty inference, but until ways are discovered of putting figures in place of letters, replacing the language of optimization by that of maximization may be just a way of fooling oneself.

Notes

1 The authors wish to acknowledge the helpful criticisms and suggestions they received in preparing this paper, from Dr Peter Sheehan, Mr Malcolm Rennie, Professor S.J. Turnovsky, and Dr K. Rivett.
2 For an extensive bibliography, see Brodbeck, M. (1968), Select Bibliography, Part Six—'Theory construction'; Part Seven—'Models and measurement'.
3 Mises, L. von (1963); also Lange, O. (1971).
4 Buchanan, J.M. (1969).
5 See Edwards, W. and Tversky, A. (1967) for surveys of such experimental work, with bibliographies.
6 See works by Samuelson, P.A. and Little, I.M.D., cited in the bibliography to this paper. See also Georgescu-Roegen, N. (1966).
7 Tullock, G. (1964), p. 403; also Baier, K. (1967).
8 See Rescher, N. (1959–60) for a defence of this view.
9 Majumdar, T. (1958).
10 For a brief and simple account of rankings and measurement-scales, see Miller, D.W. and Starr, M.K. (1967), pp. 87–98. For a fuller treatment of scaling, see Torgerson, W.S. (1958).
11 See Neumann, J. von, and Morgenstern, O. (1953), pp. 15–30.
12 Achinstein, P. (1967); Black, M. (1967); Hacking, I. (1965) and (1972).
13 The policy of maximizing expected value (or expected gain) is sometimes referred to as a Bayesian strategy, after Thomas Bayes, the eighteenth-century mathematician who studied the probable outcomes of games of chance. The policy of maximizing expected utility is sometimes called a Bernoulli strategy, after Daniel Bernoulli, another eighteenth-century mathematician, who proposed that the logarithm of the gain, rather than the gain itself, was an appropriate measure of its utility.
14 Watkins, J.W.N. (1970).
15 Pyle, D.H. and Turnovsky, S.J. (1970).
16 For a lucid and documented summary of proposed optimality-criteria for decision under uncertainty see Tisdell, C.A. (1968).
17 Neumann, J. von, and Morgenstern, O. (1953). Von Neumann and Morgenstern make the simplificatory assumption 'that the aim of all participants in the economic system . . . is money'. Consequently, it is possible for them to treat the minimax policy as applying indifferently to utility or money gains. We shall adopt the same simplifying assumption for the purpose of this exposition.
18 The lowest point of the parabola formed by a cross-section through a saddle in one plane is the highest point of a parabola formed by a cross-section in a second plane set at 90° to the first.
19 Given the simplificatory assumption that in the economic system all

participants aim solely at money (see note 17), gains in utility will precisely correspond, for all players, with money gains, so that whether a game is zero-sum or non-zero-sum will be determined by simple inspection.

20 Harsanyi, J.C. (1966), p. 620.
21 Simon, H.A. (1957), pp. 241ff.
22 Mises, L. von (1963), p. 100.
23 For a different view from ours, see Riker, W.H. and Ordeshook, P.C. (1973), pp. 50–2; see also Stanley Benn's comments on their method, Chapter 10, pp. 255–60 of this volume.
24 Weber, M. (1947), pp. 24–6, and Weber, M. (1968), pp. 115–18, for this distinction.
25 See P.S. Cohen, Chapter 6 of this volume.
26 Wicksteed, P.H. (1946), vol. 1, p. 180.
27 Boulding, K. (1967); see also Ireland, T.R. (1969), and Johnson, D.B. (1971).
28 Riker, W.H. (1962), p. 22; for a discussion of Riker's notion of 'winning', see Oran Young, Chapter 9 of this volume.
29 Scitovsky, T. de (1943), p. 59.
30 Ibid., p. 60.
31 Frohlich, N., Oppenheimer, J.A. and Young, O.R. (1971), p. 28, n. 21.
32 This assumption is taken by Marxists as evidence of the alienation of labour in capitalist society. Anyone who actually *enjoys* his work would be receiving, on classical economic assumptions, a kind of utility bonus, analogous perhaps to 'consumer's surplus'.
33 For discussions of the role of 'assumptions' in economics, see Friedman, M. (1953), Nagel, E. (1963), Machlup, F. (1964), Rivett, K. (1970). Rivett cites other recent contributions in his footnotes.

Bibliography

ACHINSTEIN, P. (1967), 'Reichenbach, Hans', in Edwards, P. (ed.), *Encyclopedia of Philosophy*, New York, vol. 7, pp. 115–18.

BAIER, K. (1967), 'Welfare and preference', in Hook, S. (ed.), *Human Values and Policy*, New York, pp. 120–35.

BARRY, B. (1970), *Sociologists, Economists, and Democracy*, London.

BAUMOL, W.J. (1972), *Welfare Economics and the Theory of the State*, London.

BAUMOL, W.J. and QUANDT, R.E. (1964), 'Rules of thumb and optimally imperfect decisions', *American Economic Review*, LIV, pp. 23–46.

BLACK, M. (1967), 'Probability', in Edwards, P. (ed.), *Encyclopedia of Philosophy*, New York, vol. 6, pp. 464–79.

BLACK, M. (ed.) (1975), *Problems of Choice and Decision*, Ithaca, New York.

BORGER, R. and CIOFFI, F. (eds) (1970), *Explanation in the Behavioural Sciences*, Cambridge.

BOULDING, K. (1967), 'The basis of value judgments in economics', in Hook, S. (ed.), *Human Values and Policy*, New York.

BRODBECK, M. (ed.) (1968), *Readings in the Philosophy of the Social Sciences*, New York.

BUCHANAN, J. M. (1969), 'Is economics the science of choice?', in Streissler, E. (ed.), *Roads to Freedom*, London.

CROSS, J.G. (1969), *Economics of Bargaining*, New York.

DAVIDSON, D., SUPPES, P. and SIEGEL, S. (1957), *Decision-making: An Experimental Approach*, Stanford.

EDWARDS, W. (1967a), 'The theory of decision-making', in Edwards, W. and Tversky, A. (eds) (1967), pp. 13–64.

EDWARDS, W. (1967b), 'Behavioral decision theory', in Edwards, W. and Tversky, A. (eds) (1967), pp. 65–95.

EDWARDS, W. (1968), 'Decision-making: psychological aspects', in *International Encyclopedia of the Social Sciences*, New York, vol. IV.

EDWARDS, W. and TVERSKY, A. (eds) (1967), *Decision-making*, Harmondsworth.

FRIEDMAN, M. (1953), 'The methodology of positive economics', in *Essays in Positive Economics*, Chicago.

FROHLICH, N., OPPENHEIMER, J. A. and YOUNG, O. R. (1971), *Political Leadership and Collective Goods*, Princeton.

GEORGESCU-ROEGEN, N. (1966), 'Choice and revealed preference', in *Analytical Economics: Issues and Problems*, Cambridge, Mass., pp. 216–27.

HACKING, I. (1965), *The Logic of Statistical Inference*, Cambridge.

HACKING, I. (1972), 'The logic of Pascal's wager', *American Philosophical Quarterly*, IX, pp. 186–92.

HARSANYI, J. C. (1953), 'Cardinal utility in welfare economics and in the theory of risk-taking', *Journal of Political Economy*, LXI, pp. 434–5.

HARSANYI, J.C. (1956), 'Approaches to the bargaining problem before and after the theory of games', *Econometrica*, XXIV, pp. 144–57.

HARSANYI, J.C. (1963), 'A simplified bargaining model for the n-person co-operative game', *International Economic Review*, IV, pp. 194–220.

HARSANYI, J.C. (1965), 'Bargaining and conflict situations in the light of a new approach to game theory', *American Economic Review*, LV, pp. 447–57.

HARSANYI, J.C. (1966), 'A general theory of rational behaviour in game situations', *Econometrica*, XXXIV, pp. 613–34.

HARSANYI, J.C. (1968), 'Individualistic and functionalist explanations in the light of game theory', in Lakatos, I. and Musgrave, A. (eds), *Problems in the Philosophy of Science*, Amsterdam.

HEMPEL, C.G. (1965), *Aspects of Scientific Explanation*, New York.

HIBDON, J.E. (1969), *Price and Welfare Theory*, New York.

HICKS, J.R. (1946), *Value and Capital*, Oxford.

HOLLIS, M. and NELL, E.J. (1975), *Rational Economic Man*, Cambridge.

IRELAND, T.R. (1969), 'The calculus of philanthropy', *Public Choice*, VII, pp. 22–31.

JEVONS, W.S. (1965), *The Theory of Political Economy*, 5th edn, New York.

JOHNSON, D.B. (1971), *The Economics of Charity*, Blacksburg, Virginia.

JOHNSON, H.G. (1968), 'The economic approach to social questions', *The Public Interest*, XII, pp. 68–79.

KLAPPHOLZ, K. and AGASSI, J. (1959), 'Methodological prescriptions in economics', *Economica* XXVI, pp. 60–74.

KOOPMANS, T.C. (1957), *Three Essays on the State of Economic Science*, New York.

LANGE, O. (1945–6), 'The scope and method of economics', *Review of Economic Studies*, XIII, pp. 19–32.

LANGE, O. (1971), *Optimal Decisions*, Oxford.

LITTLE, I.M.D. (1949), 'A reformulation of the theory of consumer's behaviour', in *Oxford Economic Papers*, NS. I, pp. 90–9.

LUCE, R.D. and RAIFFA, H. (1957), *Games and Decisions*, New York.

MACHLUP, F. (1964), 'Professor Samuelson on theory and realism', *American Economic Review*, LIV, pp. 733–9.

MAJUMDAR, T. (1958), *The Measurement of Utility*, New York.

MARSHALL, A. (1920), *Principles of Economics*, 8th edn, London.

MILLER, D.W. and STARR, M.K. (1967), *The Structure of Human Decisions*, Englewood Cliffs, New Jersey.

MISES, L. VON (1963), *Human Action*, 2nd edn, New Haven.

MISES, R. VON (1957), *Probability, Statistics and Truth*, 2nd rev. English edn, New York.

NAGEL, E. (1963), 'Assumptions in economic theory', in *American Economic Review*, LIII, pp. 211–19.

NEUMANN, J. VON, and MORGENSTERN, O. (1953), *Theory of Games and Economic Behaviour*, 3rd edn, Princeton.

NIGEL, H. (1971), *Paradoxes of Rationality: theory of meta-games and political behaviour*, Cambridge, Mass., and London.

PYLE, D.H. and TURNOVSKY, S.J. (1970), 'Safety-first and expected utility maximization in mean-standard deviation portfolio analysis', in *Review of Economics and Statistics*, LII, pp. 75–81.

REICHENBACH, H. (1949), *The Theory of Probability*, Berkeley and Los Angeles.

RESCHER, N. (1959–60), 'Choice without preference', *Kant-Studien*, LI, pp. 142–75.

RIKER, W.H. (1962), *The Theory of Political Coalitions*, New Haven.

RIKER, W.H. and ORDESHOOK, P.C. (1973), *An Introduction to Positive Political Theory*, Englewood Cliffs, New Jersey.

RIVETT, K., (1970), ' "Suggest" or "entail"?: The derivation and confirmation of economic hypotheses', in *Australian Economic Papers*, pp. 127–48.

SAMUELSON, P.A. (1938), 'A note on the pure theory of consumer's behaviour', *Economica*, V, pp. 61–71.

SAMUELSON, P.A. (1948), 'Consumption theory in terms of revealed preference', *Economica*, XV, pp. 243–53.

SAMUELSON, P.A. (1953), 'Consumption theorems in terms of over-compensation rather than indifference comparisons', *Economica*, XX, pp. 1–9.

SAMUELSON, P.A. (1963), 'Problems of methodology', *American Economic Review Proceedings*, LIII, pp. 231–6.

SCHELLING, T. (1963), *The Strategy of Conflict*, New York and Oxford.

SCITOVSKY, T. DE (1943), 'A note on profit maximization and its implications', *Review of Economic Studies*, XI, pp. 57–60.

SIMON, H.A. (1955), 'A behavioral model of rational choice', *Quarterly Journal of Economics*, LXIX, pp. 99–118.

SIMON, H.A. (1957), *Models of Man*, New York.

SIMON, H.A. (1969), 'The mathematical reduction of rationality', in Krimerman, L.I. (ed.), *The Nature and Scope of Social Science*, New York.

194

THRALL, R.M., COOMBS, C.H. and DAVIS, R.L. (eds) (1954), *Decision Processes*, New York.

TISDELL, C.A. (1968), *The Theory of Price, Uncertainty, Production, and Profit*, Princeton.

TORGERSON, W.S. (1958), *Theory and Methods of Scaling*, New York.

TULLOCK, G. (1964), 'The irrationality of intransitivity', *Oxford Economic Papers*, N.S. XVI, pp. 401–6.

WATKINS, J.W.N. (1970), 'Imperfect rationality', in Borger, R. and Cioffi, F. (eds) (1970).

WEBER, M. (1947), *Theory of Social and Economic Organization*, ed. Parsons, T., New York.

WEBER, M. (1968), *Economy and Society* (3 vols), ed. Roth, G. and Wittich, C., New York.

WICKSELL, K. (1946), *Lectures on Political Economy*, ed. Robbins, L., trans. Classen, E., London.

WICKSTEED, P.H. (1946), *The Common Sense of Political Economy*, London.

WILLIAMS, J.D. (1954), *The Compleat Strategyst*, New York.

WRIGHT, G.H. VON (1963), *The Logic of Preference*, Edinburgh.

8

Rational behaviour as a basis for economic theories[1]

C.A. Tisdell

A   The scope of the essay

The rationality of economic man is fundamental to a substantial body of economic theory. This is so whether we consider neo-classical economic theory as so expertly outlined by Sir John Hicks in *Value and Capital* or more recent developments such as those begun by John von Neumann and Oskar Morgenstern with their publication of the *Theory of Games and Economic Behavior*. Indeed, there is hardly any area of economics in which the rationality postulate is unimportant. Though it has come under increasing attack in recent years, for example from H. Simon, it still retains its hold on the subject, with increasing qualifications.

In 1945, Oscar Lange in considering the scope and method of economics stated that the postulate of rationality[2]

> provides us with a most powerful tool for simplification of theoretical analysis. For, if a unit of decision acts rationally, its decisions in any given situation can be predicted by mere application of the rules of logic (and of mathematics). In absence of rational action such prediction could be made only after painstaking empirical study of the uniformities in the decision patterns of the unit.

However, Lange overestimated the value of rational behaviour as a basis for economic theorizing. More than logic and mathematics are involved in the prediction of rational behaviour. First, one needs to know the nature of that which is to be maximized. This might only be discovered after painstaking empirical study and even then success is not guaranteed, e.g. actors might disguise their motives or not be exactly aware of them. Second, in order to predict the rational behaviour of an individual, knowledge of his feasible region is required. Logic and mathematics alone do not inform us of this region. Third, unless the relevant objective functions show some permanency, at least in their basic properties, the theory of rational behaviour is likely to be of little predictive value. Economists claim that the objective functions of economic man do have certain permanent properties, e.g. it is sometimes claimed that firms maximize profit consistently, and that the preference functions of consumers are always strictly concave. Given the permanent nature of an economic agent's objective function and his region of feasible behaviour, the postulate of practical rationality has considerable predictive power, provided the economic agent is well informed about his possibilities, and the theorist about the agent's perceptions.

It is sometimes assumed, as in neo-classical economic theory, that the economic agent is so knowledgeable that he can select a set of actions (a strategy) which cannot be bettered from his point of view. He is able to act with unbounded rationality in the restrictive sense that he knows his optimal option X and chooses X because he knows it to be optimal.

The concept of 'as if' rationality should be distinguished from the concept of unbounded rationality. The 'as if' concept is used in some economic theories. Provided an individual *consistently* acts as if he is pursuing an objective to maximum advantage, he is rational in the 'as if' sense and his behaviour can be predicted. An individual may be acting rationally in the 'as if' sense in choosing the optimal option even when he does not choose it because he knows it to be optimal.

The hypothesis of unbounded rationality has been attacked by Simon and others as inapplicable to economic life. In my view, it is more relevant than is commonly realized. Unbounded rational behaviour is possible under conditions of limited knowledge both of preferences and of the external world. In some circumstances where unbounded rationality cannot be attained immediately, it may be approached by search and attained in time. It may also be characteristic of groups on average or be ensured by selection processes.

Nevertheless, there are clearly circumstances in which unbounded rational behaviour is impossible, now or in the long term; I shall mention some of these circumstances. In section B, I consider possibilities for unbounded rational economic behaviour, on the

197

assumption that interdependence of groups of individuals is unimportant. Even with this assumption rationality postulates cannot always predict behaviour. I then relax this assumption. Using von Neumann and Morgenstern's game theory, I show that the behaviour of well-informed interdependent rational individuals cannot always be precisely predicted and, indeed, some rationality conditions are not consistent with any possible social settlement at all. Some lack or deficiency in rationality of individuals can be required for social settlements.

B Rational behaviour by individual economic agents if social behaviour is unimportant

1 Unbounded rationality

Theories of the economic behaviour of individuals are normally based on three elements:
  (i) the individual's preference ordering of his possible outcomes;
  (ii) what he believes or knows to be the available set of alternative strategies;
  (iii) a specified relationship between the agent's chosen strategy, on the one hand, and (i) and (ii) on the other.
Whether an individual acts rationally in choosing a strategy will clearly be a function of (i) and (ii), which we may call the antecedent conditions. Thus, if an individual does not know the exact relationship between his outcomes and his choice of strategy, he may be unable to choose his best strategy. Ignorance may restrict his ability to optimize.

However, neo-classical economic theory, which is a major body of current economic theory, specifies a set of antecedent conditions which make unbounded rationality possible. In this state the individual can identify his optimum optimorum and choose a correspondingly appropriate strategy. These conditions are:
  (i) The individual has a complete weak preference ordering[3] of his possible outcomes which is transitive, irreflexive and reflects the true preference of the individual.
  (ii) The individual knows of all of his available strategies and relates the outcomes exactly and correctly to his strategies.
Given the further assumption that the process of deciding is itself costless, a rational individual under these conditions will select the optimum strategy from the available set.

The conditions are rarely satisfied, however. When they are not, we are faced with the following questions:
  1 To what extent is it rational for an economic agent to attempt

to satisfy the stated antecedent conditions and put his choice problem into the above form?

2 Is it possible for an individual to choose the strategy that would be optimal under those conditions and to be sure that it is optimal?

Simon stresses[4] that it is not as a rule rational to put one's choice problem in the above form because information gathering and processing involves a cost. So, too, does calculation. Since goal-seeking behaviour involves search and calculation, goal-seeking man seeks a satisfactory outcome rather than an optimal one.

> While economic man maximizes—selects the best alternative from all those available to him; his cousin, whom we shall call administrative man, satisfices—looks for a course of action that is satisfactory or 'good enough'. Examples of satisficing criteria that are familiar enough to businessmen, if unfamilar to most economists are 'share of market', 'adequate profit', 'fair price'.[5]

Unlike economic man, administrative man uses very crude and undetailed pictures of the world and rules of thumb to reach his decisions. He has limited capacities for storing and processing information. Even if a decision-maker could be given complete knowledge of the relationship between his strategies and outcomes, it might be beyond his ability to store, use and grasp this knowledge. Nor would he have the capacity (as a rule) to order all of his possible strategies completely and transitively.

2 Discussion of the antecedent conditions for unbounded rationality

It is, I think, necessary to concede all of Simon's points. Yet, they do not render neo-classical economic theories irrelevant; for the neo-classical antecedent conditions outlined above are really much stronger than would be required to ensure unbounded rational behaviour.

An individual may not order his outcomes completely or transitively and may not perceive his outcomes and strategies completely and correctly, and yet his adopted strategy may be the best possible one. He may know from the *properties* of the objective function and the feasible set, that it is unnecessary to consider all possibilities in order to select an optimal strategy. Yet, he acts none the less with unbounded rationality, since he is able to decide on an optimal strategy even though he cannot satisfy all the neo-classical antecedent conditions.

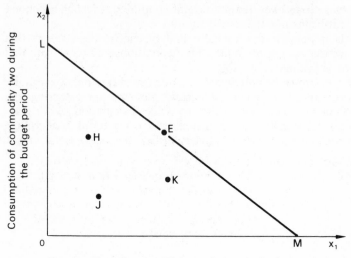

Figure 8.1

To illustrate some of the possibilities, consider a consumer first. Assume that the individual can always be made better off by a vectorial increase[6] in the quantity of two goods. Let us suppose that he has budgeted to spend a given amount on these two goods and that his problem is to select the most preferred attainable combination.

The alternative combinations of the goods (one and two) which the consumer can buy in the budget period might be represented by points on and in triangle OLM in Figure 8.1.

But given his preference ordering of the consumption possibilities *and* assuming that non-expenditure yields no satisfaction, the optimal attainable outcome for the consumer falls along the closed interval LM. Given the general ordering properties, the individual's preference ordering of bundles below and above LM is irrelevant. Intransitive orderings in these areas are of no consequence provided they are not inconsistent with the proposition that the most preferred *attainable* combination is on LM. For example, imagine that the consumer ranks H, J, and K as follows: $H > J > K$; and H and K as $H < K$. The second ordering conflicts with the first. But if E is ranked higher than H, J, and K, this intransitivity is irrelevant since E is attainable. Nor is it necessary to order the possibilities below and above LM completely. The ordering assumptions (of transitivity and completeness) of the neo-classical theory are stronger than is required to ensure the unbounded rational behaviour which is predicted.

Even along the interval LM, it may be unnecessary to order possibilities completely and transitively. The preference ordering of combinations along the budget-line LM might have a single peak and be strictly unimodal.[7] If the consumer knows this much, complete and consistent evaluation of the possibilities is unnecessary for optimizing behaviour.

Perfect knowledge of the feasible set of strategies or outcomes is also unnecessary for unbounded rational behaviour. If the consumer's indifference curves are tilted relative to the budget-line, it can be the case that his optimal consumption bundle is the one at L. Figure 8.2 indicates a case in which the individual's highest attainable indifference curve, I_1, is reached if all of his budgeted expenditure is allocated to commodity two. None of commodity one is consumed. The slope of LM shows the rate at which the goods can be exchanged in the market. However, the individual need not know this exact rate in order to choose L. The choice of L is optimal provided that the absolute slope of the budget-line is greater than the absolute slope of the consumer's indifference curve at L. Armed only with the information that the exchange-rate yields a budget-line steeper than the indifference curve at L (i.e. without knowing the exact exchange-rate) the consumer will be able to make a choice, satisfying the conditions for unbounded rationality, viz. that it is optimal, is known to be so by the agent, and is chosen for that reason.

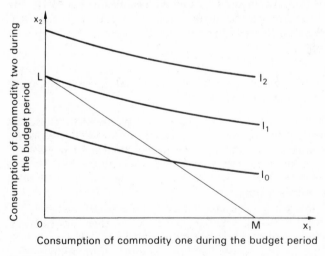

Figure 8.2

I do not know the exact price of some commodities though I have an idea (indeed, I know) the *range* in which their prices fall. My lack of knowledge about the exact prices of different types of bicycles and of luxury cars need not, given my income (and that I have a preference for comfortable transport), prevent me from acting rationally in my choice of a means of transport. Moreover, intransitivities and incompleteness in my ordering of bicycles and luxury cars may be inconsequential for my choice. In all these cases my choice can be unboundedly rational even though the strong antecedent conditions (pp. 198–9) are not satisfied. But even more significantly, I can know in advance circumstances where these conditions are not satisfied and yet my (rational) choice will be the same as if they happened to be satisfied.

Consider another example. Given the strict unimodality of its profit function, a firm need not know the profitability of all possible levels of output in order to act with unbounded rationality; it need know only about those in the neighbourhood of the output which yields a true maximum. Once an output is discovered such that profit is reduced by any and every set of small deviations from it, this output maximizes profit, and there is no need to evaluate profitability beyond its neighbourhood. However, while this indicates that the strong antecedent conditions specified are not required for unbounded rational behaviour, *the problem remains that in most instances the neighbourhood has still to be discovered.*

It is apparent, then, that the conditions for preference orderings and states of knowledge postulated by neo-classical theorists are stronger than are necessary for unbounded rational behaviour. The degree to which they can be relaxed has not been fully explored by economists.

3 Cases where immediate unbounded rational choice is impossible because of incomplete knowledge

None of the above speculation shows that unbounded optimizing behaviour is the rule. In many instances, prior knowledge is insufficient to enable the optimum to be found. It may be possible to improve this knowledge by search and computation but the cost involved in this effort is likely to make the pursuit of unbounded rationality self-defeating.

It is of interest to distinguish three choice situations:
  (a) where the individual engages in further information-gathering and processing before making a choice;
  (b) where he acts on the basis of available information;
  (c) where he acts on the basis of available information, but his

choice, besides giving him a direct payoff, yields information which has application to future choices. The last case may be the most common one. Let us consider each of those cases in turn.

(a) Further activity prior to choice

H. Simon concentrates on the case in which an individual can obtain further information prior to his choice of an action. He is dubious of all models of optimizing behaviour, including models based on expected gain and expected utility maximization:[8]

> Economic man has a complete and consistent system of preferences that allows him always to choose among the alternatives open to him; he is always completely aware of what these alternatives are; there are no limits on the complexity of the computations he can perform in order to determine which alternatives are best; probability calculations are neither frightening nor mysterious to him. Within the past decade, in its extension to competitive game situations, and to decision-making under uncertainty, this body of theory has reached a state of Thomistic refinement that possesses considerable normative interest, but little discernable relation to the actual or possible behaviour of flesh-and-blood human beings.

Since optimizing behaviour involves costly search, and payoffs are uncertain, a typical individual does not hold out for maximum rewards but is prepared to settle for a satisfactory reward; he sets himself an aspiration level. Once this level is reached, he does not search further even though his best discovered strategy may well be short of the optimal one. If after a certain amount of search no strategy is discovered which attains it, the aspiration level may be revised downward or alternatively search effort may increase.[9] Beyond this, details are not given.

Yet the type of behaviour which Simon describes is also predicted by some types of optimization theories. If the objective of the individual is maximization of expected net gain or utility and if search is required which involves cost and only probable discoveries, to maximize this value requires a stopping rule, e.g. the rule, 'if one is selling a used article, as soon as an offer better than $2 is found, accept'. It is usually rational to revise this stopping value as search continues and uncertainty is reduced. Whether or not individuals know complicated sequential optimizing procedures is beside the point. Such procedures can approximate and predict their behaviour in the 'as if' rationality sense mentioned on page 197.

203

If there is permanency in the relationships, the 'as if' rationality concept can be of predictive value even if the behaviour does not fit the restrictive concept of unbounded rationality. However, in stating this I do not rule out the possibility that some search behaviour may exhibit such rationality.

A number of economists have developed models of unbounded rationality in information-search and in the decision to cease searching and decide between the options. Thus, Baumol and Quandt mention a rule for *optimally imperfect decisions*: 'the appropriate (though not very helpful) marginal condition for what one may call an *optimally imperfect decision* ... [is] that the marginal cost of additional information gathering or more refined calculation be equal to its marginal (expected) gross yield.'[10] Since there is likely to be uncertainty about the expected values, however, the residual uncertainty would result in a random element in behaviour, i.e. random in relation to the objective world. While knowledge puts some limits on it, some randomness remains since it is not profitable (on average) to distinguish finely between the consequences of the available strategies.

(b) No further information prior to choice and no additional information of future value

Much economic decision-making is, of course, based on decision-rules—for example, cost-plus pricing—which obviate any activities of information-search and processing. Such decision-making may appear irrational unless the cost of decision-making is taken into account. Baumol and Quandt have shown how various rules of thumb when used by management do in fact maximize expected profit. The expected net gains from more refined procedures do not justify their additional cost. Under certain conditions cost-plus pricing is optimal even though the decision-procedure for each choice separately does not satisfy the antecedent conditions for unbounded rationality required by the neo-classical model. If demand is fluctuating the cost of specifying it closely in any period may exceed the gains from an improved pricing policy. Baumol and Quandt argue that 'rules of thumb are among the more efficient pieces of equipment of optimal decision-making'.[11]

In other choice situations, the agent may be interested in assessing the relationships between his options (alternative prices, say) and his end (maximum profits), may have engaged in some information-search, but must now decide on the basis of information which does not allow him to identify the optimum optimorum. In such a case, the information may nevertheless be sufficient to rule out some strategies on the grounds that choice of any of them is irrational. Even if the individual's appreciation of the possibilities does not lead him to the optimum choice, it may be possible to specify certain conditions that his behaviour would satisfy, if rational.

Take the case of a purely competitive firm which prefers greater profit to less and so wishes to maximize its profit. Its profit can be expressed as

$$\pi = px - (C(x))$$
Profit = Total Revenue—Total Cost

where p represents the price per unit for its product and x the quantity of output of its product during the relevant period. The output for the period must be determined by the firm before the price for the product is known. Output is the controlled variable of the firm and price is uncontrolled. At the time when x must be determined the exact price of its product is unknown by the firm but the total cost function is known. However, imagine that the firm is able to give an upper and lower limit for the possible price of its product. Letting p_o and p_m represent these limits for price, the firm believes that p must fall in the range $p_o \leq p \leq p_m$. Then if its marginal cost can be represented by the curve MC in Figure 8.3, it is irrational for the firm to produce an output outside the range $x_1 \leq x \leq x_m$. Given the prior limit on p, profit is certain to be greater by producing *an* output in this range, than by producing any output outside of it. Profit for x_m is certain to be greater than

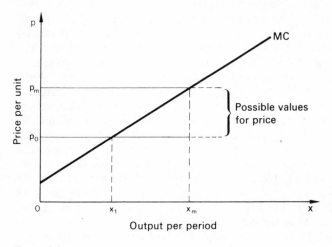

Figure 8.3

for $x > x_m$ and profit for x_1 is certain to be greater than for $x < x_1$. The smaller the band of values of prices believed to be possible, the more closely does the band of possible rational action accord with neo-classical unbounded action *provided* that the actual p is included in the predicted range. If the band tends to shift in the same direction as p, many of the neo-classical predictions about variations of supply are approximated. However, as cobweb theories of markets[12] indicate, the band of predictions does not always vary in the direction of the actual price. In order to predict market changes, economic theories require data on how economic agents form their predictions. A number of dynamic market theories, e.g. cobweb models, incorporate rather mechanistic theories about this, e.g. that firms predict that the price of the next period is the same as the last and act accordingly, or that it is a weighted average of the prices of the last n periods, and so on. In an economic world of perpetual disequilibrium, models of this type seem more relevant than neo-classical general equilibrium models.

(c) No further information prior to choice but additional information of future value

Possibly the most common economic situation is one in which the individual must make an immediate choice on the basis of information too limited to satisfy the requirements of unbounded rationality, but in which the choice not only yields an immediate payoff to the agent but also additional information which may be of future value in decision-making.

Consider the case of a firm which wishes to maximize its profit. The firm is assumed to know that its profit function is strictly unimodal[13] and stationary in time. Suppose that the firm can improve its knowledge of the profit function only by trial-and-error in production, i.e. by trying different levels of production and observing their effect on profit. It cannot, for example, purchase information or conduct market surveys, and so on, which might yield greater information. In each period, the firm produces and sells a particular quantity of output and observes its profit. In the light of these observations it is able to adjust its output in future periods. Assuming that the firm always desires increased profit, some adjustments of output are irrational. This can be illustrated from Figures 8.4 and 8.5. The firm's profit and output per period are indicated in these figures. The height of the bars in the figures indicate the observed profit at the corresponding outputs.

Consider the case of Figure 8.4. The firm first produces the output corresponding to point 1 and then the output corresponding to

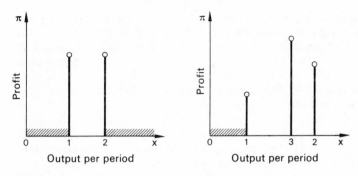

Figure 8.4   *Figure 8.5*

point 2, and observes that profit is the same in both instances. To produce an output subsequently in the banded interval, i.e. at 1 or to its left and at 2 or to its right, would be irrational, since greater profit must be achieved by producing an output between 1 and 2. As the search proceeds, the area of possible rational behaviour is liable to become smaller and smaller.

This is indicated in the example of Figure 8.5. On the basis of the first trial (the output corresponding to 1) no levels of output can be ruled out as being worthy of a trial. If 2 is subsequently tried, levels of output at and to the left of 1 can be ruled out as optimal (but no others). However, if the level of output corresponding to 3 is then tried, levels of output at or above 2 can be ruled out as sub-optimal. Thus the area of rational search is reduced to the levels of output between 1 and 2.[14]

If a decision-maker's objective function satisfies appropriate general mathematical properties, then, under stationary conditions, use of a number of search and response procedures ensures that behaviour tends to the unbounded optimum.[15] In circumstances like this, unbounded rational behaviour is approached as the number of trials is increased *provided* that the function which is to be maximized remains stationary. In general, the convexity properties of neo-classical economic models are such that in a stationary world convergence to unbounded rational behaviour is assured by the use of sensible trial-and-error procedures.[16]

The above analysis indicates that search or experimentation in some particular directions would be irrational under these conditions. However, we may also ask ourselves whether search or experiment would be rational at all. If an agent is unwilling to take the chance that profit on a new trial is lower than the highest profit already known to be attainable, search is irrational even if it is not irrationally directed. On the other hand, search or experimentation in a direction which is not irrational holds out the *chance* of greater profit not only in the trial period but in the future as well. Nevertheless, as in the above case, it may be impossible to assign a probability to the chance of finding a more profitable strategy and to estimate the magnitude of increased profitability which is involved. Within certain bounds, faith rather than rationality becomes the spring of human action.

Using the prior information about the nature of the profit function, the area of rational search can be narrowed as search takes place. Different sets of prior information enable the rational search area to be reduced in different ways.

For several circumstances in which the general nature of the objective function is known, mathematicians have suggested effective methods of search. These include Fibonacci search, search by the golden section, and various gradient methods.[17] In some problems, a number of these methods can be applied and each has different properties and uncertainty characteristics. None are irrational but neither does one method dominate the others in all characteristics which the decision-maker might feel to be important. It might be difficult or impossible to decide rationally which method should be used. Taking into account the extra costs of thinking about this and the very improbable gains, it might not be irrational to choose a search method by chance or faith once the field of possible rational methods has been narrowed down.

4   Rationality and equilibrium

In neo-classical economic models, unbounded rational behaviour occurs only if the *equilibrium* conditions of the models are satisfied. Equilibrium and unbounded rationality are inseparable in this context. Hicks makes this quite clear in *Value and Capital*: 'The degree of disequilibrium marks the extent to which expectations are cheated, and plans go astray.'[18] When the economy is in perfect equilibrium, the expectations of economic agents are fully realized and their plans are ideal; for then no one is inclined to upset the balance, since no one believes he could improve his position by a change of policy. If equilibrium is the rule, unbounded rationality is the rule. To attack the value of the concept of unbounded rationality is to attack the value of neo-classical equilibrium analysis. We live, however, in a world of disequilibrium and constant change. Conditions do not remain stationary enough to permit any substantial movements to equilibrium or unbounded rationality, and important economic decisions must be made in those circumstances. By studying only equilibrium conditions and changes of equilibria (the approach of comparative statics) we can fail to make useful economic predictions and policy decisions.

However, one can see a number of ways in which the neo-classical position can be defended. Comparative statics is of greatest value for policy and analytical purposes when the convergence to an equilibrium is extremely rapid. A neo-classical economist might hold that convergence to unbounded rational behaviour is extremely rapid because on average economic agents are well supplied with prior information. Though the world is not stationary it changes at a rate which enables unbounded rationality to be approached.

Nevertheless, a number of economists have speculated that randomness of decision-making is increasing in communities where wealth is increasing. Rational decision-making requires deliberation and other actions which take time. Time is a scarce resource. Linder,[19] building on an earlier suggestion of Harrod, suggests that time for decision-making is becoming comparatively more costly in terms of the alternatives forgone. As a result of economic progress, the value of time for consumption activities has increased and with increasing wealth the marginal disutility of a given error decreases. Hence, decisions are given less time and made on the basis of reduced evidence. In consequence, the consumer more often engages in impulse buying, is more subject to influences by advertising, persuasion and so on. The neo-classical model of unbounded rationality becomes increasingly inapplicable to consumers. Even if the time devoted to decision-making does not fall with economic progress, but even rises slightly, increases in the range of strategies, possibilities and outcomes as a result of technical progress may result in a *relative* decrease of knowledge by the individual (even if his absolute knowledge increases) so that the randomness of his behaviour increases. Increases in the shortage of time has many interesting social consequences, some of which are mentioned by Linder.

5   Incomplete preference orderings

Although incompleteness in an individual's preference ordering need not rule out the possibility of immediate unbounded rationality (see section 2) and although where it does, unbounded rationality may eventually be achieved by search (see section 3), there are circumstances in which incomplete preferences make unbounded rationality impossible. Neo-classical economists did not consider the possibility of incompleteness in preference orderings. Yet there are clearly circumstances in which rational individuals need to search and explore because of gaps in their preference orderings.

I do not know my preference for whale and seal meat, not having tested either, and there are some very fundamental matters (concerned with alternative organizations of society) about which I cannot decide my preference and so on. I cannot accept Wicksteed's view:[20]

> Any alternatives, however constituted, which could conceivably be offered to the man would find him either decisively preferring one to the other or unable to decide between them; that is to say, every conceivable alternative stands either above or below any other that you may select, or on a level with it. And the things so valued constitute the man's relative scale of preferences, the basis upon which his life is built. This scale of preferences is the register of the man's ideals, of the relative weight and value that he attaches to this or that alternative under every variety of condition.

If A and B are two attainable alternatives, it is conceivable that an individual does not know his preference ordering of A and B. He may, however, try A and then B or vice versa and develop an ordering on the basis of this experience. But is it not conceivable in some circumstances that his final ordering depends upon the sequence in which A and B are tried? Trying A first, then B, the individual might conclude that he prefers B to A; had the sequence been B then A, he might have preferred A to B. Thus, he reaches *contradictory* conclusions depending upon the sequence of the trials. The individual is mistaken in cases like this if he believes that experience will enable him to decide what he really prefers, since what he prefers will depend on the order of trial.

Choices of alternative occupations, choice of exposure to cultural experiences, choice of a partner, choice of different forms of social organization run foul of the above possibility. One reason why this is so is that the individual is *changed* by his experience; his values, aspirations and expectations are altered by his experience and observations.[21] Attempts by an individual to map out his preferences exactly may lead to their deflection. The problem is analogous to the problem of deflection of particles by observation which is discussed in quantum mechanics. Clearly, deflection is not significant in all types of search but it seems highly probable that this phenomenon is important in areas where our feelings are most strongly influenced, e.g. feelings bordering on the spiritual. A searcher can conceivably be deceived into believing that search is efficacious in *discovering* the optimal strategy even though it is the search itself that generates the preferences by which the strategy is judged best.

6 Aggregative and selective theories

Rational behaviour is sometimes claimed by economists to be characteristic of individuals in aggregate but not of any particular individual. It is an 'average' concept. For example, Hicks says that the theory of demand does study human beings but only as entities having certain patterns of market behaviour[22] and postulates an *ideal consumer* who acts according to a scale of preferences and 'chooses that alternative, out of the various alternatives open to him which he most prefers, or ranks most highly'.[23] This preference hypothesis is basic to the traditional economic theory of demand. Hicks[24] claims that:

> the preference hypothesis only acquires a *prima facie* plausibility when it is applied to a statistical average. To assume that the representative consumer acts like an ideal consumer is a hypothesis worth testing; to assume that an actual person, the Mr Brown or Mr Jones who lives round the corner, does in fact act in such a way does not deserve a moment's consideration.

However, the predictions of theories based on the average may be markedly wrong if there are considerable deviations around average behaviour in a group. It is also conceivable that all or most members of a group may be so ill-informed that the preference hypothesis is not typically satisfied.

Again it is sometimes said that forces of selection ensure that the more rational decision-makers in society obtain expanded roles at the expense of the irrational. Thus economic decisions, especially on the production side, tend to be made by rational individuals, but rational in the very limited sense of maximizing on the basis of defined objectives. Alchian[25] for example, suggests that only firms and managers that maximize profit are likely to survive in the long run and he therefore expects the bulk of managers and firms to be profit-maximizers. But this supposes intense competition. If competition is not intense, management may pursue other goals such as maximizing sales subject to a satisfactory level of profit and do so in an optimal way. It may still be acting rationally in the sense that it selects the best strategy for its scale of preferences. However, it is not under external (competitive) pressure to optimize and may in fact fail to do so; thus, for example, so called managerial slack or inefficiency may creep into the administration of the firm. On the consumption side of the economy, the concept of rationality by selection is less relevant; even here, however, more irrational individuals may tend to obtain lower incomes, and so have a smaller impact on aggregate consumption.

C Rationality of groups of economic agents and the theory of games

1 Introduction

The outcome for any one individual as a rule depends not only upon his own strategy but also upon the strategies of other individuals. Rational individuals will take account of this interdependence and this creates new possibilities many of which can be analysed by constructs from the theory of games.

As Morgenstern and von Neumann put it:[26]

> [In a social economy,] every participant can determine the variables which describe his own actions but not those of the others. Nevertheless those 'alien' variables cannot, from his point of view, be described by statistical assumptions. This is because the others are guided, just as he himself, by rational principles—whatever that may mean—and no *modus procedendi* can be correct which does not attempt to understand those principles and the interactions of the conflicting interests of all the participants. Sometimes some of these interests run more or less parallel—then we are nearer to a simple maximum problem. But they can just as well be opposed. The general theory must cover all of these possibilities, all intermediary stages, and all their combinations.

The problems dealt with in the theory of games of strategy have been largely ignored by neo-classical economists or only treated under highly restrictive assumptions such as those of the theory of perfect or pure competition. Theories of perfect competition frequently assume that the equilibrium exists and that each individual, since his trading is small in relation to the market, is faced by fixed conditions. Even traditional theories which depart from the assumption of perfect competition ignore game-like interdependence, e.g. the theories of Joan Robinson[27] and Chamberlin[28] and the standard textbook analyses of cartels, which treat these as monopolists. An early and important exception was F. Edgeworth,[29] who analysed coalitions in some detail and predicted that, as a result of the tendency for economic agents to combine, solutions to economic problems would become increasingly indeterminate. However, the traditional economic theory of market competition is deficient in so far as it does not explain the conditions under which economic agents combine. Their degree of coalition is taken as datum, not as something to be explained.

Let us consider how far the theory of games, operating with various rationality postulates, can remedy some or all of these deficiencies. In the discussion which follows, I shall be considering two questions:

1 How far can theory of games treatment of interacting agents generate determinate predictions of their behaviour?

2 How far are they dependent on or committed to unrealistic assumptions or simplifying omissions concerning the circumstances and condition of the interacting agents?

2 Individual rationality in two-person games

In a two-person zero-sum game, a loss for one player is a gain for the other. Interests of the players are diametrically opposed and there is no scope for co-operation. In this type of game, it is rational for each player to try to minimize the gain of his opponent. If any player, A, believes that his opponent, B, is able to minimize his (A's) gain for whatever strategy is adopted by A, it is rational for A to adopt the strategy which maximizes the minimum of this gain. The same is true, *mutatis mutandis*, for B. If both act in this way, the saddle-point value for the game is reached and von Neumann and Morgenstern regard this as the solution for the game.[30] As von Neumann has shown, every two-person zero-sum game has a saddle-point for either pure or mixed strategies.[31] A mixed strategy requires a player to select his strategy by chance. If all his opponent can know is the probability with which a player makes his selection, this randomization raises the player's minimum expected payoff. The rational solution requires the player to build in to his behaviour an element of unpredictability i.e. if each player wishes to maximize his (constrained) expected utility.

But as Simon has observed,[32] the knowledge attributed to the players by this theory is greater, and the attribution even more unreasonable, than in neo-classical economic theory. Each player is assumed to know all the available strategies, outcomes and preferences of the other players. In practice, each of these assumptions is likely to be violated. Once again, however, it can be argued that the assumptions are stronger than necessary for von Neumann and Morgenstern's proposed solution. Under certain conditions, strategies need only be evaluated in the neighbourhood of the saddle-point; or if the game is repeated or replicated the solution of von Neumann and Morgenstern might be approached in the limit. The arguments are analogous to those which were outlined in section B2.

Nevertheless, the formulation of the game-situation by von

Neumann and Morgenstern leaves out of account a number of strategic factors which may be important. In practice, an astute player can take advantage of other players' misperceptions and weaknesses. If an opponent does not know all of your strategy set this can be advantageous and it may be in your interest to keep him suitably ignorant. One can gain an advantage by making information selectively available to an opponent. There may also be advantages in misleading an opponent about your preferences and your probable actions. A player can sometimes obtain an advantage by tricking his opponent into believing, for instance, that he will adopt a particular strategy, while actually planning another which will be very advantageous if the opponent falls for the ruse. While economic situations rarely satisfy the conditions for zero-sum games, the strategy of misinforming competitors is common in business competition. Multi-national corporations, for example, may indicate to competitors that they intend building plants in particular countries when they have no such aim. Their aim is to deter competitors from establishing competitive plants in these countries. To carry out their ruse they may purchase land, begin negotiations with governments, etc. The point is so elementary and obvious that it is puzzling why strategic aspects of information have been given so little attention in the theory of games of strategy. Even in zero-sum games, differences in the beliefs and knowledge of the players can be decisive for the outcome of the game.

3 Three-or-more person games

Games involving three or more players hold out the possibility that a subset of players can form an alliance or coalition to their mutual advantage. This introduces new barriers to rational behaviour and may make it impossible to find any completely rational settlement for a game.

(a) The weakest von Neumann and Morgenstern rationality postulates for an n-person game

Von Neumann and Morgenstern make only modest claims for their theories of n-person games and they clearly believed their ideas to be just a starting point. They try to predict the behaviour of rational well-informed players and to narrow down the likely behaviour and outcomes by invoking successively more restrictive rationality postulates. Throughout their *Theory* they assume that coalitions and co-operative agreements are reached outside the game and that these are respected by the contracting parties.

This is a weak spot in their theory and they indicate that they would like to develop an approach which does not rely on this assumption.[33] Let us, however, accept it at this stage.

In the opinion of von Neumann and Morgenstern a group of rational individuals will co-operate if co-operation is Paretian-better than non-co-operation for that group, i.e. if at least some members of the group gain from co-operation and no individuals in it lose by it. Thus, the entire group forms a grand coalition when it is in their Paretian interest to do so.

Clearly this is a theory with limited explanatory and predictive power since nothing is postulated about the behaviour of every other possible coalition, as is done under stronger postulates. But in any case it seems to be untrue as a statement of the way rational individuals would act in even the limited range of cases covered by the theory. A group may fail to form a grand coalition when it is in their Paretian interest to do so.[34] Conflict about sharing the grand coalition payoff or mere ignorance may stand in the way of Paretian optimal agreement. Again, the costs of forming a coalition must be taken into account. Communication and discussion are not costless and if the cost tends to fall on initiators, their expected gains may be less than their cost even though, taking account of overall gains and cost of arranging a coalition, there might be a net benefit to the group. Because of this externality, it is in the interest of no set of individuals to begin the process required for a grand coalition. This difficulty is likely to be more important the larger the group since communication costs rise and individual gains from a grand coalition tend to be smaller. Enforcement of agreements may be difficult or impossible. The larger the group the more costly and difficult is it likely to be to police violations of agreements, and enforce sanctions.

There is another limitation of the theory of coalition formation. The theory of games of strategy assumes that parties can enter into coalitions and dissolve these without influencing their range of choices of strategy. Coalitions are reversible at will and do not alter the strategic possibilities of a game. In practice, however, entry into a coalition may reduce available strategies of the co-operating individual players, i.e. reduce the flexibility of the participants. In an uncertain world in which conditions are changing, individuals can often endanger their expected gains by adopting a policy which reduces flexibility.

In a business cartel for example, the members are rarely able to adopt strategies which maximize their combined profit because these mostly result in a loss of (future) options for some members. For example, joint profit may be maximized by closing down all

215

the plants of some companies in the cartel and by not advertising and selling the variety of products originally produced by some member companies. A member without productive capacity and market goodwill will not be in an easy situation to re-establish himself within the market should other cartel members take advantage of him. He is, therefore, not likely to agree to such extreme optimizing procedures for the cartel as a whole.

Yet another limitation of the analysis of coalition formation in the theory of games is its failure to take account of the effect on the behaviour of members of the experience which they obtain from membership of a coalition. Their information about other members of the coalition improves, they are subject to new social pressures as the result of their membership of a group and their attitudes may change as a result of common propaganda and information. For instance, if a worker joins a trade union his attitude towards his employer and towards non-trade union workers may change. The implications of such factors for coalition formation and the type of coalition organization which might be agreed to, require study.

It might be argued that there is one kind of coalition which does not raise some of the theoretical difficulties discussed above. Marschak and Radner distinguish coalitions in which incentives are required to ensure that individual actions are brought into line, from coalitions (teams) in which group and individual interests coincide and no such incentive is required.[35] Team situations are rare. However, there may for example be situations in which company managers, individually and collectively, desire a common goal such as maximizing the profit of their company, or maximizing the sales of their company subject to the profit of their company reaching a commonly agreed level. Each is so committed to the common goal that no incentives are required to direct the behaviour of the members of the team towards this goal.

But even in the case of a team, problems for group rationality are not absent. In a team, different members control different action variables and generally have different sets of information. A team has the problem of co-ordinating its actions and disseminating its collective knowledge. Since the dissemination of information is not costless, it generally does not pay an organization to keep its members fully informed even in respect to knowledge which could improve their appropriate response. In Radner's model, designed for studying the optimal transmission of information and actions in teams, the transmission of information is to some extent random, and the actions of the team are to that extent random.[36] He examines various procedures for sharing information. These are: no transmittal of information by members, partitioned communication, management by exception, and reporting of exceptions only. In the system which he studies, the methods are of ascending value for a group of a given size and the last method becomes relatively more valuable as the size of the group increases. It is possible then that group rationality results in an increase of randomness in a team's behaviour in relation to the outside world as the size of the organization (team) increases, and may necessitate predictable changes in its administration.

(b) Von Neumann and Morgenstern's stronger postulates— the equilibrium concept

In order to further narrow the range of possible solutions (outcomes) to a game played by rational individuals, von Neumann and Morgenstern suggest that a solution should not only satisfy the condition mentioned in the last section, but should also be a set of possible payoffs to the players which is not dominated by any other set of payoffs. One set of payoffs dominates another if there is at least one group of players which by forming an alliance can ensure that its members earn more than in the dominated set. Any rational individual would prefer to form such an alliance.

Nevertheless, the type of coalition which emerges in a game can rarely be completely explained by the rational behaviour of the participants. It is useful to illustrate this idea of a solution by taking a particular example. Assume three players, A, B, and C, in a constant-sum game and let the constant value of the game be 6 units of payoff ($6, if you like). If the players do not form any coalitions, each receives 2 units. However, if any two players form a coalition, the coalition receives 5 units *in toto*, so that the excluded player receives only one unit. Thus, by forming a coalition and co-operating any two players can gain one unit between them at the expense of the excluded player. On the basis of von Neumann and Morgenstern's theory, it follows that if communication is possible, a coalition of two players will form. But it is impossible to determine which two players will form the coalition.

How will the members of the coalition *share* their gain? Von Neumann and Morgenstern suggest that it will be shared equally so that each member of the coalition obtains 2·5 units. The three sets of payoffs (payments to players A, B, and C respectively) which form possible solutions according to von Neumann and Morgenstern's theory are:

[2·5, 2·5, 1], [2·5, 1, 2·5] and [1, 2·5, 2·5].

Other agreements on sharing are possible but, it is argued,[37] unlikely. Their argument is based upon a 'stability' property. No player will take less than he could get by going it alone (i.e. less than 1), and none will take less than he can obtain by forming a counter-coalition with another player. Imputations of the set above dominate imputations not in the set. No player is likely to break away from a coalition giving him 2·5 because the other two players (in a three-person game) are likely to form a coalition on mutually advantageous terms, e.g. they might agree to an equal division of gains and their coalition might last. This gives some support for the von Neumann and Morgenstern solution. Again, a coalition of two players should be stable for if coalitions regularly form and break down, and if breakdown is achieved at minimum cost, in the long run players achieve on average the same amount as if they had not co-operated. Thus the fruits of co-operation are frittered away. A rational player should foresee this. If his heresy will begin an unstable movement, he ought not to turn heretic if offered more than 2 by a coalition.

Thus although a coalition of two players is likely to occur there may be more indeterminancy in the payoff to individual coalition members than von Neumann and Morgenstern suggest.

We might note that in an attempt to reduce indeterminacy, some game theorists adopt the strong rationality concept (or *core* concept) that no *potential* alliance should receive less than it can obtain by forming the alliance. However, for many games (including the above zero-sum example) players are unable to obtain a set of payoffs which satisfy this condition.

4 Conclusions

In its exclusive concern with the behaviour of well-informed rational individuals, the theory of games reflects von Neumann's mathematical interests. Its implications are clearest when the interests of players are diametrically opposed, as in zero-sum games. Such situations are necessarily Paretian optimal, there is no scope for co-operation, and each player does best by following his own self-interest. Von Neumann and Morgenstern show that there exists a solution for any two-person game of this type, requiring in some cases unmixed strategies, in others mixed strategies. Given the conditions of the theory, the exact strategy or the exact probabilities with which an individual will choose his strategy can be predicted. Though in certain circumstances the only rational behaviour is *random* behaviour, it will be randomized according *to suitable probabilities*.

When more than two individuals participate in a game of pure conflict, the possibility of coalitions must be taken into account. As we have seen, given a variety of restrictive assumptions about the conditions under which coalitions are formed, predictions can be made about the coalitions that will result. But even with these restrictive assumptions, a considerable measure of indeterminacy remains—about the identity of the participants, and their respective payoffs. And on the strongest rationality postulate—the core concept—the theory is often unable to predict any possible social settlement at all.

The second weakness of the theory of games is the unrealism of its assumptions. This deficiency is most apparent in the treatment of social games involving conflict and scope for co-operation where, I contend, the theory of games has least predictive power. Game theorists have traditionally committed themselves, in dealing with these cases, to the assumption that the group will attain Paretian optimality and co-operation will make no individual worse off than he would otherwise be. But in the real world, rational individuals may frequently *not* attain Paretian optimality. It is likely that individuals will not be satisfied by anything less than a *gain* from co-operation; the cost of organizing the coalition may fall on a few individuals so that their costs exceed their benefits; conditions may be of the prisoner's dilemma type (see p. 260); and the irreversibility or inflexibility of social arrangements may lead to non-Paretian behaviour by rational individuals.

The major body of theoretical work employing rationality assumptions cannot, then, be used to generate a complete set of determinate predictions either for cases of 'isolated competitors' or for the much more common competitive situation where competitors can gain by forming a coalition. For the present, we must rest content that it can be used to predict a good deal of human behaviour, on average and within certain limits.

Notes

1 I wish to thank Stanley Benn and Geoffrey Mortimore for their useful and lengthy comments on the original draft of this essay. The groundwork of the essay was completed while I was at the Australian National University.

2 Lange, O. (1945), p. 30.

3 A preference ordering is a weak one if in addition to allowing the possibility of decided preference it allows indifference. If preferences involve a complete weak ordering then all possible alternatives are ordered and taking any two alternatives, one is either preferred to the other or the individual is indifferent about them. This rules out

circumstances in which the individual does not know whether he prefers one alternative to another.

4 Simon, H.A. (1957a, 1957b). Simon's view has much in common with those of Baumol, W.J. and Quandt, R.E. (1964).

5 Simon, H.A. (1957a), p. xxv.

6 A vectorial increase occurs if there is an increase in the quantity of at least one product and no fall in the quantity of the other.

7 A function which is strictly unimodal has a single peak and continually falls away from that peak.

8 Simon, H.A. (1957a), p. xxiii.

9 Ibid.

10 Baumol, W.J. and Quandt, R.E. (1964).

11 Ibid.

12 So called because the price-quantity observations trace out patterns on supply and demand curves which look like a cobweb. Cobweb patterns occur in the supply of agricultural produce. Farmers may react to a high price for their produce by overproducing. The overproduction depresses price and they may react by unduly reducing their output. Price then rises above equilibrium and the underproduction is followed by overproduction and so the process repeats itself with farmers being out in their predictions. Equilibrium may, but need not, be attained in the long run.

13 Profit is a single-peaked function of output and falls away continually from its peak.

14 For further analysis of the way in which search results reduce the rational direction of further search see Wilde, D.J. and Beightler, C.S. (1967), section 6.03.

15 Arrow, K.J. and Hurwicz, L. (1960). Wilde, D.J. and Beightler, C.S. (1967).

16 Arrow, K.J. and Hurwicz, L. (1960), pp. 49, 84.

17 See, for example, Box, M.J., Davies, D. and Swann, W.H. (1969), and Wilde, D.J. and Beightler, C.S. (1967).

18 Hicks, J.R. (1946), p. 132.

19 Linder, S.B. (1970).

20 Wicksteed, P.H. (1933), pp. 122–3.

21 If search takes time, and some types of search inevitably require a considerable amount of time, the decision-maker's preference may alter *independently* of his experience, e.g. due to the fact that he is maturing or growing older. His past information and experience might then only be of limited value as a guide to his future rational choice and his search need not culminate in unbounded rational behaviour.

22 Hicks, J.R. (1956), p. 6.

23 Ibid., p. 18.

24 Ibid., p. 55.

25 Alchian, A.A. (1950).

26 Neumann, J. von, and Morgenstern, O. (1964), p. 11. See also Morgenstern, O. (1935).

27 Robinson, J. (1969).

28 Chamberlin, E. (1950).

29 Edgeworth, F. (1881).

30 The saddle-point (equivalent to the centre point of some types of saddles) defines a mathematical property of the payoff function such that when one individual is minimizing his maximum loss the other individual is maximizing his minimum gain. If the interests of the players are diametrically opposed, players cannot do better than select strategies corresponding to the saddle-point and von Neumann and Morgenstern consider that these give the solution to a two-person zero-sum game involving rational players.

31 Neumann, J. von (1928).

32 Simon, H.A. (1955).

33 Neumann, J. von and Morgenstern, O. (1964), p. 224.

34 Tisdell, C.A. (1966).

35 Marschak, J. (1954) and Radner, R. (1961) and (1962).

36 Radner, R. (1961).

37 Neumann, J. von and Morgenstern, O. (1964), chapters 5 and 6.

Bibliography

ALCHIAN, A.A. (1950), 'Uncertainty, evolution and theory', *Journal of Political Economy*, LVIII, pp. 211–21.

ARROW, K.J. and HURWICZ, L. (1960), 'Decentralization and computation in resource allocation', in Pfouts, R. (ed.), *Essays in Economics and Econometrics*, Chapel Hill, pp. 34–104.

BAUMOL, W.J. and QUANDT, R.E. (1964), 'Rules of thumb and optimally imperfect decisions', *American Economic Review*, LIV, pp. 23–46.

BOX, M.J., DAVIES, D. and SWANN, W.H. (1969), *Non-Linear Optimization Techniques*, Edinburgh.

CHAMBERLIN, E. (1950), *The Theory of Monopolistic Competition*, Cambridge, Mass.

EDGEWORTH, F. (1881), *Mathematical Psychics*, London.

HICKS, J.R. (1946), *Value and Capital*, Oxford.

HICKS, J.R. (1956), *A Revision of Demand Theory*, Oxford.

LANGE, O. (1945), 'The scope and method of economics', *Review of Economic Studies*, XIII, pp. 19–32.

LINDER, S.B. (1970), *The Harried Leisure Class*, New York.

LUCE, R.D. and RAIFFA, H. (1957), *Games and Decisions*, New York.

MARSCHAK, J. (1954), 'Towards an economic theory of organization and information', in Thrall, R., *et al.* (eds), *Decision Processes*, New York, pp. 187–99.

MORGENSTERN, O. (1935), 'Perfect foresight and economic equilibrium', *Zeitschrift für Nationalökonomie*.

NEUMANN, J. VON (1928), 'Zur Theorie Gesellschaftsspiele', *Math. Annalen*, C, pp. 295–320.

NEUMANN, J. VON and MORGENSTERN, O. (1964), *Theory of Games and Economic Behavior*, New York.

RADNER, R. (1961), 'The evaluation of information in organizations', in *Proceedings of the Fourth Berkeley Symposium on Probability and Statistics*, Berkeley, 1961.

RADNER, R. (1962), 'Team decision problems', *The Annals of Mathematical Statistics*, XXXIII, pp. 857–81.

ROBINSON, J. (1969), *The Economics of Imperfect Competition*, London.

SIMON, H.A. (1955), 'A behavioral model of rational choice', *Quarterly Journal of Economics*, LXIX, pp. 99–118.

SIMON, H.A. (1957a), *Administrative Behaviour*, New York.

SIMON, H.A. (1957b), *Models of Man*, New York.

TISDELL, C.A. (1966), 'Some bounds upon the Pareto optimality of group behaviour', *Kyklos*, XIX, pp. 81–105.

TISDELL, C.A. (1968), *The Theory of Price Uncertainty, Production and Profit*, Princeton.

WICKSTEED, P.H. (1933), *The Common Sense of Political Economy*, London.

WILDE, D.J. and BEIGHTLER, C.S. (1967), *Foundations of Optimization*, Englewood Cliffs, New Jersey.

9

Rationality, coalition formation, and international relations[1]

O.R. Young

This essay deals with the links between rational behaviour and the formation of coalitions, with special reference to international relations. As such, it is concerned with questions such as: (i) when will the rational actor find it profitable to join a coalition? (ii) which coalitions will form among a group of rational actors? and (iii) what are the outstanding features of the process of coalition formation? To gain analytic leverage in dealing with these issues, it is necessary to start by defining several central concepts.

A The nature of the problem

A coalition is a set of two or more players who have explicitly agreed to co-ordinate their actions (or strategies) with respect to some specified issue area in the interests of improving their payoffs relative to what they would be in the absence of co-ordination. For a coalition to form, therefore, it must be that the prospective members can gain more in combination than the sum of the payoffs they would receive by pursuing independent strategies.

Note that this definition of coalition requires explicit co-ordination, thereby ruling out cases of tacit or accidental co-ordination.

Players are actors (including corporate entities) capable of making independent decisions in situations involving strategic interaction.[2] That is, players are behaving units whose decisions are not wholly under the control of any other actor(s). For purposes of this paper, I shall look upon actors in international relations as the states which make up the international system. This is of course a simplification, but it does not seem unreasonable as a device for getting started on the analysis of coalition formation in international relations.[3]

The concept 'rationality' refers to instrumental behaviour relating to choice. Choice occurs whenever a behaving unit selects a particular alternative from some specifiable set of differentiated alternatives. Rational choice is a subset of the overall category of choice behaviour. In a general way, the concept 'rational choice' is ordinarily used to refer to choice behaviour that is self-conscious and purposive. More specifically, let us say that rational choice involves the following conditions: (i) the behaving unit evaluates alternatives in its environment on the basis of its preferences among them, (ii) its preference ordering is transitive and stable or consistent over time, and (iii) it always selects the preferred alternative.[4]

Note that this definition of rational choice does not imply any particular assumptions concerning such issues as decision-making under conditions of risk, the role premises of the actors, and the availability of information. In this paper, I shall generally assume that players deal with risk by making use of expected-utility calculations,[5] but I do not wish to lay down any general assumptions concerning the questions of role premises and information. I shall, however, follow the practice of microeconomics and assume that the actors in international relations are co-ordinated entities that can be fruitfully looked upon as rational decision-makers.[6] Thus, I shall not enquire into the internal power structures and organizational arrangements of states in the present analysis. This is undoubtedly a rather restrictive assumption, but again it does not seem to be an unreasonable device for getting started on the analysis of the links between rational behaviour and coalition formation.

There are numerous distinguishable questions to be asked about coalitions, and it is of some importance to formulate them clearly since ambiguity concerning the exact nature of the issues at stake has detracted from the value of many previous analyses of coalition formation. Consider, then, the following list of central issues. First, *when* will coalitions form among some specified group of actors?[7] Second, which coalitions can be expected to form among the group of actors? Since the number of possible coalitions in a group of n-actors is 2^n,[8] explaining or predicting the formation of specific coalitions is obviously an analytic task of considerable proportions. Moreover, this issue generates a number of subsidiary questions. Thus, it is sometimes important to treat questions such as the size (i.e. the number of members) of the coalitions that form, the specific membership of coalitions, the processes through which a given coalition is formed, and the shifts (if any) in coalitions after their initial formation.

Third, there is the issue of the payoffs or earnings that accrue to a given coalition as a whole. While some situations are characterized by a great deal of similarity with respect to the payoffs accruing to various coalitions (as in simple games in the theory of games),[9] other situations exhibit great diversity in the payoffs going to different coalitions. Fourth, how are the earnings accruing to a given coalition apportioned among the members of the coalition? That is, what is the nature of the bargaining process within coalitions in contrast to the nature of the interactions between or among coalitions treated as co-ordinated entities? Finally, how does the rational individual actor decide whether to join a coalition at all, which coalition to join, when to join, whether to demand special treatment from the coalition in return for membership, and whether to make some payment to the coalition in return for permission to join?

Efforts to construct formal theories (in contrast to the collection of empirical data) to deal with these major issues can be grouped quite easily into several principal categories. In the first instance, there are the so-called sociopsychological theories developed by scholars such as Caplow, Gamson, and Chertkoff.[10] Though these theories are interesting and have much to recommend them, they are not based on the assumption of rationality. Instead, they rest upon assumptions about such factors as the influence of power differentials among the players and the impact of individual differences among the players (e.g. personality traits). Consequently, these theories are not directly relevant to the present analysis of the links between rational behaviour and coalition formation.

N-person game theory, by contrast, rests squarely upon the assumption of rationality, and it offers a large corpus of material that relates to coalitions and coalition formation.[11] In fact, the central role of coalition formation in situations involving more than two players constitutes one of the principal features of n-person game theory. Nevertheless, the existing work on coalitions within the framework of n-person game theory has some serious drawbacks as a focus of attention for this paper. Thus, the formal work in n-person game theory focuses predominantly on the issue of apportioning joint payoffs among specified sets of players rather than the issue of which coalitions are likely to form.[12] However, as Rapoport has argued,[13]

> seldom if ever can the behavioral scientist define payoffs
> in a conflict situation precisely enough to be realistically

concerned with the question of their apportionment.... In contrast, coalitions are often tangible and highly visible. .... The formal political process exhibits coalitions in specific situations (e.g. nominating conventions) with a precision which leaves no doubt. Large areas of international politics can likewise be described in terms of coalitions, forming and dissolving. Coalitions, then, offer a body of fairly clear data. The empirically minded behavioral scientist understandably is attracted to it. His task is to describe patterns of coalition formation systematically, so as to draw respectably general conclusions.

Moreover, the formal models of n-person game theory are predominantly static in the sense that they focus on the outcomes associated with coalition-building rather than the processes through which players attempt to put together coalitions.

However, there is another body of theory concerning coalitions which also rests squarely on the assumption of rationality but which is more directly applicable to real-world situations in the realm of politics. This is Riker's theory of political coalitions.[14] Fundamentally, this theory is an outgrowth of n-person game theory, but it exhibits several major advantages as a focus of attention for this paper. The theory deals directly with the issue of what kinds of coalitions can be expected to form rather than the issue of apportioning the joint payoff among the members of specified coalitions. Riker's work contains a large amount of material on the processes of coalition formation so that the theory is not confined to the static questions associated with outcomes. And unlike most others who have worked on theories of coalition formation, Riker has made an explicit effort to apply his theory in the realm of international relations.[15]

For these reasons, I shall concentrate on Riker's theory of political coalitions throughout the rest of this paper. This is certainly not meant as a criticism of the mainstream of n-person game theory. Nevertheless, it seems to me a reasonable simplifying procedure in the interests of moving on to some substantive issues concerning the links between rational behaviour and the formation of coalitions, with special reference to international relations.

B Riker's theory of political coalitions

Riker sets out to construct a theory capable of predicting the kinds or types of coalitions that will form among a given set of players under the following conditions:

(i) The behaviour of each player conforms to the definition of rationality set forth in the previous section.

(ii) Each player is interested in winning. Though the prize associated with victory may vary as a function of the particular coalitions that form, the requirements for winning are clearly understood by all.

(iii) The interactions of the players constitute a zero-sum game (i.e. the gains of one coalition equal the losses of the other coalition).

(iv) At the level of coalitions, the prize is indivisible (i.e. the winning coalition takes all). However, the prize can be apportioned among the members of the winning coalition, and side payments are permissible.

(v) The players form no more than two coalitions. Accordingly, one is either a winning or a blocking coalition, while the other is a blocking or a losing coalition. A minimum winning coalition is one that is rendered blocking or losing by the subtraction of any individual member.

(vi) Players are equal with respect to their ability to contribute to the victory of a coalition (i.e. they are of equal weight).

(vii) Players possess what Riker calls 'perfect information' about the past moves of all players as well as what he calls 'complete information' about the requirements for victory and the weight of each player.

(viii) The players operate in a frictionless world in which coalitions can form and disperse without incurring transactions costs.

(ix) The players belonging to a coalition can restrict the membership of their coalition if they choose.

The theory of political coalitions Riker builds on this foundation rests on a careful examination of characteristic functions for n-person, zero-sum games. A characteristic function is a collection of numerical utilities specifying the payoff that will be received by every possible coalition (as a group) which can form within a given set of players (including the grand coalition and the null or empty coalition).[16] Such coalitions must satisfy the following conditions: (i) the value of the null coalition is 0; and (ii) the value of a coalition made up of any two disjoint subsets of the players must be equal to or greater than the sum of the values these subsets could obtain playing independently.[17] In the case of zero-sum games, the characteristic function is derived by supposing that the players always separate into two, and only two, coalitions whose interests are strictly opposing.[18] Since the resultant two-person games are zero-sum in every case, it follows that the payoffs to these coalitions are simply the values of the zero-sum games.[19]

Given the characteristic function of an n-person, zero-sum game, Riker proceeds to examine this function with the objective of locating specific points on the function which can be expected to be prominent for rational players. This orientation flows directly from his emphasis on the question of what types of coalitions will form since the effort to pick out one or several particularly salient points on the characteristic function leads to expectations concerning the kinds of coalitions that will form rather than to predictions concerning the apportionment of joint payoffs among the members of specific coalitions.

The next step is to draw a clear distinction between winning and losing coalitions and to focus on that part of the characteristic function portraying payoffs accruing to winning coalitions. This concern with winning coalitions seems perfectly reasonable in the realm of politics. Moreover, in the case of zero-sum games, it does not lead to any loss of generality since the value of any losing coalition is determined as soon as the value of the corresponding winning coalition is specified. This restriction makes it a simple matter to construct a graph of that portion of the characteristic function of any n-person, zero-sum game associated with the set of all possible winning coalitions. Figure 9.1 depicts such a graph, where m indicates the smallest possible winning coalition, n is the grand coalition (which always has a value of 0 in zero-sum games), q is a measure of the joint payoff to winning coalitions, and the several curves re-

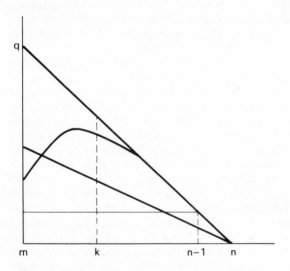

Figure 9.1

present different possible shapes for this portion of the characteristic function.

At this juncture, Riker advances the key argument that rational players will seek to form coalitions at the point where the characteristic function for winning coalitions reaches a maximum. This is so because rational players will wish to form those coalitions yielding the greatest joint payoff. Note that this argument is not sufficient to single out a unique winning coalition in a given zero-sum game, since any of a number of coalitions (i.e. coalitions with different membership) could form at the point where the characteristic function reaches a maximum. It does, however, suffice to identify a unique size (or locus on the graph) for the predicted winning coalition, thereby focusing attention on a sharply restricted set of possibilities.

Beyond this, Riker attempts to show that the peak of the characteristic function in zero-sum games will ordinarily occur precisely at the point associated with minimum winning coalitions. This argument is not implied by the preceding analysis and it strengthens the theory considerably because it specifies a unique size for the types of coalitions that rational players are expected to form in all zero-sum games. An attempt to demonstrate this 'size principle' formally constitutes the heart of Riker's work on political coalitions.[20] The resultant demonstration is open to serious criticism, but the details of the formal arguments surrounding the size principle are too technical for presentation in this essay.[21] Moreover, they do not vitiate the usefulness of Riker's emphasis on the issue of what kinds of coalitions will form in contrast to the issue of apportionment, though they do cast doubt on some of his specific conclusions.

At this point, it is possible to summarize the basic thrust of Riker's argument by setting forth his central propositions. Riker's key finding is the size principle which states that: '*In* n-*person, zero-sum games, where side-payments are permitted, where players are rational, and where they have perfect information, only minimum winning coalitions occur.*'[22] However, this size principle is formulated in purely abstract terms. Consequently, Riker attempts to translate it into 'an analogous statement about the real world'.[23] The resultant 'sociological law' asserts that: '*In social situations similar to* n-*person, zero-sum games with side-payments, participants create coalitions just as large as they believe will ensure winning and no larger.*'[24]

This sociological version of the size principle, nevertheless, remains essentially static. Therefore, to add an element of dynamism to the analysis Riker supplements his basic theorem with a 'strategic principle' which states that 'in systems or bodies in which the size principle is operative, participants in the final stages of coalition formation should and do move toward a minimal winning coalition'.[25] This strategic principle makes it possible to utilize the theory in analysing the processes of coalition formation as well as the question of what kinds of coalitions are likely to form.

C The concept of winning

Riker places heavy emphasis on the concept of winning in his analysis of coalition formation. He argues that winning is a central feature of the role premise of political man. Thus, 'What the rational political man wants, I believe, is to win, a much more specific and specifiable motive than the desire for power.'[26] Similarly, the bulk of his work focuses on the issue of what types of winning coalitions can be expected to form in n-person, zero-sum games and analogous real-world situations. Consequently, the concept of winning forms a crucial link in this theory of coalition formation. However, a little reflection suggests that the exact meaning of winning is far from clear-cut in many real-world situations, particularly in the realm of international relations.

In general, a winning coalition obtains a specifiable prize or achieves some explicit objective. In electoral situations, for example, it often seems reasonable to define the prize associated with winning as incumbency of a particular political office and the perquisites that go with it. But in less highly structured situations, like those that commonly arise in international relations, the prize associated with winning tends to be more difficult to identify. Sometimes international coalitions seek to extend the control of their members either territorially or in terms of influence on policy-making. But this equates winning with the notoriously ambiguous concept of power, a situation Riker claims to have avoided by focusing explicitly on the idea of winning.[27] In other situations, international coalitions form in order to defend their members against the actions of non-members or to deter non-members from engaging in specified actions. But this makes it difficult to judge what a coalition is able to win since it is frequently difficult to distinguish between successful defence or deterrence and mere misperceptions of threat on the part of non-members in such situations.[28] In addition, the association of winning with defence or deterrence makes it hard to distinguish between winning coalitions and what Riker calls blocking coalitions since defence and deterrence ordinarily take the form of efforts to prevent some opposing coalition from achieving its objectives. Beyond this, winning in international situations is sometimes defined operationally in terms of maximizing the number of adherents to one's own side. In the cold war, for example, the two sides often seemed to strive to maximize the size of their blocs. When situations of this kind arise, the concept of a minimum winning coalition is difficult to define intelligibly.

A related question concerns the divisibility of the prize at stake in an n-person game. The image associated with electoral politics involves indivisible prizes such as the occupancy of a given office. Thus, elections are often winner-take-all situations at the level of interactions between or among separable coalitions, even though this image is generally combined with an assumption that the prize can somehow be apportioned among the members of the winning coalition.[29] At the international level, however, there seems little reason to assume that the relevant prizes are ordinarily indivisible at the level of intercoalition interactions. Trade or territory, for example, can often be divided in such a way that each of several coalitions receives a share. Under the circumstances, it is necessary to consider situations in which there is more than one coalition that can be described as a winning coalition, though the prizes accruing to each of these coalitions need not be equal. Note that situations of this kind can arise in constant-sum games so that it is not possible to set the issue of multiple winning coalitions aside as a problem associated only with non-constant-sum games.[30]

Once the meaning of winning is clearly specified, it is important to turn to the question of the requirements for victory. That is, what does it take for a coalition to win the prize associated with victory?[31] Once again, electoral situations tend to be relatively simple in contrast with international situations. In straightforward electoral situations based on the majority principle, for example, it is an easy matter to specify the requirements for winning, though even here ambiguity tends to set in when the relevant majority is a majority of those actually voting rather than a majority of the eligible voters.[32] In international situations, on the other hand, the requirements for winning are frequently exceedingly difficult to specify with any precision. How does one specify clearly the exact nature of a coalition sufficient to achieve defence or deterrence with respect to the actions of various non-members? Similarly, what does it take to gain and maintain a certain level of political influence over the actions of some set of actors outside the confines of a given coalition? Thus, even when the prize at stake is reasonably well defined, coalition-builders in the international arena are still apt to experience problems in attempting to operationalize the concept of a winning coalition.

The requirements for victory will also be sensitive to the precise specification of the relevant players in a given game. Suppose the international system as a whole contains ten players. If five of these players can be counted on to remain neutral in a given interaction, the requirements for victory in that interaction may well be different from what they would have been if the five neutrals were active participants. Similarly, when a large number of actors can be counted on to divide relatively evenly on a given issue, a rather small coalition may be sufficient to determine the outcome despite the fact that the membership of the coalition constitutes a small percentage of the total number of players in the game. Situations of this kind violate the requirement (stemming from the definition of a characteristic function) that the players in an n-person game divide into two, and only two, coalitions.[33] But they are common occurrences in electoral politics, and certainly not unknown in the realm of international relations.

Even when the requirements for winning are relatively well known, it is sometimes difficult to determine just when victory occurs in an n-person interaction. This problem is ordinarily handled in electoral situations by the imposition of a well-defined decision rule. Thus, whichever side receives the majority of the votes on election day wins and that is the end of the game (or at least a given round of the game). But things are not so simple in many international situations. Consider the cold war as an illustration of this problem. Politicians and scholars debated for years whether the West had actually won the cold war without ever being able to reach any decisive conclusion on this question. Unlike a game with a clear-cut termination rule, the situation dragged on and on without any decisive outcome. And though it is generally agreed that the cold war is now over, it is much less clear who (if anyone) really won in this interaction.

Moreover, victory is hardly a definite or once-and-for-all phenomenon in many international situations. In electoral situations, the winner simply takes office for some period specified by the constitution and there is nothing the loser can do about it unless he decides to resort to revolutionary activities. But victory tends to be less definite in the realm of international relations. If a coalition succeeds in deterring a set of outsiders at one moment in time, this says nothing about the success of deterrence at the next moment in time. And the initial achievement of control over some actors or area external to a given coalition certainly does not guarantee the continuation of this control over time in many international situations. Thus, it may not only be difficult to pin down the point at which victory occurs, it may also be the case that victory is not a temporally precise phenomenon at all in some interactions. In such cases, the concept of winning does not bear much resemblance to our common image of winning derived from electoral politics.

It is clear, then, that the concept of winning is often problematic in the context of international relations, and this undoubtedly constitutes a serious problem for efforts to apply a theory of coalitions like Riker's to real-world situations. Nevertheless, the theory is a highly suggestive one that raises a variety of interesting issues which carry well beyond the concept of winning. In the interests of moving on to these issues, therefore, let us assume that we can successfully surmount the problems associated with the concept of winning and see where Riker's theory leads us in analysing the links between rational behaviour and coalition formation.

D Information and rationality

In translating the size principle from its abstract formulation into a sociological law applicable to the real world, Riker makes a crucial change in the required information condition. The abstract formulation explicitly assumes 'perfect information' and implicitly assumes what Riker calls 'complete information'. Perfect information is defined as follows: 'Interpreting a *move* as the act of joining a coalition, if one participant, a, knows what move or moves another, b, has made, then we shall say that a has *perfect information* about b.'[34] Complete information, on the other hand, requires that player a know 'precisely the weight of another, b' and 'precisely how much the addition of b to a coalition will alter its value'.[35]

Both these conditions are dropped in the sociological law which states that players are only expected to create coalitions 'as large as they *believe* will ensure winning and no larger'.[36] Unfortunately, this change casts severe doubts on the falsifiability of the modified size principle as a predictive proposition. Specifically, while the formation of minimum winning coalitions is perfectly compatible with the sociological law, the occurrence of larger than minimum winning coalitions does not disconfirm the law in the absence of independent observations of the relevant beliefs of the players. That is, the formation of larger than minimum winning coalitions may simply signify that one or more of the players held erroneous beliefs concerning such matters as the size of the coalition required for victory. Beliefs of this type are apt to be difficult to observe accurately on an *ex ante* basis, and Riker offers no procedural suggestions relating to this problem. Moreover, the development of such beliefs will involve psychological mechanisms quite apart from the activities associated with rational choice. Accordingly, the assumption of rationality by itself is not sufficient to determine

233

behaviour in situations characterized by imperfect and/or incomplete information.

Though he never introduces any clear-cut psychological assumption(s) to handle these problems generated by imperfect and/or incomplete information, Riker is not insensitive to the problems raised by the information condition of his sociological law. Specifically, he develops the following proposition about the connection between information and coalition formation: 'The greater the degree of imperfection or incompleteness of information, the larger will be the coalitions that coalition-makers seek to form and the more frequently will winning coalitions actually formed be greater than minimum size.'[37] However, it is easy to show that this proposition, as stated, cannot be sustained. Consider the situation of a coalition-maker who suffers from incomplete information about the other players in the game. He will be uncertain concerning the requirements for victory in the situation at hand, and he will be forced to make subjective estimates about this matter. Should his estimates be on the high side, it is true that he will seek to form a larger than minimum winning coalition. But if his estimates are substantially low, he will seek to form a coalition that is smaller than the minimum winning size, and he may discover his error only on the day of reckoning when he realizes that the coalition he has assembled is actually a losing or blocking coalition.[38] Moreover, there is no reason to conclude that coalition-makers will overestimate the requirements for victory to a greater and greater degree as the information available to them becomes progressively more incomplete.[39] Of course it would be possible to elaborate the theory further to deal with situations involving imperfect and/or incomplete information. But the argument of this paragraph serves to re-emphasize the fact that the assumption of rationality by itself is not sufficient to yield clear-cut predictions about coalition formation in situations of this type, a conclusion that seems particularly relevant to the often murky interactions occurring in the realm of international relations.

E Weights

In the initial formulation of his theory, Riker tacitly assumes that all players are equal with respect to their ability to contribute to the victory of a coalition. What this means is that the relevant resources (e.g. votes in electoral situations) available to each of the players are effectively identical. Under these conditions, it makes no difference whether one looks at individuals or resources in examining the construction of coalitions since the two perspectives will yield the same results, so long as the resources each player has to contribute are indivisible. In the real world, however, situations often arise in which individual players are not equal with respect to the resources they can contribute to coalitions, and this is particularly true in the realm of international relations where the actors are highly asymmetrical along a wide range of dimensions. To deal with inequalities of this kind Riker introduces the concept of weights and analyses situations in which the weights of the players are different. But this, in turn, raises new problems that are not easy to resolve.

To begin with, the introduction of unequal weights makes the assumption of complete information much more powerful and more difficult to accept as a reasonable approximation of reality. In electoral situations involving the principle of one man one vote, it does not seem unreasonable to suppose that players have access to complete information. But in other situations, there is no generally accepted measure of weight, and the assignment of weights tends to become a highly subjective process which is frequently controversial. Riker himself mentions international relations as an area in which the assignment of weights is apt to become 'extremely difficult'.[40] Consequently, the introduction of unequal weights tends to lead to the sorts of problems discussed in the preceding section of this paper. That is, situations involving unequal weights will often be among those in which the assumption of rationality by itself is not sufficient to yield clear-cut predictions about coalition formation.

In addition, the introduction of unequal weights raises an interesting question concerning the meaning of minimum winning size with respect to coalitions. To see this consider the following simple example. There are 100 units of the relevant resource in a given game; it takes a simple majority of these units to win, and the units are distributed unequally among the players. Given an appropriate distribution of the resources, two different winning coalitions might be as shown in Table 9.1.

Both A and B are winning coalitions, but which is the minimum winning coalition? Coalition A contains the smallest number of members required to win while coalition B involves the smallest amount of resources required to win. From the perspective of a coalition-builder (say player 1), it might be argued that coalition B is superior. Thus, if payoffs are apportioned within the coalition on the basis of relative contributions, player 1 would receive 35/51 of the prize in coalition B whereas he would only receive 35/55 of the prize in coalition A. Nevertheless, coalition A has an important feature in its favour. Thus, it might be argued that the tran-

Table 9.1

Coalition A		Coalition B	
player	*resources*	*player*	*resources*
1	35	1	35
2	20	3	10
		4	3
		5	3
	55		51

sactions costs involved in forming coalition A would be smaller than those arising from the formation of coalition B on the grounds that it requires less time, bargaining effort, and so forth to form a coalition containing fewer players.[41] And in so far as the expenditure of such things as time and bargaining resources is costly, a coalition-builder (such as player 1) might well opt for a strategy of forming coalition A rather than coalition B. Therefore, whenever significant transactions costs are present, the assumptions of Riker's basic model will not be sufficient to specify rational choices in cases where the winning coalitions involving the minimum number of players and the minimum amount of resources are not identical.

Riker himself avoids this issue by assuming that there are no significant transactions costs associated with the formation of coalitions.[42] In effect, he assumes a frictionless world in which coalitions can form and disperse in a costless fashion, with the result that he predicts the formation of the coalition with the minimum amount of resources in situations of the type discussed in the preceding paragraph.[43] Assumptions of this kind have of course been employed quite frequently in the basic theoretical constructs of microeconomics. Nevertheless, in real-world situations like many of those in international relations where the formation of an effective coalition requires substantial outlays of time and bargaining resources, there is good reason to question the extent to which predictions derived from models ignoring transactions costs are likely to correspond with empirical observations.

F Commitment

In the context of coalition formation, there is an important distinction between ironclad commitments and reversible commitments. When an actor makes an ironclad commitment to a given coalition (or proto-coalition),[44] he cannot subsequently change its affiliation, no matter how attractive later offers may be. If the existence of such a commitment becomes known to the other players, they need no longer concern themselves with the bargaining activities of that actor (as an individual actor). In the case of reversible commitments, on the other hand, actors may consider changing their affiliations at any time during the process of coalition formation prior to the application of the termination rule, and they may engage in extensive bargaining concerning the allocation and reallocation of their commitments.

Riker does not discuss the issue of commitments in detail. Yet, the distinction between ironclad and reversible commitments has an important bearing on the validity of the 'size principle'. Specifically, the combination of reversible commitments and side payments introduces the prospect of cyclical coalitions. To see this consider the well-known von Neumann-Morgenstern three-person, constant-sum game in normalized form.[45] If we label the players A, B, and C, the characteristic function of this game is as follows:

$$v(A) = v(B) = v(C) = 0,$$
$$v(AUB) = v(BUC) = v(AUC) = 1,$$
$$v(AUBUC) = 1.$$

Now suppose players A and B tentatively form coalition AUB with the idea of splitting the prize 50–50. At this point, C can offer B some payoff in excess of 0.5 to enter into coalition BUC, and it is rational for B to accept this offer since it represents an increased payoff for him. But the coalition BUC is, in turn, vulnerable to disruption by player A who is now in a position to offer C a 50–50 split to enter coalition AUC. Thus, it is clear that there is no minimum winning coalition that is invulnerable to disruption by the player who is left out, so long as commitments are reversible. Moreover, it can be shown that the phenomenon of cyclical coalitions is relevant to all essential n-person, constant-sum games in which side payments are permitted and commitments are reversible.[46]

This conclusion has several important implications for the size principle. To begin with, it suggests that some n-person interactions may not result in the formation of any stable winning coalition, let alone a minimum winning coalition. Such an outcome seems particularly likely in situations, like many of those arising in international relations, where there is no clear-cut termination rule. One way to overcome this problem is for the players to form the grand coalition and to employ some equity principle in allocating the prize among themselves. In the situation discussed in the preceding paragraph, for example, the players might agree to form coalition AUBUC on the understanding that each will receive 0·333. Though such outcomes clearly violate the size principle, there is some evidence to suggest that they occur relatively frequently in certain types of real-world situations. And it does not seem reasonable to regard the behaviour of players who proceed in this fashion as irrational.[47]

Even when the grand coalition does not form, the problems arising from reversible commitments are apt to give coalition-builders in games involving more than three players strong incentives to seek insurance in the form of coalitions larger than the minimum size required for victory. The amount of insurance sought by the rational coalition-builder will depend upon such things as his estimates of the probability of defection on the part of various participants, the utility he personally places on victory, and the costs to the initial members of the coalition associated with bringing in one or more additional members. In general, it seems reasonable to suppose that coalition-builders will seek greater amounts of insurance as the utility they place on victory increases and as their estimate of the likelihood of defection(s) increases.

G Connectedness

There are two ways in which distinguishable interactions involving the formation of coalitions may be connected with each other. First, two or more interactions occurring simultaneously may be connected in the sense that the outcome in one is a function, at least in part, of the outcomes in the others. Second, several interactions of this kind may form an iterative sequence over time such that the outcome of each interaction after the first is determined, at least in part, by the outcomes of the previous interactions.[48] In both cases, the presence of connectedness may give rational coalition-builders strong incentives to form coalitions larger than the minimum winning size.

Consider first the case of connectedness among interactions unfolding simultaneously. In such cases, a coalition-builder may well conclude that the costs of forming an unusually large winning coalition in an interaction of lesser importance are small by comparison with the gains this strategy produces in terms of advantages in some concomitant interaction he regards as more important. Strategies of this type are employed quite commonly in electoral and legislative situations. And they are also relevant in the international arena, when, for example, a set of players are engaged in several concomitant negotiations so that a powerful demonstration of dominance in one can pay substantial dividends in the others.

Consider next the case of connectedness among a set of similar interactions over time. Here a coalition-builder may well conclude that the long-term benefits of forming an overwhelming coalition in the first or first several interactions in the set are well worth the short-term costs involved in assembling one or a few coalitions larger than the minimum winning size. In electoral situations, for example, such a strategy may pay for itself by minimizing the vulnerability of the office-holder after his first several elections, thereby allowing him to cut down drastically on the costs of re-election in subsequent campaigns.[49] Similarly, in many international contexts, the acquisition of a reputation for winning decisively can pay off handsomely in the long run by minimizing the costs of maintaining various positions of power. Strategies of this general type have often been employed to great advantage by successful imperial states.

The precise effect of both these forms of connectedness on the ultimate size of coalitions will depend on a number of factors such as the relative importance the coalition-builder places on the interactions in question, the degree of connectedness among the interactions, the extent to which information about the process of coalition formation is transmitted from one interaction to the next, and so forth. Nevertheless, it seems clear that the presence of connectedness will sometimes lead to the formation of coalitions that are distinctly larger than the minimum winning size.

Riker's theory of political coalitions does not take account of this factor affecting the size of coalitions. In effect, Riker assumes that interactions are both isolated from others occurring at the same time and 'one-shot' in nature, though he does not discuss these conditions explicitly in the formulation of the theory. These assumptions are analytically similar to the assumption of 'isolated exchange' employed in some of the basic constructs of microeconomics. Assumptions of this type are undoubtedly justifiable on the grounds that the construction of theory often requires a policy of starting with highly simplified cases. Nevertheless, these assumptions are severely restrictive since they exclude several features of coalition formation which are frequently prominent in the real world.

H Collective goods

Any coalition-builder who seeks to form a coalition to achieve the provision of a collective good[50] (e.g. defence, law and order, or clean air) will experience strong incentives to assemble a coalition larger than the minimum winning size, and he may even display an interest in forming the grand coalition. This conclusion follows directly from the principal characteristics of a collective good. To see this consider the case of a 'pure' collective good, which exhibits both jointness of supply and an absence of crowding effects.[51] In this case, the addition of a new member to an existing coalition (regardless of its initial size) does not reduce the benefits accruing to the original members or increase the costs imposed on these members. At the same time, any resources the new member contributes to the coalition will serve either to reduce the size of the contributions required from the original members or to enhance the position (i.e. increase the profits) of the coalition-builder. Under these conditions, the rational coalition-builder will generally have a definite interest in expanding the size of his coalition.

However, this does not mean that there will be a tendency in such situations for coalitions to expand until the grand coalition is formed. Thus, individual members of the group may be reluctant to join a coalition of this type. This is so because any given player may conclude that if he stays out while others join, he can enjoy the benefits associated with the collective good without contributing to its supply.[52] Accordingly, the final size of such coalitions will be highly sensitive to the ability of coalition-builders to manipulate the information upon which others base their calculations or to manipulate the actual incentives faced by other members of the group.[53]

To the extent that a collective good is not characterized by total jointness of supply or exhibits crowding effects, the relationships discussed in the preceding paragraph will be mitigated. But so long as the good is collective in nature, there is reason to expect that coalitions larger than the minimum winning size will form from time to time. The implications of this conclusion are far-reaching since the supply of collective goods is of considerable importance both in the realm of international relations and in other political arenas. For example, coalitions designed to produce defence or security are concerned primarily with the supply of collective goods. Thus, their leaders will often experience strong incentives to bring in new members who can make contributions toward the collective supply of defence or security. Among other things, this suggests that Riker's theory is fundamentally a theory of offensive coalitions, which is applicable to situations where there are divisible gains to be apportioned among the members of winning coalitions and which is of only limited use in dealing with defensive alliances designed to produce indivisible benefits.

The basic reason for this gap in Riker's theory is that situations involving the supply of collective goods ordinarily violate the zero-sum condition.[54] It is not necessarily true that the gains to the winners will just equal the losses to the losers in situations of this type. In fact, the net gains of players outside the winning coalition may equal or even exceed the net gains of members of the winning coalition, unless the winners can establish an effective exclusion mechanism capable of preventing the players outside the winning coalition from enjoying the benefits of the collective good(s) supplied. Therefore, in so far as real-world situations involving the supply of collective goods are important, they challenge the realism of Riker's theory of coalitions rather than undermining the internal logic of the theory.

I Conclusion

Though there are plenty of descriptive discussions of coalition formation, comparatively little work has been done toward the formulation of rigorous deductive theories in this area. In this paper, I have discussed in a relatively informal fashion the existing theory of coalition formation which is most directly applicable to political interactions and, especially, international relations. This is Riker's theory of political coalitions. In general, this theory is a rich and suggestive source of ideas, though it only deals explicitly with a subset of the principal questions analysts often ask about coalition formation. As such, Riker's theory amply repays careful consideration and study.

At the same time, the theory in its present form displays some serious shortcomings as a basis for examining the links between rational behaviour and coalition formation. These shortcomings are of several distinct types. First, several of the central concepts employed in the theory are characterized by considerable ambiguity. This is true, for example, of the concept of winning whose operational meaning is difficult to pin down in many situations. Second, there are some significant technical problems with the 'size principle', which I have not gone into in the course of this paper. Third, efforts to translate the abstract formulations of the theory into more directly applicable sociological laws sometimes lead to serious problems of falsifiability. A case in point is the reformulation of the size principle to deal with situations characterized by imperfect and/or incomplete information.

Fourth, the theory involves a number of rather restrictive assumptions that have the effect of limiting its applicability in many real-world situations. The assumptions of ironclad commitments, zero transaction costs, and 'one-shot' interactions are all illustrations of this problem. These shortcomings are serious ones, but they should not be taken as a basis for overly pessimistic conclusions. Difficulties of this type are typical of the enterprise of theory construction in all fields. In fact, it is a principal task of theory to specify relationships precisely enough to permit the identification and analysis of problems of this sort.

Notes

1 Research for this paper was supported, in part, by the National Science Foundation under Grant no. GS-33490.
2 Strategic behaviour is the behaviour of a member of a group involving a choice of action contingent upon that member's estimate of the actions (or choices) of others in the group, where the actions of each of the relevant others are based upon a similar estimate of the behaviour of group members other than itself. The set of such behaviour on the part of two or more interacting members constitutes strategic interaction.
3 For a more detailed discussion of the actors in international relations see Young, O.R. (1972a), pp. 125–44.
4 This definition is developed at greater length in Frohlich, N., Oppenheimer, J.A. and Young, O.R. (1971), pp. 26–9.
5 For a classic analysis of the concept of expected utility, consult Friedman, M. and Savage, L.J. (1948), pp. 279–304.
6 The specific paradigm I have in mind here is the assumption that the firm can be adequately represented for some purposes as a rational profit maximizer.
7 Though players with incentives to form a coalition may sometimes fail to form one due to the effect of bargaining impediments, this issue resembles the problem of distinguishing between essential and inessential games in the theory of games. Luce and Raiffa (1957, p. 185, italics original) summarize this distinction as follows:

> It is conceivable that there are games in which no coalition of players is more effective than the several players of the coalition operating alone, in other words, that for every disjoint R and S,
> $$v(R \cup S) = v(R) + v(S).$$
> Such games are called *inessential*; any game which is not inessential is called *essential*.

8 Riker, W.H. (1962), pp. 35–6.
9 *Simple* games are 'defined by the property that (in 0,1 normalization)... $v(S) = $ [either] 0 or 1 for every coalition S' (Luce, R.D. and Raiffa, H., 1957, pp. 211–12).
10 For a general survey of these theories see Chertkoff, J.M. (1970), pp. 297–322.
11 For excellent surveys of this material consult Luce, R.D. and Raiffa, H. (1957), Chapters 7–12 and Rapoport, A. (1970).
12 Rapoport, A. (1970), p. 286. Note also the statement of Luce and Raiffa to the effect that solution concepts for n-person games (e.g. the

von Neumann-Morgenstern solution) 'are only concerned with imputations and ... do not specify the coalition structures associated with each of the imputations, or even the set of all possible coalition structures associated with imputations of the solution' (Luce, R.D. and Raiffa, H., 1957, p. 204).

13 Rapoport, A. (1970), pp. 286–7. A similar point is made in Luce, R.D. and Raiffa, H. (1957), p. 204.

14 The theory is developed in detail in Riker, W.H. (1962).

15 Ibid., ch. 10.

16 For completeness and ease of manipulation, empty sets and sets including only a single member are treated, mathematically, as coalitions in most formal analyses of coalitions. This is done to facilitate mathematical handling of the problem and should not be viewed as an alteration of the basic definition of coalition as a set of two or more players.

17 These conditions are discussed further in Luce, R.D. and Raiffa, H. (1957), pp. 182–5.

18 Ibid., p. 191.

19 In set notation, then, Riker's theory assumes that (i) $-S$ will always form in response to the formation of S; and (ii) $v(S) = -v(-S)$ for every possible coalition structure. The extent to which these assumptions constitute reasonable approximations of real-world conditions in various arenas is a matter of considerable controversy. But these assumptions are clearly incorporated in Riker's theory.

20 For Riker's derivation of the 'size principle' see Riker, W.H. (1962), pp. 247–78.

21 In addition to Riker's own analysis, consult Rapoport, A. (1970), ch. 15; Butterworth, R.L. (1971), pp. 741–5; Young, O.R. (1972b); and Hardin, R. (1973).

22 Riker, W.H. (1962), p. 32.

23 Ibid., p. 47.

24 Ibid.

25 Ibid., p. 211.

26 Ibid., p. 22. However, Riker himself is somewhat ambiguous on this criterion since he sometimes emphasizes the idea of maximizing payoffs (e.g. p. 23) even while talking about the desire for victory as the key element in the role premise of the politically rational man (e.g. p. 22).

27 Ibid., pp. 19–23.

28 For example, this issue is frequently raised in connection with the 'success' of the western policy of deterrence during the cold war.

29 Even in electoral situations, winner-take-all arrangements are hardly universal. Interestingly, this issue produced a celebrated controversy in the 1972 Democratic primaries in the United States.

30 Constant-sum games are games in which the payoffs to the players always sum to the same constant. Zero-sum games constitute a special case of the category of constant-sum games.

31 This is a crucial question in operationalizing the concept of a winning coalition. Thus, Riker defines winning coalitions operationally in terms of the requirements for winning the prize associated with victory.

32 Thus, if the relevant majority is a majority of those actually voting and

the coalition-builder is not certain how many voters will go to the polls, he will be forced to rely on estimates in deciding on the requirements for victory. A moment's reflection will indicate that this is a common problem for politicians and political leaders.

33 On this requirement see Luce, R.D. and Raiffa, H. (1957), pp. 182–5.

34 Riker, W.H. (1962), p. 78. Systematically perfect information is defined as follows: 'If all participants have perfect information about each other, we shall say that the decision system is characterized by *systematically perfect information*' (p. 78).

35 Systematically complete information is defined as follows: 'If every participant has complete information about every other, we shall say the decision system is characterized by *systematically complete information*' (ibid., p. 78).

36 Ibid., p. 47. The emphasis, however, is mine.

37 Ibid., pp. 88–9.

38 Some may wish to argue that coalition leaders will discover errors of this type before the imposition of the decision rule so that they will not attempt to form less than winning coalitions, at least in the final stages of coalition formation. However, there is nothing in the theory to guarantee this result.

39 This would require coalition-builders to make increasingly inaccurate estimates as their information becomes more incomplete. Not only is this not required by the assumptions of the theory, it also does not seem to correspond to any known empirical relationship.

40 Riker, W.H. (1962), pp. 257–8.

41 This would seem to conform to common experience in a wide range of groups, political and otherwise.

42 Riker does not really discuss the issue of transactions costs in detail. Nevertheless, his argument strongly implies an assumption of zero transactions costs. On this issue, see Riker, W.H. (1962), esp. ch. 3.

43 Alternatively, one might conclude that coalition A and coalition B both belong to the set of minimum winning coalitions.

44 A proto-coalition, in Riker's terminology, is any subset of the total group of players, when the total group is divided into three or more disjoint subsets such that no subset meets the requirements for victory (Riker, W.H., 1962, p. 104).

45 This game is discussed in some detail in Luce, R.D. and Raiffa, H. (1957), pp. 199–203.

46 In the language of formal game theory, this is equivalent to saying that such games have no core. For a discussion of the concept of the core, as well as the particular proposition at stake here, consult ibid., pp. 192–6.

47 For some related comments on ambiguities associated with the concept of rationality in games and game-like situations see Rapoport, A. (1970), pp. 72–92.

48 Situations of this type can be conceptualized as stochastic or recursive games. For a preliminary discussion of such games see Luce, R.D. and Raiffa, H. (1957), pp. 458–67.

49 Activities of this kind can be observed frequently in American electoral

politics, and I believe the same situation holds in other countries as well.

50 A collective good is any good such that (i) it cannot be withheld from any member of a specified group once it is supplied to some member of the group and (ii) it can be shared by more than one individual.

51 The concept 'jointness of supply' refers to situations in which a single production unit is capable of supporting a multiplicity of consumption units. Likewise, the concept 'crowding' refers to situations in which the provision of a collective good to additional individuals detracts from or dilutes the value of the good consumed by the original recipients. For a thorough discussion of these, and related, concepts consult Head, J.G. (1962), pp. 197–219.

52 This is the so-called 'free rider' problem. For extended discussions of this phenomenon see Olson, M.Jr (1965), and Frohlich, N., Oppenheimer, J.A. and Young, O.R. (1971). [See also ch. 10, section B-Eds.]

53 This issue is discussed from different perspectives in Olson, M.Jr (1965) and Frohlich, N., Oppenheimer, J.A. and Young, O.R. (1971).

54 Frohlich, N., Oppenheimer, J.A. and Young, O.R. (1971), pp. 130–2.

Bibliography

BUTTERWORTH, R.L. (1971), 'A research note on the size of winning coalitions', *American Political Science Review*, LXV, pp. 741–5.

CHERTKOFF, J.M. (1970), 'Sociopsychological theories and research on coalition formation', in Groennings, S., Kelley, E. and Leiserson, M. (eds), *The Study of Coalition Behaviour*, New York, pp. 297–322.

FRIEDMAN, M. and SAVAGE, L.J. (1948), 'The utility analysis of choices involving risk', *Journal of Political Economy*, LVI, pp. 279–304.

FROHLICH, N., OPPENHEIMER, J.A. and YOUNG, O.R. (1971), *Political Leadership and Collective Goods*, Princeton.

HARDIN, R. (1973), 'Hollow victory: the minimum winning coalition', mimeographed essay, Fels Center of Government, Philadelphia, Pennsylvania.

HEAD, J.G. (1962), 'Public goods and public policy', *Public Finance*, XVII, pp. 197–219.

LUCE, R.D. and RAIFFA, H. (1957), *Games and Decisions*, New York.

OLSON, M.JT (1965), *The Logic of Collective Action*, Cambridge, Mass.

RAPOPORT, A. (1970), *N-Person Game Theory*, Ann Arbor.

RIKER, W.H. (1962), *The Theory of Political Coalitions*, New Haven.

YOUNG, O.R. (1972a), 'The actors in world politics', in Rosenau, J., Davis, V. and East, M. (eds), *The Analysis of International Politics*, New York, pp. 125–44.

YOUNG, O.R. (1972b), 'The limits of the size principle', unpublished MS.

10

Rationality and political behaviour

S.I. Benn

A Political theory and the economic example

It was a basic postulate of the Utilitarian political science of Jeremy
Bentham and James Mill that political actions can be best understood as rationally calculated means to advance the actor's interests.
Though this view of political motivation persisted in the English
liberal tradition of political theory, it came to be treated with
increasing scepticism under the influence of writers like Walter
Bagehot, who emphasized the importance of custom in a political
culture; of sociologists like Pareto, Michels, and Mosca, who
explored the non-rational elements in political motivation; and of
Graham Wallas, who entitled Chapter I of *Human Nature in
Politics* (1908) 'Impulse and instinct in politics', and Chapter II
'Non-rational inference in politics'. Subsequent developments
in political sociology, reinforced by the pervasive doubt of the
rationality of men's beliefs and actions generated by Freud, have
persuaded many that explanations of political behaviour in terms
of rational calculation are naive and superficial. But the intellectual
fashion may now be changing once again. An increasing number
of studies have appeared since the early 1950s whose authors,
impressed by the theoretical achievements of economic science,
try to apply an analogous methodology to politics. Some, indeed,
like Mancur Olson Jr and James Buchanan, are economists
moving across from a concern with public finance and welfare
economics into what is often termed 'political economy'; others,
like William Riker, have seized on game theoretical accounts of

coalitions and bargaining as models for political theory. This mode of analysis has been confined so far mainly to political behaviour in constitutional democracies. This is readily understandable, not only because these are close to home, but also because there are obvious analogies with market economies; political parties take over the role of competitive firms, and a mass electorate the role of the consuming public with votes rather than money to spend, demanding policies and welfare in return for electoral support. Although some sociologists have tried to use the exchange model more widely,[1] it certainly seems most at home when applied to the bargaining of committees and caucuses, to the adoption of platforms by candidates and parties, to voting, and to readiness to participate in political activity. The claim that a theory of political behaviour can be formalized as a theory of rational choice seems more plausible if one has this kind of thing in mind, rather than the Nuremberg rallies or the Chinese Cultural Revolution.

Fundamental to this quasi-economic (or praxeological[2]) approach is the concept of rational action. It might appear, therefore, that such theories challenge the opinion that affect, rather than calculation, is what counts in political decision. How far this is true depends, as we shall see, on the strength of the rationality postulates employed. Some writers, like Anthony Downs, Mancur Olson Jr, and Gordon Tullock,[3] do claim that one gets much further with a strong explanatory concept of rationality than many have supposed; but they allow, too, that some political behaviour really is irrational or non-rational. Riker and Ordeshook,[4] by contrast, seem to be making a far more sweeping claim. Their aim, it seems, is to develop a theory of rational choice so inclusive that no part of political behaviour falls outside its explanatory scope. Their rationality requirements are correspondingly weaker. I shall argue that the disagreement, which appears at first sight to be about facts—whether political behaviour is always rational, or sometimes irrational or non-rational—is really methodological; they are engaged on quite different enterprises.

B Anthony Downs: role-rationality and the democratic voter

I shall start with Downs's account of the role of voters in a democratic system, as an example of an explanatory theory using strong rationality postulates. His purpose, he says, is to provide 'a behavior rule' for governments 'by positing that democratic governments act rationally to maximize political support',[5] comparable therefore to the rules provided by economic theory to predict the actions of

247

consumers and firms. A corresponding postulate is that political support will be forthcoming under predictable conditions, since voters also act rationally. Downs does not claim that this is an account of how governments or voters universally behave; rather,[6] '...[like] all theoretical constructs in the social sciences, it treats a few variables as crucial and ignores others which actually have some influence'.

It tells us, he says,[7]

> what behavior we can expect if men act rationally in politics. Therefore it can perhaps be used to discover (1) in what phases of politics in the real world men are rational, (2) in what phases they are irrational, and (3) how they deviate from rationality in the latter.

One can detect several distinct though related senses of 'rationality' in Downs's book. The first refers to a general, relatively non-technical concept: a person is rational in this sense who has a transitive, connected preference ordering, and who acts to maximize his utility-income. For the purpose of his theory, Downs then distinguishes *personal* from *political* rationality. It may be personally rational for a man to vote for a particular party to placate his wife, if placating his wife is more important to him than the success of one party rather than another. *Politically* rational action, by contrast, is defined as[8] 'action which is efficiently designed to achieve the consciously selected political or economic ends of the actor'. Downs gives no general specification of what ends count as political or economic; we shall see in a moment how he arrives at particular instances. Placating one's wife is clearly *not* an end of this sort, since he characterizes voting for that reason as irrational for the purpose of the theory, since it[9] 'employs a political device for a nonpolitical purpose'.

Downs's concept of rational political action is both consequentialist and, in some not very clearly defined sense, 'selfish'.[10] Politically rational agents are held not to be[11] 'interested in policies *per se* but in their own utility incomes'; and though Downs tries to leave room for altruistic motives,[12] they must be interpreted in terms of the agent's attempts to maximize his own utility-income, rather than that of the person benefited. It would not count as rational, presumably, to vote for A because one thought he would be glad to be prime minister, nor as an expression of solidarity or loyalty either to him or to some principle. From these general conditions for political rationality are derived specific substantive rationality requirements for different roles in the political system.

This use of a concept of what I shall term 'role-rationality'[13] is methodologically interesting. Consider a game of bridge: suppose North bids in an eccentric way, because he wants to capture the interest of a bystander. From North's 'personal' standpoint, his action may be completely rational; from the point of view of the game it would be irrational, because not appropriate to the goals inherent in the idea of the game. Anyone not knowing North's exogenous motivation would be perplexed to give an account of the bidding, in terms of a strategy likely to maximize the kind of gains specified by the game. For an observer trying to understand what appears to be a move in the game of bridge, rather than, for instance, in a game of courtship, it would be reasonable to take, as an initial postulate, that the move will be intelligible in terms of the goals of *bridge*; only when that assumption breaks down would it be reasonable to look elsewhere. This, I take it, is Downs's strategy in trying to understand a system of democratic government; rational moves will be directed to what he takes to be the institutionalized goals of the game; if with that assumption he succeeds in explaining what actually occurs (and he claims that in large measure he does), there is no need to look elsewhere for explanations.

Downs examines the role-rationality conditions for governments and party leaders, as well as voters. I shall confine my attention, however, to the rationality of voters, since my object is not to assess Downs's theory of democracy, but only to illustrate one way of employing strong substantive rationality postulates in theory-construction.

Downs's account of the rationality of voters specifies two conditions. In the first place, applying the general condition of political rationality to the voter's case, he concludes that a voter will act with political rationality if he[14] 'casts his vote for the party he believes will provide him with more benefits than any other'. Acting in this way is rational, presumably, because the voter is then using his political role to maximize the kind of utility-income that it is paradigmatically capable of maximizing. This condition is taken to entail that if the party whose programme the voter fancies most in general terms has no chance of winning, it will be irrational for him to vote for it, since a losing party will not benefit him at all. I shall call this condition the 'political rationality condition for voter's role-rationality'. The second component of a voter's rationality is more closely related to his electoral function, as Downs conceives it. Having specified that the purpose of elections in a democracy is to select a government,[15] he derives as a condition for a voter's rationality that 'his actions enable him to play his part in selecting a government efficiently'. I shall call this the 'functional condition for a voter's role-rationality'.

Downs seems to think that the voter could not satisfy the functional condition unless he also satisfied the other. But this is surely not the case. For given some appropriate rule for aggregating individual votes into a social choice, voters who cast valid ballots could be voting to select a government, even if they voted at random. Downs would consider such voting inefficient presumably because 'selecting a government' conceals a further far-reaching condition. Introducing his discussion of the problems of coalition governments, he declares:[16] 'every democratic government must somehow obtain the voluntary consent of a majority of voters before it can legitimately govern'. An electoral system that produced governments whose legitimacy in these terms was doubtful would not be fulfilling its purpose. And random balloting would not, one supposes, count towards consent.

Even with this consent condition added, it would still be possible for a voter in a two-party system to meet the functional condition for role-rationality without being politically rational. For if each citizen voted for the party he preferred, regardless of its chance of winning, and regardless, therefore, of the benefits he expected actually to get from voting for it, he could still expect that a government would be elected that could claim to have the consent of a majority at least of those voting. Only in the case of multi-party systems is the exercise of political rationality necessary to voters' functional role-rationality. If, in such a system, voters voted for the parties they preferred regardless of expected benefits, a government to which a majority consented would very probably not emerge. Such an outcome would be likely only if each confined his choice to parties with a reasonable chance of forming a government, and selected from among these the one he expected to benefit him most, even though he would have *otherwise* preferred some other party. It would seem to follow from Downs's conditions that a rational voter cannot knowingly vote for a loser, except, perhaps, as a move in a long-run winning strategy.

But political rationality in voting is very difficult in a multi-party system all the same, because it involves having some expectation about how others will vote. Assuming that they too are rational, and that no one has a dominant strategy, the electoral game may be one with no determinate solution, because voters are involved in a regress of interacting expectations. Add to this uncertainty the possibility that no party will form a majority, so that the voter must also predict the coalition that will be formed, and to vote rationally becomes formidably difficult, if not logically impossible. Under these conditions, voters might actually be tempted to vote for the party they prefer, even knowing that there is little chance of its forming a government. Downs comments:[17] 'From the point of view of our model [from the point of view, that is, of elections considered as 'direct government selectors'] the complexity of behaving rationally has led them to behave irrationally.' Downs concedes that voting in this way may be 'the rational thing for them to do as individuals', but he can hardly be using the strict consequentialist sense of 'rationality', since expressive voting does not *ex hypothesi* promise *any* valued outcome at all. It is, instead, a kind of principled '*Hier steh' Ich*'.

Downs draws the moral that, under certain conditions, a multi-party system will make it impossible for voters to perform their roles rationally. But perhaps, in moving on from two-party to multi-party coalition systems, Downs has failed to notice a change in the purpose of elections, or even, perhaps, in the point of the game. Downs recognizes, indeed, that in such systems[18] 'voters do not directly elect the government...they elect members of a legislature, who in turn choose a government by majority vote'. He still insists, however, that the system requires that the majority of citizens shall have consented to the government so formed, even though another stage has intervened in the choice procedure. The objects of the voter's choice would therefore remain, in principle, the same. But perhaps a different idea of consent is at work in the multi-party game: the purpose of elections in these systems may be to constitute a legislature, as the central market place in which groups bargain, and in which policies are formed by consultation, discussion, and accommodation. Out of this emerges a government committed to a very wide and diverse range of interests. It is at least plausible that a rational citizen might see in such a system his best chance of getting his interests fairly considered, given that social decision-making is necessarily a matter of accommodation and compromise between conflicting interests. It would then be rational to give his consent to the system, and, derivatively, to governments that are generated by it, even ones he had not voted for. In such a system, indeed, it may be rational for the voter to vote for the party he prefers, knowing that it cannot form a government alone, but knowing, too, that its influence on policy outcomes will be roughly proportional to the number of votes it can collect and to its capacity to combine constructively with others. Such a model would demand of the voter political ends more like those assumed by another, more traditional model of democracy, where voters express support for the party ideologically closest to their own attitudes—a choice that according to Downs's model is irrational.

There is room, in fact, for diverse opinions about the point of a given political game, and therefore about the point of its institutions. The purpose of an election is a matter for fairly free interpretation as the purpose of taking a trick in bridge is not. Suppose, for instance, that voters saw the game as a struggle to the death between forces of good and evil; or perhaps like a football match with local supporters' clubs cheering on the teams, simply for the fun of competition; or even as a way of ensuring government by good and wise men: each interpretation would demand something different from the rational voter, because it ascribed to him a different function. None of them would require him to adopt as his end in voting the maximization of the expected benefits to him from the government that is elected.

The difficulties of accounting for what happens in multi-party systems, using a Downsian analysis, may be due, then, not to any defect in rationality on the part of the voters, or even to any defect generated by the system, but simply to an explanatory model that ascribes to voters, in these cases at least, an end which it is not rational for them to have. In these cases, the role-rationality for voters would have to be specified differently.

C Downs and Olson—the doubtful rationality of participation

Downs's postulate of rationality is in more serious trouble than this. Downs admits[19] that a citizen who behaved as though his vote alone determined the election would be acting, in his terms, most irrationally. Since this probability is minute, a rational voter's 'party differential'—roughly the importance to him of one party's success rather than another's—must be so heavily discounted, in assessing the expected utility of casting a vote, that if voting involves any significant cost (in discomfort, effort, opportunities forgone) it would be irrational to vote.[20] Equally, it is irrational to take any trouble to inform oneself about the parties or the issues. Now this is, in its way, a powerful thesis, for it explains as the outcome of *rational* behaviour, political apathy, ignorance, and abstention, the readiness to accept political stereotypes, to accept uncritically the ideological guidance of opinion–leaders, the disproportionate influence of special interests who do not have to incur special costs to inform themselves—all those features that good democrats have for years deplored as flaws in a rational, democratic society. But if men are really rational, this, says Downs, is precisely what we should expect.

This argument is objectionable on two counts. First, it would almost always be personally irrational, in Downs's sense, for any-one to vote at all, i.e. to choose to act, whether rationally or otherwise, in the role required of him by the political system. On Downs's account, what the democratic game stipulates as rational behaviour would almost always be personally irrational. And that sounds disturbingly like saying that it is an irrational game.

The second objection is that the theory makes false predictions. For on Downs's showing, a rational electorate would be expected to register *no* votes, and the system would promptly collapse. Instead, general elections in England have been known to muster a voluntary turnout of over 80 per cent. So Downs tries a supplementary hypothesis—that rational citizens want democracy to work well so as to gain its benefits; that one return the rational voter gets from voting, besides influencing to a minute degree the outcome, is the continuous satisfaction of living in a democracy; this is his 'long-run participation value'.[21] For some, but not all, this will outweigh the voting cost. But why? Downs argues that since each individual knows that he himself would be a loser if the system broke down,[22] 'he resists the momentary temptation to let short-run individual rationality triumph over long-run individual rationality. Surely, such resistance is rational.' Surely in the case of mass electorates it is *not*; for I am no more the crucial agent in securing the long-run gains than in determining the party that will govern me. It may well be rational for democratically minded citizens to vote—but not for the reasons that Downs alleges.

Mancur Olson's book is an elaboration of the abstentionist consequences of a Downsian conception of rationality, save that Olson realizes that the consequences follow, not from the postulate of self-interested action but from the situation of individuals in large groups, provided that they are[23] 'rational in the sense that their objectives, whether selfish or unselfish, should be pursued by means that are efficient and effective for achieving those objectives'.

Olson rests heavily on the distinction between collective and non-collective goods. He defines a collective (or public) good as:[24]

any good such that, if any person X_i in a group $X_1 \ldots X_i \ldots$ X_n consumes it, it cannot feasibly be withheld from the others in that group . . . those who do not purchase or pay for any of the public or collective good cannot be excluded or kept from sharing in the consumption of the good.

It is irrational for a person so placed to devote resources to paying for the good. Even a philanthropist would do better to take his share free, and use his money for a charitable purpose.

From this general postulate about the rationality of the 'free rider', Olson derives his main thesis:[25]

> Unless the number of individuals in the group is quite small, or unless there is coercion or some other special device to make individuals act in their common interest, *rational, self-interested individuals will not act to achieve their common or group interests.*

They will do so only if there is some positive or negative selective incentive, 'offered to the members ... individually on the condition that they help bear the costs or burdens involved in the achievement of the group objectives'. Nor in the absence of such incentives, will they form group organizations to promote group interests. To those who argue that a rational person would support an organization that acted in his interests because he would know that if he didn't, others wouldn't either, Olson replies that this is like saying that prices in a competitive market would never fall below monopoly level because each firm can see that if one firm increased output, they all would!

Olson directs his principal thesis at a variety of targets. Pluralists have supposed that any large group with collective interests to defend would organize; but because individuals have no selective inducement to make voluntary sacrifices, latent groups remain latent, even when exploited, and the theory of counteracting power collapses. This is especially true of poorer people, for whom the cost of organizing is proportionately high; for them in particular, participation in collective defensive organizations is *individually* irrational. Rational, too, is[26] 'the absence of the sort of class action Marx predicted'. The rational thing for the bourgeois and the proletarian alike is for each to ignore his class interests (to which his own efforts would make little difference) and spend his energies on his personal interest. Anarchists like Bakunin and Kropotkin were equally mistaken in supposing that[27] 'the need...for organized... co-operation after the state was overthrown would ensure that the necessary organization and group action would be forthcoming'.

Olson's thesis, and Downs's, too, is that a great deal of political behaviour hitherto considered irrational, on a strict means/ends maximizing interpretation of 'rationality', is not irrational at all, but precisely what one would expect of rational people. The difficulty is that we are led to regard the behaviour of those who do participate, who loyally turn out to party meetings, vote conscientiously, spend long hours informing themselves about political issues, as even more mysteriously irrational than we formerly thought the apathetic to be; political conscientiousness now begins to look like merely 'expressive' or ideological behaviour, with no rational end-orientation.

D   The methodological significance of strong and weak concepts of rationality in action

Every political theorist who employs a rationality model analogous to the economists' is confronted with the question what to say about expressive or ideological action. Strikes and boycotts apart, the activities of individuals in market situations are rarely ideological; or at any rate, economists have not felt the necessity to make a place for such action in their explanatory theories. Politics is different. A characteristic of ideological behaviour is that it expresses a principle, an attachment to a moral idea, or a loyalty towards some group or individual or movement. Weber distinguished sharply[28] between means/end rationality *(Zweckrationalität)* and value-rationality *(Wertrationalität)*, regarding the former as the purer case of rationality, the latter as verging on affective or traditional behaviour, precisely because no specifiable reason for action could be found outside the act itself. The only possible reason would amount to a different or wider description of it, subsuming it under some broader-valued principle.

Now there are two possible strategies for dealing with 'value-rational' action. Downs's method is to place it firmly outside the category of rational action. It is irrational to vote for a party's principles, unless one does so as a short cut, using its ideology as a clue to the benefits one can expect to get from voting for it. Even this would be rational only in the short term; for in the long run one learns by experience what can be expected of it.

Downs sees himself as setting up a strong explanatory hypothesis, yielding testable predictions as well as explanations, and vulnerable, therefore, to falsifying instances. Some action, therefore, must count as irrational. So it would be open to him to admit that voters have non-*zweckrational* motives for wanting to vote, knowing they have small chance of doing anything that will make a difference to the outcome. He could still claim, however, that, once at the polling station, the choice would be just such a maximizing, *zweckrational* one as his theory requires; for though it might be personally irrational to adopt the active role of voter, one could still choose in accordance with the rationality conditions of the role, once having chosen to choose at all.

An alternative strategy is to extend the range of conditions that will count as costs and benefits, so as to absorb the ideological considerations—and any other besides—into a portmanteau concept of 'satisfaction'. This is the methodological proposal made by Riker and Ordeshook. They claim that writers who treat voting as[29] 'an irrational act in that it usually costs more to vote than one can expect to get in return', do so because of 'an incomplete and misleading specification of a citizen's calculus'. Left out of account is the utility attaching to the act of voting itself, irrespective of electoral or policy outcomes. Or rather, only the negative component, the cost of going to vote, is taken account of, whereas there are 'substantial' private benefits to be included, such as 'the satisfaction of complying with the ethic of voting', which, according to Riker and Ordeshook, is significant for anyone 'socialized into the democratic tradition'. Besides this, there are satisfactions derived 'from affirming allegiance to the political system', 'from affirming a partisan preference', from 'affirming one's efficacy in the political system', and so on. Taking account of these satisfactions 'the decision to vote by those who have been socialized to vote is a rational decision' even granting that any single voter's differential influence on the outcome is infinitesimal.[30]

Once it has been shown that no system could actually work with only the slender motivation postulated by Downs and Olson to induce men to do what their political roles demand of them, the next move natural to a cost-benefit analyst is to catalogue whatever additional utilities could be derived from participation. A theory is then elaborated by searching for every aspect of a possible change in an actor's situation to which he could possibly attach some positive or negative value, putting these all into a formula, and asserting it as a truth that when the net expected utility of acting to make that change is positive, the agent will make it; and if negative, not.

I want to consider five possible criticisms of this procedure.

(a) Lumping together as 'satisfactions' all the varied considerations that may weigh with a voter suggests the psychological error that Geoffrey Mortimore and I alluded to in Chapter 7, section E; namely, that people only do things because they aim to get some kind of personal satisfaction out of them. People get satisfaction from doing some things only because they believe them to be the things to do for quite other reasons. To represent someone as 'calculating net satisfactions' who is weighing the satisfaction of a half-hour in the pub against the boring duty of a visit to the polling station is surely to misdescribe the kind of conflict he has to resolve.

Riker and Ordeshook might well reply that this criticism misinterprets their enterprise. Their theory is an exercise in translation, to enable the result of empirical investigations conducted within diverse conceptual frameworks to be brought together within a single theory.[31]

[Many] empirical generalizations concerning participation in general and voting in particular—generalizations that commonly consist of correlations between some measure of participation and variables such as socio-economic status, race, religion, region, and so on—can be reinterpreted as generalizations about the properties of these probabilities and utilities. Thus, as we seek to reinterpret empirical research as the attempt to measure and to account for the values of the parameters of this calculus, we supply a focus to research that currently lacks a rigorous theoretical perspective.

The basic rationality postulate of the theory, that political action is aimed at maximizing net expected utilities, is thus not a psychological hypothesis but a logical truth which implies the procedural requirement that every consideration influencing a decision must be expressed in terms of a calculus of utilities and probabilities. This can be interpreted as the prescription: If net costs seem too heavy to make an act plausible, seek to explain it by coming up with a compensating benefit; if the expected net benefits seem plausibly large enough to warrant action that nevertheless does not take place, look for a countervailing cost.

(b) Brian Barry is critical of this kind of theory.[32] 'It is no trick', he says, 'to restate all behaviour in terms of "rewards" and "costs" ... it does not in itself provide anything more than a set of empty boxes waiting to be filled.' He is clearly sceptical of the value of a theory that is incapable of empirical refutation; and this scepticism is shared by Olson.[33] Barry's description of this kind of theorizing, though accurate, is *not*, however, a conclusive objection to it. Formal explanatory schemata, not themselves empirically testable, can contribute significantly to science if they suggest ways in which observations can be related to one another, low-level generalizations brought together under higher-level laws, new hypotheses derived from established generalizations, and so on. Some schemata are heuristically more valuable than others.

(c) To possess the heuristic properties of a good schema, however, a theory must yield empirically refutable predictions when empirical data are fed into it. It is doubtful whether the theory elaborated by Riker and Ordeshook would meet this requirement. Supplementing the somewhat simplistic cost-benefit analysis of Downs with a variety of other satisfactions accruing to voters, they formalize propositions that, roughly interpreted, say things like: an elector will not abstain when the sum of the expected utilities accruing to him if he votes, including those directly accruing from the act of voting, is greater than the utility of any alternative to voting. If these utilities could be measured empirically or inferred from some other evidence than the behaviour to be explained, the theory might serve the purpose Riker and Ordeshook claim for it. But they concede that their analysis does not tell how this is to be done.[34] Of what use then is a theory which suggests no practical way of summing the list of satisfactions on which it depends, or even of establishing with any assurance that any given voter enjoys them, and which yields predictions that no one knows how to falsify? Without a way of replacing the symbols in the formulae with values that can be operated with arithmetically, the theory can do little more than direct the researcher's attention to the wide range of possible pro and con considerations which, differently combined in different groups, might account, but in only a rough sort of way, for observed statistical differences in behaviour.

(d) Criticizing the use of all-embracing rationality models, Brian Barry claims[35] that the value of the 'economic method' is that, from simple premises, interesting predictions can be derived by the use of logic and mathematics. If however people's moral principles, such as a belief in a just price, were written into 'the competitive equilibrium' model as sources of satisfaction, nothing of interest could be inferred from it. 'In other words, there are no interesting deductions to be drawn from the interaction of given "tastes" in a market; the price can simply be read off from the universal "taste" for a certain price.' Explanatory attention would shift to how people came to have such 'tastes'.

Now this is an odd criticism; for though it is true that from unanimous acceptance of a principle one can infer directly the collective outcome, this is a consequence of unanimity, not of people's acting on principle. Barry seems to be running together two different points; first, that if someone has absolute moral principles, one does not have to infer how he will act from the expected utilities he attributes to outcomes; to translate his principles into the language of utility and preference orderings yields none but truistic inferences. Second, if everyone agrees to a course of action because they all prefer that to any other, one needs no further premise from which to infer what they will do.

Now neither point will sustain the conclusion that nothing of interest could be derived from including 'principled interests' in a praxeological or 'economic' analysis of politics. In the first place, one can entertain considerations of principle without their being absolute; a person may 'trade-off' the importance he attaches to a promise, for instance, against the value he attaches to the results of breaking it. Having assessed his options by both criteria, he can arrange them in a single order of preference, and make a rational decision. (See Chapter 7, section E.) Of course, to say that a rational agent can do it is not to overcome our objection ((c) above) that because one doesn't know how to compute the net utilities in practice one cannot predict how he will act. But this difficulty is not peculiar to principled considerations; if it seems more feasible to compare outcome-utilities, this is possibly because in economics, the paradigm of such studies, relevant net utilities are often computed in terms of financial profit and loss. But there is no reason to expect similar methodological conveniences to be available in assessing the outcomes studied by political scientists.

Riker and Ordeshook do recognize, however[36] (though only in a tailpiece to an appendix to their chapter entitled 'The assumption of rationality'), that someone may be so passionately devoted to a given outcome that no matter how tiny the chance of achieving it, its expected utility would outweigh that of any alternative. In such a case, its utility to him would not be commensurable with other goals, since it cannot be ordered cardinally with them. And they recognize, too, that 'many of the objects ordered in the political sphere' are 'passionately desired or hated' in this way. 'Choices involving only "ordinary" political goals, such as election victory, economic policy, and so on, can usually be ordered cardinally... it may not be possible...with extraordinary goals, such as those involving questions of peace and war, personal safety, race, caste, and the like.' This might be taken as an admission that political situations do occur in which some goal or value is of such overriding importance that a praxeological analysis could yield nothing of interest.

The second point I attributed to Barry was that if everyone agrees on principles one need only 'read off' what will be done. This is simply not an objection to the method under review. Barry seems to overlook the possibility that everyone may have principles, but not all the same ones, or that some people act on principle while others maximize outcome-utilities. If the operational problems of utility-measurement could be overcome, an 'economic theory' might, in principle, accommodate such difference and yield interesting predictions, just as the theory that accommodates the differences in consumers' tastes, and aggregates the conflict of the market, yields interesting predictions about the allocation of resources. In politics, this would be a way of dealing with what I suppose to be the reality of political parties—that even among their leaders there are both vote-maximizers and doctrinaires, and that the policy outcome is the result of interaction between them, not simply of an entrepreneurial concern for vote-profits, as Downs postulates. It seems at least plausible, for instance, that theories could be constructed specifying conditions under which doctrinaires or 'politicians' would come out on top. If Brian Barry is correct[37] in thinking that Goldwater gained the Republican nomination because the activists preferred losing with him to possibly winning with a moderate, we clearly need a theory to supplement Downs's, that will predict outcomes of the conflict of rationalities.

(e) These somewhat hypothetical advantages may be outweighed by a real taxonomical loss. My argument has suggested that *Zweckrationalität* and *Wertrationalität*, though capable of figuring together in a praxeological theory, are nevertheless opposite poles of a continuum. It may be more important to keep them conceptually distinct than to reduce one to the other by representing *Wertrationalität* as a concern not to feel uncomfortably guilty after doing wrong, analogous to a prudent concern not to overeat. Political action in the *zweckrational* style is sufficiently different from the *wertrational* style for one to expect clear differences between the political cultures and systems in which each predominates. So recognizing rather than obscuring the difference may well have the advantage of making possible a taxonomy otherwise unavailable.

E   The rationality of avoiding the necessity to play irrational games

The dilemma confronting Olson's rational members of large latent interest groups is that though there exists a course of action which each knows would be beneficial to him, it would be irrational for any of them to take it unless he had *special* inducements. Consequently, Olson argues, the provision of collective goods is always below the optimum level; it would be to everyone's advantage to increase it, yet to no one's advantage to pay *his* contribution for the sake of it alone. So the aggregation of individual rationalities seems to produce a state of affairs that is not Paretian optimal. Olson's is a special case of the game theory problem of the Prisoners' Dilemma: the case of the two prisoners not allowed to communicate, who are presented with the punishment matrix in Figure 10.1, and are invited to confess to a crime; either one's confession would incriminate both.

If Row, trusting Column not to confess, himself confesses, he does well. But conversely, if Column trusts Row, and so betrays him, *he* will do well. There is for each, however, a dominant strategy, for if Row confesses, he is better off whatever Column does than he would be were he not to confess. But because the same is true of Column, too, they finish up both confessing and getting 5 years apiece. But they need only have suffered 1 year apiece, had they been able to trust one another.

Figure 10.1

The game of Chicken (see Figure 10.2) that could model international brinkmanship, industrial conflict, or Hobbes's state of nature is worse even than the Prisoners' Dilemma.

Assuming that the values assigned to the outcomes are as indicated (and whether they ought to be is another question), there is no dominant strategy, and therefore no assurance that independent rational choice will not maximize mutual disaster, let alone fail to reach Pareto optimality. Note that these dilemmas spring not only from lack of communication, but from *rational* behaviour in the Hobbesian condition of no trust. Luce and Raiffa comment:[38] 'There should be a law against such games.' And sometimes there is. Rational men, who expected to find themselves regularly in such a dilemma, would have an interest in agreeing to providing selective incentives that would alter the individual payoffs, making the co-operative strategy dominant for every player. This is why unionists agree to the 'closed shop'. According to Hobbes, it is the reason that a rational man would have for agreeing to government by a sovereign guarantor, who would furnish the selective inducement to

Figure 10.2

261

participate in providing the collective goods of peace and personal security, by threatening to punish anyone not choosing the 'stand-off' strategy. Rational men, in short, have a reason to engage in a preliminary positive-sum co-operative game, of which the payoff is the avoidance of the need to play Prisoners' Dilemma and Chicken games.

Riker and Ordeshook generalize this analysis, using the notion of 'external costs'. External costs are the limitations on an individual's capacity to achieve his goals resulting from another's choices. If, therefore, the consequence of anyone's freedom to do a is an external cost for everyone else (the case of pollution, for instance) but his own doing a adds only imperceptibly to his own inconvenience (since others are polluting anyway), then no one has an inducement not to do a.

Provided agreements are enforceable, this problem could be solved in a small community, simply by direct negotiation; the larger the community, the more difficult this becomes, and the greater the need for a predetermined collective decision procedure that substitutes regulation for free options. This substitution is, according to Riker and Ordeshook, what characterizes the political process. It happens when the external costs to some relevant majority of individuals (the regulators) of leaving some action freely open to everyone exceeds the costs to the regulators of having that option denied to them. If the option in question were that of not contributing to some collective good, then the external cost to each individual of others' abstaining would be the loss to him of the utility of that good, since the cost of providing it for himself alone would exceed its benefit to him. So if the cost to the regulators of having to contribute is less than their expected gain from the good, regulation will occur and the good will be provided.

Buchanan and Tullock[39] have made this the starting point of an interesting exercise in the theory of democratic constitutions. They take for granted some initial distribution and protection of rights (including property) and the enforceability of agreements. Given, then, the need for an arrangement to avoid Prisoners' Dilemma situations, what collective decision rule, they ask, could rational participants agree to that would assure to each the maximal achievement of his goals? Under what constitution would regulation freeing him from the costs imposed by others' pursuing their goals, stop short at the point at which its benefits no longer compensate him for the corresponding loss of opportunity to pursue his own?

Buchanan and Tullock acknowledge two objectives;[40] the first is to explain 'the emergence of a constitution'; I discuss this later.

The second is to produce a 'theory of constitutional choice' which has 'normative implications', but 'only in so far as the underlying basis of individual consent is accepted'. Constitutions might be appraised by utilitarian criteria if we could make interpersonal comparisons of utility; without such comparisons, we can still assess them by their acceptability to rational individuals; for if an individual thought he could do better under some different constitution than one proposed, he would withhold consent to it and go on bargaining until either he got better terms or found he was wrong. So any arrangement that all could rationally agree to would be Paretian optimal. In this respect it is like the allocation of goods effected by free exchange in the economists' competitive market.

The political equivalent of free exchange is, indeed, a rule of unanimity, combined with the opportunity for side payments and log-rolling. For under such arrangements, every decision would be the most favourable that each could hope for in the circumstances; otherwise he could improve his situation by vetoing it. A person might agree to a ban on polluting the stream, though it will involve him in costly sewage disposal, provided the others will compensate him, or if there are at least corresponding costs to him from others' activities, whether of the same or different kinds, that he can buy off by agreeing to pollution control.

The drawback of the unanimity rule is that bargaining involves not only heavy costs in time and energy, but also from the capacity of the individual who holds out to exploit his bargaining position. Accordingly, because there are advantages to be gained from social decisions, it will be worth a rational man's while to accept a decision-procedure short of unanimity, even though it will not guarantee that every decision would be optimal for him, in order to save himself bargaining costs. He will need, however, to consider carefully what risks he can afford to take. Some of his less highly regarded interests he will be prepared to submit to the hazards of simple majority decision. Others he will want to safeguard by qualified majorities, which approach the rule of unanimity as the chance increases that regulation would affect adversely interests he considers vital. And precisely because the constitution settles the conditions under which all first-order concerns will be regulated, unanimity will be needed for any fundamental amendment to it.

Buchanan and Tullock deny that no rule could command unanimity. It might be difficult to achieve among rational individuals where differences in condition give rise to differences of interest. So laws enacted under the constitution, regulating particular forms of action and opportunities, will be controversial. But at the level of constitutional acceptance, none can be sure[41]

263

what his own precise role will be in any one of the whole chain of later collective choices that will actually have to be made. For this reason he is considered not to have a particular and distinguishable interest separate and apart from his fellows ... [he] will not find it advantageous to vote for rules that may promote sectional, class, or group interests. ... His own self-interest will lead him to choose rules that will maximize the utility of an individual in a series of collective decisions with his own preferences on the separate issues being more or less randomly distributed.

Buchanan and Tullock have followed the tradition of the social contract theorists; rational individuals with conflicting preferences and interests agree that they would be better off for having a collective decision-procedure, even if particular determinations were imperfect. But for procedural cost considerations and the heavy externalities arising from free bargaining, they would do best by free exchange; as it is, it pays to risk a certain amount of unsatisfactory collective decision-making.

Buchanan and Tullock claim that their theory is not only normative, but[42] 'an explanation for the emergence of a political constitution from the discussion process conducted by free individuals attempting to formulate generally acceptable rules in their long-term interest'. It seems highly improbable that they intend this as a statement about the actual historical origins of political constitutions, at least if by 'free individuals' they mean men and women. For though the representatives of the thirteen former colonies may have thought along these lines in drawing up the United States' Constitution, and other federations and supra-national bodies like the EEC may have been created in a similar way, there is little resemblance between this model and the historical origins of the British Constitution, or of most other unitary states. Some constitutions have been adopted by referendum, but few unanimously.

The most plausible interpretation is to treat the model as a kind of extended metaphor: modern states are 'as if' they had emerged from the kind of discussion process the authors envisage. This would be to adopt a strategy similar to Hobbes's: Depict the characteristic goals and capacities of rational men, and infer from these the dilemmas in which without regulative institutions they would necessarily find themselves. Infer the political solutions and institutions that it would be rational for them to adopt. Using these as an ideal type, examine existing institutions to discover how far they can be held to correspond in form and in function; to the degree that they do, one has provided both a functional explanation and a justification for them. To the extent that they do not, they are found defective by a standard that one can claim to be universally relevant, because derived from universally applicable rationality postulates. The defect might be explained by some intervening variable, such as a countervailing ideology that confuses people's assessment of the outcome: but this must be taken, both normatively and scientifically, as a deviation from the paradigm, in need of both special explanation and special justification.

F Conclusion

The conclusion suggested by my analysis of praxeological or 'economic-style' theories in political science, is that there is a place for strong explanatory theories, incorporating 'role premises' related to political systems of certain particular types. These would be 'theories of the middle-range', suggesting explanation of political behaviour in systems satisfying certain general stipulative conditions such as a fairly high degree of consensus; for then consequences count more than ideologies.

I have suggested grounds for doubting whether the scope of such theories can be usefully extended by weakening the rationality postulates, at least until someone comes up with a practical suggestion for making utilities of very different kinds commensurable. Until then, there will be an abundance of formulae but few testable hypotheses.

One general objection might be added to the specific ones made in this paper. This kind of theory centres attention on choices of means to ends, and quite neglects the forces making for the adoption of one set of ends rather than another. When 'ends' are taken to include fulfilling one's political obligations, respecting legitimacy, being a good citizen, and so on, the exclusion from the theory of any account of political end-formation is a serious omission. Riker and Ordeshook appeal frequently to the influence of being socialized into a democratic tradition to account for the utilities said to be derived directly from political participation.[43] But this process is exogenous to this theory: the ends are its inputs, not its outputs. In the view of many political scientists and sociologists, to explain value-formation, political socialization, and the development of a political culture, is central, not peripheral for political science: not only do men's apperception of their system condition the demands they make on it and the way they work it; the acculturation process itself shapes that apperception. On this interpretation, what the 'political economists' study are but the ripples; the underlying political swell requires other concepts and other methods.

A further limitation of the method is its inability to say anything about the sources of change in a political culture. Just as economic theory cannot predict the changes in taste that take place with economic growth, so political theories modelled on it say nothing, for example, about the consequences for British politics of the change in the British citizen's understanding of his political status with the entry into the EEC. Nor does it have anything to say about the conditions for the growth of a political consensus in a developing country like Nigeria or New Guinea. Since these conditions must largely be outputs of the political system itself, there is something very limited about a methodology that can treat them only as exogenous factors.

Notes

1 See, for instance, Blau, P.M. (1964).
2 For an account of 'praxeology', see Chapter 7 in this volume.
3 See Downs, A. (1957), Olson, M. Jr (1965), and Tullock, G. (1968), ch. 7.
4 See Riker, W.H. and Ordeshook, P.C. (1973).
5 Downs, A. (1957), p. 20.
6 Ibid., p. 34.
7 Ibid., p. 33.
8 Ibid., p. 20.
9 Ibid., p. 7.
10 Ibid., p. 27.
11 Ibid., p. 42.
12 Ibid., p. 37.
13 This term is not used by Downs; but it is used by Frohlich, N., Oppenheimer, J.A. and Young, O.R. (1971), p. 29, in a sense similar to mine. See also Chapter 7 in this volume, section E.
14 Downs, A. (1957), p. 36.
15 Ibid., p. 24.
16 Ibid., p. 142.
17 Ibid., p. 153.
18 Ibid., p. 143.
19 Ibid., p. 244.
20 Ibid., p. 274.
21 Ibid., p. 270.
22 Ibid., p. 268.
23 Olson, M. Jr (1965), p. 65.
24 Ibid., pp. 14–15.
25 Ibid., p. 2. Note that in a small group, one man's contribution can make a perceptible difference to the likelihood of success. He therefore has an inducement to contribute to provide collective goods.
26 Ibid., p. 105.
27 Ibid., p. 131.
28 This distinction is explored in Chapters 6 and 7 in this volume.

29 Riker, W.H. and Ordeshook, P.C. (1973), pp. 62–3.
30 While not questioning the truth of this last supposition, Riker and Ordeshook suggest that voters may often believe this influence to be much larger than it really is, so that, given the probability subjectively assigned, voting may be practically rational anyway. Whether this belief is rational is another matter; but these authors pay little attention to the problems of epistemic rationality. Their method of coping with apparent practical irrationality is commonly to attribute the action to misattributions of probability, or some other epistemic failure.
31 Riker, W.H. and Ordeshook, P.C. (1973), p. 69.
32 Barry, B. (1970), p. 15. Barry's criticisms are directed at an earlier statement, in Riker, W.H. and Ordeshook, P.C. (1968).
33 Olson, M. Jr (1965), p. 160.
34 Riker, W.H. and Ordeshook, P.C. (1973), p. 69.
35 Barry, B. (1970), pp. 15–16.
36 Riker, W.H. and Ordeshook, P.C. (1973), p. 43.
37 Barry, B. (1970), p. 109.
38 Luce, R.D. and Raiffa, H. (1957), p. 97.
39 Buchanan, J.M. and Tullock, G. (1965).
40 Ibid., p. 7.
41 Ibid., p. 78.
42 Ibid., p. 7.
43 E.g. Riker, W.H. and Ordeshook, P.C. (1973), pp. 60–1:

> One essential element of our explanation is that the paradox of participation is solved by the construction of an ideology of obligation. . . . Thus, we learn that voting is an element of good citizenship, and the desire to be a good citizen leads many to vote even though the public consequence of this act (that is, its efficacy) is thought to be small. One result of political socialization, then, is the augmentation of the public consequences of one's acts with private consequences.

Bibliography

BARRY, B. (1970), *Sociologists, Economists, and Democracy*, London.
BLAU, P.M. (1964), *Exchange and Power in Social Life*, New York.
BUCHANAN, J.M. and TULLOCK, G. (1965), *The Calculus of Consent*, Ann Arbor.
DOWNS, A. (1957), *An Economic Theory of Democracy*, New York.
FROHLICH, N., OPPENHEIMER, J.A. and YOUNG, O.R. (1971), *Political Leadership and Collective Goods*, Princeton.
LUCE, R.D. and RAIFFA, H. (1957), *Games and Decisions*, New York.
OLSON, M. JR (1965), *The Logic of Collective Action*, Cambridge, Mass.
RIKER, W.H. (1962), *The Theory of Political Coalitions*, New Haven.
RIKER, W.H. and ORDESHOOK, P.C. (1968), 'A theory of the calculus of voting', *American Political Science Review*, LXII, pp. 25–42.
RIKER, W.H. and ORDESHOOK, P.C. (1973), *An Introduction to Positive Political Theory*, Englewood Cliffs, New Jersey.
TULLOCK, G. (1968), *Towards a Mathematics of Politics*, Ann Arbor.

11

Can ends be rational? The methodological implications

S.I. Benn and G.W. Mortimore

A Introduction

In Chapter 4 three requirements for rationality in action were
distinguished:

    (a) rationality in the beliefs on which the agent acts;

    (b) formal practical rationality in the agent's choice, which was
taken to consist in its relationship to his beliefs about his choice-
situation and to his ends;

    (c) the rationality of the ends for the sake of which the agent
acts.

The last requirement was deferred for later discussion, and is the
subject of the present chapter.

It was suggested in Chapter 4 that explanations in terms of a
man's ends were at the same time explanations in terms of his
attitudes to various end-states—where 'attitude' embraced such
things as his desire to preserve his honour, motives like ambition,
and consumer preferences (p. 95). 'Attitude', as we have used the
term in this book, also covers such things as hatred and approval
which are perhaps not so straightforwardly identifiable with being
in favour of an end-state coming about. What remains to be discussed, therefore, is how a man's attitudes can be rational or
irrational.

Several of the papers in this collection have already touched on
rationality requirements for attitudes. Robert Abelson's paper
reveals social psychologists to be especially concerned with attitudes like approval and hatred. One theory he there discusses takes

an individual to exhibit rationality in his attitudes to an associated set of objects if he brings these attitudes into a certain *relationship* with one another, specified as balance or consistency. Economics and its derivative disciplines focus, by contrast, on wants and preferences: but as we have seen in Chapter 7 many of the accounts of rationality in these disciplines are similarly *relational*, the key relationship being the transitivity of preference ordering.

In the last section of Chapter 7, and again in Chapter 10, however, we observed that technical theories of rational action may stipulate certain substantive requirements, limiting what might count for the purposes of the theory as the ends of rational action. A very common, general stipulation confines rationality to the pursuit of consequential end-states, either relegating normative considerations, such as a concern for telling the truth, or acting justly, or preserving one's artistic integrity to the non-rational sphere, or translating such considerations into satisfactions the agent will enjoy from meeting normative requirements. Besides such general restrictions, however, technical theories designed to have considerable explanatory power over a relatively narrow range of behaviour commonly stipulate quite specific ends; for instance, a theory explaining the pricing policy of entrepreneurs in a market economy will stipulate that only profit-maximizing behaviour will count as rational; or rational voting may be confined to casting one's vote to elect a government likely to be of benefit to the voter. We have called such stipulative restrictions on ends requirements of 'role-rationality' (see Chapter 7 and Chapter 10).

'Role-rational' stipulations prescribe the ends appropriate to an agent *in respect of a role*; but of course a given agent may have many roles, some of which he values more highly than others, some of which, indeed, he would prefer not to occupy at all. There is no intrinsic irrationality in not accepting as one's own the end appropriate to a role for which one feels no concern. It cannot be inferred from any of the theories in question, therefore, that *simply as a rational agent* one is committed to pursuing the ends ascribed by the theory to the bearer of such a role.

In this paper we shall be examining the question: is there any sense in which we can say that there is a certain attitude A (whether to certain consequential end-states or more generally) which it is rational (or irrational) for *any* person to have, irrespective, that is, of any role or property or attribute that he has which is not necessary to him simply as a person? Now one might make such a claim if one could show that there were some other attitudes that any person would have simply as agent, and if having those attitudes rationally committed him to having attitude A, too. We shall call this sense in which one might say that it is rational for anyone to have attitude A, a *relational* sense, since it is rational only in relation to some attitude antecedent to A. An alternative possibility is that there may be some sense in which it would be rational (or irrational) for any agent to have some attitude A irrespective of any antecedent attitude. We shall call this a *non-relational* sense. We shall be concerned, not so much to suggest an answer to these questions, as to explore their relevance for the social scientist. To simplify our discussion we will leave aside attitudes like hatred and disapproval and concentrate on attitudes like wants, desires and preferences, focusing specifically on the central aspect of these attitudes—the disposition of the wanter to pursue the wanted end-state, acting for the sake of bringing it about.

B Relational conceptions of a rational end

R.S. Peters's *Ethics and Education* includes an attempt to show that there is a set of ends and attitudes, such as having true beliefs, freedom to choose the optimal course, and respect for persons, to which anyone is committed who asks what there are reasons for doing.[1] The antecedent attitude or interest expressed in asking the question carries with it a relational commitment to these other attitudes. But what antecedent attitude *is* expressed by this question?

On one interpretation, the attitude is not simply a concern about *doing* whatever there is a reason for doing, but a concern to grasp the reason itself. It might then be plausibly argued that anyone with these concerns could not condone suppression of discussion which prevented him from hearing arguments, nor coercion which prevented him from doing something which he knew there were reasons for doing. Such an argument would amount, then, to a claim that certain antecedent attitudes carry a rational commitment to other ends. However, the concern to grasp reasons for choice is surely an attitude which is constitutive of rationality in a person. So even if the argument goes through, it shows only that certain ends are rational, in a relational sense, for any *rational* agent. They would not be rational, in that sense, at least, for anyone disposed to act on impulse who disclaimed any interest in being rational.

Peters's interest in such concepts, it should be noted, is not primarily explanatory or predictive but prescriptive: he is aiming at an ethical justification for having certain ends in education. Supposing his argument could be upheld, however, it could have significant implications for social scientists too. A sociologist or a social psychologist might find in it a taxonomy capable of distinguishing people with rational attitudes, and capable of sustaining an operational theory about the conditions under which persons come to have rational concerns. It might be possible, too, to determine under what conditions a person who possessed the antecedent attitudes constitutive of rationality might nevertheless reject— rationally or otherwise—the other attitudes that Peters claims are relationally-rational for such a person to have.

Such a theoretical programme would be fairly narrow in scope, however, precisely because it would apply only to people with the rational concern to grasp reasons. This attitude is probably rather uncommon; it would certainly not sustain a theory as general in its application as those examined in Chapters 7–10. While such theories generate explanations and determinate predictions by stipulating some restrictions on the content of the ends that an agent can rationally have, the less restrictive the theory the wider the range of behaviour it will embrace. If the requirements are too strong, its explanations and predictions will be remarkably determinate, but the events predicted would hardly ever occur. The rationality models commonly employed by social scientists are weaker than the one we have been considering precisely because they aim to catch in their conceptual net a far wider range of human behaviour.

Peters's argument would apply more widely, however, if it were interpreted rather differently. The attitude expressed in asking for reasons may be simply a concern to *do* what there are reasons for doing, rather than to know what the reasons are. The discussion of formal practical rationality in Chapter 4 suggests that a man might be rational in this sense if he acted by rule of thumb, or on the advice of an expert, provided he had reason to think that this policy was the way to select the optimal course, the one, that is, that there was a reason for choosing, even though he did not himself know the reason. Are there any ends or attitudes to which any person would be rationally committed by this attitude?

Peters seems at times to argue that the list of attitudes mentioned earlier could be derived from this weaker condition. Suppose, however, someone claimed that, his own judgment being notably fallible, he would have a better chance of succeeding in doing whatever there was a good reason for doing if he entrusted himself to some authority—a priest, say, or an efficiency expert. No doubt this would require an initial concern to have true beliefs and liberty to choose the right priest or expert. Whether thereafter one would be more likely to optimize by following instructions implicitly, or by retaining the right to make one's own judgments and one's own blunders, seems, however, a contingent question. So a regard for freedom and true belief cannot be something to which a chooser is committed simply by virtue of his formal practical rationality. A similar objection could be made out against the claim that an optimizing agent is committed to any of the other ends which Peters lists.

An argument rather similar in type is suggested by John Rawls:[2] merely by virtue of having any ends at all, one is committed to a kind of relational meta-end, the maximal achievement of whatever ends one has. Rawls adds the rider that someone with this meta-end would be rationally committed to adopting some overarching life-plan that would assign an order of importance to all lesser ends. This notion does not add much beyond a consistency requirement over time, though it might be taken to imply, too, certain second-order ends, like that of keeping one's options open, and maximizing available general resources, useful whatever one's life-plan.[3] It is by no means clear, however, that there are any resources that it would be rational to maximize whatever one's life-plan. If rational life-plans could range from Gandhi's to John D. Rockefeller's, what should be maximized? The attitudes that are rationally related to the mere fact of having any ends at all seem too broadly specified to be of much use to the social scientist, whatever their value to the moralist.

We have considered so far accounts which try to identify certain very general ends that are shared by all agents, or perhaps by all rational agents, and which argue that certain other ends are relationally rational, given these. We have expressed some doubt whether a social scientist could get a great deal out of such notions. Something might be made, perhaps, of an account specifying the ends to which someone is committed by having the concern to grasp reasons for choice—the concern that constitutes him a rational person; but it would apply to only a very restricted range of behaviour and people. We shall now explore, therefore, the possibility of a non-relational sense in which an attitude might be thought to be rational, to see whether that might prove more fruitful.

C   Non-relational rationality of ends

1   The philosophical issues

It may be argued that there obviously is a sense in which an individual's end can be rational by virtue of something other than its relationship to his other ends and attitudes, since certain restrictions on the content of ends are conventionally built into our concepts of rationality as applied to actions and agents. A man simply does not satisfy the criteria of rationality, it may be suggested, if he pursues for its own sake an end like the removal of greenness from the world. However, there is always a temptation to use the concept of rationality, with all its honorific force, to back up what may be simply the received view about the ends men ought to pursue. What has to be shown is that the conventional criteria for using 'rational' of ends do not reflect a particular ethical opinion about the ends worth pursuing, which can no more claim to be rational than any alternative view. The only way we can decide this is surely to consider how we might conceive of an individual's displaying rationality or irrationality in having something as his end.

The natural strategy is to see whether ends can be rational or irrational in any of the senses in which actions or beliefs can be rational or irrational. We have encountered two conceptions of rationality in previous discussions.[4] The first focuses on the individual's *reasons* for belief or action. Irrationality is attributed if he has no reasons, if his reasons are bad ones, or if there are good reasons to believe (or do) something else. Rationality consists in acting or believing for reasons which are (or which it is reasonable to think are) good reasons. It is the capacity to grasp that certain considerations are reasons, and the disposition to be influenced by those considerations.

There can, of course, be reasons for pursuing something as an end. My reason for seeking an academic qualification can be my belief that it will enhance my career prospects. This reason is, however, a relational one; it is concerned with the connection between a mediate end (the qualification) and a further end—the desired career. The question we are posing is whether anything could count as a non-relational reason for an end.

The second conception of rationality focuses on the content of, say, an individual's belief and suggests that the proposition rationally demands rejection, or rationally compels assent. Irrationality is exhibited in accepting the former and failing to assent to the latter. To extend this conception to ends, we need the idea that certain states of affairs, by virtue of their content, *demand* to be pursued (or not to be pursued) by the rational agent.

Either extension of the notion of rationality would challenge the view that practical rationality can only be manifested in grasping and acting on end-dependent reasons. Accordingly, to contrast with the notion of formal practical rationality, we shall call them notions of substantive practical rationality.

2   Hume and Weber

A clear rejection of the possibility of substantive practical rationality is given in David Hume's account of the operations and functions of reason.[5] Reason, on Hume's account, is the faculty for grasping logical relationships between concepts and propositions, and the only rationality which can be displayed in the pursuit of an end is epistemic rationality in the agent's beliefs about his end, and the ways of achieving it. This view depends on Hume's sharp distinction between ideas (a notion which appears to cover both concepts and propositions) and passions (a notion roughly equivalent to our broad notion of attitude). Ideas are the province of reason, which can lead a man to beliefs about the existence and nature of the things which become the objects of his passions. Whether they *do* become the objects of his passions, given those beliefs, cannot in principle be affected by the operations of reason. And reason cannot be conceived as an independent motivating force, opposed to the passions, just because 'its proper province is the world of ideas'. Thus, concludes Hume, 'it is not contrary to reason to prefer the destruction of the whole world to the scratching of my finger'.

The Weberian doctrine of value-freedom *(Wertfreiheit)* in science and in the social sciences in particular is the counterpart in that area to the Humean account of the limits of rationality. This is the orthodox contemporary view, and runs roughly as follows: while the scientist can intelligibly and usefully postulate, as part of an explanatory theory, that people pursue their ends rationally, he cannot intelligibly postulate that they pursue rational ends. Equally, an agent's having an irrational end cannot be a fact into which a scientist can appropriately enquire; at most, he can enquire into an agent's failure to order his ends rationally. Weber states the limitations of 'rational or empirical' science in the following terms:[6]

(1) the indispensable means, and (2) the inevitable repercussions, and (3) the thus conditioned competition of numerous possible evaluations in their *practical* consequences, are all that an *empirical* discipline can demonstrate with the means at its disposal. ... Even such simple questions as the extent to which an end should sanction unavoidable means, or ... how conflicts between several concretely conflicting ends are to be arbitrated, are entirely matters of choice or compromise. There is no (rational or empirical) scientific procedure of any kind whatsoever which can provide us with a decision here. The social sciences, which are strictly empirical sciences, are the least fitted to presume to save the individual the difficulty of making a choice. ...

In consequence, though a person's ends (or attitudes) can of course provide the explanation of his actions, and can themselves be genetically explained, there is no set of ends that has a privileged status as rational, and there is no special, methodological model in which some ends, as substantively practically rational, figure in some especially explanatory way.

That is not to say, of course, that a scientist acknowledges no values; on the contrary, he accepts the canons of value-free inquiry precisely because he has committed himself to theoretical ends, to the exacting set of values constituted by his interest in being epistemically rational.[7] One undertakes that kind and degree of value-commitment in electing to practise seriously as a scientist. But the notion of the value-freedom of science means that, having its own theoretical ends, science is neutral as between other end-orientations. And, according to Weber, scientific inquiry cannot furnish reasons for adopting scientific inquiry as a form of life; so even these theoretical interests of science can be no more than hypothetical values, depending on an ultimate choice or commitment which might itself be sociologically or psychologically explicable, but for which no reasons can be adduced.

The value-free canon is presently under attack by some morally committed critics of this orthodoxy. It is morally indefensible, some argue, that scientists should disclaim responsibility for their discoveries; no one is entitled to have regard only to theoretical values.[8] Moreover, the events that social scientists study concern human persons, not guinea pigs; it is irresponsible and inhuman to adopt towards them a morally neutral stance on the alleged ground that science cannot generate any rationally certified value-commitment. There are a variety of ethical positions from which such criticisms might be argued; for instance, that there are objective values that, given good faith, can be perceived intuitively, or that can be accepted on authority, and that reasons are neither necessary nor can be rationally sought for adopting them. Or it might be argued that no matter how someone comes by his moral values, he would not be justified in suspending moral judgments on his findings simply because he happened to be a social scientist sitting at his desk.

None of these arguments would constitute a challenge to the thesis that there are no rational ends. What is needed is an account of how rationality or irrationality could be exhibited in pursuing something as an end, which significantly extends the Hume-Weber account of the scope of reason.

3   Alternatives to Hume and Weber

There are two broad lines of attack on the Hume-Weber view which

275

are developed in two major traditions of thought about rationality in the pursuit of ends—the Kantian and the Aristotelian. Both challenges start with the notion of reason as a normative faculty exercised, for example, in operating with norms of inference and canons of rational choice. And both pose the question: Was Hume correct to suggest that the norms of reason are exclusively concerned with propositional belief and inference? We can only answer this question if we can give an account of the conditions which qualify a norm as a norm of reason. At this point the two challenges offer different, though not incompatible accounts.

(i) The first suggests that what distinguishes norms of reason from norms of other kinds (moral, aesthetic, etc.) are the concepts used in formulating them. The norms of epistemic rationality concern the logical relationships between concepts and propositions; and they bring to bear a battery of notions like 'logical commitment', 'implication' and 'consistency'. These are the terms we use to say why a proposition demands rejection by an epistemically rational believer, or why one proposition provides an epistemically good reason for believing another. One move against Hume is to suggest that such terms can be used in non-epistemic areas, too: for example, we might extend the notion of commitment to embrace the relationship between an individual's choice on the one hand, and, on the other, his wants and his beliefs about getting what he wants. We might then seek to use members of this family of concepts to show how a man can exercise his reason in grasping that there are reasons for pursuing a certain end, or in grasping that a certain end demands to be pursued.

The logical notions just considered may be thought to have special epistemic associations. There are, however, other concepts which are characteristically used to invoke norms of reason but which seem to have no such special associations. The concepts of impersonality and universality, for instance, come into play wherever an individual does, or believes, or wants x for a reason which he takes to be a prescriptive reason for doing, believing, or wanting x. The prescriptive notion of a reason itself generates these very general norms of rationality. A further move against Hume might take the form of extending these general rationality requirements to ends and attitudes.

(ii) The second account of what qualifies a norm as a norm of reason suggests that the norms of reason are united by their relation to two *tele* of human life—belief in what is true and achieving what is best. Practical rationality is then understood as the capacity for appreciating what is good and worthy of pursuit, and for pursuing it as an overarching end in action. On this view the epistemic and practical are parallel areas of rationality—on a level with each other. And appreciating which ends are worthy of pursuit is a paradigmatic exercise of reason.

In the remainder of this paper, we shall explore some attempts to develop the concept of rationality in these directions, not so much to assess their validity and success (for to do justice to them would require a far more elaborate examination than we can provide here) but rather to ask what differences it could make to the practice of the social sciences if such an attempt turned out to be feasible.

D An Aristotelian view of ends and social science

1 The good for man

In the *Nichomachaean Ethics* Aristotle develops an account of practical rationality which is broadly on the lines of (ii) above.[9] Everything, says Aristotle, has its characteristic end (or *telos*).[10] The modern conception of an end, as aim or objective is, however, only one component of Aristotle's conception of a *telos*. This includes, besides, the idea of some state to which the thing naturally tends, as well as the idea of that state of the thing that would warrant saying that it is good of its kind. A man is good if he does well what his nature, i.e. his particular capacities, make him peculiarly fit to do.[11] This we might term his natural function. But man's function as man is not like that of an instrument for some extrinsic end (as the capacity and activity of both cobbler and leather-knife are instrumental to making shoes), but is rather some activity done for its own sake. Because a man is uniquely rational, man's end—that state in virtue of which men might be distinguished as good or bad specimens of men—must be some state of rational activity. For whereas a man's power to draw carts would qualify him as only a poor specimen of a draught animal, in his capacity for rational thought and action he is, as a species, incomparable.

Rational activity, together with the satisfaction in recognizing that something worthwhile is being well done, constitute that active state of a man that Aristotle calls *eudaimonia* (generally though inadequately rendered as 'happiness').[12] *Eudaimonia* is that about a man's life that makes it good—a life to be valued. But, as we suggested earlier, to say that it is man's *telos* is to say that there is a tendency to realize it in all men. Now to speak of a tendency in plants or animals to achieve some developed state would be to point simply to a normal growth pattern. But where, as with a man, we are concerned with an intentional agent, a tendency towards *eudaimonia* will presumably be exhibited, if at all, in intentional action. What, then, are we to say about the man who pursues objectives, like honour or pleasure, which are not *eudaimonia*?

The agent can be represented as deficient in rationality in either of two ways, and it is not absolutely clear which view Aristotle himself took. On one interpretation of his argument, the failure is in substantive practical rationality, in failing to grasp that particular features of a certain kind of life constitute reasons for having such a life as one's end, and that a way of life which does not manifest them is inadequate on that account. What perplexes the Humean is to find a kind of consideration, other than an agent's actually 'going for' it, that could provide a reason for pursuing an end. Aristotle's answer, according to the first interpretation, is that anyone with a proper understanding of the notion of an ultimate end—of an end valuable without reference to some further end— would be able to derive from that notion substantive criteria for recognizing what can count as such an end. Aristotle maintains that if we are not to be involved in an infinite regress, there must be some ultimate end which is somehow self-certifying; according to the present interpretation, Aristotle is arguing that the concept of an ultimate end puts substantive restrictions on ends that could count as ultimate.

Aristotle's method of establishing the substantive practical rationality of having *eudaimonia* as an ultimate end is to examine possible alternative candidates, such as honour and pleasure, and to show that for reasons deriving conceptually from the idea of an ultimate end, these could not qualify. An ultimate end must indeed be pleasurable, since for something to be an end it must be attractive, and anything that held no promise of pleasure could not be that. But an ultimate end must also have properties like self-sufficiency, so that it could not be pursued for the sake of something else; it must be satisfying, in the sense that having hit on the form of life that embodies it, one would have no inclination to change to some other. In this way criteria are elicited from an analysis of the very notion of what it is to have an ultimate end which narrow the possible candidates down to the one form of life—the eudaimonic.[13]

It is by no means clear, however, that this was Aristotle's own view of the matter. For the way in which we have just put it suggests that ends are rather like means—to be deliberated about, and selected on their merits. For Aristotle, the end of a thing—its *telos*— is not only something to aim at, it is also that to which the thing necessarily tends, and which defines what is good for it. So according to Aristotle, we do not deliberate about ends, precisely because ends cannot be chosen. They are, on the contrary, the considerations that govern deliberation. So if we stress this part of Aristotle's argument, it seems to follow that the notion of practical rationality, with its issue in decision, cannot extend to the pursuit of ultimate ends. *Eudaimonia* is not the most eligible of ends; it is that end to which man tends, inasmuch as he is a man. The reasons we cited earlier—the pleasurableness, the self-sufficiency, the satisfying property of *eudaimonia*—now appear not as reasons for *having* it as an end, but as evidence for believing that the eudaimonic life is the kind of life for which men do in fact strive.

But how can this be, since many men strive for wealth, pleasure, and honour instead?[14] Aristotle's reply must be that such men misapprehend the nature of the good for man, and consequently the nature of man himself. This is the second account of the failure in rationality that we mentioned earlier. Seeking the immediate aims that they do, they are indeed seeking *eudaimonia*, but are mistaken in believing that in attaining them they would really be enjoying *eudaimonia*. The rational enterprise of grasping the end of man would not then be a practical one at all, but an epistemic one. The man who pursues honour or pleasure is not making the wrong choice; he is pursuing *eudaimonia* all right, but with a mistaken view of what constitutes *eudaimonia*. According to this second account, Aristotle is not offering us a conception of substantive practical rationality, for he is not offering reasons for having *eudaimonia* as an end. He is providing reasons instead for judging *eudaimonia* to be the end to which all men tend; and for saying that only one amongst the variety of forms of life at which a man might aim is worthy of the description '*eudaimonia*'.

2   The implication for social science

On either interpretation, the Aristotelian account would, if true, allow the social scientist to evaluate and recommend ends as rational, without being open to the charge of introducing a subjective and personal judgment into his work. The restraints which Weber imposed on social science in the passage quoted above (see p 274) would no longer apply. On the first interpretation, the social scientist would be able to commend an end, not for purely relational reasons, but on the grounds that anyone who grasped the notion of an ultimate end would see that the end in question qualified as such. On the second interpretation, he would be in a position to commend ends as rational, on the grounds that they were wholly or partly constitutive of that end (in Aristotle's view *eudaimonia*), to which all men tend.

The implications of the Aristotelian approach for explanation and theory-building are more complex. On both interpretations, the Aristotelian account would allow the social scientist to explain and predict an individual's pursuing certain ultimate ends, by attributing rationality to him. In each case, a discrepancy between the rational and the actual would enable the social scientist to formulate explanatory questions about the conditions responsible for the failure of rationality. But the explanatory postulate, and the explanatory questions, would be very different, according to which interpretation of Aristotle we accept.

On the first, to attribute rationality to agents is to attribute substantive practical rationality, i.e. the grasp of the notion of an ultimate end and the disposition to pursue as ultimate ends only those ends which are eligible to be pursued as ultimate ends. The explanatory questions posed by instances of substantive practical irrationality would concern the conditions under which individuals attain both an understanding of the notion of an ultimate end, and the capacity to assess, correctly, possible ends in terms of the standards incapsulated in that notion. If, therefore, we could elicit substantive criteria for an ultimate end, it would add substantially to the agenda of social science. Weberian psychiatrists, social psychologists, and anthropologists can and do enquire into the causes of breakdowns in formal practical rationality, into the conditions for developing it, into the problems of societies in which its development is inhibited, or in which breakdowns are common. If it turned out that many people also adopt irrational ends, failing to grasp what is implicit in their having any purposes at all, a corresponding list of questions would suggest itself in relation to substantive practical rationality and irrationality.

On the second interpretation, rationality in the pursuit of ends would consist in rational belief about the end to which all men tend, that they seek under the aspect of their good, and that, when found, will satisfy them. Aristotle, as we have seen, identified this as *eudaimonia*, but we are interested here only in the explanatory and theoretical implications of the idea that there may be *some* such end, discoverable by some form of inquiry. Irrational ends would then raise questions about the conditions under which men form correct beliefs about their own natures, their intrinsic needs, and the objects that would satisfy them. When they hold irrational beliefs of this kind, is this, perhaps, because there are elements in society that set out deliberately to mislead them, or is there something about a society's organization, as Marx argued, that is responsible for their having 'a false consciousness'? What social conditions are necessary if men rational by nature are not to misapprehend their own natures, seeking the good where it is not to be found?

Social criticism or research programmes that seem to rely on the notion of rationality of ends rarely differentiate between the practical and the epistemic approaches. Social psychologists like Laing[15] and Fromm,[16] for instance, want to reformulate descriptions of social deviance to explain it in terms of the frustrations of persons trying to respond rationally to the demands of a society that promotes irrational ends. Such critics could be saying either that the deviant is resisting adopting ends because he knows, however dimly, that there are good reasons for not adopting them; or they may be saying that he cannot find in these ends the properties of the end to which all men tend.

Similar notions are commonly found in criticisms of the 'consumer society'.[17] These suggest not only that consumer values are somehow unworthy, but that they are not such as a rational man could accept as his end. A structural defect in society alienates man from himself: the attempt at self-conscious reflection on his own nature produces only a distortion and his rational faculty atrophies so far as his grasp of his own nature and ends are concerned. So he fails either to see that the ends promoted by the society are not worth pursuing, or to grasp that they are inherently unsatisfying to a human being and therefore not the things he (or anyone else) is looking for in life.

Each interpretation of the Aristotelian argument would also have its own special consequences for the character of the social sciences as disciplines. On the first account, the role of philosophical analysis would be far more central than the positivists allow. For to provide a characterization and analysis of purposive behaviour, to elicit what concepts a person must possess in order to engage in it, to delineate the categories, therefore, that any adequate description of purposeful action would have to employ, is essentially a philosophical task.

On the second account, the procedure for establishing what ends are rational would be rather different. Aristotle thought one could establish the *telos* of a thing, that to which it naturally tends, by reflecting on its essence—a mainly conceptual exercise. Few social scientists today, and not many philosophers, would think much of this as a research programme. But one might still maintain that there is in fact an underlying common element which men attribute, correctly or incorrectly, to all their diverse ends, and for the sake of which they believe them worth pursuing, and that this element could be discovered by a combination of empirical research and analysis. So a social scientist might elicit from a survey of men's actual objectives and, even more, from their apperceptions of their objectives, whatever it was that gave point and coherence to all purposive action, even to action aimed at goals where it was not to be found. For understanding how such mistakes could be made, what the agent saw that made it attractive to him and enabled him to believe in it as an end consistent with his own nature, would also reveal the nature of a rational end.

It should be noted that Weberian explanations and predictions need not be invalidated by an extension of the notion of rationality to ends. Someone's actions could still be explained as formally rational if they were appropriate to his beliefs and to his ends, whether the latter were rational or irrational. Radical critics commonly allow, indeed, that though men in our society pursue worthless and factitious goals, they may do so with a high degree of formal practical rationality. Adding the substantive dimension to practical rationality could open up new questions and new disciplines; it need not invalidate the Weberians' answers to old questions.

E   Rationality and moral ends

1   Kant and rational freedom

Kant's central concern was to show that the human will could be free to determine its own ends, rather than submit to the determination of passion, desire, or inclination. Kant's view is that the human will is only freely determining its ends if it is conforming with, and acting out of respect for, the requirements of rationality. His philosophical enterprise thus consists in an attempt to show what these requirements are, and how the will can be influenced by them.[18]

Just as there are rational criteria for the acceptance of beliefs, so for Kant there are rational criteria for assessing a man's ends. Indeed, there is a family resemblance between them. Reasons for belief are impersonal; logical norms of inference are to be applied irrespective of someone's inclinations to believe this or that; and a reason for believing something is a reason for anyone's believing it. Analogously, Kant claims that a consideration cannot be offered as a reason to justify one's own actions, or to criticize and advise others, without its carrying with it certain rational commitments. The promise-breaker cannot offer his personal motive, 'because it suits me', as such a reason. For it to count as a reason, it would have to be stated impersonally: 'because it suits whoever made the promise'; and adducing such an impersonal consideration as a reason commits one to 'willing' a state of affairs in which everyone acts on that consideration. In Kant's terminology, an individual who breaks a promise because it suits him is acting in accordance with the maxim 'let me break a promise whenever it suits me', and rationality requires acting only on maxims that one can conceive and will to be universal laws.[19] The promise-breaker must thus ask himself whether he can conceive and will the state of affairs where everyone breaks his promises when it suits him. Though Kant's notion of 'willing' is an obscure one, we can take it that it at least involves having a pro-attitude to that state of affairs. The question whether an individual is to break a promise when it suits him turns, therefore, into the question whether he is prepared to adopt this state of affairs as his end. The requirement that one act only on maxims which one can will to be universally accepted laws ('the categorical imperative') is the supreme requirement of both morality and rationality in action.

The final stage in Kant's argument is to show how willing such an impersonal end-state could be held to be rational or irrational. Here Kant distinguishes two types of rational requirement. First, the end-state has to be conceivable. Now one of the very best reasons for not pursuing a state of affairs as an end is the impossibility of bringing it about. It may be plausibly suggested, however, that it would be logically impossible to pursue something as an end unless one believed that it could be brought about; if that is so, the irrationality involved in not meeting Kant's requirement is the epistemic irrationality of believing something that is logically impossible. In any case, this requirement of rationality only identifies ends which are rational in the sense 'not irrational'; it does not show that there are reasons for pursuing them, nor that they demand to be pursued by any rational person. To show that an end is rationally compelling, using this requirement, we would have to show besides that no alternative ends to it could be conceived.

Kant's other rationality requirement for assessing end-states turns out to be end-dependent and relational. He argues, for example, that I cannot will a state of affairs in which no one helps anyone in distress because I have a concern for my own happiness.[20] It appears, then, that in considering whether I can will the impersonally characterized end-state to which my reasons for action commit me, I ask whether it is compatible with my other ends.

We have suggested already that for Kant, rationality is a condition for freedom or autonomy. In Kant's view, if an act could be causally accounted for in terms of inclinations and desires it would be a heteronomous rather than an autonomous act. Nor would it be autonomous if it were adopted as a rational means to a desired end—for the desire would still be a contingent cause of the act. Only an action chosen by an agent because it meets the requirements of rationality could be truly free or autonomous.

Why then should we concern ourselves with acting on reasons which satisfy the requirements of substantive rationality that Kant prescribes, thereby satisfying the conditions for autonomy? Is autonomy itself a rational end to pursue? On Kant's account the free or autonomous individual has both the capacity and the disposition to grasp reasons for action, and to act upon them. Is it rational, then, for an individual to seek to develop and preserve his autonomy? While it is not easy to say for certain how Kant answers this question, some sections of his ethical works suggest the following.

Man simply cannot be indifferent to freedom because, as self-conscious agent, he knows himself under the aspect of chooser. Any person reflecting upon his own experience will find that he cannot give an account of the reality he knows without making and using a conceptual distinction between himself, as a willing, experiencing centre, an ego independent of natural, causal determination, and the world of things. The very idea of having an end presupposes, indeed, the possibility of choice, rather than being causally determined by attractions and repulsions.

But even though conscious of this distinction we are still quite capable of letting ourselves be heteronomously determined; we can respond to the external stimuli that attract or repel us, without reflection, and without having a reason for acting that could be stated as a universal maxim. Even though we discover, from reflecting on our experience, that we can and do exist as choosers, we also discover that we sometimes act impulsively or reactively. Why, then, should we regard as a rational end the perfecting and preserving of our autonomy, rather than suppressing this capacity in favour of spontaneity and immediacy of response? Kant tries to bridge the gap in the argument by appealing to the notion of acting consistently with our nature. To choose not to be free would be to turn one's back on what one is committed to by being conscious of oneself as a chooser: a chooser cannot consistently choose to be heteronomous.[21] The value of autonomy, as manifesting a free and rational will, is something to which we are committed by accepting the categories of choice and action in thinking about ourselves. Since we cannot rid ourselves of them, we cannot rationally adopt ends that do not take account of them.

What kind of inconsistency could this be? Why can I not consistently acknowledge that I am capable of grasping reasons for action and acting on them, yet deliberately set out to avoid using this capacity, hoping perhaps that it will wither away? One possibility is that when I conceive of myself as a chooser I am also aware of myself as having the *disposition* to act for good reasons. It is integral to my nature as chooser that I have ends and that I care about doing whatever is supported by good reasons in terms of those ends. If this is so, could I consistently be indifferent to developing and preserving both my capacity to act on reasons, as well as my capacity and disposition to grasp what count as reasons for action?

If this is Kant's argument, the claim that it is rational to have autonomy as an end remains at best a relational one, dependent on a concern to have rational traits. Even as a relational argument, however, it is open to the same objections as we brought against the second interpretation of Peters's account in section B (see p. 271). There is no necessary connection between a disposition to do whatever is supported by good reasons, and having a concern to decide for myself what that is. Consciousness of a capacity to choose, and a disposition to do what is best in terms of my ends, would be compatible with choosing heteronomy, if that seemed the best way to ensure that one did whatever there was a good reason for doing. So the gap between consciousness of oneself as a rational chooser and having autonomy as an end has not been bridged.

2 The application of the Kantian view in Piaget's developmental theories

Kant's line of thought has branched in various directions. The existentialists, for instance, have seized on the need to safeguard freedom of choice, but, virtually accepting Hume's critique of rationality, identify freedom as the state of a person who realizes the arbitrariness of all ends and makes a personal existential commitment to ends selected *without* reason. Others see autonomy as the outcome of a process of exploring the ends and attitudes one happens to have, tracing them back however to a few ultimate ends in the light of which one then constructs a consistent set of mediate ends. Still others, truer to Kant's own conception, conceive of autonomy as the state in which the agent exercises the capacity to adopt a set of ends which he can see conform to such requirements of reason as impersonality and universality.

Kant's conception of autonomy has had a notable influence on developmental theories in educational psychology. In the first place, it has provided a foundation for Jean Piaget's taxonomy of development. Piaget claims to have shown that there is a normal process of moral development, in which a child passes progressively through a standard set of stages, ordered by his increasing grasp of the conceptual requirements of rationality (see R.S. Peters's account of this in Chapter 12). Differing degrees of rationality, corresponding to whether more or less exacting conditions of impersonality and universality of ends are satisfied, would then provide ways of classifying stages in the development of personality towards the rational ideal of autonomy.

Besides a taxonomic scheme, Piaget offers an explanatory theory. If rational autonomy is taken to be the normal outcome of the process, one can enquire on the one hand into the conditions that are necessary to, or which encourage, normal development, and on the other, into those that inhibit and frustrate it. In this, of course, it is no different in principle from any other developmental hypothesis. Its particular interest as a hypothesis about rationality lies in the claim that the stages correspond not only to a growth in the capacity to grasp complex concepts but also in the capacity to abstract from self-centred desires, and that this is a development in a capacity to operate with logical norms. According to Piaget, therefore, a person who can see nothing except from his own point of view, and one capable of seeing what a situation would be like from another's point of view but not caring for that person's interest, would alike be suffering from a retarded development of rationality. Richard Peters draws attention in Chapter 12 to weak points in Piaget's theory—notably to the slide from epistemic decentering to moral decentering.

Suppose, however, that Piaget could substantiate his claim that there is a process of development not only in the capacity to make inferences, but in the capacity to grasp and assess reasons for action by reference to such criteria as impersonality; he would then have provided not only a taxonomic and explanatory schema, but an evaluative one, too. For if by a process of natural maturation, working through an expanding capacity to grasp how and what considerations could count as reasons for action, a normal person came to have a concern to be rationally autonomous, then anyone who did not come to accept this as an end would be defective or retarded, not merely in moral sensibility, but also in his achievement as a rational being. And this would be both a description and an evaluation.

The logical standing of Piaget's theory as an explanatory hypothesis, like that of any developmental theory, is not easy to determine. As R.S. Peters points out, talk about development presupposes an end-product. But if only some members of a class do in fact attain the final stage, what reason is there for taking a particular sequential development to be the norm? Since many more acorns rot into little piles of humus than ever make oak trees, why should not humus be taken as the normal end of acorn development? Or why not the fallen trunk on the forest floor? Why is senescence decay rather than development? In biology, a developmental theory can have very great explanatory power if the stages, like juvenility, sexual maturity, and adulthood, can be so defined that they apply to a very wide diversity of species, and the processes by which the organism passes from one stage to the next have much in common. In the case of human personality development, however, the choice of a particular sequence as normal development and a particular stage as maturity might be thought to depend on some evaluative commitment extrinsic to scientific enquiry. In the case of Piaget's theory, however, it might be plausibly argued that because the developmental process includes coming to grasp the reasons for having rational autonomy as an end, anyone who is himself rationally developed would have a reason for rating above others any developmental process by which persons attained rational autonomy, and for rating that stage above earlier stages, stages of decay, and stages on different sequences not leading to rationality. This would provide from within the theory a reason for selecting the development of rational autonomy as the norm, rather than any other of the many possible series of sequential stages through which different men do in fact pass.

We have referred to Piaget's theory as one concerning the development of certain capacities. For a developmental theory of this kind to provide a genuinely explanatory hypothesis, it must satisfy the following requirements:

(i) The criterial conditions for the achievement not only of the end stage, but for each intermediate stage of the development, must be clear and coherent.

(ii) The theory must specify, for each stage, the antecedent conditions of the individual necessary if he is to reach that stage. These conditions may be physical states of the individual, as for instance a certain physiological structure may be a necessary condition for acquiring sexual capacities. Or the necessary conditions may themselves be capacities. An instance of a theory of the latter type is Kohlberg's account of the development of rational capacities, according to which progress to the next developmental stage requires that the individual possess certain antecedent intellectual resources and capacities.

(iii) It must be possible to determine whether the subject possesses the necessary conditions for progressing to the next stage, independently of whether he actually does move on to it. For we need to be able to distinguish the subject who possesses them, but does not progress on account perhaps of unfavourable environmental conditions, from the subject who does not possess them at all.

(iv) The theory must provide an account of environmental conditions necessary if the subject who does possess the necessary conditions is actually to move on to the next stage.

(v) It must provide an account of the common environmental conditions that tend to prevent progress to the next stage, even when all the other necessary conditions, both of the individual himself and of his environment, are satisfied.

(vi) If the theory is to identify failures to attain either the end-state or any intermediate state, it must be possible to recognize the lack of a capacity appropriate to that state by some criterion other than performance. For otherwise one could not distinguish the non-performer who lacks the capacity from the one who merely lacks the will.

Piaget was clearly aware of the need to satisfy (i) and (ii). It is less clear that his account will meet the requirements of (iii). We mentioned above, however, that Kohlberg has suggested that the antecedent condition for acquiring further capacities consists in an appropriate conceptual equipment. On Kohlberg's view, the sequence of stages of rational development is a logical sequence, so that the capacity to grasp a certain set of conceptual relations necessarily waits upon the capacity to grasp more primitive ones. Only someone with the capacity to understand addition can acquire the capacity to understand multiplication.

A theory that could clearly specify, first, the criteria for rational autonomy and, second, the antecedent conditions of the subject for developing it through a predeterminable succession of stages, would be equipped to sustain a practical research programme to discover the environmental conditions necessary for the development of autonomy, and conditions liable to inhibit it. We might then begin to account for the seeming failure of so many individuals to reach this final stage of development in rationality.

3 Jürgen Habermas—rationality, freedom, knowledge, and interest

The Kantian emphasis on autonomy through the rational choice of ends is developed in the work of Jürgen Habermas, who in effect combines Kant's view that freedom consists in rationality with Aristotle's claim that rationality is man's natural end. We do not claim that the account that follows is an accurate representation of Habermas's thesis: his exposition is too opaque and some links in his argument too uncertain for any summary to be more than a rational reconstruction. We have tried, however, to state a thesis recognizably akin to Habermas's, selecting, however, the features that bear most directly on the question of the rationality of ends.

Habermas begins with Kant's problem: For action to be rational it must be unadulterated with any sensual interest or natural desire; but how, asks Kant,[22] 'can reason, without any other motives taken from elsewhere, be practical by itself', i.e. capable of initiating action? The very distinction between reason and desire that enabled Kant to propose impersonality and universality as criteria of pure practical rationality drove a wedge between knowing what was reasonable, and being motivated to behave rationally, i.e. for non-end-dependent reasons.

Habermas finds the germ of a solution in Fichte's claim[23] that 'the highest interest and ground of all other interest is interest *in ourselves*'. The genesis of this interest is biological; like all living things, men have an instinctual interest in self-preservation. In man's case, this issues not only in a disposition to control and therefore to understand his environment, but also by a process of self-reflection to understand himself. For to manipulate the environment to one's advantage one must understand the nature of the self to be advantaged. Now the truth that emerges from this self-reflection is that man's nature is objectively given only in the formal respect that he is a species that constitutes itself, shaping himself according to his understanding of himself in the world. So 'the interest of self-preservation cannot aim at the reproduction of the life of the species automatically and without thought',[24] because thought grasps the nature of the self to be preserved and, in grasping it, modifies and creatively extends it.

Through self-reflection man becomes aware of himself as cognitively rational, creative, and, in potentiality at least, autonomous. By this process the subject frees himself from the 'dogmatic enslavement' implied in comprehending oneself as a mere product of nature. 'The dogmatist ... lives in dispersal as a dependent subject that is not only determined by its objects but is itself made into a thing.'[25] But the dogmatist has not grasped the specific self-constitutive nature of man.

Now Habermas has given an illuminating account of what it is to be a self-conscious chooser. But since rational autonomy is not a feature of every man, but something that men can have to a greater or lesser degree, something indeed to be valued and accepted as an end, one still needs to bridge the logical gap between having an awareness of the possibility of autonomy and the rationality of having it as one's end. Habermas is not content to rest on the alleged mere matter-of-fact, that human beings have an instinct to preserve themselves, that issues contingently in an interest in autonomy. 'The human interest in autonomy and responsibility', he says,[26] 'can be apprehended a priori'. But his account of the *a priori* argument is sketchy and obscure. It depends on the proposition that the point of language is 'universal and unrestrained consensus'. It seems that we should be acting inconsistently as users of language if, while engaging in an activity the point of which depends on the shaping of agreement in belief and action, through the exchange of reasons that can be grasped by the free intellect, we did not also value the capacity necessary for its success. It is by no means clear, however, that this is the only point of language-use. After all, one way of constraining masses of people into consensus is also by the use of language. However, Habermas's argument would need much more elaboration than it gets before one could assess its value for bridging the logical gap between having the capacity for autonomy and having a reason for pursuing it as an end.

4 Hegel and the rationality of historical ends

Habermas's anthropology puts a great deal more stress than did Kant on man's social nature, and on the development of self-knowledge as something that applies to the species as well as to the individual—indeed, to the individual only through his culturally-formed self-awareness as a member of a species. It was largely the work of Hegel that added this new dimension to Kantianism.[27]

For Hegel, man's history was the evolving consciousness of a self-forming social species, a consciousness that by the exercise of rationality progressively imposes its own intelligible order upon the stuff of the universe; with its extending comprehension, the human species absorbs, as it were, the natural universe into its own rational nature. Equally, man's own understanding of himself is concretely expressed in his institutions, normative structures informed by ideas and values, that evolve as man's self-perception evolves. Precisely because Hegel conceived of the universe as intelligible only by virtue of the ideal schemata devised by man, its conscious component, and because he believed the succession of these schemata to follow a rational, dialectical pattern analogous to the inferential sequence of logical argument, Hegel believed that, rightly comprehended, the history of man would display a rational necessity behind the apparent contingency of events; the ends and values characteristic of each stage of cultural development would be seen as stages in the emergence of an autonomous self-conscious species. Man's *telos*, then, would be the realization of rational autonomy. But this would not be merely a natural tendency, an inbuilt direction, as it were, in human evolution; its logical necessity could be demonstrated, at least after the event, at each stage of its development, by showing the logical relations between the central ideas informing that stage and those of antecedent stages. The ultimate end—rational freedom—was apparent, Hegel believed, both from contemplation of history and from a proper philosophical understanding of the nature of self-conscious being.

If the rationality of man really did provide a clue to historical development, as the Hegelians say it does, positivist social science would indeed be self-excluded from a great range of important questions for the science of man. Accepting agents' ends uncritically, and concentrating only on means and their relation to agents' beliefs about their decision-situations, the historian and the social scientist would never come to ask: What is the significance of this decision, this social movement, this state's hegemony, in the enterprise of human self-understanding and of human freedom? Equally, they could never provide as an explanation for a group's success that the realization of its ends was required for the evolving pattern to enter its next phase. For the Hegelian, ends consonant with historical development would be rational, and would be achieved; others, running counter to the thrust of reason, would fail. Nevertheless, such an explanatory scheme would not displace a positivist one; for the question 'How did it happen?' could still be asked and answered in a positivist way; but a new question: 'Why did it have to happen?' would be added, and answering it would require the notion of rational ends.

But the rationality of historical agents was not, according to Hegel, necessarily a subjective rationality; the historian may perceive the cunning of history where the statesman, who is its agent, does not. Nevertheless, Hegel did see the process as one of increasing self-awareness; the very fact that the historical *telos* was towards the rational autonomy of mind (or spirit) guaranteed that men would not always be sleepwalkers. Rational ends that men pursued only half-wittingly were rational only by reason of their role in promoting the greater self-awareness and autonomy of the species. And Hegel believed that his own philosophical system was, in this respect, the great breakthrough. By the exercise of philosophical understanding, the rational will has become aware of itself as its own rational end.

F Conclusion

We have not attempted in this paper the lengthy and difficult task of assessing the philosophical programmes that might rebut the limitations on social science imposed by Humean-Weberian

positivism. We have simply sketched the outlines of these programmes and suggested some differences that it would make to
social science if they could be successfully carried through. There is
little reason to suppose, however, that the effect would be to
invalidate the method or falsify the findings of positivist science;
one could still assess the formal practical rationality of means and
the epistemic rationality of belief, predict and explain actions using
those categories, prescribe optimal strategies for given ends, and
so on, whether those ends were rational, irrational, or non-rational.
The explanatory and predictive questions to which economists,
historians, sociologists, and social psychologists currently address
themselves would remain, therefore, virtually unaffected. For if men
seek irrational ends, their actions could still be explicable using the
formal practically rational models; and there is little enough reason
to suppose that most men's ends are, to any great degree, substantively rational. Even if there were reasons for adopting certain ends
as one's own, it could be argued that, men being what they are,
someone's actually adopting such an end was as much a subject for
explanation as someone's not doing so. It is only on some further
hypothesis, that men as individuals—or as a species—have a
tendency towards rationality, that the idea of substantive practical
rationality might generate new explanatory questions and procedures or predictive possibilities. Theories like Piaget's and Habermas's, that claim to recognize such a tendency in human beings,
do profess to open up new problems in just this way. But we should
expect such theories to be important, not in sciences like economics,
where the problems are to explain particular acts and social phenomena like price movements, and the processes would be much the
same whether the ends were rational or not, but in social sciences
concerned with the development of rational traits whether of
individual men and women or of cultures.

Of course, if we go beyond explanation and prediction, and
consider the prescriptive or advisory function of the social scientist,
the notion of the rationality of ends could be important even in
those sciences hitherto employing only formal rationality models.
An economist might no longer be confined to advising on means;
for there might then be more to say about a policy of maintaining
full employment, for instance, than that it would tend to promote
inflation: there might be reasons for saying that stable currencies
and incomes were less important as ends than providing everyone
with a job, and that a government that took a different view must be
failing to grasp all the relevant considerations. There is no reason
to suppose, however, that the arguments necessary to establish
such prescriptive claims would be any easier to formulate or more

reliable in practice than those by which economists who accept Humean-Weberian limitations warrant their merely hypothetical prescriptions. An opportunity to ask bolder questions is not itself a guarantee of right answers.

Notes

1 Peters, R.S. (1966), Part Two; see especially pp. 121–6, 154–6, 161–6, 180–2, 213–15.
2 Rawls, J. (1971), ch. VII, § 63. See also Fried, C. (1970), ch. 3.
3 Rawls, J. (1971), p. 93.
4 See Chapter 1, p. 13, and Chapter 4, p. 96, of this volume.
5 Hume, D. (1888), bk II, part III, section III.
6 Weber, M. (1949), pp. 18–19. See also Myrdal, G. (1958), and Nagel, E. (1961), pp. 485–502, for discussions of value-neutrality in social science.
7 Weber, M. (1948).
8 See, for instance, essays by S.M. Willhelm and Alvin W. Gouldner, in Horowitz, I.L. (ed.) (1965).
9 See Aristotle (1961), I, VI. 5–13, VII. 13, X. 5–8. For a recent treatment on similar lines, see Flynn, J. (1973).
10 Aristotle (1961), I. 1.
11 Ibid., I. 7.
12 Ibid., X. 6–8.
13 Ibid., I.7.
14 Ibid., I.5.
15 For instance, Laing, R.D. (1967), pp. 97–9, 116–17. See also Laing, R.D. (1965), and Laing, R.D. and Esterson, A. (1970).
16 Fromm, E. (1955).
17 Reich, C.A. (1971), and Marcuse, H. (1955) and (1964), might be interpreted as making this kind of a point. See also Mills, C. Wright (1967).
18 Kant, I. (1948).
19 Ibid., pp. 88–92.
20 Ibid., p. 91.
21 Kant, I. (1927), I.I.III, 'Of the motives of pure practical reason', pp. 164–82. See also Kant, I. (1964), pp. 77–111.
22 Kant, quoted by Habermas, J. (1972), p. 202.
23 Fichte, quoted by Habermas, J. (1972), p. 206.
24 Habermas, J. (1972), p. 288.
25 Ibid., p. 208.
26 Ibid., p. 314. Albrecht Wellmer (1971), p. 80, quotes in translation the following passage from an unpublished work by Habermas:

> No matter how the intersubjectivity of mutual understanding may be deformed, the design of an ideal speech situation is necessarily implied with the structure of potential speech; for every speech, even that of intentional deception, conforms to the idea of truth. And this idea can only be disclosed by returning to the structure of unlimited

and non-repressive communication. When we master the means of construction of an ideal speech situation, we can conceive the mutually interpreting ideas of truth, freedom, and justice....

27 In addition to Hegel, G.W.F. (1942) and (1949), see Plamenatz, J. (1963), pp. 129–268, and Avineri, S. (1971), for expositions and discussions of Hegel's view of the relation between rationality and world history.

Bibliography

ARISTOTLE (1961), *Nicomachean Ethics*, trans. Ross, Sir David, London.

AVINERI, S. (1971), 'Consciousness and history: List der Vernunft in Hegel and Marx', in Steinkraus, W.E., *New Studies in Hegel's Philosophy*, New York.

DEARDEN, R.F., HIRST, P.H. and PETERS, R.S. (eds) (1972), *Education and the Development of Reason*, London.

ELLUL, J. (1965), trans. Wilkinson, J., *The Technological Society*, London.

FLYNN, J. (1973), *Humanism and Ideology—An Aristotelian View*, London.

FRIED, C. (1970), *An Anatomy of Value*, Cambridge, Mass.

FROMM, E. (1955), *The Sane Society*, New York.

HABERMAS, J. (1972), trans. Shapiro, J.J., *Knowledge and Human Interests*, Boston.

HAEZRAHI, P. (1968), 'The concept of man as end-in-himself', in Wolff, R.P. (ed.), *Kant*, London.

HAMPSHIRE, S. (1959), *Thought and Action*, London.

HAMPSHIRE, S. (1965), *Freedom of the Individual*, London and Dunedin.

HEGEL, G.W.F. (1942), *Philosophy of Right*, trans. Knox, T.M., Oxford.

HEGEL, G.W.F. (1949), *The Phenomenology of Mind*, trans. Baillie, Sir James, London.

HOROWITZ, I.L. (ed.) (1965), *The New Sociology*, New York.

HUME, D. (1888), *A Treatise of Human Nature*, ed. Selby-Bigge, L.A., Oxford (repr. 1964).

KANT, I. (1927), *Critical Examination of Practical Reason*, in Abbott, T.K. (trans.), *Kant's Theory of Ethics*, London, 6th edn.

KANT, I. (1948), *Groundwork of the Metaphysic of Morals*, in Paton, H.J. (ed. and trans.), *The Moral Law*, London.

KANT, I. (1964), *The Metaphysical Principles of Virtue*, trans. Ellington, J., Indianapolis.

KOHLBERG, L. (1969), 'Stage and sequence: the cognitive developmental approach to socialization', in Goslin, D.A. (ed.), *Handbook of Socialization: Theory and Research*, Chicago.

LAING, R.D. (1965), *The Divided Self*, Harmondsworth.

LAING, R.D. (1967), *The Politics of Experience* and *The Bird of Paradise*, Harmondsworth.

LAING, R.D. and ESTERSON, A. (1970), *Sanity, Madness, and the Family*, Harmondsworth.

MARCUSE, H. (1955), *Eros and Civilization*, Boston.

MARCUSE, H. (1964), *One-Dimensional Man*, London.

MILLS, C. WRIGHT (1967), 'Culture and politics', in Horowitz, I.L. (ed.), *Power, Politics, and People*, New York.

MYRDAL, G. (1958), *Value in Social Theory*, London.

NAGEL, E. (1961), *The Structure of Science*, New York.

PETERS, R.S. (1966), *Ethics and Education*, London.

PETERS, R.S. (1972a), 'Education and human development', in Dearden, R.F., Hirst, P.H. and Peters, R.S. (eds) (1972).

PETERS, R.S. (1972b), 'Reason and passion', in Dearden, R.F., Hirst, P.H. and Peters, R.S. (eds) (1972).

PETERS, R.S. (1973a), 'Freedom and the development of the the free man', in Doyle, J.F. (ed.), *Educational Judgments*, London.

PETERS, R.S. (1973b) 'The justification of education', in Peters, R.S. (ed.), *The Philosophy of Education*, London.

PIAGET, J. (1965), *The Moral Judgment of the Child*, New York.

PIAGET, J. (1968), *Six Psychological Studies*, London.

PLAMENATZ, J. (1963), *Man and Society*, vol. II, London.

RAWLS, J. (1971), *A Theory of Justice*, Cambridge, Mass.

REICH, C.A. (1971), *The Greening of America*, Harmondsworth.

STRETTON, H. (1969), *The Political Sciences*, London.

WALTON, K.A. (1967), 'Rational action', *Mind*, LXXVI, pp. 537–47.

WARNOCK, G.J. (1968), 'The primacy of practical reason', in Strawson, P.F. (ed.), *Studies in the Philosophy of Thought and Action*, London.

WEBER, M. (1948), 'Science as a vocation', in Gerth, H.H. and Mills, C. Wright (eds), *From Max Weber—Essays in Sociology*, London.

WEBER, M. (1949), *The Methodology of the Social Sciences* (ed. and trans. Shils, E.A. and Finch, H.A.), Chicago.

WELLMER, A. (1971), 'Some remarks on the logic of explanation in the social sciences', in *Royal Institute of Philosophy Lectures, Vol. IV, 1969–70—The Proper Study*, London.

Part Three

Rational persons

12

The development of reason

R.S. Peters

The organization of moral values that characterizes middle
childhood is, by contrast, comparable to logic itself; it is the
logic of values or of action amongst individuals, just as logic is
a kind of moral for thought.[1]

A Introduction

I take it as axiomatic that, in talking about development, there must
be a prior conception of the end-product, and that the processes
which contribute to it must be sequential.[2] In the case, however,
of human development, if its physical aspects are disregarded,
there is an additional condition which derives from the fact that
the processes are processes of learning. This involves coming up to
a mark in a variety of respects as an outcome of past experience,
and between the attainment and the learning processes there must
be some intelligible connection. It is unintelligible, for instance,
that an understanding of Euclid could develop out of learning
experiences of standing on one's head, unless, say, the posture
were conceived as drawing one's attention to angles and their
relationships. It is an empirical question, of course, which particular
experiences help individuals or people in general to reach the
particular level of mastery, or understanding; but the outcome
dictates certain types of experience.

Now much of the more precise experimental work in child
psychology has been done within the old stimulus-response type of
conceptual framework on the assumption that the development

of thought can be explained in terms of variants of the old principles of association such as recency, contiguity, frequency, etc. My view is that such principles explain certain forms of human behaviour but, in the main, those that are non-rational or irrational. At best they are to be regarded as primitive precursors of thought that may impede the later development of rationality.

I propose to ignore also physiological findings about the development of the brain, even though these deal, of course, with necessary conditions for the development of rationality. Theories such as those outlined by Woodward,[3] and the influential views of Miller, Galanter, and Pribram[4] make use of a model of the nervous system, which is thought appropriate to deal with types of behaviour that the old stimulus-response approach could not handle. As, however, this model credits the nervous system with plans, strategies, information, etc., it seems conceptually corrupt from the outset. For all such concepts are only properly attributable to conscious agents. Such models may suggest fruitful hypotheses, but their findings can all be translated into more straightforward terms. Indeed, Woodward uses such models mainly to corroborate and supplement Piaget's findings.

The basic structure of my account of the development of rationality will be provided by the work of Piaget.[5] This is not simply because he has devoted most of his life to just this topic; it is also because he throws out at times certain suggestions about connections between the use of reason and its social context that I find both stimulating in themselves and appropriate as supporting some theses which I propose to advance in this essay.

B The end-product of the development of reason

In this section I shall give an account of the main features that mark a man out as rational. This will provide an account of the end-product of the developmental process, and so enable us to judge whether Piaget does justice to the complexity of the phenomenon of rationality, and whether he provides an adequate explanation of its development.

1 Intelligence, rationality, and reasonableness

(a) Intelligence and reason

Piaget thinks that in his work he is tracing the development of intelligence. In a way, he is right; for though rationality involves much more than intelligence, it can be viewed appropriately as a development of it. We only describe thought and behaviour as intelligent or unintelligent in a situation in which there is some kind of novelty in relation to the belief structure or established behaviour routines of an agent. If a person, or animal for that matter, is just carrying out some established routine, questions of the behaviour being intelligent or unintelligent do not arise. Suppose, then, that something novel or unexpected turns up. The person who exhibits intelligence can do what Piaget calls 'assimilate' it. By that is meant that he deals with it by fitting it into his existing belief structure because of some similarity which he grasps. Alternatively, if the novelty is too discrepant to be dealt with in this way, he 'accommodates' to it by making some adjustment to his expectations.

What additional features do being rational or reasonable possess? For we talk quite happily of animals and very small children as being intelligent or stupid, but we do not talk of them as being reasonable or unreasonable, rational or irrational. The difference is surely that we can understand rational behaviour and belief as informed by general rules. It is behaviour and belief for reasons— and for reasons of a certain kind. Rational behaviour and belief spring from the recognition, implicit or explicit, that certain *general* considerations are grounds for action or belief. Thus, the development of rationality allows an individual to transcend the present— to emerge from a level of life in which his actions and beliefs are determined by the particular immediate impulses and perceptions of his current experience. Current and future actions and beliefs come to be influenced not just by what occurs here and now, but by what an individual believes has been or will be the case in the past or in the future. The clearest cases are perhaps when an individual forms predictive beliefs on the basis of past observations, or makes plans for the future on the basis of various expectations.

This transcendence of the present is, of course, implicit in the more primitive use of intelligence, in that both perception and action are unintelligible without the use of concepts; we always see something as something and want it under some aspect. There is, therefore, an implicit relating to the past and future by means of general concepts. But in reasoning this relating is extended and made explicit. Inferences made in choosing or forming an opinion, and arguments to justify one's action or beliefs, all tacitly invoke rules which mark out certain general considerations as relevant grounds.

There is another way in which rationality involves the transcendence of the present. The considerations which influence the rational man need not and usually will not contain any temporal reference. The force of the consideration that p, will not depend on *p*'s being the case *now*. This second aspect of the transcendence of the present is linked with other ways in which rationality allows of the transcendence of the particular—the emergence from a level of life in which what determines actions or beliefs are considerations about the identity of persons or things, or of time and space. All this emerges clearly if note is taken of what the use of reason is usually contrasted with—authority, revelations, tradition. In these cases what is right or true is finally determined by appeal at an ultimate level to some particular man, body, or set of practices; it is not determined by appeal to general considerations. In the use of reason, by contrast, identity, as well as time and place, come to be seen as irrelevant sources of considerations.

Thus both 'rational' and 'reasonable' presuppose a background of reasoning which is not necessarily present when we talk about behaviour or beliefs as being intelligent or stupid. 'Stupid' is used simply when there is no grasp of a similarity which provides the basis for assimilation or of a difference too glaring to warrant it. There can, of course, be reasoning in cases where we use the term 'stupid' and the reasoning itself can be intelligently or stupidly done; but there does not have to be.

(b) 'Reasonable' and 'rational'

There are certain distinctions to be made between 'rational' and 'reasonable' which are particularly important for one of the theses which I propose to develop in this paper. They are embedded, I think, in the ways in which we ordinarily use these terms. But even should counter-examples be produced, I shall not mind. For the point of examining ordinary usage is not to spot some linguistic essence but to take one route to explore distinctions which may prove important in the context of a thesis.

How, then, do 'rational' and 'reasonable' differ, given that they both presuppose a background of reasoning? They obviously do, as can be gleaned by considering their opposites. 'Irrational' functions almost as a diagnosis, and requires special explanation. 'Unreasonable' is a much milder and more common complaint and does not seem to be associated in the same way with summoning the psychiatrist for advice. The difference, surely, is that 'rational' and 'irrational' have application to situations in which someone could have conclusive reasons for belief or action. 'Irrational' is usually applied to cases where there is a belief or action with no good reason or in the face of reasons. The irrational man is presumed to be aware of the considerations which would normally be deemed conclusive for believing or doing something; but, because of something that comes over him, he cannot bring himself to believe or do what is appropriate. Or alternatively, he believes something fervently, for which there is not the slightest evidence or does something for which there is no discernible reason. To call a man unreasonable who believed that his hands were covered in blood when the blood could not be seen and when he had washed his hands in hot water with detergent in it, would be to make too feeble a complaint. For 'unreasonable' is a weaker kind of condemnation: it presupposes that a person has reasons for what he believes or does: but it suggests that the reasons are very weak, and that he pays little attention to the reasons of others. A man who is unreasonable has a somewhat myopic or biased viewpoint; he either wilfully turns a blind eye to relevant considerations or weights them in an obtuse and idiosyncratic way. It would be unreasonable, for instance, to believe that it is not going to rain simply because there are patches of blue sky about, or that one will contract pneumonia simply by getting caught in the rain without an umbrella. Generalizations are used, but there is little attempt to test them or to consider them critically. The individual tends to be attached to beliefs that suit him, or that are based on authority, hearsay or a narrow range of considerations. It is a level of life to which epithets such as 'bigoted', 'short-sighted', 'prejudiced', 'wilful', 'pig-headed', 'obtuse', have obvious application.

Many of these epithets apply to actions in which there is the same suggestion of a limited form of reasoning with sketchy attention to evidence and to relevant considerations. It is unreasonable, for instance, to insist on driving from London to Birmingham by car if all one wants is to get there as quickly as possible; for there is the inter-city train service. Similarly it is unreasonable to do the football pools as the appropriate way of acquiring the money for one's summer holiday. In the sphere of emotion the same point holds. It is unreasonable, but not irrational, to be afraid of being shot at by a gamekeeper near a 'Trespassers Will Be Prosecuted' notice. It is unreasonable, but not irrational, to be jealous of one's son if he begins to occupy some of one's wife's time and attention.

The second important difference between 'unreasonable' and 'irrational' is that the former has a more explicitly social connotation. 'Reasonable' suggests a willingness to listen to arguments and relevant considerations advanced by others in public argument. There is, however, a second and stronger sense of 'reasonable' which implies that an individual is disposed to take account of the claims to consideration that other individuals have—that is, he is to some degree impartial in dealing with situations in which the rights and interests of others are at stake. 'Irrational' has no suggestion of a failure to give this kind of impartial consideration to the claims of others.

The possibility of a slide from the first to the second sense of 'reasonable' will prove to be very important in our understanding and appraisal of Piaget's treatment of the development of rationality in a man's practical life.

2   The publicity and objectivity of reason

The reference to the social aspect of 'reasonableness' introduces another cardinal feature of 'reason' which is its publicity. It is very easy to think of reasoning as the operation of a private gadget, or as the flowering of some inner potentiality. But this is an untenable view; for though there is a sense in which, as a mode of consciousness, it is private to the individual, its content and procedures of operation are public possessions. By that I mean that the concepts fundamental to its operation are shared concepts; children are introduced to them from the very beginning of their lives as social beings. They structure the experience of the world for them from the very start. With the learning of language, which is one of the main vehicles of reasoning, children are initiated into rules of syntax as well, which are also public possessions. Furthermore developed types of reasoning, which involve criticism and the production of counter-examples, can best be understood as the internalization of public procedures, and the different points of view of others. The individual, who reasons in this developed sense, is one who has taken a critic into his own consciousness, whose mind is structured by the procedures of a public tradition. He can adopt the point of view of what G.H. Mead called 'the generalized other'. This is a reflection in his consciousness of social situations in which the point of view of others has in fact been represented.

There is another public feature of reasoning which is crucial to its objectivity when it is applied to the world as in science, history, or morality. In these forms of reasoning, different points of view confront one another, each supported by reasons. But what counts as a reason depends not only on public rules embodied in concepts, syntax, and forms of inference which structure common forms of discourse, but also upon there being some forms of experience which are generally taken to terminate disputes. In science, for instance, consensus can be reached on matters in dispute only because there is a prior understanding that what the research workers can all hear or see shall count as evidence for anyone. Similarly, in practical reasoning, it is because we respond alike to situations of danger, frustration, suffering, and the like, that we are able to agree in deliberation on what is to count as a reason for acting. Without such shared experiences and responses, neither explanation nor deliberations could get under way, since there would be nothing on which one could rely as an unproblematic anchoring point of discourse.

3   The norms of reason

It has been usual, since the time of Hume, to contrast reason with passion. But, as I have argued elsewhere,[6] this contrast is a mistake. Integral to the life of reason are a related set of norms or standards with a range of correlative attitudes and concerns. What marks off rationality, as a level of life distinct from the non-rational, the irrational and the unreasonable, is the continual influence and interaction of these norms and concerns. I shall distinguish three aspects of the operation of the norms of reason.

(a) There is, first, the influence of the rational individual's concern for consistency and the avoidance of contradiction. This concern can be manifested in two ways in which a rational man forms and modifies his beliefs. He has to resolve and remove any putative inconsistencies between his existing beliefs and assumptions and any discrepant 'incoming' experience or piece of information. If something turns up which is novel he has either to latch on to some feature or similarity which will enable it to be subsumed under his existing assumptions, or, if it is too discrepant to be fitted in, he has to make an appropriate alteration to his assumptions. The second demand of the requirement of consistency is, of course, that in forming beliefs by an inference from antecedent convictions and assumptions, the individual avoids drawing conclusions which are inconsistent with his premises.

In the sphere of action the rational man, in choosing means to his ends, can be understood as concerned to secure consistency between his choices and his ends; and if he is acting on rules, between his choices and his rules. The demand for consistency is implicit in the requirement of reason that willing the end commits one to willing the means. One paradigm of rationality is the man who has a number of ends which cannot be simultaneously achieved: in devising a plan or schedule whereby the ends of highest priority are achieved, or all his ends are secured over a period of time, he can be seen as avoiding unnecessary conflict between his ends and as avoiding choices which unnecessarily conflict with and frustrate some of his wants. Presupposed by such rationality in choice is the agent's consistently ranking his ends and his rules in some order of priority. There is also a process—analogous to the adaptation

305

of assumptions to some novel item of experience—of modifying one's ends and rules in the light of circumstances. Rationality is, for example, evinced in qualifying an absolute disapproval of lying when confronted by a case where exceptional circumstances incline one to think that there are overriding grounds for lying— e.g. the immense amount of suffering likely to be brought about if the literal truth is told on a particular occasion.

(b) The rational man also has a well-defined sense of what counts as a relevant consideration in the various contexts of belief-formation and choice. What counts as relevant can be given in a generalization, as for instance a meteorological generalization which indicates relevant grounds for the prediction that it is going to rain: or it may be given in a rule of conduct that indicates, say, the circumstances in which one ought to be polite. To accept such standards of relevance is to be disposed to take account of the considerations in question when they crop up, and to reject as partial or arbitrary choices or beliefs based on other considerations, such as may be suggested by extrinsic attractions or aversions. Rationality is also usually held to commit a man to rejecting as arbitrary *particular* considerations of time, place and identity. If one is considering whether it is going to rain, the mere fact that it is 10 a.m. and the place Christchurch does not count. Some additional features characterizing the time and place of the prediction have to be added. Similarly if one acts on the rule that one ought to be polite, the mere facts that it is 10 a.m., that one is in Christchurch and that one is talking to Mr Brown, have to be disregarded. Similarly, rational prudence involves taking no account of purely temporal considerations. As Sidgwick put it: 'Hereafter as such is to be regarded neither more nor less than now'. There must be other than temporal considerations, even if they are as crude as 'if you wait you won't be able to have it at all' or 'if you wait there will be more of it'.

(c) Finally, fully developed rationality involves not a comparatively passive taking account of considerations which are forced on one's attention, but an active enquiring and critical spirit. Many of the central norms of rationality relate to such activities. Thus the tendency to adapt assumptions to novel situations develops into the conscious attempt to check assumptions—nurtured, perhaps, by a caution born of past experience of being in error. This becomes of outstanding importance in systematic developments of reasoning about the world as in science or history. For instead of just being brought up short by the givenness of the world and having to accommodate to it if the novelty is to be dealt with, the individual becomes much more concerned about the warrants for his stock of assumptions and rules. He pays explicit attention to what Bacon called 'the negative instance'. He makes sure that his assumptions and rules are well-grounded. And, in activities such as science he makes explicit attempts to overthrow them by imagining counter-examples and seeing whether his assumptions and rules can stand up to such tests. He looks for evidence.

The same development can be discerned, too, in forms of practical reasoning, such as morality. Consider an individual who, through first-hand experience, becomes sensitive to the suffering brought about by social practices. No longer able to accept them uncritically, he sets about ruthlessly examining them against principles that common human experience establishes as relevant grounds for evaluation and decision.

Reasoning thus entails the recognition of the normative demands of consistency, relevance, impartiality and the search for grounds for belief and decision. It can readily be seen, too, that if it is going to operate in ways which are compatible with its overarching *tele* of discovering what is true and what is best, other norms enter in. Clarity in stating assumptions is necessary if issues relating to consistency, relevance and respect for evidence are to be raised. Honesty is also required; for cheating would be completely counterproductive in the context of the determination to check the assumptions and rules concerned.

What status is to be accorded to these norms which are definitive of the use of reason? One can, in the fashion of a true English gentleman, say with Ryle that the individual is now subject to certain characteristic scruples.[7] One can talk less modestly about the intellectual virtues of consistency, clarity, impartiality, sense of relevance, and demand for evidence or about the ethics of belief governed by the conviction that truth matters. Or one can talk about the rational passions that characterize the concern for truth.[8] These are just different ways of drawing attention to a group of values that are inseparable from the developed use of reason.

4 Action and will

In the sphere of action there is a continuum of virtues generated by the demands for consistency, relevance and the active search for grounds for belief and decision. They are closely connected with the concept of a self that endures through time. As we have seen, rationality in action is manifested in choosing means to ends, in the scheduling or planning of a series of choices over time in order to satisfy a number of conflicting wants, and in the delay of gratification which is demanded by plans which give no special priority to the present. All such deliberation and planning involves the use of reason; and is subject to the demands of consistency and relevance, and the requirements of active rationality.

In putting such plans and policies into action, it is often the case that there is scope for the exercise of an additional family of virtues, which are intimately connected with what is often called 'the will', 'having character', or 'strength of character'. The virtues are those such as integrity, courage, perseverance, and resoluteness. They are connected with reason in that all imply some kind of consistency in sticking to a principle or pursuing a policy or plan. The administrator refuses to abandon justice by accepting a bribe; his secretary heaves herself out of bed when the alarm goes with thoughts of the importance of being at the office on time flitting through her numbed consciousness. There is also the implication that these principles or policies are adhered to in the face of counter-inclinations or temptations. To give an account of such actions, which William James described as actions in the line of greatest resistance, reference must be made to the affective aspects of the demands of reason inherent in consistency and relevance as well as to the affective aspects of the principles and policies concerned.

C Piaget's theory of development

In the previous section, I have examined the principal components and the structure of the concept 'reason'.[9] Reason is the end-product of the process of development which is the subject of the rest of this paper. In particular, I shall examine critically the theory of development offered by Piaget. In this section I shall sketch the main outlines of the theory, focusing on those features that bear upon the distinction I have made between 'rationality' and 'reasonableness', on the publicity and objectivity of reason, on the acceptance of the norms of reason, and on the relation between the development of reason and action and will. These elements have figured prominently in my own account of the end-product; in my view it is the development of these features that most needs to be explained.

Piaget distinguishes four stages, which I shall consider in turn.

1 0–2: The Copernican revolution of early childhood

The first stage is what Piaget calls the intellectual revolution of the first two years. The child now apprehends the world as one in which enduring objects existing in time and space stand in causal relations, though causality is at first interpreted purely in terms of agency. At the earliest stage, the child's consciousness is egocentric, since[10]

> there is no definite differentiation between the self and the external world. ... The self is at the centre of reality to begin with for the very reason that it is not aware of itself. ... The progress of sensori-motor intelligence leads to the construction of an objective universe in which the subject's own body is an element amongst others and with which the internal life, localized in the subject's own body, is contrasted.

It is only with the emergence of the concept of enduring objects that the child is able to objectify emotions and to differentiate them by reference to objects. The concept of a 'means to an end', which presupposes causality, also emerges at this stage. This is a prerequisite of any kind of rational action.

The thought of the very young child is non-rational in so far as it is not subject to such categories. One of Freud's most important contributions to psychological theory was just this distinction between primary and secondary processes; for he argued that the mind of the very young child is ruled by wishes in which there is no proper grasp of means to an end, and of enduring objects in a space-time framework having causal properties in relation to other objects.

At the primary Freudian level thought is determined purely by the affectivity of the wish. This makes possible a primitive form of associative thinking determined by affectively loaded similarities between objects in which no account is taken of their identity as substantive entities as distinct from their pleasing or displeasing features; there is no grasp of temporal or spatial considerations or of causality, which presupposes a sense of time and of objects having stable characteristics. Without these concepts one could not have the capacity for rational belief or for the postponement of gratification which is indispensable to rational action. As Freud postulated the continuance of primary thought processes even in the adult, a more precise plotting of this intellectual revolution is very important. Some lapses from rational belief and action could be explained, Freud suggested, in terms of disruptions brought about by the persistence of this more primitive form of thought.[11] People succumb to impulses prompted by these unstructured wishes. And some more enduring forms of irrationality, such as schizophrenia, might be linked with the failure to acquire elements of the secondary conceptual apparatus, e.g. the concept of oneself and others as enduring objects, the distinction between appearance and reality.

2 2-7: Pre-operational thought and moral realism

The next stage in Piaget's developmental account is of great significance for the social aspects of the development of reason; for it
is at this stage (roughly 2–7) that language is acquired and 'Thought
becomes conscious to the degree to which the child is able to communicate it.'[12] In this stage, according to Piaget, the child
internalizes rules that are imposed on him by adults. What exactly
is meant by 'internalization' is no clearer than the way in which
it actually happens. But this stage is of crucial importance in the
development of man as a purposive, rule-following animal. Children
somehow grasp, from the inside as it were, what it is to follow a
rule. Language is obviously of great importance. It is a means of
formulating rules, and a device for teaching children to follow
them. But for the child himself the use of language still has partly
an ego-centric function. As Luria[13] has also demonstrated, the use
of monologue helps the child to perform tasks as an adjunct to
action; also, when children of this age talk together, their 'con-
versation' has the character of a collective monologue. But, on the
other hand, language, together with imagery, enables the child to
represent and rehearse actions, to reconstruct the past, and to
anticipate the future. It helps, too, to unite the child with others
as it is a vehicle for concepts and ideas that are public. It aids his
socialization as well as providing a tool for individual projects.

The affective life of the child parallels this development in
thought. He has interests of a predominantly practical character.
He learns to evaluate himself and to develop levels of aspiration.
Feelings are interchanged as well as words, and fellow-feeling
develops for those who share his interests. There is also respect for
older people—especially parents—which, at this stage, is a mixture
of affection and fear. Obedience is his first moral precept and values
take the form of rules which are heteronomously accepted. What
matters about them is their formulation rather than the intent
which may inform them.

However, accommodation to others and to reality is still very
rudimentary; for the child's thought is characterized by what
Piaget calls 'intuition', in which judgments are made on the basis
of perception rather than reason. 'One quality stands out in the
thinking of the young child: he constantly makes assertions without
trying to support them with facts.'[14] This stems from the character
of his social behaviour, from his ego-centricity in the sense of a lack of
differentiation between his own point of view and that of others.
'It is only vis-a-vis others that we are led to seek evidence for our
statements. We always believe ourselves without further ado until

we learn to consider the objections of others and to internalize such discussions in the form of reflection.'

3 7–12: Concrete operations, autonomy, and will

The next stage of concrete operations (roughly 7–12) is the crucial one for the development of reasoning proper. The child becomes able both 'to dissociate his point of view from that of others and to co-ordinate these different points of view'.[15] True discussions between children are possible and 'ego-centric' language disappears almost entirely. 'One is hard put to say whether the child has become capable of a certain degree of reflection because he has learned to co-operate with others or vice-versa.' The child is no longer so impulsive; he thinks before he acts. But this reflection is a kind of internal dialogue, that parallels actual discussions which the child holds with parents and peers. He has taken the objector, as it were, into his own consciousness.[16] This fertile suggestion is, of course, as old as Plato who described thinking as the soul's dialogue with itself. It was also one of G.H. Mead's main contributions to developmental psychology.

The crucial difference in the child's thinking at this stage, which differentiates it from intuitive thought, is the capacity for reversibility or a rigorous return to the point of departure. When judging whether a flat cake of pastry weighs as much as a ball constructed out of the same amount of pastry, the child does not just go on what he can see. He can, as it were, return to the starting point and grasp that a ball can be remade from the material of the flat cake. He can objectify his own performances, both physical and intellectual, and conceive of himself going back to the beginning again, and perhaps doing them differently. This permits a range of rational operations.[17] It also permits what Piaget calls the 'decentering' of ego-centricity.

Piaget thinks that it parallels the capacity to see a situation from another's point of view, to go over the situation again, as it were, employing perhaps a different type of operation. It is thus possible to transcend the sense-bound character of pre-operational thought.

The construction of logic now begins. 'Logic constitutes the system of relationships which permit the co-ordination of points of view corresponding to different individuals, as well as those which correspond to the successive percepts or intuitions of the same individual.'[18] Piaget associates with this stage the development of a morality of co-operation and personal autonomy, in contrast to the intuitive heteronomous morality of the small child. 'This new system of values represents, in the affective sphere, the equivalent of logic in the realm of intelligence.'[19]

R.S. Peters

The morality of co-operation, replacing that of constraint, is one consequence of the child's new capacity to decenter. He sees that rules are alterable and, by his new-found ability to look at them from other people's point of view, is able to adjust his behaviour to others on a basis of reciprocity. He can also operate on his own rules and re-think them, thereby developing towards autonomy for himself and respect for others as rule-makers. The terms used to formulate a rule matter less than the intent which informs it; for the individual is now aware of himself and others as having intentions which are expressed in behaviour. The sense of justice based on strict equality takes the place of the previous emphasis on obedience. Thus, honesty, a sense of justice, and reciprocity form a rational grouping of values that can be compared to the 'groupings' of relations or concepts that characterize logic.

At this stage of development, there emerges, as an equivalent to the regulative operations of reason, the will as a regulator of the affective life.[20] A young child will persevere in an activity when his interest is engaged; but interest is an intuitive regulator, not an intellectual one. Will, by contrast, is a kind of organization of the emotions into a higher order motive, that transcends the momentary interest. So when a duty is momentarily weaker than a specific desire, the act of will consists not in 'following the inferior and stronger tendency; on the contrary, one would then speak of a failure of will or "lack of will power". Will power involves reinforcing the superior but weaker tendency so as to make it triumph'. Will acts, therefore, like a logical operation, when the conclusion of a piece of deductive reasoning is at odds with what appears to be the case; operational reasoning then corrects the misleading appearances by referring to previous states that are the grounds for the conclusion. Correspondingly, an act of will involves a decentering or detachment from the pressure of immediate interest, and so a decision taken in harmony with the personality as a whole.

4   Formal operations

The final stage is that of formal operations, which develop in adolescence. Logical operations, formerly restricted to concrete reality, to 'tangible objects' that could 'be manipulated and subjected to real action', can now be performed on general ideas, hypotheses, and abstract constructions. Going beyond the logic of relations, classes, and numbers, the logic of propositions is now possible, in which the system of inference is an abstract translation of that governing concrete operations. The adolescent starts by using this new range of abilities in the service of ego-centric assimi-

312

lation, but gradually learns to accommodate these systems to reality. He learns to predict and to interpret experience by theorizing instead of indulging in metaphysical ego-centricity.

What Piaget calls the 'personality' of the individual now emerges which results from autosubmission of the self to some kind of discipline. Rules and values are organized in the light of a life-plan. There is a de-centering of the self which becomes part of a co-operative plan dictated by ideals which provide standards for the operation of will.

D Critique of Piaget's account

In what follows I shall begin by focusing on Piaget's account of the development of rationality in an individual's practical life. In later sections, I shall redress the balance by concentrating on his account of epistemic rationality.

1 Rationality and reasonableness

I shall begin my critique by considering how far Piaget's account pays due attention to the distinctions noted earlier between the notions of rationality and reasonableness and between the two senses of 'reasonable'.

(a) The explanation of unreasonableness and irrationality

Piaget's system permits a convincing account to be given of people who are unreasonable but not downright irrational. If there is some kind of fixation at the early ego-centric stage beliefs tend to be infected with the arbitrariness and particularity characteristic of pre-operational thought. Little attempt is made to fit them into a coherent system or to test them out reflectively. Behaviour is governed by wants and aversions of an immediate, short-term character. The viewpoint of others impinges but little. Indeed the behaviour of others is seen largely in a self-referential way as it impinges on, threatens, or thwarts the demands of the greedy restless ego. The emotional life is not organized by stable senti-ments. It tends to be gusty, and dominated by powerful self-referen-tial emotions. There is, too, a bastardization of will which is exhibited in wilfulness and obstinacy.

If, on the other hand, the fixation is at the transcendental stage of 'moral realism', the love of rule-following, of doing the right thing, is very much to the fore. The capacity for reasoning is enlarged because of the beginnings of classification and the desire to assimilate things into an established pattern. But another dimension of un-reasonableness becomes possible because of the sanctity attached to what is established, which is reinforced by the fear of disapproval. The individual can be dogmatic, prejudiced and censorious because what is right is, for him, what is laid down by the group or by some-one in authority. He is capable of a range of emotions beyond the ken of the purely ego-centric man—loyalty, trust, shame. He can show courage, determination, and other qualities of will in sticking to the code which he reveres. But he does so in a heteronomous way because of his fear of disapproval.

To explain the genesis of unreasonable behaviour I have used the Freudian conception of 'fixation', used by Freud himself in his later theory of the super-ego to explain distinctive forms of irra-tionality.[21] He was trying to explain the fact that some children seem to develop much more rigorous standards than their parents. This leads to obsessions and compulsions, which are irrational in the sense that rules are followed in a way which has no warrant in the situation. He tried to explain besides the fact that many people have a picture of themselves—what Adler called a 'guiding fiction'—which is quite out of keeping with the traits which they in fact exhibit. In his theory of character development, too, Freud was trying to explain not the genesis of character in the sense of what Kohlberg calls 'the bag of virtues' which people possess, nor 'having character', which, is connected with virtues such as integrity, determination and courage, but rather the occurrence of various forms of irrationality. His contribution was in the tradition of characterology which goes back to Theophrastus. Either there is a subordination of traits to a dominant one, as in the sketch of the penurious man (Freud's anal character); or a whole range of traits is portrayed as being exercised in an exaggerated or distorted manner, as in the case of the pedant. Freud spotted similarities between these styles of rule-following and various forms of neurosis and assigned a common cause to both in his theory of infantile sexuality. Reason completely fails to exercise the 'decentering' function in relation to rule-following postulated by Piaget: the agent shows no capacity for impersonal appraisal of his behaviour, for making the kind of assessment that might be made by someone not centrally involved.

(b) Reasonableness

However, while Piaget allows for the kinds of belief and action which fall between the downright irrational and the totally rational, he gives no attention to the distinction between the two notions of reasonableness, outlined in section B1(b)—between reasonableness as the disposition to take account of any relevant considerations advanced by others, and reasonableness as the disposition to give impartial consideration to the interests of others and their claims concerning those interests. The critical stage for Piaget in the development of reason is the stage of concrete operations which is characterized both by reversibility in thought and the ability to see other people's point of view, to internalize their criticism and so on. This is a thoroughly acceptable idea which stresses the public character of reasoning. It was not, of course, Piaget's discovery; but he demonstrated the details of this development in a brilliant way. He does not, however, make anything of the important distinction between seeing things from the point of view of others (what he calls de-centering) which is essential to objectivity, and having *regard* for the point of view of others which presupposes some degree of active sympathy for them. He takes no account, in other words, of the possibility that a person might become a rational egoist. He assumes that a rational person will also be reasonable. In this respect, like Kant, he was a child of the Enlightenment.

The absence of any proper account of the development of sympathy is also a failure of Piaget's more specific work on moral development.[22] He makes mention, of course, of sympathy in the sense of the fellow-feeling that a child has at the heteronomous stage for those who share his interests. But this is really a feeling of fraternity rather than active sympathy for another individual. Sympathy, also in the sense of being able to reverberate in response to another's display of feeling, is presupposed in his account of de-centering. For without this capacity it would be difficult to give any account of taking another's point of view in the affective realm. But both these forms of sympathy are possible without any concern for another person. And this, surely, is what a reasonable person must have in the second social application of the concept of 'reasonable'. For without this would his sensitivity to the claims of others be explicable? He would, of course, have a concern about consistency; he might appreciate, too, 'intellectually' that another person might have good reasons for his claims. But would this be sufficient to explain the fact that people are moved to act by consideration of the claims of others, especially if they are in conflict with their own? At this point, as is well known, Kant introduced the rational emotion of respect as explaining how people are moved to act out of consideration for law (i.e. consistency) and for other people as sources of law. But this raises the question in another form. For can a convincing account be given of the genesis of the 'moral' emotion of respect without postulating a 'natural' basis for it in compassion?

315

The same criticisms can be made of Piaget's account of emotional development. Some people, of Augustinian leanings, are prepared to argue that there is a group of self-referential emotions, such as envy, jealousy, and pride, which are extremely unamenable to education. They have, perhaps, a more Hobbesian view of human nature than Piaget. They may credit human beings with a general tendency to think of themselves first and foremost. Thus the objects or situations which are picked out by the specific appraisals of situations, which form the cognitive core of all emotions, always include some thought of oneself. This is perhaps an extreme view; but there is sufficient basis for the doctrine of original sin to suggest that, though human beings are capable of being moved by other types of emotion, ego-centricity in this sphere is not just a skin that can be sloughed off in middle childhood. We may ask, then, for a justification for regarding the transcendence of ego-centricity as an aspect of the development of rationality, and for an account of the way the grip of ego-centric emotions can be loosened.

Presumably, the grip of such emotions can be loosened by the development of what Koestler[23] calls the self-transcending emotions, such as love, awe, the sense of justice, and respect. But are the ego-centric ones just precipitates of the ego-centric period of early childhood? Or are they a more stubborn strand in the fabric of human nature? Or are they mainly the product of acquisitive, individualistic societies? Do we have just partially to 'de-centre' them, e.g. by transferring pride to human achievements in general such as science or poetry, instead of directing it towards more trivial objects such as personal appearance and possessions? Or is it possible for them to slip from us like some of our childhood fears? Obviously they can be unreasonable or irrational in the sense that they can be felt for objects to which we have little claim or for situations which we have had absolutely no hand in bringing about (e.g. a man who feels proud of the sea). But can the development of reason alone rid us altogether of such self-referential emotions?[24] Indeed is our being subject to such emotions as distinct from our directing them towards inappropriate objects, a matter just of being unreasonable or irrational? Is not lack of subservience to them connected with the development of moral, religious, and aesthetic emotions of which Piaget takes no account?

2 Will and autonomy

Piaget had two connected insights both of which were rather vitiated by his elaboration of them. First, he saw that reasoning is basically a social matter and is only explicable in terms of the public acceptance of norms. 'Logic', he says, 'is a kind of moral for thought'. But he then inappropriately, as I shall later argue, proceeded to attempt an explanation of its development in terms of an equilibrium model.

Second, he saw the logical or rational aspects both of morality and the organization of personality in terms of will. But he had too thin a concept of rationality to do justice to this insight. Thus his account of moral development, as has been seen, was marred by his failure to distinguish two applications of the concept of reasonableness, the formal and the substantive. The same sort of defect is to be found in Piaget's account of will which he sketches as a solution to the problem posed by William James, that the virtues of will such as courage, integrity, perseverance, and resolution involve action on principles in the face of strong counter-inclinations. Piaget assumed that there is a disengagement of affectivity from the self and a submission to discipline defined by the laws of co-operation.[25] These, like Rousseau's General Will, provide the assistance required to conquer insistent counter-inclinations. But why should there be this disengagement from the self? Surely rational egoists can exhibit great strength of will. They 'de-centre' from instant gratification, however strong the immediate urge, and act in terms of prudence. McDougall, when confronted with James's problem, gives an answer in terms of support for duty from the self-regarding sentiment.[26] Why should not this provide an organization of personality which is as capable of reinforcing duty as the Kantian type of ideal assumed by Piaget? As Hoffman points out,[27] Piaget's data relate only to the individual's judgment of others. Why should he evaluate his own behaviour in the same way? Impartiality may require it. But why should he not make a case for being specially placed with regard to the development of his own interest as others, too, are placed with regard to the development of theirs? Unless concern for others is written into the 'moral point of view' what is objectionable about a society of rational egoists?

There is, too, an even more fundamental valuative point underlying Piaget's whole account of personality development in which autonomy functions as the end-point. Kagan and Kogan[28] ask whether field-independence, which goes with autonomy, is a socially desirable form of development. Field dependents, they claim, are much more alert to the social nuances that surround them. They are better at remembering social words and faces. They are quicker at attaining consensus in a group, and more adept at interpersonal accommodation. They are, in brief, more likely to adapt harmoniously to society, whereas field independents tend to

317

be more aloof, awkward in personal dealings, and more prone to take a line of their own. If these different styles of cognitive functioning do depend on early family circumstances, they are in principle amenable to training. But which style should parents encourage?

Piaget, as a child of the Enlightenment, assumes that autonomy is the obvious ideal. And, though he acknowledges the importance of the social environment, he assumes that it merely hastens or impedes the development towards autonomy which he regards as almost a logically necessary sequence. There is a sense, of course, in which he must be right. For how could a child become autonomous if he had not first passed through a previous stage of rule-conformity when he learnt what it is to follow a rule? But there are some societies which definitely discourage development towards this final stage. By processes of shaming and indoctrination their members are prevented from developing very far towards autonomy. There are thus important valuative assumptions underlying not only Piaget's assumptions about the principles which give content to the organization of personality, but also his assumptions about the autonomy which structures its form.

This raises major questions in ethics about the status of Piaget's developmental findings. Kohlberg, as a matter of fact, regards them as providing the basis for bridging the gap between 'is' and 'ought'.[29] To discuss this suggestion would open up vast issues which would require another paper to clarify.

3   Publicity and objectivity

It is often said that Piaget's biological preoccupations led him to neglect the social aspects of the development of reason. This is perhaps true of his account of the early experience of the child which is dominated by the model of assimilation and accommodation. But it certainly is not true of his account of the development of concrete operations in which, in his conception of 'decentering', he made a brilliant, if unoriginal, attempt to link the development of reason with reversibility and the capacity to adopt the standpoint of others. This is crucial to any account of the publicity and objectivity of reasoning.

There is, however, an omission in his account of objectivity, which parallels his failure to account for the development of reasonableness as distinct from rationality. This is connected with his predominating interest in logic and mathematics as the paradigms of reasoning, together with a Kantian type of moral system in which justice and consistency are the basis of all the virtues.

Logic and mathematics are unusual forms of reasoning, in that the possibility of agreement on the outcome of a process of reasoning depends wholly on the acceptance of the canons of valid deductive inference. Rational agreement in most other developed forms of reasoning depends, besides, on a common acknowledgment of what is to count as a ground from which inferences can relevantly be made, and by which judgments can be properly supported. Scientific reasoning, for instance, depends upon the employment of sense organs, yielding evidence on which there can be agreement, since it is accessible to any observer and because anyone can appreciate its bearing on the truth or falsity of the propositions to which it relates. A similar point can be made about moral reasoning. The development of virtues such as justice and truth-telling could be fitted into the Piagetian scheme, as involved in 'decentering', because these might plausibly be grounded on formal conditions of rationality, like the exclusion of the irrelevant, impartiality, and so on. But the development of a fuller conception of morality, which depends not merely on conceding to others the claims one makes on one's own behalf, but also a concern and respect for them, is possible only as one becomes sensitive and sympathetic to their sufferings and to their attempts to make something of their lives. And for this Piaget's account, which stops short at the capacity for looking at things from another person's standpoint, is inadequate.

The problem of objectivity is raised still more acutely by certain other forms of reasoning, notably those involved in religious and aesthetic judgment. Piaget deals with it only in the most general terms: one becomes capable of objectivity as one develops the capacity to look at situations from the standpoint of other subjects, likely to be differently affected by them. And from the appreciation of a diversity of viewpoints there can develop a capacity for the impersonal assessment of situations—for viewing them as *anyone* might, whose personal interests were not affected by them. Now this is necessary, but not sufficient for an account of reasoning. For there are still different modes of reasoning that need to be distinguished, each with its characteristic canons, determining what is to count in support of an inference of that specific type. Piaget considered science as well as logic and mathematics, but it raised no difficulty for him since he was able to rely on the fact that all men palpably possess sense-organs; and it is at least plausible to envisage men peering out on a public world of objects, which would consequently supply the content of a shared experience. But though the existence of objects to gaze at may be one condition for objectivity, it cannot be a necessary one. For the notion of objectivity can be applied just as readily to judgments made from a moral, a religious, or an aesthetic point of view. It may well be argued, therefore, that the shared responses of scientific observers are only a special case of what a repertoire of shared responses is like, and of the way it makes objective judgments in any field possible. Responses like the experience of awe in the face of contingency may supply a similar grounding for religious reasoning, and others like the sensitivity to suffering may similarly underpin moral reasoning, each in its own area providing a ground for agreement on objective judgment, corresponding to the evidence of the senses in science.

If this point about reasoning were accepted the way would be open for posing two further types of developmental problem which are of considerable educational significance. First, there would be a genetic story to be told about the origins of these shared responses and about their transformations at the different stages of development. This would be like asking, in Piaget's system, how the sporadic curiosity of the child becomes transformed into the disciplined search for the truth of the scientist, or how spontaneous sympathy becomes transformed into a steady concern and respect for others. Second, there would be the problem of setting out the norms which are constitutive of 'directed thinking' in these other modes of experience, e.g. neatness and elegance in the realm of the aesthetic. A developmental account would then have to be given of the emergence of sensitivity to them.

4   Equilibration and the norms of reason

One of the most important questions to which Piaget's theory gives rise is why children progress through the various stages until they reach the end-point of autonomous beings making use of formal operations.

(a)   The stimulation of social conditions

He links such development, of course, with social conditions which favour assimilation and accommodation by providing stimulation and novelty. His account of the role of language and his postulated link between the development of reasoning and critical dialogue should lead him to welcome the findings of sociologists such as Bernstein[30] and Klein,[31] who link the use of generalizations involved in reasoning, the tendency to plan for the future, and the general capacity for abstract thought with the different types of language and methods of social control employed in different strata of society.

A particularly interesting substantiation of this influence of the social environment on 'cognitive stimulation' is to be found in the study of Bruner and Greenfield.[32] The Wolof, a tribe in Senegal, were investigated for their ideas about the conservation of continuous quantities. Those who had not been exposed to the influence of western schooling were unable to make distinctions such as that between how things are and how the individual views them. They had not the concept of 'different points of view' so important to operational thought. Also, the concept of conservation is achieved much earlier by the Tiv, a tribe in Nigeria, whose children are encouraged to experiment with and manipulate the external world, unlike those of the Wolof. If the Wolof child wants to know anything he is told to ask someone, not to try to find out for himself. The child's personal desires and intentions, which might differentiate him from others, are not encouraged. What matters is conformity to the group. Thus the social pressures of the Wolof discourage the interaction with the environment which Piagetians regard as crucial for cognitive growth.

On Piaget's view, of course, the sequence of stages in the development of rationality is culturally invariant, and follows a *logical* sequence. Hypothetico-deductive thinking, for instance, presupposes a stage of classification; for without observed regularities there would be nothing to explain by reference to hypotheses. In a similar way the achievement of autonomy presupposes a stage at which an individual learns what it is to follow a rule. But this account of the invariant stages of development is consistent with the view that different social environments provide features which are more or less stimulating for such development. There will thus be individual and cultural differences in the rate and extent of development along a logically hierarchical sequence of stages.

However, Piaget holds that social conditions are not the crucial determinants of development; they merely facilitate or impede a progression that is to be explained in another way. Kohlberg, indeed, has elaborated this thesis about the connection between the social environment and 'cognitive stimulation' in his account of class differences and in his cross-cultural studies which reveal different rates and levels of development.[33] Why then do some children, with similar social backgrounds, remain 'embedded', as Schachtel[34] calls it, with a conventional heteronomous outlook? This issue is raised in a concrete way by the vast amount of research that has emerged from the experiments by Witkin[35] and his associates on individual differences in cognitive development. Witkin claims that individuals have very different capacities for analytic thinking and for abstracting from concrete perceptual situations. This influences the control of impulse, and the capacity for personal relationships, as well as intellectual skills. It is claimed that these abilities depend not on the development of linguistic sophistication, but most probably on early familial factors.

(b) Equilibration

But why, in general, should *anyone* progress towards autonomy? For it is a progression in defiance of the deep-seated need for the security that a stable conformity provides. What general motivation is there for this type of development? Piaget's answer can be summed up in one word—equilibration. In his early work, in which he was particularly concerned with the way in which reasoning proper emerges from the kind of intelligence which men share with animals, Piaget used the biological model of assimilation and accommodation to cover both biological and rational processes. 'Assimilation' covers both nutrition, in which food is literally taken into the stomach, and understanding some new item of experience by subsuming it under existing assumptions. 'Accommodation' is used, too, both in its biological sense of fitting into an environment, and in an extended sense to describe the way in which a child adapts his concepts and assumptions to cope with some new experience that is too discrepant to be dealt with by his existing ones. In addition Piaget supposes that there is a general tendency towards stability, possessed by all organisms, which enables the organism to maintain a balance between assimilation and accommodation. This he calls 'equilibration'. The tendency of the body, demonstrated by Cannon, to maintain homeostasis, is paralleled by that of the mind to maintain the individual's framework of belief, his behaviour routines and the rules informing them (what Piaget refers to as his 'schemata'), a more dynamic type of equilibrium. There is not a return to an existing equilibrium state but a constant movement towards new ones. A succession of strategies is developed for dealing in an affectively organized way with cognitive perturbations of increasing complexity as the child grows older. The entire process of cognitive development thus 'consists of reactions of compensation to perturbation (relative to previous schemas) which make necessary a variation of the initial schemas'.[36]

I have argued elsewhere[37] that this type of extension of the postulate of homeostasis is either a piece of metaphysics rather than science, or a redescription which does no explanatory work. Mischel,[38] too, has criticized this biological version of it using similar arguments. Homeostasis functions as an acceptable explanation at the physiological level only because it is possible to specify the deficit states that initiate the behaviour and the mecha-

nisms by means of which equilibrium is restored, in ways independent of the behaviour explained. But in Piaget's theory, which
transfers this type of explanation to the mental level, this is not
done. It is claimed that the individual is prompted to assimilate or
to accommodate by becoming aware of momentary disequilibrium
between his schemata and the novel situation encountered. But
such states of mental disequilibrium can only be identified by
reference to the content of the schemata whose activity they explain.
In other words, it is only by grasping the incoherence between what
the individual already knows and the new material that one can
understand that there is a problem for him. It seems then, that
'the tendency towards equilibrium' is simply a somewhat misleading
way of talking about the disposition to remove inconsistencies
and get rid of contradictions. But nothing is added to our understanding of this disposition by introducing the model of restoring
equilibrium at the mental level. To call this an attempt to re-establish
equilibrium is not to explain why dissonance or inconsistency is
motivating. It is simply to draw attention to its motivational
properties by an inappropriate redescription.[39]

(c) Assimilation and accommodation

In my view, we can go no further in explaining the development
of rationality than the ascription to man of two basic and closely
related dispositions to respond to his experience. There is, first,
assimilation—the constructive, classifying aspect of thought, the
tendency to impose a conceptual scheme on experience and to
generalize on the basis of similarities. Allied with this is the disposition to accommodate or to modify the scheme and the generalizations in the light of recalcitrant experience and information.
The development of each process brings the various norms of
reason into play. Assimilation can be seen as a tendency to strive for
consistency in imposing a conceptual scheme on experience,
picking out significant similarities. Assimilation requires, therefore,
a sensitivity to the relevance or irrelevance of similarities from
which a reflective concern to avoid arbitrariness and partiality
can develop. We have already seen that the demand for consistency
is at work in the process of accommodation—the tendency to
dwell on the novel or the discrepant and to adapt one's beliefs and
assumptions accordingly. The development of accommodation
involves the insistence on relevance, as distinct from purely associative similarities, the demand for clarity so that differences
cannot be slurred over, and the demand for evidence or independent
confirmation of the generalization that has been advanced.

The primitive processes of accommodation and assimilation, then, generate thought as distinct from mere daydreaming or free association, i.e. a directed mental process guided by a concern, however primitive, for some basic requirements of consistency and relevance. I would want to argue that it is a conceptual truth that individuals with a tendency to assimilate and accommodate will be brought to think by features of their environment which are novel or discrepant (in terms of their conceptual scheme and/or generalizations).

There are a variety of interesting questions about these early stages in the development of reason which Piaget did not ask. For instance, in the development of reason the tendency to accommodate is of particular importance because of its connection with checking, criticism and looking for the negative instance. Psychologists have constructed a scale of reflection-impulsivity on which individuals show considerable and important differences.[40] For some children go for the first hypothesis that comes to mind; others reflect and check before committing themselves. They are more mindful of the possibility of the negative instance. This tendency seems to be a general one that is consistent over a variety of tasks. It affects the accuracy of recall and reading as well as the validity of reasoning. But it can be modified by training and by being exposed to models. What is the explanation of this basic difference between people that is so essential to the development of reasoning? The probable explanation is the extent to which children are afraid of making a mistake, rather than the strength of the desire to succeed; for this desire often occasions carelessness. This hypothesis is supported by some experiments, by a cross-cultural study, and by evidence from pathology.

(d) The norms of reason

The above account of the development of rationality puts the emphasis squarely on the acquired grasp of various norms of reason. Now Piaget acknowledges the norms involved in the life of reason: he insists as much on the normative features of logic as on the logical features of morality. Yet, when confronted with the problem of explaining the development of rationality and giving an account of the motivation of the rational man he attempts to underwrite his account by a model taken from physiology.

Nonetheless, there are the materials in Piaget's account for a more adequate approach. Piaget properly puts the twin processes of assimilation and accommodation at the centre of his account and, as we have seen, many of the central attitudes and norms of reason can be plausibly traced to the individual's initial dispositions to assimilate and accommodate. And while the equilibrium model is open to the criticisms I have discussed above, it can be seen as a misleading way of giving a central place to the general norm of consistency which is immanent in the processes of assimilation and accommodation. Piaget's recognition of the normative nature of reason opens the way for a satisfactory account of the motivation of the rational man; for the norms of consistency, relevance and the active search for grounds are, of course, motivating. But any complete account of rational motivation would need to distinguish at least two kinds of motivation. On the one hand there is the sheer enjoyment of construction, of getting things clear and right. This is, as it were, the hedonistic side of the ethics of belief. But, on the other hand, there is the more obligatory aspect, the demand that confusions and inconsistencies be removed, that conclusions be checked, that evidence be sought, and that irrelevance be expunged from argument.

The above is, however, no more than the bare outlines of a suggested approach to the development of rationality: substantial problems remain. For let us suppose that rationality does emerge from the primitive dispositions to assimilate and accommodate—tendencies for which an evolutionary account might be given in terms of their survival value. How does this combination of classifying and caution evolve into the conviction that one ought to be consistent, that one ought to look for the negative instance? How does a love of order become transformed into Kant's categorical imperative? How does caution about making mistakes emerge into what Russell calls 'cosmic piety', into the conviction of the givenness of the world and its regularities and the demand on man that he should check and re-check his assumptions? In brief what is to be made, in an explanatory system, of the *telos* immanent in the development of reason, that truth matters?

The difficulties about such explanations parallel the difficulties in ethics generally about giving naturalistic explanations in terms of concepts such as 'want'. For we are really concerned with the emergence of the ethics of belief out of the ego-centric, hedonistic world of the young child. 'Belief' is a concept that has a foot in both worlds; for though it is descriptive of a psychological state, in its developed form, where it is distinguished from expectations, which animals also have, it can only be explicated by reference to the acceptance of norms. For belief is a state of mind *appropriate* to what is true. But it is not the case that believers always *want* to find out what is true. Rather they feel that they *ought* to do so. The pursuit of truth as an absorbing activity characteristic of

325

scientists and other academics must be distinguished from the state of mind of any reasonable being who feels that, though it may be a bit of a bore, and though it may interefere with his wants, he ought to look into the evidence for some of his cherished assumptions.[41] This can only be represented as a case of wanting if the concept of 'wanting' is made purely formal so that it becomes analytic that, if anyone does anything, this must be something that he wants to do. And the fact that this move has often been made by naturalists to bridge the gap between interpersonal moral values such as justice and human wants adds little to its plausibility in the field of the intellectual virtues. Indeed it is even less plausible; for whereas there obviously is a conceptual connection between action and some concept of 'wanting', the connection between knowing, believing, doubting, etc., and such a concept is much more problematic.

Those who want to preserve some kind of naturalistic status for the intellectual virtues might admit the normative aspects of the final product but they might give an explanation of this in terms of socialization. They might point to the fact that many cultures or sub-cultures discourage curiosity,[42] which may explain the limited development of reasoning in some people. Encouragement of curiosity involves not only approval of sporadic inquisitiveness, but also insistence on standards for its operation which become incorporated in a social tradition such as that of science. So social approval supporting traditions is the source of the normative aspect of the intellectual virtues. It transforms idle and sporadic curiosity about the explanation of things into self-critical reactions if explanations are not rigorously examined.

There are two difficulties about this type of explanation. The first was made very pertinently by Hume in the context of the attempt to explain morality in terms of a sense of duty, which was instilled in people by society. For this leaves over the problem of why society should attach such approval to some forms of behaviour rather than to others. There must, he argued, be some first-hand form of judgment to which attention is drawn by this social reinforcement, which generates a second-hand type of approval. And this is a judgment of the importance of consistency, etc., not just an expression of its attractiveness.

There is, second, the distinctiveness of such first-hand judgments from the second-hand conformity. In moral development generally a person may first of all behave justly because he is susceptible to rewards and punishments, and then to praise and blame. But he reaches a stage when he sees 'for himself' what makes a rule right or wrong. He sees the wrongness of causing suffering or of exploitation and judges social practices in the light of this first-hand type of appraisal. And, it is argued, the sort of guilt experienced when he does wrong or contemplates it, is qualitatively different from the guilt which is associated with the fear of punishment or of disapproval. The same sort of point can be made about the intellectual virtues. There is all the difference in the world between feeling that one ought to abandon a cherished belief when confronted with conclusive evidence against it, just because there is such evidence, and feeling that one ought to abandon it because one will not stand well with one's colleagues if one sticks to it. Skinner[43] suggests that scientists, who allow themselves to be swayed by consequences that are not part of their subject matter, will find themselves 'in difficulties' because other scientists can easily check up on them. Their alleged 'finely developed ethical sense' is therefore a feature of the environment in which they work. But why do scientists make a fuss about cooking results in the service of self-interest? Why is their disapproval attached to this lack of authenticity in the first case? Surely because science, as an activity, is only intelligible on the assumption that truth matters. So we are back again at our starting point, namely the status of the norms definitive of the operation of reason which the person who cares about truth accepts as required by his quest. My tentative conclusion is that no attempt to reduce such virtues to naturalistic wants is plausible. Man is potentially a rational being and, as such, comes to subject his beliefs and actions to the normative demands of reason. The intellectual virtues are expressions of the normative demands of reason on his sensibility.

E Conclusion

My main criticism of Piaget has been that, though he stresses the normative features of logic, he also tries to explain logical thinking in terms of a purely naturalistic conception of man. Thus his account of the development of reason does not just raise the usual doubts about giving a purely naturalistic account of conduct in the sphere of practical reason. It also raises even more fundamental questions about the status of man in the natural world as a creature that develops beliefs. Human beliefs and behaviour cannot be made intelligible without the basic postulate of the rationality of man. But this, in its turn, can only be made intelligible if we write into rationality the responsiveness to normative demands. What type of developmental account is appropriate for explaining the transition from the biological beginnings of reason to its norm-ridden end-product? Piaget's natural history of mind explicitly raises this question but does not solve it. It merely locates more precisely the points of perplexity.

Notes

1 Piaget, J. (1968), p. 58.
2 See Nagel, E. (1957) and Peters, R.S. (1972c). For a sustained defence of this starting point in relation to conceptual development see Hamlyn, D.W. (1967) and (1971).
3 Woodward, W.M. (1971).
4 Miller, G.A., Galanter, E. and Pribram, K.H. (1960).
5 The general background of Piaget's work will be assumed but, for the purpose of this paper, there will be a concentration on Piaget, J. (1968); for in this article, in which he reviews his work up to 1940, there is the most explicit attempt to link cognitive development with social and affective development, which is of particular relevance for the theses advanced in this paper.
6 See Peters, R.S. (1972a).
7 See Ryle, G. (1972).
8 See Peters, R.S. (1972a).
9 For a fuller explanation of more of its facets see Dearden, R.F., Hirst, P.H. and Peters, R.S. (1972).
10 Piaget, J. (1968), p. 14.
11 See Peters, R.S. (1972a), pp. 218–23. See also Peters, R.S. (1965).
12 Piaget, J. (1968), p. 19.
13 Luria, A.R. (1961).
14 Piaget, J. (1968), p. 29.
15 Ibid., p. 39.
16 Ibid., p. 40.
17 Ibid., pp. 48–54.
18 Ibid., p. 41.
19 Ibid., p. 41.
20 Ibid., pp. 58–60.
21 See Peters, R.S. (1960).
22 See Hoffman, M.L. (1970), in his definitive article on 'Moral development', who also makes this criticism. The same type of criticism is made of Kohlberg's extension of Piaget's theory in Peters, R.S. (1971), pp. 246–7, 259.
23 Koestler, A. (1966), pp. 273–85.
24 See Peters, R.S. (1972b), especially pp. 474–80.
25 Piaget, J. (1968), p. 61.
26 See McDougall, W. (1942), ch. IX.
27 Hoffman, M.L. (1970), pp. 280–1.
28 See Kagan, J. and Kogan, N. (1970).
29 Kohlberg, L. (1971).
30 See Bernstein, B.B. (1972).
31 See Klein, J. (1965).
32 See Greenfield, P.M. and Bruner, J.S. (1969).

33 See Kohlberg, L. (1968), (1969), (1971).
34 See Schachtel, E. (1959).
35 See Witkin, H.A. *et al.* (1962).
36 Quoted by Mischel as his translation of Piaget, J. 'Apprentissage et connaissance', in Greco, P. and Piaget, J. (1959), p. 50 in Mischel, T. (ed.) (1971), p. 326.
37 Peters, R.S. (1958), chapters 1, 3, 4.
38 Mischel, T. (1971).
39 Berlyne (see Berlyne, D.E., 1960, 1965) indulges in a similar piece of metaphysics or redescription by extending the old drive theory to cover intrinsic as well as extrinsic motivation. Human beings have a 'drive to solve a problem' as well as hunger and sex drives. But there is the same problem of specifying the conditions of drive arousal independently of the problem-solving type of behaviour that they are supposed to explain. No specific internal conditions are specifiable and the appropriate environmental stimuli cannot be identified independently of the cognitive state of the problem-solver. There is, too, the objection that the mechanical model of 'drive' nullifies the important distinction between valid processes of thought and processes that simply proceed by chance associations—a distinction that Berlyne himself wants to preserve by his characterization of directed thinking by notions such as 'legitimate' and 'appropriate' steps in the solution of a problem. But the model of man as a purposive rule-following animal cannot be reconciled with the model of an entity 'driven' by 'mechanisms'.
40 See Kagan, J. and Kogan, N. (1970), pp. 1309–19.
41 See Peters, R.S. (1973).
42 See Klein, J. (1965), vol. 2.
43 Skinner, B.F. (1972), p. 174.

Bibliography

BERLYNE, D.E. (1960), *Conflict, Arousal, and Curiosity*, New York.
BERLYNE, D.E. (1965), *Structure and Direction in Thinking*, New York.
BERLYNE, D.E. (1970), 'Children's reasoning and thinking', in Mussen, P.A. (ed.) (1970), vol. 1, pp. 939–81.
BERNSTEIN, B.B. (1971–2), *Class, Codes and Control*, London vol. 1, 1971, vol. 2, 1972.
CLIFFORD, W.K. (1947), *The Ethics of Belief*, London.
DEARDEN, R.F., HIRST, P.H. and PETERS, R.S. (eds) (1972), *Education and the Development of Reason*, London.
GOSLIN, D.A. (ed.) (1969), *Handbook of Socialization Theory and Research*, Chicago.
GRECO, P. and PIAGET, J. (1959), *Apprentissage et Connaissance*, Paris.
GREENFIELD, P.M. and BRUNER, J.S. (1969), 'Culture and cognitive growth', in Goslin, D.A. (ed.) (1969), pp. 633–57.
HAMLYN, D.W. (1967), 'The logical and psychological aspects of learning', in Peters, R.S. (ed.) (1967).
HAMLYN, D.W. (1971), 'Epistemology and conceptual development', in Mischel, T. (ed.) (1971), pp. 3–24.

HARRIS, D.B. (ed.) (1957), *The Concept of Development*, Minnesota.

HOFFMAN, M.L. (1970), 'Moral development', in Mussen, P.A. (ed.) (1970), vol. 2, pp. 261–355.

KAGAN, J. and KOGAN, N. (1970), 'Individual variation in cognitive processes', in Mussen, P.A. (ed.) (1970), vol. 1, pp. 1323–42.

KLEIN, J. (1965), *Samples from English Cultures* (2 vols), London.

KOESTLER, A. (1966), *The Act of Creation*, New York.

KOHLBERG, L. (1968), 'Early education: a cognitive developmental view', *Child Development*, vol. XXXIX, pp. 1013–62.

KOHLBERG, L. (1969), 'Stage and sequence: the cognitive-developmental approach to socialization' in Goslin, D. (ed.) (1969), pp. 347–480.

KOHLBERG, L. (1971), 'From is to ought', in Mischel, T. (ed.) (1971), pp. 151–235.

LURIA, A. (1961), *The Role of Speech in the Regulation of Normal and Abnormal Behaviour*, New York.

MCDOUGALL, W. (1942), *An Introduction to Social Psychology*, 24th edn, London, pp. 150–79.

MILLER, G.A., GALANTER, E. and PRIBRAM, K.H. (1960), *Plans and the Structure of Behaviour*, New York.

MISCHEL, T. (1971), 'Piaget: Cognitive conflict and the motivation of thought', in Mischel, T. (ed.) (1971), pp. 311–55.

MISCHEL, T. (ed.) (1971), *Cognitive Development and Epistemology*, New York.

MUSSEN, P.A. (ed.) (1970), *Carmichael's Manual of Child Psychology*, New York.

NAGEL, E. (1957), 'Determinism and development', in Harris, D.B. (ed.) (1957), pp. 15–24.

PETERS, R.S. (1958), *The Concept of Motivation*, London.

PETERS, R.S. (1960), 'Freud's theory of moral development in relation to that of Piaget', in *British Journal of Educational Psychology*, vol. XXX, pp. 250–8.

PETERS, R.S. (1965), 'Emotions, passivity, and the place of Freud's theory in psychology', in Wolman, B. and Nagel, E. (eds) (1965), pp. 365–83.

PETERS, R.S. (ed.) (1967), *The Concept of Education*, London.

PETERS, R.S. (1971), 'Moral development: a plea for pluralism' in Mischel, T. (ed.) (1971), pp. 237–67.

PETERS, R.S. (1972a), 'Reason and passion', in Dearden, R.F., Hirst, P.H. and Peters, R.S. (eds) (1972), pp. 208–29.

PETERS, R.S. (1972b), 'The education of the emotions', in Dearden, R.F., Hirst, P.H. and Peters, R.S. (eds) (1972), pp. 466–83.

PETERS, R.S. (1972c) 'Education and human development', in Dearden, R.F., Hirst, P.H. and Peters, R.S. (eds) (1972), pp. 501–20.

PETERS, R.S. (1973), 'The justification of education', in Peters, R.S. (ed.) (1973), pp. 239–67.

PETERS, R.S. (ed.) (1973), *The Philosophy of Education*, Oxford.

PIAGET, J. (1968), *Six Psychological Studies*, London.

PIAGET, J. (1970), 'Piaget's theory', in Mussen. P.A. (ed.) (1970), pp. 703–32.

RYLE, G. (1972), 'A rational animal', in Dearden, R.F., Hirst, P.H. and Peters, R.S. (eds) (1972), pp. 176–93.

SCHACHTEL, E. (1959), *Metamorphosis*, New York.
SKINNER, B.F. (1972), *Beyond Freedom and Dignity*, London.
WITKIN, H. *et al.* (1962), *Psychological Differentiation*, New York.
WOLMAN, B. and NAGEL, E. (eds) (1965), *Scientific Psychology*, New York.
WOODWARD, W.M. (1971), *The Development of Behaviour*, Harmondsworth.

13

Psychosis and irrationality

R. Brown

A Particular actions and beliefs

We sometimes wish to explain the economic and social behaviour of either individual agents, or of groups of agents, by estimating its divergence from action rational in whole or in part. But to do this we have to be able to recognize, and characterize, various kinds of irrational activity—various kinds of failed or flawed action. We also have to be able to distinguish such failures from non-rational behaviour, behaviour that is, which is neither rational nor irrational.

Sometimes, however, it is suggested that many apparent cases of failed or flawed action are misclassified. It is suggested, for example—to take the cases with which I shall be concerned—that psychoses are not forms of purely irrational behaviour, as is so commonly claimed, but, instead, are non-rational, or alternatively, are at least partly rational. All three views, like the similar ones on neurotic behaviour, are represented in the literature.

Thus it has been argued that psychotic behaviour is only apparently irrational, that closely examined it will turn out to be rational given the agent's understandably mistaken but irrationally held beliefs. Anyone else with those beliefs and similar preferences and opportunities, it is said, would behave in the same bizarre yet basically rational way. Psychotic behaviour is rational because if the beliefs on which the behaviour is based were true, the behaviour would be the most likely means to produce the intended outcome without also producing side effects that outweigh its desirability.

Other people have claimed that psychotic behaviour is neither rational nor irrational; that, instead, it is non-rational. It is behaviour which was not, and could not have been, consciously planned, since it does not make sense to say either that it was or was not done for a reason, that is, the agent's own reason.

Still other writers have argued that psychotic behaviour is simply irrational. The agent's repressed reasons are his reasons none the less, for unless he can be brought to acknowledge them as his own bad reasons, his therapy cannot be successful. But to have bad reasons means, in this case, to have acted for reasons which were bound to result in the use of unsuccessful means. It is thus to have acted irrationally to some extent.

The suggestion, then, is that we look again at the nature of particular psychotic beliefs and actions with a view to re-characterizing, and hence re-classifying, them. To take up this suggestion fully would be to try to chart the relationship between being mentally ill and being not rational. If we could become clearer about this connection, we should be in a better position to describe and assess the use of rationality as a therapeutic ideal in psychiatric treatment. However, my contribution here to this question will, and must, be limited to some basic points about the ascription of irrationality, rationality, and non-rationality to psychotic beliefs or behaviour.

1   Kraepelin's patient

Let us consider how psychiatrists have in fact interpreted psychoses, beginning with, but not limiting ourselves to, the family of disorders labelled 'schizophrenias'. They are the most common of the psychoses among many groups of people, the most spectacular in symptom, the most resistant to treatment, and the most serious in their social effects. We begin with a patient whose schizophrenia is discussed by R.D. Laing. He first quotes Kraepelin's well-known description of a man in a state of catatonic excitement:[1]

> The patient I will show you today has almost to be carried
> into the room, as he walks in a straddling fashion on the
> outside of his feet. On coming in, he throws off his slippers,
> sings a hymn loudly, and then cries twice (in English), 'My
> father, my real father!' ... The patient sits with his eyes shut,
> and pays no attention to his surroundings. He does not look up
> even when he is spoken to, but he answers beginning in a low
> voice, and gradually screaming louder and louder. When
> asked where he is, he says, 'You want to know that too? I tell
> you who is being measured and is measured and shall be
> measured. I know all that, and could tell you, but I do not

want to.' When asked his name, he screams, 'What is your name? What does he shut? He shuts his eyes. What does he hear? He does not understand; he understands not. ...' At the end, he scolds in quite inarticulate sounds.

Of this account Laing remarks that Kraepelin took note of the patient's 'inaccessibility'; Kraepelin wrote of the patient: 'Although he undoubtedly understood all the questions, *he has not given us a single piece of useful information. His talk was ... only a series of disconnected sentences having no relation whatsoever to the general situation.*' Laing interprets the patient's behaviour rather differently. He writes:[2]

> What does this patient seem to be doing? Surely he is carrying on a dialogue between his own parodied version of Kraepelin, and his own defiant rebelling self. ... Presumably he deeply resents this form of interrogation which is being carried out before a lecture-room of students. He probably does not see what it has to do with the things that must be deeply distressing him. ...
>
> What is the boy's experience of Kraepelin? He seems to be tormented and desperate. What is he 'about' in speaking and acting in this way? He is objecting to being measured and tested. He wants to be heard.

Laing is suggesting here that the patient's behaviour has a point: some of what he says and does is a witting protest against Kraepelin's treatment of him. The patient's behaviour exhibits some degree of organization; it has a rationale; it is done for the sake of an end, that of indicating that he is not being treated with the simple respect due to him. The patient's actions show at least a minimal degree of rationality, and perhaps more. For the agent does what he does because he grasps that it is a way of bringing about *one* of his ends. Moreover, according to Laing, the agent acts for a reason to which he assigns a certain weight—his right to complain of shabby treatment—even though he may or may not think that what he does and says is the best way of pursuing that end. In fact, on this account the patient's behaviour is rational to a considerable extent. Some of it looks non-rational only because we have not understood that he was *acting out*, in the form of a dialogue, what it was that he thought and felt and wanted. Once we understand this, Laing might say, we see that the patient may or may not have chosen the most effective means available to him of communicating with us. But his behaviour was less than fully rational only to the extent that he used means which were not the best open to him. His behaviour was reason-based rather than being wholly non-rational as Kraepelin thought.

2   Expressive actions and end-directed behaviour

The crux of Laing's argument is this: at least some of the behaviour of Kraepelin's patient is both rational and expressive. It is rational because done for the sake of one of his ends. It is expressive, Laing suggests, because the patient acts out what he thinks and feels about Kraepelin's treatment of him. The patient's expressive behaviour is end-directed, for he mimics Kraepelin in order to express his thoughts and feelings about him. On Laing's view, the patient is neither irrational nor non-rational, since the mimicry is both intentional and done for a good reason.

Obviously, the correctness of this view depends simply on whether the patient's expressive behaviour *is* end-directed. Much expressive behaviour is not, of course. An angry man who throws his arms about, clutches his head and scowls, is often, and perhaps usually, not acting in these ways because scowling and head-clutching are activities which he is pursuing for their own sake or for the sake of some further end. They are often, and perhaps characteristically, not reason-based activities at all. True, they constitute part of his anger, and he may be acting rationally or irrationally or non-rationally in being angry on that occasion. But the question of the rationality of his being angry on that occasion is quite different from that of the rationality of the ways by which that anger is expressed. Scowling, for example, is neither a rational nor irrational way of expressing anger; the constitutive parts of a rational activity need not themselves be either rational or irrational, for they may be non-rational.

On the other hand, some expressive behaviour is end-directed in that it not only shows what the agent feels and thinks but is performed for the sake of doing exactly that. Showing gratitude by doing a favour or taking revenge by doing an injury are typical instances of expressive behaviour which is sometimes performed merely for its own sake: that is, for the sake of the agent expressing his state of mind. However, much expressive behaviour is performed for the sake of some further end. Expressing anger or hate or fear in order to obtain a desired response from someone else is an obvious example. So is displaying a particular emotion and attitude, or acting out a specific wish, only in order to satisfy certain conventions of expressive behaviour.

Expressive behaviour, whether or not directed to satisfying particular conventions, can be judged, by means of those conventions, to be more or less appropriate to the occasion. A display of genuine grief is appropriate to the Christian grave-side, but even genuine grief is unwelcome if it takes the form of prolonged hysterical laughter. Crocodile tears are preferable. However, it may still be irrational of a given agent, at a specific time, either to be in a specific conventionally appropriate state or to show that he is. Similarly, it may be irrational of a particular person, at a given time, not to observe the conventions, not to behave expressively as expected, and even irrational of him not to be in the conventionally appropriate state. Again, a person may be irrational to let any expression of his state appear on a given occasion, no matter what the occasion conventionally demands. There are, in short, many differences between (a) the rationality (or irrationality or non-rationality) of expressing one's state on a given occasion, and (b) the rationality (or irrationality) of trying to satisfy the conventions of expression on any given occasion.

Now, on Laing's account, someone might argue, the behaviour of Kraepelin's patient in the lecture hall was irrational only in that he did not use the most effective means of communication available to him. The audience found him incomprehensible and this could not have been his intention. He was irrational in failing to satisfy the conventions of expression appropriate to the occasion. But to this claim it can be retorted that the important question is simply this: 'Was the patient's behaviour end-directed or not?' However, nothing in Kraepelin's actual description permits us to give an unequivocal answer to this question. Laing writes:[3]

> Kraepelin asks him his name. The patient replies by an exasperated outburst in which he is now saying what he feels is the attitude implicit in Kraepelin's approach to him: What is your name? What does he shut? He shuts his eyes. . . . You don't whore for me? (i.e. he feels that Kraepelin is objecting because he is not prepared to prostitute himself before the whole classroom of students), and so on. . . .

Clearly, the claim that the patient 'is now saying what he feels is the attitude' of Kraepelin is of no help here. The patient is not saying anything in the sense of giving a verbal account of his beliefs and attitudes; he is merely expressing his resentment by hostile mimicry and scolding. Since compulsive mimicry—which need not be consciously end-directed—is characteristic of certain forms of schizophrenia, the patient's mimicry may not be end-directed at all. The question at issue here is whether the patient's behaviour merely expresses his state of mind or whether the patient does what he does *in order to* express his state of mind. These two alternatives—the latter a case of end-directed behaviour, the former not—are simply straddled by Laing's remark that the patient is 'saying what he feels is the attitude' of Kraepelin. The fact that the patient himself cannot tell us whether his behaviour in the lecture hall was end-directed is strong evidence that it was not. For the most likely reason why he cannot tell us is that he did not know at the time and, because of confusion of thought, cannot tell us now. But if the patient did not know at the time whether or not his activity was engaged in for the sake of an end, and cannot tell us now, he did not and does not know what he was trying to do.

Of course, there is the possibility that his behaviour was directed to an unconscious end, so that the patient was not aware of the connection between it and his behaviour. But neither Kraepelin's account nor Laing's discussion offers any evidence for this conclusion. The presence of unconscious goals is usually inferred either on theoretical grounds or from repeated instances of characteristic patterns of activity, activity which has the properties found in goal-seeking. In the present case, all the likely theoretical grounds are under dispute, since there is basic disagreement as to the nature of schizophrenia. And we simply have no information about repeated instances of the patient's behaviour.

3 Irrational actions

In what ways, then, are the schizophrenic's *actions* irrational—assuming for the moment that his illness is largely non-organic and that he is able, sometimes, to act on the basis of reasons?

Consider Laing's patient named 'David'. One reason that he gave for not being able to act spontaneously was that it put him at the mercy of other people, and he realized that he was afraid to take that risk. Why was he afraid? Because he did not trust them, and he knew that he did not. David lacked trust, says Laing, because he had never developed into an independent person able to tolerate the risks inherent in personal relationships. That tolerance is learned, normally, by a person being placed in certain sorts of situations at appropriate stages of his development. If something goes wrong and these situations do not arise, then simply knowing this, as David did, may help the agent very little in coping with the effects of their absence. He has not learned what he should have learned early in life, namely, that some people can be trusted. He has now, somehow, to learn to trust or rely on his psychiatrist, and to be encouraged by the success of this relationship to go on to rely on more and more people. The patient may even understand that he has to undergo this process in order to change, want badly to change, but not be able to take the initial risk of actually placing trust in another person. And given the patient's condition, he cannot establish a trusting disposition in himself without first actually participating in a relationship of trust.

One way, then, in which the agent, David, was irrational was in his having an irrational trait, in his being disposed not to rely on people. It was irrational because David wanted desperately to achieve aims, as we shall see later, which could not be realized in the absence of his willingness to rely on at least some people. But the actions which his trait led him to perform were not merely ill-adapted to realizing some of his most important ends; the actions were a positive hindrance. They frustrated the realization of his other highly desired ends. David had become so sensitive to taking the slightest risk of being hurt by other people that he did not give any weight to his other goals. He did not consider their claims in competition with his lack of trustfulness, for set against the latter they remained largely unexamined. David not only mis-calculated the risks which he ran of being hurt by other people, he did so at the cost of ignoring some of his own goals. Because he miscalculated as a result, in part, of remediable inattention, his actions and disposition to those actions were irrational.

There is another, closely related, way in which patients like David can be irrational in their actions. The patient can take thought and conclude that there is not much risk of being hurt by other people if he relies on them. But when he attempts to act on his conclusion, he finds that his deep-seated fears prevent him from doing so. His disposition not to rely on people prevails over his knowledge that the risks are slight. This class includes those people who in the course of therapy come to understand their plight, want to change it, but cannot bring themselves to take the initial risk, however slight they know it to be. People in this situation act irrationally since they do not follow the course of action which they have decided is the better of the two in their case. They are guided in their actions by factors whose inferiority as reasons in the situation has already been agreed upon by the agents themselves.

There is, of course, still another way in which the actions of the psychotic person can be irrational—irrational either for one person in particular or irrational for any person at all. Actions can be directed toward ends which it is irrational to try to achieve, or rational to try not to achieve. These ends may be either causally or logically impossible to achieve. Or the ends may simply be im-possible in theory, or in practice, for the agent to confirm as having been attained. A characteristic example of the latter is that of the schizophrenic's 'intentional project of self-annihilation'. This project cannot be carried through except by the patient doing what is impossible in practice, observing his own physical death, since he does not merely wish to commit suicide, but to satisfy himself that he is in a state of complete psychological and physical security.

Again, it is impossible in practice, contrary to what some patients wish, to reach a state of complete and permanent anonymity, to remove all risk of misunderstanding and pain from personal relationships, never to have disturbing thoughts and feelings, to achieve permanent emotional security by developing a secret personality. Such aims as these are irrational because it is rational to believe that they are impossible to realize or confirm. True, none of these ends is self-contradictory. But some of them, like eliminating all risk of pain and disturbing thoughts, or reaching a state of complete and permanent anonymity, would require for their achievement the total control of the agent's environment, of his responses to it, and of his responses to his own internal states. Such control would be unrecognizable: how could it be known to exist? Of course, someone might make total control of this kind a regulative ideal in his life. And if there were no other weighty reasons against adopting such an ideal—although in fact there are—it would not be irrational of the person to try to realize his ideal as much as he could. However, it would be irrational of him to believe, and to act on the belief, that his ideal could be realized completely. For if he had the desires, information, and abilities that would make it, *prima facie*, rational of him to adopt the ideal, he would already be in possession of good reasons for thinking that it could not be fully achieved by anyone.

But what sorts of other reasons are there against adopting such a regulative ideal, or more generally, against pursuing these unattainable ends? One obvious reason is that the attainment of these ends would make impossible the pursuit or attainment of other ends which are important to the agent. The fantasy of total control (the desire to be omnipotent) would purchase a defence against all insecurity at the expense of being able to feel danger or excitement, to feel and act spontaneously, or even to feel any desires at all. If, as Laing thinks, the psychoses are malformed strategies, or specialized forms of role-playing, for coping with the agents' failure to achieve ends like being secure, independent, spontaneous, creative, and self-respecting, then the 'success' of the strategy or role-playing is obtained by relinquishing these ends, not by achieving them. To the extent that the psychotic strategy results, as it does in some cases, in the agent giving up his original ends in favour of perpetuating the strategy itself, and making its maintenance his end, the strategy may, but need not, become self-defeating. The psychosis may worsen under this regimen, and the agent deteriorate so much that no sign of strategy remains.

4 Irrational beliefs

(a) What does the psychotic believe?

One fundamental problem which arises immediately about irrational beliefs is that of discovering exactly what it is that the psychotic agent believes. The sensations, feelings, perceptions, and thoughts of the advanced schizophrenic, for instance, are so unusual, and his personality so fragmented, that it is difficult to identify his beliefs. He has lost the capacity to use ordinary classifications systematically and consistently, to confine himself to coping with one problem at a time, to be precise; and most important of all, he has lost any interest in making himself understood.

Norman Cameron gives such examples of schizophrenic utterances, as:[4] '"A boy threw a stone at me to make an understanding between myself and the purpose of wrong-doing", and "I was transferred due to work over here due to methodical change of environment"'. Cameron does go on to say that[5]: 'Taken in the frame of the individual patient's life and his known fantasies, these sentences can be translated into more precise socially current forms.' But the problem, as Kurt Goldstein says, is that:[6]

> It is often difficult or impossible to find out in direct conversation or in the investigation of isolated capacities something about the ideas, the hallucinations, and the feelings which govern the patient's behaviour. During the execution of the performance tests these factors come into the foreground adventitiously, incidentally, without conscious intent on the part of the patient.

What occurs, then, is an incompatibility between the patient's words and his actions. Thus:[7]

> Patients who were attentively trying to solve the sorting problem often made statements about what they were looking at, or had just done, which grossly contradicted the perceptual pattern or the action. They made groups on the basis of colour, and declared the principle to be that of form, and vice versa. ... It was evident that their behaviour disorganization permitted the coexistence of incongruous and even competing responses, in relation to the same things, without any tendencies toward fusion or compromise.

The diffuseness, vagueness, and idiosyncratic nature of his speech are allied with the schizophrenic's reluctance to draw conclusions and make decisions. It is difficult to discover what he thinks on any given issue not merely because he cannot express his thoughts appropriately, but because he is afraid to commit himself to a definite view.[8]

Thus:[9] Patients are met [writes Thomas Freeman of depressives]

who are afraid that in some way unknown to them they may have done something which will harm others. However, close questioning indicates that the patient does not believe consciously that he is responsible for what he imagines may be happening. For example, a woman patient ... said, 'I feel I am causing all the trouble that is going on ... people seem to be difficult and awkward. They look sort of queer ... I feel people are looking at me. I feel as if people are saying I am God but I am not God, I am just myself ... I was praying there wouldn't be a war.'

There is, says Laing, a further hindrance to our finding out what it is that a given psychotic person believes. He sometimes deliberately conceals what he thinks. Laing writes:[10] 'A good deal of schizophrenia is simply nonsense ... to create boredom and futility in others. The schizophrenic is often making a fool of himself and the doctor. He is playing at being mad to avoid at all costs the possibility of being held *responsible* for a single coherent idea, or intention.'

There is another aspect of the problem of identifying the beliefs of a psychotic agent. It arises when we ask, 'What are we to make of the bizarre remarks of the advanced psychotic: that accusatory voices pursue him everywhere, that his thoughts are being scanned by radar, that his body is made of a transparent substance, that he is invisible, that he is dead?' Are we to take it that the agent believes these remarks to be literally true: that other people can look through him as they can look through an ordinary window, that he is dead as his great great grandfather is dead? Or does he expect his listener to give these remarks a special, non-literal interpretation? Or are they not assertions at all—neither literal nor metaphorical—but mere utterances, non-rationally based, whose form coincides with that of rational speech? That is, one aspect of the problem of identifying the psychotic's beliefs is that of determining which of his utterances are assertions of his beliefs: which of them are intended by the agent to describe what he thinks and feels, whether put literally or metaphorically. The problem is illustrated by a patient of whom Searles wrote:[11]

when he now referred, in a puzzled way, to a certain chair in
the nearby living room as being his younger sister Marian, of
whom I knew him to be fond, I realized that, although he
insisted he meant this literally, as usual, his puzzlement
indicated that he was struggling to see *in what sense*—namely, a
metaphorical one—this was actually true. . . .

On the kind of view taken by Laing, the correct answer to our
questions is that the psychotic's remarks are usually metaphorical
and incomplete. They need to be given a special interpretation—
require the aid of a gloss—for they encapsulate complex sets of
judgments which contain many private and condensed references.
The author of these remarks, it is said, is trying, indeed, to describe
his thoughts and feelings. The account which he himself gives is an
adequate description of his situation, then, if he is properly understood. The psychiatrist's basic task, on the Laingian view, is to
learn to understand what the patient is trying to tell him by both
his words and deeds.

For example, to the schizophrenic his being visible is both
dangerous and necessary. It is dangerous because to be visible to
other people is to risk being an object of their observation and
hence of possible attack by them: 'there is a constant dread and
resentment at being turned into someone else's thing, of being
penetrated by him, and a sense of being in someone else's power
and control'.[12] It is safer to be invisible and inaccessible. At the
same time there is often a '*need* to be seen and recognized' since, as
one patient put it, 'other people provide me with my existence'.
'On his own, he feels that he is empty and nobody. "I can't feel
real unless there is someone there. . . ."'[13] This is the situation
in which the schizophrenic patient says, on the one hand, 'My
every action is being watched, my thoughts are being monitored,
my enemies can see into me', and on the other hand, complains
that he is invisible, dried up, remote, unreal, dead. In saying that
his thoughts are being scanned by radar, the patient is trying to
describe how his thoughts seem to have no particularly intimate
connection with him, how he does not feel that they are related to
him in any way different from the thoughts of other people. He is
also suggesting, of course, that the process is malevolent and dis-
ruptive; he is fearful of what is happening to him and tries to
explain it. But when he defends himself by isolating himself from
his invisible enemies, he finds himself threatened with extinction,
since there is then no one to assure him that he is alive. At this
point he says that he is emotionally empty, that his brain has been
removed, that he is only a shadow.

According to Laing, the aptness and accuracy of such remarks is clear. They describe, with some feeling, the patient's view of his situation. He is, in fact, often remote from us, emotionally deadened, a quietly hostile observer of his own thoughts, sensations, and failure of ordinary feelings. His body is not dead, but this is irrelevant for him because he no longer takes his body to be part of himself; it is no more part of him than the chair on which he sits. On this sort of interpretation, 'I am dead' means roughly, 'I believe that I am no longer functioning as a person'. And for that claim there are said to be more than adequate grounds. Because there are thought to be such grounds, it is, on this view, not open to us to argue that his specific beliefs are all, or for the most part, inadequately supported by the evidence available to us. Many of the propositions he asserts, when properly understood, are true even though the patient himself is unable to support them adequately.

(b) The agent's account of himself

Now to this interpretation it can be immediately and correctly replied that the patient is not simply trying to *indicate* the state of his mind and feelings with the aid of special, metaphorical uses of language. He is also trying to *account* for his condition, and his explanations for what he thinks and feels—or fails to think and feel—are an essential part of his description. He is unable to form rational beliefs about his condition. If he were not increasingly convinced of the literal truth of his explanatory account of what is happening to him, he would not be psychotic. He might have visual and auditory hallucinations, and suffer from simple delusions, but he would quickly recover. It might seem to him, temporarily, that a host of voices uttered obscene messages, that his peculiar bodily sensations and dreadful emotions and thoughts were the result of outside interference by malevolent forces. The voices would not overwhelm him, however, and he might soon interpret them as projected fears and desires. He might systematically and critically set about examining his plight in much the same way as he might if he were subject to attacks of malaria. The fact that often the agent cannot do this because he is a prisoner of his own account is what creates his psychotic illness. He actually believes, and continues to believe, that he hears the voices of torturers, that people look at him with suspicion, that the touch of his hand is dangerous to other people. These and many other of his beliefs are simply false. Thus even after the agent's account is properly understood, so that the therapist grasps what the patient is trying to tell him, it is still the case that much of the agent's account is wrong, and that many of his beliefs are irrational—irrational for anyone with relevant evidence to hold, and often, though not always, irrational for him in particular to hold.

But to claim that many of the agent's beliefs are irrational is not to claim, of course, that they cannot be the result of the agent's bewildering family background. For if the Laingian view is correct, the schizophrenic's thought and behaviour are largely produced by the family situation in which the agent is placed, by the distortions of truth with which the agent has had to cope from infancy. Laing and Esterson write of the mother of their patient Claire:[14]

> What Mrs. Church says she says is bewilderingly incongruent with what she says. She repeatedly maintains, for instance, that she forgets things and lets bygones be bygones, advising Claire to do the same. But she 'forgets' things in a peculiar way. She recounts them at length and qualifies her account by saying that she forgets them. After one such story from twenty years back, she said, 'I think of *those* things, Claire—I mean I forget it and let it pass.'
>
> Unless one has a vantage-point outside this relationship, it must be very difficult to know where one is. She says, 'I am doing X'. She then does Y; then she says she had been doing X, and expects Claire not to perceive that she had done Y.

Thus it may be true that the schizophrenic person is made so by the confusing and distorting family relationships in which he grew up. All the supposed symptoms of schizophrenia—confusion of ego boundaries, autistic withdrawal, impoverishment of affect, auditory hallucinations, catatonia, and paranoia—may be the result of the agent struggling to make sense of a senseless situation. Nevertheless, it is also true that the agent's struggles are unsuccessful. He fails to make sense, psychologically speaking, of his situation, and his symptoms unmistakably reveal this. Of course, his original beliefs, as we shall illustrate presently, may have been rationally based: he may have had the best reasons available to him at the time, given his age, opportunities, and family situation. But it does not follow that it was rational of him to cling to those beliefs after new evidence became available to him. He remained fixed in beliefs and practices which additional evidence made increasingly inappropriate and irrational for him to maintain. This almost complete inability to respond appropriately to new evidence and new reasons, to be sensitive to changes in information, is characteristic of psychotic persons.

B The psychosis as a whole

1 Reasons for being psychotic

Clearly, we can ask two related questions about the rationality of psychotic people. One is the question, 'Does the psychotic act and believe, to any significant extent, on the basis of reasons, whether good or bad?' The other is this: 'Did the agent have his reasons, adequate or inadequate, for trying to become, or for being, psychotic?' That is, was his psychosis a rational, or reason-based, adaptation to his circumstances as some non-psychotic personality system might be? To ask whether a person can have reasons for being psychotic is to suggest either that his psychosis is the result of his own deliberate policy or is the outcome of unconscious wishes, drives, and beliefs which he acted upon unwittingly. It is to suggest that there were some considerations which he took into account in forming his psychosis. And it is also to raise the question whether an agent can have reasons of which he is unconscious, whether, for example, he can treat certain apparent facts as reasons for his actions while unaware that he does so.

The answer to this last question does not depend upon whether we are asking about justificatory reasons or explanatory reasons. True, an agent cannot *look* for the best justificatory reasons for a course of action open to him without being aware of what he is doing. The search for the best reasons requires him both to pick out relevant factors and to grade them as reasons in an appropriate and rational way. And the rational grading of reasons cannot be done unconsciously, for the grading will only be rational if the principles of selection are open to criticism by the agent, and such criticism is a conscious, intentional activity. However, it does not follow from the impossibility of an agent unconsciously *searching for* justificatory reasons that an agent cannot unconsciously *treat* certain states of affairs as justificatory reasons for people's actions.

He can rely, in his practical reasoning, on *p* being a justificatory premise for a conclusion while refusing to accept that he does so. A man may refuse to assent to the statement that deliberate violation of an unpopular law on abortion is morally permissible, and yet show in many other ways that he regards acts violating it as justified.

Similarly with respect to explanatory reasons, an agent cannot search, unaware of what he is doing, for the reasons which he took into account and upon which he acted in a particular case. He must ask himself the question 'Were these my reasons for what I did?'; and incorporated in this is the further question, 'Did I, at the time, take such-and-such circumstances to be (justificatory) reasons for me to act as I did?' Neither the framing nor the answering of these questions can be carried on unconsciously by the agent. On the other hand, an agent's actions can make it clear that he took certain justificatory reasons for granted even if he would not assent to the claim that he did so. Thus a man may reject the suggestion that his habitual failure to pay his alimony promptly is the result of his belief that women of independent means ought not to receive an income from their separated husbands. His refusal to recognize this as the reason upon which he acts may be that he refuses to accept the fact that his wife has left him. His belief about independent women receiving an income is the major premise p in a practical syllogism; the minor premise is that his wife has left him; and the conclusion is his failure to pay his alimony.

But however a man's refusal to recognize his reason p is to be explained, there may be abundant evidence that he has relied on p as a justificatory reason for his actions. He may fiercely resist all attacks on p, show surprise when his close friends who also hold this belief do not always act upon it, and he may pay his alimony promptly when his wife's independent means are temporarily cut off. Hence a man can act on the basis of certain reasons while unaware that they have been his reasons.

Let us return to the more general problem of whether a person can have reasons, conscious or unconscious, for trying to become, or for being, psychotic. Laing describes his patient David as a person whose psychotic illness appears to be the result of the patient's own deliberate policy. David was an eighteen-year-old university student who dressed in a defensively eccentric fashion and seemed to have hallucinations. 'He had always been a very good child, who did everything he was told and never caused any trouble. His mother had been devoted to him. He was inseparable from her.'[15] After his mother's death when he was ten years old he kept house for his father. 'He did the housework, cooked the meals, bought most of the food. He "took over" from his mother or "took after" her, even to the extent of showing her flair for embroidery, tapestry, and interior decoration.'[16]

It became apparent that he felt himself always to be playing a part in which he overcame his 'shyness, self-consciousness, and vulnerability' by concealing his own self and displaying only 'what his mother wanted him to be'—his public personality. His goal was 'to make the split between his own self (which only he knew) and what other people could see of him, as complete as possible',[17] never to give himself away to anyone else. However, he had always liked to dress himself in his mother's clothes and play women's parts in front of a mirror. As time went on he discovered that 'he could not stop playing the part of a woman. He caught himself compulsively walking like a woman, talking like a woman, even seeing and thinking as a woman might see and think.'[18] The only way he could escape from doing this—from identifying himself with his mother—was to adopt the role of a fantastically dressed eccentric. He did not know why this was so, but it did provide what he wanted—a way of detaching himself from his mother's ever present influence.

The case of David obviously raises the following question: In what respects was it irrational of David, given his situation, information, and abilities, to adopt as a policy of behaviour the making of 'the split between his own self (which only he knew)' and his public personality 'as complete as possible'?

Laing's description suggests that David deliberately and knowingly adopted this as his aim. *If* he did, and was not merely impelled by unconscious reasons or by organic disturbances, then he both valued his goal (self-protection from his mother's enveloping attentions) and chose one of the few—perhaps the only—means of achieving it open to him. He was not overcome by panic or impulse though he was goaded by fear. He chose means which, given his age, experience, and information, it could well have been rational of him to believe were at least as adequate to some of his ends as any other means open to him. He could not be expected, as a child, to realize that while his procedure might be successful in the short run it might be very costly in the long run. Nor could he be expected, as he grew older, to assess the continuing consequential effects of his role-playing: loss of identity, weakening of relationships with other people, loss of ability to cope in a practical way with the environment, fantasies of disappearance, persecution; finally, emotional and intellectual petrification. Yet the very accumulation of these effects over time reduced both the boy's ability to acquire rationally-based beliefs about alternative means, and his ability to evaluate ends different from the one which in fact he was pursuing.

It looks, then, as though it was rational, to a quite substantial degree, for David to adopt means which we now know were highly likely to isolate him, to a dangerous degree, from other people. David's actions exhibited some degree of practical rationality because they were based on the rational belief that he could protect his autonomy, for the moment, by adopting a false personality. This belief was at least rational in part, given his false beliefs that everyone was, like himself, a constant actor, and that his own adoption of a false personality would not itself eventually destroy the autonomy of his hidden or true personality. While his actions were inappropriate to achieving some of his long-term ends, he was not in a position to know this, and so neither his actions nor beliefs were strongly irrational.

2 Adopting and maintaining a psychosis

To say this much about people like David, however, is not to suggest that he, or anyone else, could wittingly or unwittingly adopt a psychosis and then maintain it as a way of life. Nevertheless, there is a weak sense in which a psychosis can be deliberately formed. It is that in which an agent, after learning something about psychosis, might deliberately expose himself to certain conditions that he thought were likely to prove traumatic. He might wish to become psychotic, and take whatever steps he thought would produce this condition in himself. If his means were effective, his end would be realized. But in doing this, the agent would merely be placing himself in a position as favourable as possible for the development of a psychosis. He would not be actively developing his illness himself. After exposure he could only hope for the best (or worst) —could only hope for aid from factors over which he had no control. The illness, if it appeared, would simply *happen* to him from that point on. Thus while a person could (rationally or irrationally) initiate the process of becoming psychotic, could rationally or irrationally try to become psychotic, he could not actively maintain and implement it as a policy: as he could implement, for example, a policy of aiding aboriginal peoples. Long before the psychotic process had been completed, the person would have lost the ability to maintain (monitor, criticize, and correct) it. Hence, even given that the psychoses are non-organic in origin, the question 'Could an agent ever have his own reasons for being, or trying to become, a psychotic personality?' has a dual answer. For taken as a whole, *being* psychotic, as contrasted with *trying to become* psychotic, is neither rational nor irrational, since it cannot—logically cannot—both be entered into and maintained on the basis of the agent's own reasons, conscious or unconscious. It does not logically lie within his power to do more than to expose himself to known causal conditions, e.g. certain drugs.

3 Psychosis as a rational adaptation

There is another interpretation of the question whether it can ever be rational for a person to become psychotic. A psychosis may well be a rational adaptation to the agent's circumstances in the sense that it happens to produce effects which are at least as beneficial to him as any other course of action that he might adopt. A man who is hopelessly imprisoned, or about to suffer extreme torture, or the lone survivor on an ocean rock, may be better off mad than sane, just as in similar situations he may be better off dead than alive. He may be, but need not be. In any case, the question 'Is his psychosis a rational adaptation to his circumstances?' assumes, first, that psychosis can be, on some occasions, a neurological reaction to intolerable circumstances of stress, and second, that such a reaction is adaptive because its role in a system is, for example, to protect the agent from further stress, as fainting protects him from unbearable pain.

However, both assumptions are debatable. The psychoses may turn out to be purely biochemical in origin. If so, the agent's intolerable circumstances might well not be a causal factor in his illness. But even if they should prove to be, it obviously would not follow that the illness was an *adaptive* mechanism. To demonstrate this, we should have to be able to specify the properties and boundaries of the system in which psychoses were thought to play a role; and, further, we should have to specify the precise mechanism through which the psychoses fulfilled their adaptive function. At present we can do no more than state these two assumptions. Until we can do more, the dictum 'psychoses are rational adaptations' has no cash value at all, for the psychoses have not yet been shown to be either reason-based activities or adaptive mechanisms. Hence, there is no point in adding these deficiencies to those of the first interpretation of our question. It has still not been shown either that the agent has his own reasons for *being* psychotic—though he might have reasons for trying to become so—or that his psychosis is in any sense an adaptation, rational, irrational, or non-rational, to his circumstances.

4   Advanced psychosis as conflicting sub-systems

Now, obviously, having an advanced psychosis is not having a social way of life; it is more like not participating in a social way of life, not conforming to any system of social conventions. The agent becomes increasingly isolated and insulated from other people. He increasingly cannot recognize them, understand them, or empathize with them. Nor can he dependably recognize various features of his natural environment and cope with them in such a way as to satisfy his needs. Psychoses, unlike neuroses, can engulf the entire personality. The agent develops a pseudo-system of thought and action which makes it difficult, and sometimes impossible, for him to participate in any way of life, including the one which he tries to provide for himself by means of his pseudo-system. For such systems are failures as systems. They are failures not merely because their agents suffer so much that they become medical patients. The pseudo-systems fail because they are internally incoherent and often disintegrate. They do not function as *systems*.

Characteristically, each of them is a loosely affiliated collection of conflicting sub-systems—called 'sub-systems' because the collection is the lineal descendant of an earlier unified system and is associated with the same physical body. By a process of positive feedback the person's psychological defences have become so elaborate that they imprison him. He can no longer act, think, or feel except within their increasingly restrictive confines. His preference schedule is wildly inconsistent. In short, his ability to do as he wishes and to be the kind of person he admires is drastically and progressively reduced. Yet this outcome is not what he wanted initially, nor is it what he wants in his lucid moments. He struggles, without hope, to free himself from his condition. But he can neither abandon his defences nor tolerate life within them.

The conflict between the agent's sub-systems is so deep and far reaching that he is compelled to act it out in the form of his psychosis. Thus 'the stupor of some catatonic schizophrenics seems to be a dramatization of the idea of death, and some states of ecstasy represent the dramatization of being born again'.[19] Yet this acting out, this way in which he shows his mental condition, is not, as Laing seems to suggest, the agent's chosen, but inappropriate, means of communicating with us. His acting out is a symptom; it is not *chosen* by him, and it is not his means of communication however well it indicates his plight. His means of communication increasingly disappear with the development of his illness. As Crowcroft says of the advanced schizophrenic,[20] he 'cannot sort out or understand his experiences because he cannot distinguish himself from the world'. In the end, he becomes unable to describe his situation by means of word, deed, song, or code. He cannot do this either to himself or to other people, since his ability and desire to do so are lost in the same 'flight from reality' which leads him to his psychotic refuge. In this last stage of illness the agent is neither a believer nor a chooser. He no longer believes and acts on the basis of his own reasons. He does not and cannot take certain states of affairs to be justificatory reasons for his beliefs.

Thus the question arises, 'How can we identify the agent who is said to believe p?' For sometimes we may be at a loss to know to whom the word 'he' refers in such remarks as 'He believes p'. When the patient abdicates responsibility for his ideas and intentions, as many advanced psychotics commonly do, we can no longer count on him to draw inferences consistently. And when we cannot count on this, and its related set of dispositions to appropriate action, we lose the ability to assign beliefs to *him* as an integrated believer. We cannot say what it is that *he* believes. If we then try to assign specific beliefs to some part of his personality, perhaps to Voice No. 1, the same evasive manoeuvres may recur. That personality fragment itself may sub-divide into two parts, or alter radically, so as to avoid the imputation of settled belief to it. Hence in the case of the advanced schizophrenic one of the logically necessary conditions for the ascription of either rational or irrational beliefs is not satisfied. This condition is the exercise of a capacity to systematically relate propositions and value judgments by means of their logical and evidential relationships, and to try to act intentionally in accordance with that system. For the performances of the advanced schizophrenic are not regularly the intended outcome of his beliefs and attitudes. He both loses control over some of the movements of his body and loses much of his capacity to perform organized sets of goal-directed actions. In brief, the agent's personality is not stable and integrated enough for us to say that he believes anything in the sense of his displaying consistent and regular responses of the appropriate sorts. Much, but not all, of his behaviour becomes non-rational rather than irrational.

At this point we might be tempted to suggest that the agent's illness, in so far as it decreased the range of his ends, also decreased his ability to reflectively assign weights to the 'full range of his ends'; and that therefore the disease had made him less rational because more of his activity had become non-rational. However, this suggestion cannot be correct. There is no necessary logical connection between the narrowing of the variety of his ends and his ability to weigh reflectively the ones which he still possesses. At best, the connection is contingent though common. The agent's irrationality, if any, must consist in his pursuit of ends which it is irrational for him or perhaps for anyone to try to achieve, or in his failure to pursue ends which it is irrational for him not to try to achieve. If the illness caused the agent to become fixated on these ends, or caused him to pursue these ends because of irrational beliefs produced by the illness, then, and only then, the illness caused him to behave irrationally.

C The physiological explanation

Suppose, now, that we alter the basic causal assumption under which we have proceeded so far. That assumption is that the psychoses are chiefly, or at least importantly, non-organic ('dynamic') in origin. If we now assume, instead, that they are chiefly or importantly organic, what difference will this make to the answers we have given to our questions about the rationality of psychotics?

Let us begin with a useful distinction. Some of the agent's delusional beliefs will represent his misguided attempts to explain the altered character of his experience—to explain such things as his general suspiciousness, auditory hallucinations, delusional perceptions, thought broadcasting, thought interference, and emotional blunting—in terms of his own reasons. But some of the agent's mistaken beliefs will not be such rationalizations. These other mistaken beliefs will be his acceptance of perceptual hallucinations and illusions as genuine. His emotions and attitudes, therefore, will be the direct causal outcome either of his perceptual disorders, e.g. fixation on particular sense-qualities of objects, or of his disorganized thought with its over-inclusion and extreme literalness. Since the agent's ability to perceive normally and his ability to think normally deteriorate together, it is not possible for him to maintain a critical attitude toward his perceptual experience.

If we now ask 'In what does the agent's irrationality or nonrationality consist?' we must be clear as to whether our question refers to his explanations or to that which he is trying to explain. For example, the irrationality of a person taking himself to be constantly exuding a putrid odour is different from that of a person who explains the presence of the odour as a punishment for his sexual guilt. The former may have no explanation to offer; his irrationality may consist only in his mistakenly taking himself to have a putrid odour, although this irrationality may be of several different kinds. Thus, it may be that while in fact he has a distinctive odour, he has no good grounds for characterizing it as putrid, since by tests the odour can be shown to be indistinguishable from other odours which he calls 'musky'. Or it may be that his olfactory receptor cells or olfactory bulb can be shown to be inoperative, so that his claim cannot be a report on the scent of his respiratory air. In contrast, the person who gives a pseudo-explanation not only attributes the odour to himself but believes, in addition, the truth of the various false statements which make up his explanation, and believes them, by hypothesis, on clearly inadequate grounds. Moreover, both the agent's perceptual beliefs and his inferential beliefs (his rationalizations) are highly resistant to rationally based change. It is not that he suffers hallucinations and illusions which, if he were given therapeutic support, he might be able to recognize as afflictions. Rather, his ability to recognize his perceptual disorders is diminished as they increase, for his thought becomes disordered at the same time as his perception does.

Thus if we proceed on our present assumption—that schizo-phrenia and the other functional psychoses are neurophysiological disturbances—we are still left with a variety of possible questions, and hence of possible answers, concerning the agent's rationality, irrationality or non-rationality. But the relative frequencies of these three answers will change over the course of the agent's illness. Even the most deteriorated psychotic will show some end-directed, or reason-based, behaviour, and thus some behaviour which it is either rational or irrational for him to exhibit. Of course we may not know whether a given belief or action is reason-based, but that is not at issue. The simple point is that organically determined psychoses no more produce completely non-rational beliefs, actions, and attitudes than dynamically determined psychoses produce only reason-based behaviour. To put it even more strongly: from the fact that a person suffers from an organic brain disease like senile dementia it does not logically follow that his beliefs, actions, and attitudes are non-rational, i.e. not based on his own reasons, to a greater extent than those of someone afflicted only with what is now called a 'functional' psychosis. Non-rational behaviour is behaviour to which the expression 'reason-based' is logically inapplicable. But the expression can be logically inappli-cable to behaviour which is produced by either physiological or psychological causes. Catatonia, for instance, whether neurological or functional, is not exhibited for the agent's own reasons; the agent does not bring it about that his limbs remain wherever they are placed and that they cannot be moved voluntarily by him.

We must distinguish, then, between knowing that a psychotic illness has a neurophysiological cause and knowing that any one of its symptoms, or its causal consequences, is non-rational. Knowledge of the one does not entail knowledge of the other. A similar lack of entailment holds between knowing that a psychosis is functional and knowing that any one of its symptoms, or causal consequences, is reason-based. In point of fact, organic mental diseases—brain lesions for example—often have the causal effect of greatly narrowing both the variety of ends which the agent pursues and the variety of means which he employs in order to realize them. Even so, the agent can often display end-directed behaviour and his ends can appear on his preference schedule. The agent's ends are ones to which, on reflection, he would wish to give some weight. If the agent has fixated on some few activities, like those connected with a persecutory anxiety for example, his preference schedule will be brief but his means may still be efficient. As in the case of functional mental states, an organic psychosis increases the agent's irrationality only if it causes him to hold irrationally based reasons for pursuing those ends. It might, for example, cause him to suffer perceptual illusions on which he based irrationally held beliefs; and these beliefs might influence the attitudes he had toward certain ends. But if no such irrationally based reasons are present, then under the conditions assumed—that is, excluding consideration of the rationality of the agent's means—the psychosis does not increase the agent's irrationality.

However, it is clear that both organic and functional psychoses must include *some* non-rational behaviour, and that the proportion of such behaviour must increase with the development of the psychosis. For whatever the origin of the psychosis, the same elements of the clinical picture may be present. In both sorts of cases there may be ideas of reference, persecutory delusions, hallucinations, and misidentifications; from these, in both cases, a delusional reality may be produced, and this delusional system may be supported by rationalizations. But in advanced chronic syndromes, these pseudo-reasons of the patient become increasingly superfluous with the fragmentation of his perception and thought. He simply loses the ability to recognize, formulate, or to act upon, reasons of his own, and it does not matter whether these be good or bad, genuine or rationalizations. The conflicting sub-systems into which his personality eventually disintegrates represent non-rational, not irrational, behaviour.

In both the organic and functional psychoses, then, the agent's earlier limited area of irrational behaviour can develop into an extensive area of non-rational behaviour. This process of development takes place independently of the type of cause which produces it. Thus 'a neurophysiological disturbance' and 'a malformed strategy for coping with the agent's failure to attain certain ends' are both characterizations of a story with one unhappy ending. Of course the two characterizations differ in a very important respect: they may classify differently any given piece of behaviour, any given trait of an agent, any particular type of process. Thus on the one view, a patient who has paranoid schizophrenia might be said to be the product of unresponsive parents: on the other view, he might be said to be the product of his reticular over-activity. If we set aside the question of interaction between causes of these two sorts, then we can interpret David's failure to trust anyone, for example, either as a learning deficiency arising from his early family life, or as the causal effect of the repeated disruption of his central process by a dominating sensory input. On the first interpretation, David's lack of trust can be either rational or irrational. On the second interpretation, it cannot be either of these. But notwithstanding this, whichever general account we choose—whether we assimilate the advanced functional psychoses to reason-based neuroses or to physiological disturbances of the nervous system—the behaviour that both accounts try to explain will be non-rational to an important extent.

Notes

1 Laing, R.D. (1965), pp. 29–30.
2 Ibid., pp. 30–1.
3 Ibid., p. 30.
4 Cameron, N. (1944), p. 54.
5 Ibid., p. 54.
6 Goldstein, K. (1944), p. 29.
7 Cameron, N. (1944), p. 58.
8 Kasanin, J.S. (1944), p. 131.
9 Freeman, T. (1969), pp. 150–1.
10 Laing, R.D. (1965), p. 164.
11 Searles, H.F. (1950), p. 571.
12 Laing, R.D. (1965), p. 113.
13 Ibid., pp. 113–14.
14 Laing, R.D. and Esterson, A. (1970), p. 87.
15 Laing, R.D. (1965), p. 70.
16 Ibid., p. 70.
17 Ibid., p. 71.
18 Ibid., p. 72.
19 Crowcroft, A. (1967), p. 118.
20 Ibid., p. 119.

Bibliography

CAMERON, N. (1944), 'Experimental analysis of schizophrenic thinking', in Kasanin, J.S. (ed.) (1944).
CROWCROFT, A. (1967), *The Psychotic*, Harmondsworth.
FREEMAN, T. (1969), *Psychopathology of the Psychoses*, London.
GOLDSTEIN, K. (1944), 'Methodological approach to the study of schizophrenic thought disorder', in Kasanin, J.S. (ed.) (1944).
KASANIN, J.S. (1944), 'Concluding remarks', in Kasanin, J.S. (ed.) (1944).
KASANIN, J.S. (ed.) (1944), *Language and Thought in Schizophrenia*, Berkeley.
LAING, R.D. (1965), *The Divided Self*, Harmondsworth.
LAING, R.D. and ESTERSON, A. (1970), *Sanity, Madness, and the Family*, Harmondsworth.
SEARLES, H.F. (1950), *Collected Papers on Schizophrenia and Related Subjects*, London.

Part Four
Social rationality

14

The rationality of societies

P.H. Partridge, S.I. Benn and
G.W. Mortimore

A   Individual rational conduct and social rationality

1   The problem introduced

Earlier papers in this collection have amply demonstrated that the criteria for ascribing rationality to individuals' actions and beliefs are by no means beyond dispute. There is nevertheless a widely accepted core of meaning to such ascriptions. We shall show in this paper that there is no corresponding consensus, even in the most general terms, on the criteria for ascribing rationality to whole societies or social systems, or to particular institutions, traditions, and customs within a society. For although social thinkers seem generally agreed that whether systems and institutions are rational is a matter of considerable importance, there has been no more agreement about the meaning of this concept than there has been about the nature of the 'good' or the 'just'. Our aim in this paper is to show how certain disputes in social theory are related to differences of opinion about the criteria for such assessments.

We shall look in section A3 at the account commonly given by social theorists of individual rationality in action and belief, since their accounts of the rationality of societies are clearly modelled on it. In section B we look first at social rationality concepts reducible in one way or another to individual rationality, and then at others that seem to postulate a social agent analogous to the individual agent. In section C we shall consider a view which rejects the standard account of individual rationality in ways important for its application to institutions and societies. Finally, in section D, we consider possible reasons for thinking that individual rationality may be inconsistent with the rationality of societies or institutions, or that rational institutions may frustrate development of individual rationality.

2 Two ways of attributing rationality

Some of the obscurities of the subject can be removed by a preliminary distinction. We shall say that an individual's actions and beliefs are rational$_1$ if he acts (or believes) for good reasons. So an agent's acts are rational$_1$ if he has reasonable grounds for believing them appropriate to his ends, and does them on that account; and his beliefs are rational$_1$ if he has reason to believe that they are grounded on relevant considerations (evidence, direct experience, etc.), and accepts them on that account. Rationality in this sense is attributable primarily to agents and credents, and only by derivation to their actions and beliefs. It refers to the particular manner in which they act (or hold their beliefs), i.e. on considerations that they believe to be reasons for what they do (or believe).

An act may be rational in an impersonal sense, however, if it is the rational thing for an agent to do—whether or not he does it, or does it on account of its being rational. We shall call this 'rationality$_2$'. A punter may back the horse with the best chance of winning—and may indeed win—but have acted irrationally$_1$ if he selected it because he found its name euphonious. Nevertheless, the horse he chose was the rational$_2$ one to choose, given the available information and the desire to back a winner. The rationality$_2$ of an action depends not on the manner in which the agent performs it, but on whether the action satisfies the appropriate requirements of reason applied to antecedent beliefs and goals. A person does what is rational$_2$ when he chooses the course he would have chosen had he acted rationally$_1$, whether his choice satisfies the other conditions for rationality$_1$ or no. While we shall not insist on this distinction at every point of this paper, it will be useful in explaining, for instance, how one might claim that, given a set of imputed ends, social practices well-adapted to achieving those ends might be considered rational$_2$, even though these practices discourage the making of rational$_1$ judgments by individuals. The rationality$_2$ of certain practices might actually depend, indeed, on individuals, habitually acting in a non-rational$_1$ manner.

3 The standard account of individual rationality

(a) The account of rational$_1$ actions most frequently elaborated by social scientists focuses on the relation between the agent's action and his ends. Take a couple of typical definitions.[1]

An action is rational to the extent that it is 'correctly' designed to maximize goal achievement, given the goal in question and the real world as it exists. Given more than one goal (the usual human situation), an action is rational to the extent that it is correctly designed to maximize *net* goal achievement. When several actions are required to attain goals, rationality requires *coördination*; that is, the actions must be scheduled and dovetailed so that net goal achievement is not diminished by avoidable conflicts among the actions.

Second, Oakeshott (giving an account of rationality he is preparing to attack):[2] 'The view we are to consider takes *purpose* as the distinctive mark of "rationality" in conduct ... "[Rational]" conduct is behaviour *deliberately* directed to the achievement of a *formulated* purpose and is governed solely by that purpose.' It involves a 'separately premeditated selection of the means to be employed'. It excludes capriciousness, 'impulsive conduct', 'conduct ... not governed by a deliberately accepted rule or principle or canon', 'conduct which springs from the unexamined authority of a tradition', conduct pursuing 'an end for which the necessary means are known to be absent'.

In his list of exclusions Oakeshott tendentiously strengthens the model of rational conduct he is setting up to attack. However, these two accounts include the chief primitive elements in the standard account of rational individual conduct. These include: the seeking of premeditated goals, formulated in advance of acting; a disposition to calculate means to achieve designed ends; the deployment of beliefs about causal relations in the choosing of means; the choice of an action (or of a plan co-ordinating a set or sequence of actions) for the purpose of maximizing goal-achievement. These might be termed criterial requirements of practical rationality. Besides these, there are certain criterial requirements of epistemic rationality, notably, an empirical-scientific approach in forming beliefs about possible means, including a concern for grounds for belief, and a disposition to question beliefs for which no grounds could be adduced. One might distinguish, too, certain preconditions for the satisfaction of both kinds of criterial conditions; for instance, if natural and human behaviour were unpredictable, there could be no rational expectation that any given course of action would achieve any goal, and consequently no reason for adopting one course of action rather than another.

(b) Individual rationality is also commonly held to require

consistency and the avoidance of contradictions. There are two notions of consistency which have figured prominently in accounts of rationality and irrationality in societies. The first derives from the notion of acting (or believing) for a reason. Reasons for action are logically universal in their scope; a set of relevant conditions for doing A on some occasion is a reason for doing A on all similar occasions. So a statement that a consideration is a reason for doing A can always be formulated as a rule—that A shall be done whenever that consideration obtains. And since rationality consists in acting and believing for reasons, it is easy to see why Oakeshott included acting according to rules in his account of the standard notion.

The notion of rationality as rule-conforming, though highly formal, has nevertheless important negative implications, namely, that purely self-referential facts, like one's fancies, that may otherwise influence judgment, are not reasons unless the rule makes them so. For though one may indeed act consistently on the principle: when offered a bowl of fruit, select the piece one fancies most, it is not always rational to build such self-referential principles into one's rules of action. We shall argue later that this consideration accounts for part at least of the Weberian view that being governed by rules is a characteristic feature of rational bureaucracies.

Of course, the consistent application of rules is not a sufficient condition for rationality. The rule may be too rigid; features of a case that, on other criteria of rationality, would be held to distinguish it in a relevant way from the paradigm defined by the rule might not be admissible under it. It is in such cases that the law is said to be both irrational and unjust, since it requires the judge to treat unlike cases as if they were similar. An individual who ran his private life by such rules would be insensitive, undiscriminating, or hidebound; his judgment would be determined by criteria of one sort only where reasons of other sorts (of morality, for instance) should be overriding. And these are frequently cited as characteristics of authoritarian personalities, rather than of the critical, autonomous personalities that we generally associate with rationality.

The second consistency requirement is the one that is invoked to criticize the irrationality of believing two contradictory propositions. The irrationality here is not that a consideration is treated in one situation as a reason for believing something, but disregarded in another that is similar in all relevant respects. It is rather that there is a contradiction within a person's beliefs deriving from their content and from the logical norms governing them, not from his reasons for holding them. The notion of consistency in this case applies to the propositions themselves, and only by derivation to a person's believing them. If one believes both p and not-p, that belief is inconsistent and irrational because the propositions are inconsistent, because there are logical norms that declare that, as contradictories, they cannot both be true. It is this second consistency requirement, rather than the one related to reasons for believing and acting, that seems to provide the basis for the Hegelian notion of the rationality of societies, and for Marx's conception of social contradictions, that we refer to later in section B2(b).

B The rationality of societies and institutions, and the model of individual rationality

Our first step (B1) in extending the model of individual rationality to social entities, both to institutions and to whole societies, will be to examine concepts that rely on the means/end aspect of rational action, beginning with concepts that reduce pretty straightforwardly to the means/end rationality$_1$ of individuals, moving by stages to notions that, while still analogous to it, are not reducible to it. The concepts examined in B2 link more closely with the consistency conditions of the model, stressing non-arbitrariness or absence of internal frustration ('contradiction').

1 The rationality of social entities and the pursuit of ends

(a) Social entities that promote the rationality$_1$ of individuals

(i) The rationality of social organization has been linked most closely to the rationality of individuals in Max Weber's account of the increasing rationalization of capitalist society. In our terminology, Weber's capitalist society involves the development of both the practical and the epistemic rationality of its members. Deliberative choice, based on propositions about the causal connections between acts and outcomes, takes the place of emotionally expressive or traditional behaviour. The beliefs on which choices are based are empirically or scientifically verifiable: thus Weber links progressive rationalization with growing scepticism about the existence of magical, unknowable, incalculable, and uncontrollable forces.

Weber associated with this development the emergence of a rational bureaucracy, of an organization that made likely the appointment of officials who in deliberation and decision would employ empirico-scientific methods. Thus a certain kind of society might be rational if it fostered the rationality$_1$ of individual members, and irrational if it inhibited it.

363

(ii) A society of rational$_1$ men might not be a rational society in another sense, however, if it so structured their relations that their efforts at goal-maximization, no matter how rational$_1$, were mutually frustrating. Social organization would be rational in this sense, therefore, if, without necessarily fostering the rationality$_1$ of its members, it provided maximum opportunities for them to exercise rational choices. The *laissez-faire* liberal economists' model of a competitive market system, where allocations simply emerged with no co-ordinated planning from the interaction of rational$_1$ individual choices, would count as a rational society in this sense if, as they claimed, it maximized overall goal-satisfaction.

Paul Diesing's notion of the rationality of 'an integrated social system' seems to be of this kind too. Diesing argues that[3] '(a)n integrated social system is a rational one, since it is effective in making action possible and meaningful, and the integrative trend in social systems is a trend toward rational social organization.' Diesing takes social integration to involve such things as the internal consistency of roles, fit between pairs of roles, continuity in the sequence of roles (his analysis of social structure is largely in terms of role theory), compatibility with the non-social environment, and so on. He appears to take it for granted that conflicts between goals, interests and demands, and the incompatibilities or lack of adjustment between separate institutions, necessarily diminish social rationality, and must always result in the reduction of individual goal-achievement. (This is not self-evident. We revert to this point in section C.) Certainly, any resources that individuals have to devote merely to fending off rivals, or defending their own resource base, are costs that might be eliminated by the integration of ends and means. So Diesing takes a legal system to be rational because it not only provides accepted ways of settling disputes when they arise, but also, by defining and enforcing rights and obligations, it is more effective than force, bargaining, and negotiation in preventing disputes from arising. Similarly, it has been argued that democratic legislative processes are more successful than dictatorships in securing agreement through discussion on the goals to be pursued through political action, the distribution of resources between competing goals, and the like, and that this is one mark of their rationality.[4]

(b) Rational social entities as forms of organization it would be rational$_2$ for each member to choose

If a form of organization such as Diesing envisages, or such as the classical economists envisaged in the market model, yields optimal outcomes for its members, it can be said to be rational in another sense. For under certain conditions it would then be rational$_2$ for each member of a society, given the chance, to choose or accept such an organization, and to act within its structure of roles. If, for instance, every worker sought a certain living wage as his primary goal, and a complex industrial enterprise, in which each worker was assigned a specialized function, provided his best chance of getting it, it would be rational$_2$ for him to accept it, and his role in it.

The notion of a rational society in this sense, however, extends beyond societies that maximize returns to rational$_1$ behaviour. The difference between the views of Diesing, and writers like Adam Ferguson, Adam Smith, Edmund Burke, and Frederick Hayek clearly illustrates this, and brings out the difference, therefore, between the implications of the present concept, and that discussed in B1(a)(ii). For while Diesing's integrated society, like the market model, falls under both, the social arrangements recommended as rational by these other writers do not. Instead, they seem to make it a causal condition of the rationality$_2$ of social institutions and practices that individuals operate with only a modified rationality$_1$. These writers defend the rationality of established traditions (and of deliberately following traditional modes) by asserting that there is often a 'wisdom' embodied in traditions, greater than any the individual could expect to acquire for himself, and not apparent to the individual with his circumscribed experience. This sort of view is well put in the well-known passage in Burke:[5]

> We are afraid to put men to live and trade each on his own
> private stock of reason; because we suspect that this stock in
> each man is small, and that the individuals would do better to
> avail themselves of the general bank and capital of nations
> and of ages.

Only with 'pious awe and trembling solicitude' would a rational individual venture to touch the social institutions in which reason and prejudice are so strongly blended.

The truth of Burke's doctrine can be more readily assessed if it is re-expressed in our terms. Traditions, he claims, embody the experience and wisdom of past generations, while innovations embody the beliefs and assumptions of a few persons only. Assuming, then, that the goals to which individuals attach fundamental importance do not change, traditional institutions will be rationally$_2$ suited to achieving them, having evolved through a long process of experimental and piecemeal adaptation. For any given individual, therefore, it is practically rational$_2$ (he will 'do better', i.e. it will be the course that maximizes his own goal-achievement) not to adopt as a goal maximum epistemic rationality in the selection of means, nor to deliberate too much upon the order of his preferences. Epistemically rational$_1$ procedures rarely yield epistemically rational$_2$ beliefs; equally, a deliberate ordering of preferences does not yield a practically rational$_2$ ordering of goals. So one does better (is practically rational$_2$) to fall in with accepted prejudices and traditional practices. Anyone who grasps the truth of this principle and acts upon it would also exhibit a certain degree of individual practical rationality$_1$, though without conscious deliberation about preference ordering, and at the cost of giving up epistemic rationality$_1$. We shall look critically at this thesis later on. Our purpose for the moment is simply to exhibit the relation between the concepts of social rationality and individual rationality that it seems to require.

(c) Social rationality and compatibility with man's nature

The rationality of a society has often been connected with its capacity to satisfy what are taken to be standard or central human needs and potentialities. This connection has been especially emphasized in our own time, when the connection between social progress and economic growth and technological development, and the associated manipulative and calculative notions of rationality, are frequently challenged.[6] The rationality of societies, institutions and policies is judged more by the manner in which they affect the moral and intellectual quality of the life they impose upon men; rationality appears not as a technical but as a moral category. It is, nevertheless, a case of the type just examined in B1(b), with this added feature: in those cases a society was to be deemed rational if it was such that a person would rationally$_2$ choose it, whatever the goals or interests he happened to have; in the present case the relevant idea of man's nature, understood as a set of potentialities or needs, limits the kind of goals a man could reasonably have, or the forms of activity that he could choose, supposing he had a rational grasp of his own nature. Consequently, a society would be rational in the present sense only if it made possible the pursuit of ends and activities such as a man who understood his own nature would choose. If, besides, that nature is defined in terms of the capacity to become a free and rational agent,[7] then no society could be rational in the present sense that inhibited the development of that capacity, i.e. that made it impossible that a man should actually choose that society in a rational$_1$ manner. And radical critics of our society claim that since it systematically distorts man's understanding of his own nature, a rational₁ choice of such a society is indeed impossible.

The most familiar of such theories rest on the conception of 'alienation'; the most famous of them that of the early Marx. For Marx, of course, capitalist production is irrational because it is in contradiction to the human essence which is 'free conscious activity'. Man expresses himself through productive labour, and its products; man 'produces himself not only intellectually, as in consciousness, but also actively in a real sense and sees himself in a world he made. In taking from man the object of his production, alienated labour takes from his *species-life*, his actual and objective existence as a species.' Thus, the appropriation by the capitalist of the products of labour means 'degrading free spontaneous activity to the level of a means; alienated labour makes the species-life of man a means of his physical existence'. That is, under the regime of private ownership of the means of production man's labour is not free but coerced labour; he produces not directly to satisfy his own needs, but to produce the means to satisfy other needs; productive labour which ideally is the expression of his essence, the 'objectification' of his own character, is something determined and imposed upon him by what controls his activity and is in that way alien to him. Division of labour is also a denial of the human essence or 'species being'; as Marx puts it in *Capital*, volume I, it 'converts the labourer into a crippled monstrosity by forcing his detailed dexterity at the expense of a world of productive capabilities and instincts'. Again, man is in essence a social being; he produces and realizes his essence (or objectifies himself in the world he himself makes) in co-operation with others, but private appropriation and division of labour divides men and sets them in opposition to one another. Men are alienated not only from their labour and its products, but from their fellow men: 'The positive overcoming of *private property* as the appropriation of *human* life is thus the positive overcoming of all alienation and the return of man from religion, family, state, etc., to his *human*, that is, *social* existence.'[8]

This of course is a rationalistic view in the special, technical sense, that it purports to be able to discover the essences of things and to display the discrepancies between essence and actual existence. So the theory of natural rights was a rationalistic position in this sense, proclaiming the essential (or 'inalienable') rights of man. Locke argued (though with qualifications) that it would be irrational for men to accept institutions that deprived them of their natural rights. One could similarly argue that a rational₁ man who understood his true nature could not accept any institution that subjected him to conditions that prevented him from realizing it, i.e. from being what he would be at his best. So if it were possible to validate an account of the human essence, this would provide a criterion, satisfying the conditions of generality and objectivity that rationality is usually said to imply, for judging institutions rational or irrational.

In modern philosophy and social thinking generally this kind of rationalism (or 'essentialism' as Popper calls it) is strongly contested. So if one wants to connect the 'rationality' of institutions with the way they affect the quality of human living, one may be forced back to weaker positions, some of which we have already sketched. For example, the rationality of social arrangements may be taken to depend on their providing the certainty, regularity and predictability necessary if individuals are to plan any course of conduct rationally. As Popper puts it, 'the creation of traditions, like so much of our legislation, has ... [the] function of bringing some order and rational predictability into the social world in which we live .... Every rational action assumes a certain system of reference which responds in a predictable or partly predictable way.'[9] So one might argue that the predictability that accrues from efficient organization, stable social integration, etc., enhances man's freedom by increasing his capacity to achieve the purposes he chooses for himself.

Or we might start from human potentialities which we take to be of special moral or psychological importance (e.g. spontaneity, creativity, the capacity for initiative, sociability) and, without claiming these to be *the* essence of man but simply capacities that do often manifest themselves in favourable circumstances, consider how particular institutions and forms of social organization express or inhibit them. Those characteristics of capitalist society denounced by Marx and many others since may very likely mutilate certain human potentialities (while no doubt satisfying many other needs); but no doubt any possible form of social organization would be hospitable to some human potentialities and inhospitable to others; every society may involve some kind and measure of alienation as Marx describes it. And, of course, social arrangements and institutions affect different individuals and social classes differently. But if we discard the notion of a human essence and we select, possibly for moral reasons, some particular human qualities or potentialities as our point of reference, what justification do we have for continuing to invoke the standard of rationality? We may agree with Marx that capitalist production involves the alienation of the worker from his own productive activity, its product, and his fellow-men, agreeing too that on moral grounds all this is bad;

but in what sense can we say that it is *irrational*? Using the different and narrower criteria that Weber applies to bureaucracy and in industrial organization (see B1(a) and B1(d)), these features of capitalist society might well be entirely rational.

Nevertheless, some measures of consensus about 'human nature' do emerge over time. For example, there would be a wide consensus now that no men are slaves by nature. Traditional inequalities between persons of different race, and in the roles attributed to men and women, on the grounds of differences in their capacities, potentialities, sources of fulfilment, are being eroded partly by processes of argument. If we ask: 'Are men by nature assembly-line operators?', we find no equal consensus; nevertheless, assertions that work which is mindless repetition and routine is dehumanizing are nowadays more frequently made and seem to be received with more sympathy. Similarly, most people nowadays would agree that warfare is an irrational institution, not simply because of profit and loss calculations, or out of a concern to 'maximize goal-achievement', but also for reasons related to the quality of human life, to the brutalizing associations of war, much as apologists for war would once extol its 'ennobling' characteristics. This sense of rationality, then, which presupposes premises concerning human nature, human potentialities, the morally good life for man, has been too pervasive to be omitted from any catalogue of what philosophers and social thinkers have meant by the rationality of societies.

(d) Rationality$_2$ of a social system, irreducible to individual rationality, and in relation to goals predicated of the system itself

We now turn to conceptions of social rationality which take it to be analogous to individual rationality rather than reducible to statements about the rationality of the society's members.

An organization may require each of its members to confine himself to one highly specialized function, insufficient on its own to achieve the goals of the organization; the organization's goals may not then be his goals, and the means it employs may not be selected by the individual members, who may have little idea how their functions contribute to the goals of the organization. In that sense, the rationality of the organization may be achieved at the cost of the individuals' capacity for rational behaviour, i.e. of their capacity to deliberately select the best means to their own ends. This is suggested by the example given by Karl Mannheim of what he calls functional rationality[10]—viz., the organization of a military unit, and the disciplined specialized actions of the individual members and sections of a unit for the purpose of efficiency in battle.

A similar idea seems to underlie some (though not all) of what Weber has in mind in his account of the growing rationalization of industrial societies. According to Weber, the main characteristics of a rational bureaucratic structure included the following: (a) there is a graded hierarchy of offices, functions, and authority within the organization; (b) the functions and authority attached to each office are specified by rules; (c) officials are appointed, not elected, and there is a career structure through which they move by merit or seniority; (d) officials are appointed to their offices on the basis of their technical qualifications; (e) bureaucratic structures are characterized by a high degree of impersonality, manifest, for instance, in the separation of the personal life, interests, and avocation of the official from the duties and rights attached to his office, and in the application to particular cases of technical rules or general rules of law.[11]

Weber emphasizes not only the growing 'intellectualization' accompanying social operations, noted in B1(a) above, but also the intensified specialization of functions, the closer relationships between a man's function and his technical qualifications, the hierarchical organization of authority (one of the rational functions of which is the definition and co-ordination of the powers and duties of the specialized workers and officials), and so on. Now the capacity to make deliberate choices for the realization of purposes or goals is at the heart of the standard conception of rational behaviour; yet as Marx, Weber, and many others have pointed out, division of labour, specialization and bureaucratic organization normally require some suppression of the personal initiative or autonomy of the individual member. Thus, social rationality does not always coincide with individual rationality (at least in the standard sense), and indeed may often suppress it. Social rationality becomes an impersonal characteristic; and, when the integration of individual functions and roles within an organization or group, and the integration of organizations or institutions with one another for the sake of achieving 'social' ends has not been effected by any act of planning, by deliberate human design, we may wonder to whom the quality of rationality is to be attributed.

This difficulty can be overcome, in part, by our distinction between rationality$_1$ and rationality$_2$. For as we pointed out in Section A2 of this paper, while rationality$_1$ applies primarily to agents, rationality$_2$ is attributed primarily to the content of decisions, or, equally, to practices and institutions, from the standpoint of their appropriateness to presupposed ends. Supposing the end for which an army exists is the fighting and winning of battles, its effectiveness under a certain range of conditions (and therefore its practical rationality$_2$) may well be inversely proportional to the extent to which its rank and file members are disposed to deliberate in a rational$_1$ manner, and directly proportional to their acceptance of hierarchical authority, each soldier confining the exercise of his judgment to the narrow field allocated to his role. And though ascription of ends to institutions is itself problematic, it might be argued that for some kinds of institutions like armies (if not for all), to understand something as an institution of that kind is already to attribute to it a general class of ends, such as to be victorious in battles. So the idea of that institution would already presuppose certain conditions for rational$_2$ organization. Though a bureaucracy's end might be less circumscribed, there may be certain second-order ends, like flexibility, the capacity for processing masses of information, for resisting subservience to some particular group of clients, etc., which are necessary conditions for its being able to carry out any of the very varied goals that might be set it. Bureaucracies having the stated Weberian properties might then be particularly well adapted in these respects. In the case of some institutions at least, there seems little difficulty in being able to say 'what they are for'; and in these cases, rationality$_2$ seems at least an intelligible notion. However, ends cannot be assigned in the same way, or so readily, to all institutions, least of all, perhaps, to the complex structures that we loosely call 'societies'.

(e) Rationality$_1$ of a social system in relation to goals predicated of the system

Attributing rationality to societies may seem, at first sight at least, to endow organizations and institutions with the capacities for considering ends and deliberating about means implied in our notion of rationality$_1$. Modern social scientists and philosophers are generally sceptical about the usefulness of such an attribution; it has its place, however, in the history of social theory, and may still be ideologically important. Rousseau writes in *The Social Contract* as though one might attribute to a face-to-face society an end—the public good—even though none of its members adopted that end as his own. This General Will would manifest itself if individual voters addressed themselves to discovering and attaining the general good rather than to satisfying their personal preferences. Rousseau strongly suggests, however, that the General Will continues to exist, albeit mutely, even when individuals are concerned only with their own preferences. It is doubtful whether this view could be coherently stated—unless it were interpreted to mean that citizens voting on public policies, could and should aim at public goods benefiting all or most citizens, the needs of everyone being impartially considered. If all individuals deliberated impersonally and voted in this way, their aims could be identical, their collective policies, if based on epistemically rational beliefs, would be rational$_1$, and their decisions unanimous. Even so, to argue that because the collective decision was rational$_1$ in all its parts, it was therefore not merely rational$_2$ but also itself rational$_1$ would be to commit the fallacy of composition.

While such talk of social rationality may often be figurative only, some such notion as Rousseau's undoubtedly survives in a good deal of populist democratic ideological thinking. There are also writers who, stressing the notion that parliamentary government is government by collective deliberation (a rational process), infer that it yields a socially rational$_1$ decision taken by a collective entity, claiming that because a deliberative process is not just a confrontation of interests, but one in which opinions may be altered, and even a consensus formed, it is not fanciful to talk of a collective mind at work.

2   Rationality, consistency, and contradictions

We shall now turn to social rationality concepts in which the notions of consistency (noted in A3(b) above as constituents of the standard model of individual rationality) play a major role.

(a) Social rationality as non-arbitrariness, or rule-consistency

According to Martin Albrow, the application of general rules to particular cases is much more central to Weber's idea of social rationality in law and administration than the idea of efficiency in attaining the goals of an organization. Such a procedure is, he says, 'for Weber, intrinsically rational', and he quotes the sentence from *Wirtschaft und Gesellschaft* where Weber says that '[bureaucratic] authority is specifically rational in the sense of being bound to discursively analysable rules'.[12]

For Weber, general rules may be technical rules (their use being related to *zweckrational*), i.e. means/ends (modes of action) or rules expressing values or norms of conduct (connected with *wertrational* action). If we ask why, in legal judgment or in administration, the settling of particular cases by the application of general rules is a more rational form of procedure than imaginable alternatives (e.g. tossing a coin, trial by ordeal, guidance by the feelings of the judge or administrator), we can invoke two criteria habitually associated with rationality. First, a general rule is a reason for action that is publicly discussable, capable of being argued for or against on more or less objective grounds. Second, control by general principles or rules at least aspires towards consistency. Rule-governed procedures divorce the interests and standards that guide an official's decisions in his private and in his official capacities, and substitute impersonal criteria for individual judgment that could otherwise be distorted by personal interests or idiosyncracies. This feature of bureaucratic structures thus makes for consistency in the decisions of any one official; it tends also to narrow the discrepancies between different officials dealing with very similar cases, so that the bureaucracy's output of decisions does not appear capricious and arbitrary. Consistency in administration also contributes to predictability, and thus to the rational calculation by individuals of means to ends.

Of course, strict adherence to rules, of the kind that Kafka satirized, whether in judicial or administrative processes, is notoriously liable to lead to what many, using different criteria, judge to be 'irrationalities'. This, in effect, is one of the simple points made by critics who are unhappy about Weber's notion of bureaucratic rationality. If the rules are absurd, how can it be rational to apply them consistently? And even rules that seem appropriate enough to standard cases may result in anomalies when strictly applied to other cases that, by the informal criteria of private judgment, ought to be distinguished from the standard cases but are not.

Legislators attempt to meet such problems practically by delegating powers of discretion to administrators. But this is to abandon in principle precisely the rule-bound consistency that Weber exhibits as a condition for rationality. Where a decision is discretionary, unrelated to publicly avowed criteria, there is no way of assessing the rationality of either the decision or the criteria. If, however, it can be traced back to a rule, we shall be inclined to call both rule and decision rational if, after enquiry and deliberation, the rule appears justified by reasons. The same kind of consideration will apply to other features of society. If all that can be said, for instance, for the capitalist's direction of the labour of the worker, or for denying the worker any part in deciding the goals of the organization, is that these inequalities of function and opportunity are matters of luck, historical circumstance, or the power to enforce them, many will want to say that no grounds have been shown in support of the *rationality* of the established arrangements; that it has not been shown that there is any 'reason' in them. On the other hand, it may be claimed these inequalities are related to differences in men's capacities; or that those who are confined to manual or routine tasks in general do not aspire to the sort of role that requires initiative and responsibility; that it is false to suppose that their aspirations are stifled by existing institutions; or that capitalist organization provides the greatest 'net satisfaction' of mankind's dominant goal, the improvement of the material conditions of life. Such grounds adduced as justificatory reasons will, of course, be debated and controverted. Some will claim that the alleged facts are not facts; or if they are, that they are insufficient to provide a reason for actual social arrangements.

(b) The rationality of societies understood as internal consistency

We have already discussed Marx's view that within the capitalist system there is a contradiction between the human essence and actual forms of human existence. The notion of contradiction is used in a second way, however, by both Hegel and Marx; for contradictions are held to exist within the various institutions and practices of societies at various stages of their development. This idea of social contradiction is familiar enough; it is frequently used of poverty in the midst of plenty, of the deliberate destruction of food that occurred in the 1930s in societies containing hungry millions, and so on. 'The contradictions of capitalism' is one of the most familiar Marxian phrases. Thus, the dynamic of capitalism leads to an increasing socialization of processes of production which contradicts the central capitalist institution of private ownership and control of the means of production; capitalism, by the organization of production which it necessitates, provides the necessary conditions for the formation of the revolutionary class that will overthrow it; capitalism requires the increasing 'immiseration' of the working class, which affects the capitalist's ability to dispose of the products of industry.

The notion of a 'social contradiction' has been so loosely defined and applied (by Marxist and other writers) that it would be too large a task to distinguish the different kinds of social situations which are said to be 'contradictions'. We shall venture only a few brief comments. First, both Hegel and Marx (to the extent that he follows Hegel) assimilate social to logical relationships, and treat institutions as steps in the development of reason in history as though history were an inferential argument. Of course, institutions which have coexisted within a society for a period of time cannot be said to be contradictory in the same logical sense as can propositions (or concepts) which mutually exclude each other; nor do we suggest that Hegel believed they did. The analogy to logical-epistemic consistency might be more plausibly developed in his case by concentrating not on propositional contradictions as such, but rather on the coexistence of contradictory beliefs. And this, of course, is quite possible. Indeed, Hegel's philosophy of history can fairly be understood as a progressive sequence of such contradictions and their resolution.

Societies may be said to embody contradictions in another sense, however, and one more important perhaps for Marxist theory. Marxist examples of 'social contradictions' generally seem to refer to situations in which men's efforts in social activity result in mutual frustration. This comes about when their apperceptions of their social relations lead them to expect that the pursuit of certain mediate goals will result in the satisfaction of their needs. These expectations, and perhaps the needs themselves, are generated by the social order. But the system is such that though for any one individual it could be said that he correctly assesses what he must do, given the system, to attain his goals, the interaction of the efforts of all individuals can end only in collective frustration.

Consider this highly simplified model: suppose the workers believed they must work for wages paid by capitalist entrepreneurs in order to earn their food; suppose the entrepreneurs believed that to earn a profit they must pay out less in wages than they get in return for selling the product; then, if there were no one but the workers to buy the product, it would be impossible for the capitalist to sell all his output at a price per unit higher than he paid his workers, impossible therefore for him to make a profit, impossible therefore for him to continue indefinitely employing all the available workers. Such a system would be grounded on unrealizable expectations, even though any particular individual's perception of his options and their likely outcome would be as correct as they could be, given the system of expectations. And no *single* individual could alter that system. Equally, the attempt by all parties to keep such a system going (and there might be contingent exogenous forces, like the exploitation of foreign markets, to keep it going for a while, despite its incoherences) might result in the emergence of defensive modifications, like monopoly industry, or state regulation, which would make the society's apperception of its own reality even more fantastic, and so generate expectations and personal policies even less capable of consistent realization. Like all prisoners' dilemma games, it would be irrational to play this one if one had the option of changing it. But changing the game is not only revolutionary, but requires that the parties achieve a clear understanding of their dilemma.

In some respects the sense in which one might call arrangements of this sort irrational comes close to the idea that a society might be irrational$_2$ if it could not be rationally accepted by its members (see B1(b) above). It has, however, two further features: first, the Marxist model includes within it the idea that the social relations themselves generate the society's unrealistic self-image, and therefore the expectations and the goals of the individual agents, so that the system guarantees its own irrationality$_2$; second, it includes a notion of development, so that the incoherencies of expectation and aim lead to a dramatic and explosive denouement, when the players finally achieve awareness of the game they have been playing, and change it.

C A view that rejects the standard model of rationality— Michael Oakeshott: rationality without premeditation

In this section we present a view of rationality that appears to depart from the standard model at a crucial point—that which identifies practical rationality with the calculation of means to premeditated ends. Michael Oakeshott characterizes the standard model as an 'abstract and attenuated' rationality. His main objection is to the way 'rational conduct' so envisaged is related (at least in his version of the model) to established and traditional arrangements and modes of conduct. It is, he claims, as if the rational actor can withdraw from the real processes of social activity in order to cogitate his purposes and deliberate about means for achieving them, subsequent action deriving only from this process of thinking. '[It] is preposterous ... to maintain that activity can derive from this kind of thinking, and it is unwise to recommend that it should do so by calling activity "rational" only when it appears to have this spring.' '[If] "rationality" is to represent a desirable quality of an activity, it cannot be the quality of having independently premeditated propositions about the activity before it begins.'[13]

The positive points Oakeshott wishes to make are that purposes or ends arise out of, are suggested by, the activities in which we are already engaged: existing forms of activity suggest them and ways of attacking them. As he puts it (speaking here of scientific enquiry as an example of behaviour):[14] 'It is the activity itself which defines the questions as well as the manner in which they are answered.' 'Both the problems and the course of investigation leading up to their solution are already hidden in the activity.' Both purposes and the resources for achieving them are alike provided by existing or traditional modes of behaviour. Oakeshott's conclusion is that the quality we have in mind (or should have in mind) when we speak about activity as rational is *'faithfulness to the knowledge we have of how to conduct the specific activity we are engaged in'*.[15]

Now there are two truisms, one logical the other empirical, that together account for the persuasive power of Oakeshott's argument. In the first place, it is true that only by experience of a practice, at least at second hand, can one come to know not only *how* to act, but also what things there are to do. The uninitiated do not make scientific discoveries; equally, even radical revolutionary activity in politics can be related in some way to a tradition. Taken in an extreme form, therefore, the notion of a form of activity premeditated without reference to *any* practice is irrational because logically inconsistent with the concept of 'activity', whether as standard-governed or as purposive behaviour. Standards and purposes must alike be learnt. Second, it is practically impossible that a society could change all, or even a substantial part of its customary practices at one stroke—at least if it is to avoid the costs of social collapse. Even in revolutions, a great majority must (in John Macmurray's phrase) 'go on living the daily life'. Now these points are so clearly true that it is hard to imagine any serious social thinker denying either of them; unfortunately, Oakeshott is not at all punctilious in identifying his targets, or in demonstrating that they do make the assumptions he imputes to them.

Relying on these truisms Oakeshott has been led so to overstate his position that he is left with no theory of political and social innovation—a fact only partly concealed by his obscure and dubious idea that innovations are 'intimated by existing traditions of behaviour'. Absorbing all innovation into traditional behaviour, he is left with no convincing way of distinguishing what would ordinarily be regarded as an innovation from strictly conservative action. For, of course, the truisms cannot imply that social imagination and inventive thinking have no role in politics. A practice does not constrain to one particular course of action, nor would Oakeshott claim that it did. Rather it suggests ('intimates') what counts as a problem, and possible approaches to solutions. The radical creative thinker—and actor—is the one who exploits these resources with the greatest ingenuity—even daring. In any case, traditions or practices are never as monolithic as Oakeshott seems to suppose; indeed there may be parts in a state of tension with one another, and what is 'intimated' by one may be quite impracticable given the predominant force of others in the society. Contemporary yearnings for 'participatory democracy' may lead nowhere in practice, but could scarcely be ruled out as not intimated by existing traditions of political behaviour. Nor can one always tell in advance which aspirations are capable of being achieved in time; the range of permissible innovation would be drastically restricted if all aspirations with a prospect of less than certain success were excluded. And if one takes a pluralistic view of society, it can be rational, in any case, to persist with 'lost causes', if only because such persistence may restrict the spread of other, undesirable movements. Because of their emphasis on integration, most contemporary accounts of social rationality attend too little to the rationality criteria for societies structurally maintained by the opposition of traditions and interests.

D Social rationality and individual irrationality or non-rationality

We have seen, in Section B of this paper, how for many writers rationality may be attributed to institutions only if the institutions foster the rationality$_1$ of individuals, by enabling them to pursue their ends without mutual frustration, or by making their environment predictable, or by stimulating the development of individual rational capacities. But there have been indications, too, that for some other writers, individual rationality cannot necessarily be inferred from social rationality, and, for still others, so far from being a necessary condition for social rationality, it may actually make it impossible. We shall now take up these themes explicitly.

1 Burke and the rationality of traditional behaviour

According to Burke, a widespread disposition among individual members of a society to look critically at traditional institutions and practices could result only in the undermining of the stability of the social structure, without which life would be unpredictable, and passions unrestrained. The capacity for individual rationality$_1$ was so limited, that any attempt to rely on it rather than on 'useful prejudices' as a condition for social order, would be practically irrational. Social rationality$_2$ required, then, that individuals act non-rationally, conforming without critical deliberation to the requirements of established custom. Their conduct as individuals would then be rational$_2$.

Now we conceded, in discussing Oakeshott's views, that at any particular time the greater part of the behaviour of most of the members of a society is bound to be supported by traditional, or at least well-established, modes of behaviour, pursuing purposes already embedded in the institutions and forms of activity by and to which they have been moulded; and they will accept as a matter of course that what they do will in all likelihood lead to the results their experience leads them to expect. Whether or not this sort of behaviour is rational, it is hardly to be called irrational.[16] And it would be irrational to take as a model of social rationality a society in which any substantial number of members persistently question established arrangements and modes of behaviour, ask to be assured of the rational grounds and justification of existing customs or institutions, project and make choices between alternative purposes or ends; for such a mode of life cannot be reconciled with necessities of human and social existence. It would suffer, at the very least, from an unusual measure of unpredictability (or be a sad case of social *anomie*). By contrast, a society characterized by 'the despotism of custom' (to use Mill's phrase) would exhibit a very high degree of predictability. Some of the standard criteria of rational behaviour may cut both ways.

But it is impossible to convert these general platitudes into general precepts for the guidance of political behaviour. So far as any particular tradition or institution is concerned, we can easily think of dozens of reasons why it may no longer embody *present* wisdom or rationality. It may have established itself gradually in response to conditions that no longer exist, or when resources for action did not exist which now do exist; it may have been fashioned in accord with beliefs or values no longer respected within the community, or imposed or fostered by groups possessing superior power for the advancement and protection of their special interests (women's liberationists would argue that that certainly applies to the traditional roles assigned to women).[17] A general appeal to tradition may usefully draw attention to general considerations about the difficulties of innovating, of getting a new habit of behaviour established, about the almost inevitable attendance of unforeseen and unwanted consequences (a point on which Popper places great emphasis),[18] and about the advantages of the degree of certainty supposedly attaching to tradition-based behaviour. But precisely because a society's problems and interests change, a general appeal to the reason embedded in tradition will carry little weight.

2   Critics of the technological rationality of institutions

The incompatibility of social and individual rationality is a recurrent theme, not only in traditionalist but also in recent radical writings critical of industrial technological society. Jacques Ellul, for instance, in defining 'technique', which he regards as the characteristic feature of modern society, writes:[19] 'In our technological society, *technique* is the *totality of methods rationally arrived at and having absolute efficiency* (for a given stage of development) in *every* field of human activity.' This technique is directed not to the ends of individual human beings, nor to any ends that could be attributed even indirectly to 'human nature'. Organization is alleged to generate its own ends simply as a product of its own operation. So 'all men are constrained by means external to them to ends equally external'.[20] 'Humanity seems to have forgotten the wherefore of all its travail, as though its goals had been translated into an abstraction or had become implicit; or as though its ends rested in an unforeseeable future of undetermined date. ... Everything today seems to happen as though ends disappear, as a result of the magnitude of the very means at our disposal.'[21]

Marcuse, like Ellul, sees the 'post-industrial' social system operating with what he calls 'technological rationality', but directed to the satisfaction of individuals' wants. But these wants are factitious or pseudo-needs, generated and implanted in the individual by a system that requires that he be motivated by them, so that the system may function. Through these needs the individual is disciplined to labour by 'repressive rationality', a socialized disposition to repress the spontaneous desires, to repudiate the gratification of the senses that would destroy the fabric of bourgeois society if indulged. There can be a formal (or technical) rationality, then, that merely reflects and, indeed, fosters the individual's alienation, his failure to understand his own nature and to adopt goals that are consistent with it. Marcuse contrasts this Weberian concept of rationality with another:[22]

> If reason means shaping life according to men's free decision on the basis of their knowledge, then the demand for reason henceforth means the creation of a social organization in which individuals can collectively regulate their lives in accordance with their needs. ... [The] philosophical construction of reason is replaced by the creation of a rational society.

Marcuse is evidently operating with a formal and a substantive concept of rationality. A society is only formally rational when its organization can be described as rationally adapted to the factitious needs that it does itself generate. For it does so at the cost of substantive individual rationality, inducing individuals to seek ends inconsistent with their true essence. A society would be substantively rational if it liberated human potentialities—or, at any rate, those potentialities that Marcuse chooses to see as the essential ones.

The role—and the precise characterization—of individual rationality is never very clear in Marcuse's work. The stress on the creative impulse and spontaneity suggests that, if rationality is part of man's essence, it must be understood in some sense that plays down the element of deliberation and means/end optimization, emphasizing instead conditions for expressing and fulfilling his erotic nature. By contrast, C. Wright Mills identified the capacity to reason with 'the nature of man' in an unequivocal and basically Kantian way.[23] 'The increasing rationalization of society', he writes, 'the contradiction between such rationality and reason, the collapse of the assumed coincidence of reason and freedom— these developments lie back of the rise into view of the man who is "with" rationality but without reason, who is increasingly self-rationalized and also increasingly uneasy.' The 'adaptation of the individual and its effects upon his milieux and self results not only in the loss of his chance, and in due course, of his capacity and will to reason; it also affects his chances and his capacity to act as a free man.' '... [In] the extreme development the chance to reason of most men is destroyed, as rationality increases and its locus, its control, is moved from the individual to the big-scale organization. There is then rationality without reason.' If we put this in terms of our own distinctions, Mills appears to be saying that the rationality$_2$ of twentieth-century society, in relation to a limited range of ends that do not include individual rationality$_1$, tends actually to inhibit individual rationality$_1$, producing what he terms 'The Cheerful Robot'.

E Conclusion

Because 'rationality' is generally an honorific term, its meaning tends to shift, according to whether a writer is disposed to acclaim or condemn a particular style of behaviour or organization. The account of rationality that we have taken as standard was elaborated and enthusiastically endorsed by writers of the eighteenth-century Enlightenment, for whom 'Reason' was a handy critical weapon with which to attack the assumptions of traditionalist society in which aristocratic and clerical privileges and institutions were strongly entrenched. The Age of Reason was an age of radical criticism. Exploiting a familiar dialectic, however, an opponent like Burke could turn their conceptual weapon against them by selecting enough of the features of the standard account to make his usage familiar and intelligible, yet dispense by implication with other conditions that the rationalists considered criterial, defending thereby precisely what they were out to upset. With Weber, however, we encounter a genuine attempt to formulate the concept for value-

381

neutral, taxonomical purposes. But precisely because many of the features that Weber treated as criterial conditions for rational organization were ones that critics of technological, bureaucratically structured societies condemned (as, indeed, did Weber himself), 'rationality' became ambiguously charged. In the work of one and the same author one may find a society described and condemned at one point as rational (but in our rational$_2$ sense), and elsewhere as irrational, in the sense that it inhibits or frustrates the rationality$_1$ of individuals. But individual rationality is then generally taken to include not only the formal conditions of epistemic and practical rationality, but also the acceptance of a set of ends or values deemed appropriate to man's nature. These shifts in meaning while confusing are not beyond mapping; we have tried in this paper to chart a way through some at least of this conceptual jungle.

Notes

1 Dahl, R.A. and Lindblom, C.E. (1953), p. 38. This model does in fact provide stronger requirements than the simplest account of rational$_1$ action, in that it specifies that a rational action must be 'correctly' designed to maximize, whereas the standard account is here assumed to require only that there be good reasons for believing that it will maximize.
2 Oakeshott, M. (1962), pp. 83–5.
3 Diesing, P. (1962), p. 85.
4 Cf. Pennock, J.R. (1964).
5 Burke, E. (1790), p. 359.
6 See, for example, Hampshire, S. (1972).
7 This notion is examined at greater length in Chapter 11 of this volume, 'Can ends be rational?'
8 Marx's concept of the alienation inherent in capitalist relations of production is most fully developed in *Economic and Philosophic Manuscripts* of 1844. The main passages from this work are conveniently assembled in Easton, L.D. and Guddat, K.H. (1967), pp. 283–314. See also Easton, L.D. (1970).
9 Popper, K.R. (1963), p. 131.
10 Mannheim, K. (1940), p. 54.
11 For a summary of Weber's account of the ideal-typical rational bureaucratic organization, see Albrow, M. (1970), pp. 37–45.
12 Albrow, M. (1970), p. 63.
13 Oakeshott, M. (1962), pp. 90–1.
14 Ibid., pp. 97, 99.
15 Ibid., pp. 101–2.
16 Cf. Schutz, A. (1970).
17 Cf. Coleman, S. (1968).
18 Cf. 'Towards a rational theory of tradition', in Popper, K.R. (1963), pp. 120–35.

19 Cf. Ellul, J. (1965), p. 1, 'Note to the reader'.
20 Ibid., p. 429.
21 Ibid., p. 430.
22 Marcuse, H. (1968), pp. 141–2.
23 Mills, C. Wright (1967), pp. 169–70.

Bibliography

ALBROW, M. (1970), *Bureaucracy*, London.
BURKE, E. (1790), *Reflections on the Revolution in France*, in *Works*, vol. II (Bohn edn, London, 1855).
COLEMAN, S. (1968), 'Is there reason in tradition?', in King, P. and Parekh, B.C. (eds), *Politics and Experience*, Cambridge, pp. 239–82.
DAHL, R.A. and LINDBLOM, C.E. (1953), *Politics, Economics, and Welfare*, New York.
DIESING, P. (1962), *Reason in Society*, Urbana.
EASTON, L.D. (1970), 'Alienation and empiricism in Marx's thought', *Social Research*, XXXVII, pp. 402–27.
EASTON, L.D. and GUDDAT, K.H. (trans. and eds) (1967), *Writings of the Young Marx on Philosophy and Society*, Garden City, New York.
ELLUL, J. (1965), *The Technological Society*, London.
HAMPSHIRE, S. (1972), 'Russell, radicalism and reason', in Held, V., Nielsen, K. and Parsons, C. (eds), *Philosophy and Political Action*, New York, pp. 258–74.
MANNHEIM, K. (1940), *Man and Society in an Age of Reconstruction*, London.
MARCUSE, H. (1968), *Negations*, Harmondsworth.
MILLS, C. WRIGHT (1967), *The Sociological Imagination*, New York.
OAKESHOTT, M. (1962), *Rationalism in Politics*, London.
PENNOCK, J.R. (1964), 'Reason in legislative decisions', in Friedrich, C.J. (ed.), *Rational Decision*, New York, pp. 98–106.
POPPER, K.R. (1963), *Conjectures and Refutations*, London.
SCHUTZ, A. (1970), 'The problem of rationality in the social world' (1943), in Emmet, D. and MacIntyre, A. (eds), *Sociological Theory and Philosophical Analysis*, London, pp. 89–114.
WEBER, M. (1968), ed. Roth, G. and Wittich, C., *Economy and Society (Wirtschaft und Gesellschaft)*, New York.

15

Rational social choice

G.W. Mortimore

A Introduction

This paper is concerned with the ways in which a number of social theorists have used the notion of rationality to assess social choices. Each theorist advances one or more conditions as requirements of rationality in social choice, and considers a social choice to be acceptable and worthy of approval only if it satisfies such conditions. I shall examine some of the rationality requirements proposed, and ask why they should be taken as grounds for supporting or approving a social choice.

'Social choice' is here understood in a technical sense which is common in recent work in political economy and welfare economics.[1] In this sense, the process of social choice may be either a collective decision procedure like a voting system in which each individual contributes his own personal choice between alternative social arrangements; or the workings of an institution like a market economy in which the outcome—a certain distribution of income, say—can be attributed to the individual choices of consumers and producers within the market; or the decisions of someone 'acting for society'—an official, say, or a dictator. Thus, a social choice may be between alternative political constitutions, economic systems, distributions of wealth, arrangements for health care, foreign policies, and so on. Social theorists frequently use the notion of rationality to assess both the processes of social choice and the social choices which are the outcomes of these processes. Kenneth Arrow's primary concern in *Social Choice and Individual*

Values is with the possibility of democratic social choice processes issuing in rational social choices. James Buchanan and Gordon Tullock in *The Calculus of Consent* consider the varieties of political constitution which might be the outcome of a rational social choice. John Harsanyi in a number of papers on social choice, and John Rawls in *A Theory of Justice*, attempt to develop an account of a rational social choice which might be used as a general criterion for assessing all social choices.

These writers share a good deal of common ground. They are individualists, holding that talk about the rationality of social choice only makes sense if it translates into talk about the rationality of individuals choosing and acting. They are exclusively interested in the practical rationality of choice as distinct from the rationality of the beliefs on which a choice is based. Their interest is in the technical notion of formal practical rationality. As we have seen in Chapter 7, this notion, as applied to a choice, is to be analysed in terms of the two conditions:

(i) the agent's preferences satisfy the formal requirements of connectedness, asymmetry and transitivity

(ii) his choice is optimal, given his preference ordering of the outcomes of the options, and his knowledge or belief about these outcomes.

My interest in this paper, then, will be in how notions of rationality in social choice are to be understood in terms of this notion of individual rationality.

B Arrow's notion of collective rationality

1 Individualism and the social choice function

On the individualist view, we cannot attribute preferences to societies, for societies are not to be treated as agents. Yet, as we have seen, social outcomes like distributions of wealth or political arrangements can be viewed as the outcome of a 'social choice' process, with individual agents' preference orderings and choices as inputs. In such a process, the function which characterizes the relationship between such inputs and the social choice outcome, is usually referred to as the social choice function. The function may actually figure as a voting rule in a voting system, for example the majority voting rule; or as the rule by which an official takes account of individuals' preferences in making a decision 'on behalf of society'. Or it may simply characterize the systematic relationship between input and output in an arrangement like a market— between the input of consumers' preferences, for example, and the consequent distribution of commodities.

Arrow's General Possibility Theorem for social choice functions purports to show that there can be no social choice function which satisfies both a requirement of 'collective rationality', and certain mild and uncontroversial ethical requirements.[2] Since one of his ethical requirements is a minimal condition for democracy, Arrow's conclusion is that 'the doctrine of voters' sovereignty is incompatible with that of collective rationality' (p. 60); and this has understandably excited a long series of attempts to show where Arrow has gone wrong.

Arrow's rationality requirement is that for any set of alternatives and for any set of individual preference orderings of those alternatives, the social choice function shall generate a weak ordering of the alternatives from the individual preference orderings. A weak ordering is defined as satisfying two axioms:

I (connectedness): For all x and y, either xRy or yRx

II (transitivity): For all x, y and z, xRy and yRz imply xRz

where x, y and z are variables standing for alternatives and R is the constant 'is preferred or indifferent to'.[3]

One way to understand this requirement of collective rationality is to think of the social choice function as generating a social ordering of the alternatives. In the case of individuals, rationality requires that their preferences are connected and transitive; and therefore constitute an ordering. Arrow's Axioms I and II are the corresponding rationality requirements for a social ordering. But for an individualist like Arrow, there is no social agent to whom a social ordering could be ascribed. In any case, the collective rationality requirement is applied to social choice functions which characterize the relationship between inputs and the social choice output of social choice processes like voting systems. So Arrow's requirements have somehow to be understood as requirements concerning the *choices* generated by a social choice process.

Arrow does seem to suggest that the connectedness and transitivity conditions are requirements for the rationality of the social choices emerging from a social choice process (pp. 106f.); though he offers curiously little help in understanding these requirements in individualist terms. We might interpret them in either of two ways: as conditions under which choices are made in a rational way, or as conditions under which what is chosen is something which it is rational to choose, irrespective of whether rationality was exhibited in choosing it. Though the first might seem to involve the notion of a social agent capable of rationality, this is not really the case, for at least two important categories of social choice can be conceived as choices made by individuals acting in their capacity as public officials. Voting arrangements can be conceived as issuing in prescriptions, executed by officials 'acting for society'; and an official may arrive at a decision independently by deriving an ordering of alternatives from considerations about individuals' preferences, his deliberations and choices thus reflecting a given social choice function. Despite his occasional references to markets, it appears that Arrow's attention is mainly focused on one or both of the above types of social choice process (p. 107). For a process of either kind, we can ask of any social choice function whether it would always permit an official to act rationally.

Alternatively we might ask, not whether the choice process will generate choices which are rationally made, but whether it will generate choices which it is rational to make. Analogously, we might ask of an investigatory process, not whether it will produce beliefs held for good reasons, but whether it will produce beliefs which there are good reasons to entertain. Talking of a social choice as a rational choice in this second way would not commit us, then, to ascribing rationality to a social or individual agent making that choice.

In what follows I shall consider whether, on either account, Arrow's requirements are recognizable individualist requirements of rationality.

2 Connectedness

I shall take Arrow's first axiom to be equivalent to:

For all x and y, at least one of xPy, xIy, yPx

where P stands for 'is preferred to' and I for 'is indifferent to'. Arrow speaks of Axiom I as the condition that 'some social choice be made from any environment' (p. 118); but there seem to be two conflicting tendencies in his interpretation of the requirement. On one hand, it seems to be intended to exclude some social choice functions, on the ground that in some environments they would generate no choice. We can understand this line of thought readily enough in individualist terms, if we consider a social choice process which generates prescriptions of the form xPy ('Do x rather than y') on which an official then has to act. If the decision-rule generates no such prescription, the official has no basis for choice, and presumably must arbitrarily plump for an alternative. His choice will not reflect a social preference ordering and since, as an official, this is the only kind of preference ordering on which he can act he will fail to satisfy one of the requirements for choosing rationally. His choice will similarly fail to satisfy the basic requirement for being a choice which it is rational to make, for—from the official point of view—there is no reason to make it.

However, Arrow also displays a tendency to treat Axiom I as a requirement which logically could not be violated (p. 119). For, he suggests, a society always ends up in some state of affairs or other after the operations of a social decision-process, and we can always think of that state of affairs as a social choice. But this is an odd suggestion. Some social choice functions do not generate a social ordering of some sets of alternatives from some sets of individual preference orderings of those alternatives. It is true, of course, that when these functions are embodied as decision rules in a social choice process, some state of affairs always prevails after the operation of that process (assuming the society continues to exist). But this 'choice' has not been generated by the social choice function: it exists in default of any determinate prescription emerging from that function. Little sense can be made, therefore, of the idea that such a choice has been made rationally, or is a rational choice to make.

What, then, of the application of Arrow's requirement to markets, where there is no official acting on the prescriptions of the choice process, and where the input of individual preferences always generates a social choice? There is clearly no individualist sense in which we can say that the choice was rationally made. The most we can say is that the social choices generated by a market are ones it would be rational for an individual to make if he were operating with the social choice function which characterizes the operations of the market.

3 Transitivity

I shall take Axiom II to be equivalent to:

For all x, y and z, xIy, $yIz \rightarrow xIz$
$$xIy, yPz \rightarrow xPz$$
$$xPy, yIz \rightarrow xPz$$
$$xPy, yPz \rightarrow xPz$$

Arrow claims that Axiom II is a requirement for consistency between a number of successive social choices. His central aim in formulating the axiom seems to be to rule out the possibility of a choice process generating the following series of choices, which he regards as obviously inconsistent.

$$y\{x/y\} \quad z\{y/z\} \quad x\{z/x\}$$

where $y \{x/y\}$ stands for 'y chosen from the set of alternatives x and y' (pp. 2–3).

There are two problems with Arrow's claim. First, satisfying

Axiom II is not sufficient to rule out the choice series Arrow regards as inconsistent. For a series of paired alternatives x/y, y/z and z/x, the prescriptions xIy, yIz and zIx would satisfy Axiom II. Yet an official would not be acting inconsistently with these prescriptions if he made the choices, $y\{x/y\}$, $z\{y/z\}$ and $x\{x/z\}$.

One obvious remedy is simply to introduce a further axiom which directly concerns social choice, thus:

For all x, y and z, if $y\{x/y\}$ and $z\{y/z\}$, then $z\{z/x\}$.

But this raises the second problem: Are the choices $y\{x/y\}$, $z\{y/z\}$ and $x\{x/z\}$ really inconsistent and irrational? The paradigm of the kind of intransitivity with which Arrow is concerned is the intransitive series of choices generated by the application of the majority rule in a society where there are overlapping majorities (see Table 15.1).

Table 15.1

Voters	Preferences		
A	yPx	zPy	zPx
B	yPx	yPz	xPz
C	xPy	zPy	xPz
Social choice	yPx	zPy	xPz

Now there would surely be no inconsistency or irrationality in this succession of choices if between the second and third choices A changed his ranking of x, y and z from $zPyPx$ to $xPyPz$. For the third choice would then take the society to a state of affairs x, unanimously preferred to z, and preferred by a majority to y. If preferences remain unchanged, however, the official whose official end is to satisfy the preferences of the majority makes a series of self-stultifying choices. For at the end of the series he has chosen a state of affairs x to which y, a state of affairs which he has rejected in a previous choice, is socially preferable according to the majority rule.

Another way of understanding Arrow's rationality requirement is to see the series of choices as an opportunity for the official to make a choice between the three options x, y and z. But this is a choice which an official cannot make rationally under the conditions specified in Table 15.1 if he is operating with the majority rule as his optimality criterion, for no one of the alternatives is optimal. Similarly, Axiom II may be understood as a requirement for rationality in a *single* social choice between three alternatives. For if a social choice process is capable of generating the decision prescriptions yPx, zPy and xPz, no rational official faced with a single choice between x, y and z will be able to deduce a determinate prescription to guide his choice.

4 The rationality of social choice processes

Because of the obscurity of Arrow's account, a good many of his critics have misunderstood his collective rationality requirement. Thus, Buchanan takes him to be defining social rationality as social choice *in accordance with* a social choice function and objects that this commits Arrow to postulating a social group with 'an organic existence apart from that of its individual components', to which the social choice function is ascribed.[4] But this involves two misunderstandings. First, Arrow's collective irrationality is manifest not in an inconsistency between choice and social choice function as Buchanan seems to think, but in the failure of a social choice function to generate any choice at all, or in its generating inconsistent and self-stultifying choices. The second misunderstanding consists in taking Arrow's rationality requirements to imply a collective chooser. We have seen already that there is no difficulty in interpreting it in individualistic terms.

I have so far taken Arrow's collective rationality requirements to concern the rationality of the social choices generated by the social choice process. We might also interpret them, however, as requirements for a social choice process being itself one it would be rational to choose. For it might be argued that if the purpose of a social choice process is to generate choices, and to generate choices which are not self-stultifying, it is rational for individuals to choose a social choice process which meets Arrow's requirements. This point has been disputed by a number of critics.[5] For one thing, even if we accept that intransitive social choices are to be avoided, a rational individual need not require that a social choice process generate transitive choices under all logically possible conditions; it would be sufficient if it did so under all foreseeable conditions. Buchanan suggests, indeed, that we could regard a series of intransitive choices over a period, in a community where there are overlapping majorities, as the best way of giving every individual in the community a chance to live, for some time at least, under a state of affairs which he prefers to the alternatives.[6]

I shall not pursue the question of whether it would be rational for individuals to choose a social choice process which is collectively rational in Arrow's sense. I want instead to consider the ways in which an account of rational social choice as a choice rational individuals would jointly make, might be used as a criterion for assessing the acceptability of social choices.

C Social choice by rational individuals

Arrow's requirements for rationality in social choice demand only that a choice bear *some* functional relationship to individual preferences, and that it be consistent (in the sense discussed earlier) with other choices. A more powerful criterion is needed if we are to identify a particular constitution, say, or a distribution of welfare as *the* rational social choice from the available alternatives. The suggestion considered in this section is that a social choice is acceptable if and only if it *would* be a rational social choice *under certain specified conditions*; and that an alternative would be a rational social choice if and only if each member of society could and would rationally choose it.

1 Buchanan and Tullock

In *The Calculus of Consent* we find Buchanan and Tullock asking how rational individuals would choose between alternative constitutions. They ask this question as a way of determining which constitution satisfies an ethical criterion which can be stated in two parts (pp. 14–15):

(i) A state of affairs is better than another if and only if a change from the former to the latter can be shown to be in the interest of all parties.

(ii) A state of affairs is in the interest of all parties if all would agree to it.

This criterion might be thought to have very restricted usefulness as a standard for assessing social choices, since unanimity on questions of social choice is comparatively rare. However, Buchanan and Tullock hold that it *can* suffice as the basic criterion of social choice if one recognizes that it need be used to assess only the second-order choice between alternative social choice processes, i.e. constitutions; first-order social choices between policies can be assessed in terms of the constitution from which they emerge (pp. 92–6). They believe that individuals will normally choose unanimously between constitutions, because each individual will normally be uncertain 'whether he is likely to be in a winning or losing coalition on any specific issue' arising under a constitution and will assume 'that occasionally he will be in one group and occasionally in another' (p. 78). Under these conditions they say an individual will 'find it advantageous' to vote for rules that promote the interests of everyone. Indeed, given this uncertainty about the future, the individual 'is not considered to have a particular and distinguishable interest separate and apart from his fellows'.

(a) The conditions of uncertainty

Let us look first at the conditions of uncertainty under which individuals are said to make their constitutional choice. There seem to be four separate matters about which one might be uncertain:

(i) whether one is or will be a member of some group given an especially powerful position by a given constitution (e.g. a constitution with an electoral system weighted in favour of electors in rural areas);

(ii) what one's interests are or will be;

(iii) what proposals affecting these interests will come up;

(iv) what others' interests are or will be with respect to these proposals.

Clearly, these kinds of uncertainty at the stage of constitutional choice may be important influences. If a rational individual were uncertain whether he would remain in a rural area, he would hesitate about voting for a constitution favouring the rural elector. Even if he knew that he would remain a member of the constitutionally privileged group of country dwellers, he would not vote for a constitution giving a decisive voice to them if he were unsure how country dwellers will vote on issues affecting his interests. And even if he knew that he shared certain interests with them, he might not know how many other non-shared interests would be better served by another constitution.

But I doubt whether the kind of blanket uncertainty which Buchanan and Tullock postulate is always, or even mostly, a feature of constitutional choice. Surely it is common for individuals to be sure (and to have a right to be sure) that they have a *community of interests* with members of a group. And they commonly know, too, that their membership of one interest group is going to have much more significant effects on their welfare than their membership of others. Even were that not the case, each individual, whatever his state of uncertainty about his group membership, interests, etc. will be able to identify one alternative which will indubitably favour him over others—a constitution which gives him dictatorial powers. Buchanan and Tullock anticipate this objection, and give a two-part reply. First, they insist that he 'would need to be almost omniscient concerning the whole set of issues that might arise' (p. 79). But this is an odd thing for them to say. Given that a man's interests are furthered if and only if he moves to a preferred state of affairs, he needs no prescience about future issues to be justifiably certain that he will be best-off if he is dictator.

Their other comment is that a dictatorial constitution (or indeed any constitution favouring a small group) could not be agreed to by everyone at the stage of constitutional choice (p. 79). But how does this meet the objection that when dictatorial constitutions figure amongst the alternatives there is no constitution which would be preferred by everyone to all the alternatives because a different dictatorial constitution would be preferred by each person? Their point seems to be that a rational individual choosing between constitutions under normal conditions will only consider alternatives which could command universal assent, and this rules out dictatorial constitutions. However, this amounts to the introduction of a further criterion for the assessment of constitutions. For it appeared at first that Buchanan and Tullock were interested in identifying the constitution which each individual would prefer with a view solely to its implications for his preferences. It now appears that they are interested in the constitution individuals would prefer from the limited set which could gain everyone's assent. If this further restriction could be developed in a non-circular way, the postulated conditions of ignorance would not be required for the conclusion that rational individuals will reject any constitution which favours one group over others. As far as I can see, however, the constraints of ignorance are given central place in the main statement of their argument, and the constraint deriving from the necessity to secure others' agreement is only introduced as an afterthought.

(b) Rational choice

Let us now consider the adequacy of their account of rational choice under the postulated conditions of uncertainty. Are Buchanan and Tullock correct in supposing that rational individuals under the postulated conditions of uncertainty will reject constitutions which favour certain sectional groups? On their account, individuals in this state of uncertainty will assume that they are as likely to be on the winning side as on the losing side; and that exceptional gains on particular issues are no more likely than exceptional losses on others. This is certainly in line with one common view of the rational basis for choice under conditions of complete uncertainty, though it is a view which has recently been challenged by John Rawls.[7] But if Buchanan and Tullock are to take this line, how can they hold that rational individuals will reject constitutions which favour sectional interests? Only, it seems, if they assume that it is rational for individuals to pursue a maximin policy rather than to maximize expected utility.[8] For choosers maximizing expected utility would select the constitution which promised the greatest aggregate net benefit to the whole community. But it is doubtful, to say the least, whether egalitarian constitutions always operate to produce greater aggregate net benefits than constitutions which favour sectional groups.

It should be apparent, therefore, that Buchanan and Tullock require at least three further substantial arguments to justify key moves in their account of rational choice between alternative constitutions: the first to justify their contention that constitutional choice is normally made under the postulated conditions of uncertainty, the second to show that it is rational under such conditions to choose on the basis of certain probabilistic assumptions, and the third to support their implied view that a maximin policy is a more rational policy in such circumstances than maximizing expected utility.

2 Rawls and Harsanyi

In *The Calculus of Consent* an account of rational social choice between constitutions is used as a way of determining what types of constitution satisfy ethical criteria. I shall now consider whether a *general* account of rational social choice, as the choice rational individuals could and would make under certain conditions, could be developed as an *independent* criterion for assessing social choices.

The obvious difficulty in the way of any such general account is that we cannot assert that x is the rational social choice from $\{x/y\}$ in this sense, if x and y are things for which individuals might have widely different preferences. It might thus appear that the only general thing we can say about rational social choice is that something is a rational social choice if and only if everyone prefers it. This, the Paretian account, would be a criterion of extremely restricted usefulness. However, a number of recent writers—pre-eminently Harsanyi and Rawls—have developed accounts which apparently circumvent this difficulty. Adopting an approach parallel to that of Buchanan and Tullock, they consider the choice that individuals would make under certain specified constraints, including conditions of ignorance.

Harsanyi is interested in giving a general account of rational social choice between any set of alternatives under two conditions of ignorance.[9] The first is that the chooser is ignorant of anything about these states of affairs except the distributions of preference-satisfaction prevailing under them. Thus his account is effectively an account of the distribution rational choosers would select from the available alternatives. The second condition is that the chooser is ignorant of his location in each distribution. This condition is clearly a requirement for unanimity in choice. Rawls, on the other hand, is concerned with the principles rational individuals would choose to have adopted as the publicly accepted basis for making social choices.[10] However, he considers the choice that would be made by individuals who know only that they have preferences but who are ignorant of their content. He thus assumes that an individual's choice between principles will be exclusively determined by his judgment about the effects of their adoption on the resources that will be available to him for satisfying his preferences (pp. 62, 92–5). Presupposed in his account, therefore, is a view of how rational individuals would choose between alternative distributions of such resources; and this background account of rational social choice is capable of the same general application as Harsanyi's account of choice between distributions of preference-satisfaction. Like Harsanyi, Rawls considers the choice that would be made by individuals ignorant of their location in these distributions.

Thus Harsanyi and Rawls, in their different ways, give an account of social choice between states of affairs of restricted kinds. The kinds chosen are precisely those in which any rational individual would have the same interest. Any rational individual necessarily aims to maximize the satisfaction of his preferences, and since rationality involves willing the means to one's ends any rational individual aims to maximize his resources for preference-satisfaction. Both writers secure unanimity in choice by supposing it to be made by individuals ignorant of their location in the distributions.

How a rational individual will choose between alternative distributions of preference-satisfaction or resources will depend on the answers to two questions.

(i) What would be the rational decision policy under such a condition of ignorance? Rawls argues that under such a condition it is rational to choose, not on the assumption that one has an equal chance of occupying each situation, but rather to be primarily concerned to safeguard oneself against being in the worst-off position (pp. 161–75). Indeed, the ranking that Rawls derives reflects the choices a rational individual would make if he were certain of occupying the worst-off position. According to Rawls, if some individuals are better off than others in state x, rational individuals will choose x in preference to an alternative in which individuals are equally well off, *if and only if* the worst-off individual in x is better off than he would be if everyone were equally well off. Harsanyi, on the other hand, considers that a rational individual would assume that he had an equal chance of occupying each position, and—maximizing expected utility—would choose the alternative yielding the highest average level of preference-satisfaction.

(ii) Would rational choosers make ordinal or cardinal comparisons of how a man fares under alternative distributions of preference-satisfaction, and would they make them interpersonally? There are, notoriously, disagreements about the ways in which the satisfactions arising from different states of affairs can be compared. According to an ordinalist, all that can be said is how individuals rank x in relation to alternatives; according to a cardinalist, we can say how high up the individual's preference scale x takes him. And some cardinalists also allow for interpersonal comparisons of the levels of preference-satisfaction, under given states of affairs. Distributions of resources can obviously be characterized cardinally and comparisons can be made of the resources available to different individuals.

The importance of one's assumptions about the possibility of cardinal interpersonal comparisons can be simply illustrated. Consider how individuals will choose between two distributions of utility (preference-satisfaction), believing that they have an equal chance of occupying each position in whichever state is chosen. If all that can be said about each of the states is that individuals are better- or worse-off under other states of affairs, then rational individuals will choose between them according to the majority principle, i.e. will choose whichever state of affairs makes the majority better-off. For this is the state which gives them the maximum chance of being better-off. If, however, individuals can make interpersonal cardinal comparisons of how individuals fare under alternatives, they are in a position to consider which alternative maximizes expected utility. If we make the assumption that it is rational to choose the alternative with maximum expected utility, then the rational choice under the conditions specified will be the alternative with the maximum average level of utility.

We have, then, the Paretian account of rational social choice, and a number of accounts which consider choice under special conditions.

Could any of them function independently as a criterion for evaluating social choices? To answer this question we need to consider the practical force of 'x is a rational social choice' on any of these accounts. How could this consideration be a reason for individuals choosing x, or supporting the social choice of x? Now to say that x is the rational social choice in the Paretian sense entails that every individual has a reason to make or support it, viz. that x is the optimal option in terms of each individual's ends. But does the rationality of a social choice on Rawls's or Harsanyi's accounts imply anything more than that an individual *would have* a reason to make it *if* he laboured under the peculiar conditions of choice which are written into the account? What possible bearing could it have on the choice of an individual who knows he will be better off under y, to point out that if he were ignorant of where he were to be located in x or y it *would* be rational for him to choose x?

3 Principle-dependence

(a) Harsanyi

Harsanyi's aim in developing his account of rational social choice is to identify the social choice function rational individuals would use in making their choices under the specified conditions of ignorance. As we have seen, he argues that each individual would choose so as to maximize expected utility (and, therefore, average utility). But what, then, does Harsanyi regard as the force of this social choice function as a general criterion for assessing the acceptability of social choices? Is it of significance *because* it picks out the rational social choice? And what is the evaluative significance of pointing out that something is a rational social choice, on Harsanyi's account?

It appears that for Harsanyi 'x is a rational social choice' has practical force just in so far as the consideration indicates that x is the social choice demanded by certain moral principles. The background moral principles with which Harsanyi appears to be operating specify that social choice should be a function of:
  (i) only facts about the relationships between the alternatives and individual members of society;
  (ii) only facts about their preference-satisfaction under the alternatives;
  (iii) facts about *every* individual's preference-satisfaction, irrespective of any other fact about him.
Harsanyi's principles also specify the ethically desirable functional

relationship between these considerations and social choice. His two fundamental principles seem to be:

The fact that any individual's preference-satisfaction is greater under x than y counts in favour of x.
Each individual's preference-satisfaction is to be given equal weight.

In order to show the practical relevance of Harsanyi's account of rational social choice, therefore, we would need to argue *independently* for these principles. Then why not assess social choice by directly applying these principles? Why introduce the account of rational social choice at all? There are two reasons. First, it fills out and makes determinate various of the principles—particularly, the principle of equal consideration. The notion of equal consideration is spelt out as the kind of consideration any rational self-interested person would give to each position if he were ignorant of whether he would occupy it. And second, the account provides a single determinate principle for picking out the choice demanded by these moral standards—on Harsanyi's view, the principle of maximizing average utility or preference-satisfaction. The ultimate justification of the latter, then, is not that it selects social choices which are rational but that it selects choices demanded by what Harsanyi takes to be principles constitutive of the moral point of view.

It is interesting to compare Harsanyi's approach with the recent work of David Richards, a disciple of Rawls.[11] Richards's aim is the Rawlsian one: to formulate a set of principles which rational individuals would choose under specified conditions of ignorance. But he takes something very like Harsanyi's view of the practical force of 'x would be rationally chosen...'. To show that a set of principles would be rationally chosen under the specified conditions is, on Richards's view, to show that they are demanded by certain very general moral principles or considerations (pp. 79–91). The most general is the precept that persons be treated as persons, an ideal which is in turn spelt out by Richards in terms of human equality and the fortuitousness of differences. Richards suggests that considering the principles which individuals would choose under specified conditions of ignorance is a way of filling out these general ideals and making them determinate, and of drawing from them a set of more specific principles. He takes the same view as Harsanyi of the status of the general background principles. They are, he contends, built into the concept of morality. 'Morality involves treating persons as persons.'

Neither Harsanyi nor Richards argues for their contention that one set of principles represents *the* concept of morality or the moral point of view; and it may well be suggested that it is an arbitrary stipulation designed to put anyone who questions the writer's preferred principles into the position of questioning *morality as such*. This point might be reinforced by pointing out that Harsanyi and Richards take rather different views of the implications of the moral point of view. Harsanyi, as we have seen, emphasizes the requirement of equal consideration, spelt out in terms of the average utility social choice function. Richards, following Rawls, rejects the principle of average utility and advances a principle which demands an *absolute level* of consideration for each individual—in essence, that no individual should gain at the expense of any other.

(b) Rawls

Rawls's account contains a different suggestion about the practical force of '*x* is a rational social choice'. In his view, the rationality of a social choice is a consideration with practical force because it indicates that the social choice in question is compatible with or promotes the realization of each individual's rational nature; and this latter is an ethical good.[12] Rawls's view is simply summarized in three propositions:

(a) The expression of one's nature as a free and equal rational being is a supreme good.

(b) One is expressing one's nature as such if one is acting on principles 'that would be chosen if this nature were the decisive determining element'.

(c) A man's nature as a free and equal rational being is the decisive determining element only if 'the principles he acts upon are not adopted because of his social position or natural endowments, or in view of the particular kind of society in which he lives or the specific things that he happens to want'.

A man's nature as a free, equal, and rational being is therefore the decisive determining element when he adopts principles under the conditions of ignorance—ignorant of the content of his preferences and of his position under future states of affairs.

Now it is easy to understand how one expresses one's nature as a free, equal and rational person in adopting principles under the veil of ignorance. Everyone rationally and freely adopts a principle with no one enjoying any special advantage by knowing which principle will best promote his ends. But if, instead, I live according to principles that *would have been* chosen under the conditions of ignorance, while yet enjoying full knowledge of my preferences and position in society, in what sense am I then expressing my nature as a rational being? For with full knowledge of preferences and position it may not be rational of me to assent to these principles. Surely I express my nature as a rational being only in *actually* adopting principles.

A defence is perhaps available to Rawls, given a certain modification in his position. The argument might run: *social* rationality is the sort of rationality in choice which is compatible with everyone's exercising an equal degree of rationality in making the same choice. And this can be exhibited only in a choice based on such general considerations as that one has *some* preferences (though of unspecified kinds) and will occupy *some* position in society. I can then realize my rational nature if, even in conditions of full knowledge, I adopt my principles without taking account of the content of my own preferences and of my position in society.

It seems possible to articulate a coherent concept of social rationality along these lines, so that it follows that social rationality can only and always be realized if one lives under principles that would be adopted under the conditions of ignorance. What now seems open to doubt, however, is whether the achievement of social rationality is desirable. Is it really desirable or commendable that a man makes his social choices without regard to the content of his ends or the contingent facts of his position in society, and motivated by an exclusively egocentric concern with the achievement of his ends? If Rawls's account does involve valuing social rationality above an agent's individual rationality in pursuing his particular ends, the practical force of '*x* is a rational social choice' would seem to be as principle-dependent as on Harsanyi's account.

4 Moral reasons

I shall now examine a way in which we might assign *independent* practical force to '*x* is a rational social choice'. The suggestion is that showing that rational individuals would choose *x* on the basis of consideration *R* under specified conditions amounts to showing that *R* is a moral reason in favour of *x*. This is an ambitious claim and it is not possible here to do more than sketch the argumentative strategy that would be needed to justify it. The central moves in this strategy would be to argue for two propositions:

    (i) An account of rational social choice under certain conditions of ignorance isolates just those considerations which could and would appeal to any rational individual simply by virtue of his rationality, and which would motivate any rational individual to make the same choice.

(ii) If we examine the notion of a moral reason we will find that it is the notion of a consideration which would appeal to *any* rational individual, irrespective of his particular attitudes and desires and simply by virtue of his rationality.

Let us examine each in turn.

The accounts we have considered concentrate on choice between distributions of preference-satisfaction (Harsanyi) or resources (Rawls), by assuming that the chooser is ignorant of or unconcerned about any other features of the alternatives. This can plausibly be regarded as a way of isolating the considerations that would influence a rational chooser, when he is influenced by only those preferences which *any* rational individual would have. Rationality, as we have seen, is a disposition to choose options which are well-adapted to satisfying one's preferences. Any rational individual, then, in choosing between x and y, is concerned with the degree to which his preferences are satisfied under x and y, and with the amounts of resources for preference-satisfaction which he will enjoy under x and y.

But how are we to view the second special feature of these accounts of rational social choice, namely, the assumption that the individual is ignorant of his location in these distributions? On the suggested account of the notion of a moral reason, a consideration can only be properly advanced as a moral reason if it *could in principle* motivate any rational person simply by virtue of his rationality, and would motivate any rational person in the same way. Now it is again plausible to argue that only a consideration which would motivate any individual ignorant of his location in alternative distributions satisfies these two requirements. Take the consideration that the average level of preference-satisfaction is higher under x than y. If Harsanyi's account of rational social choice were true it would follow that this consideration could in principle motivate any rational person. For if it is offered to a rational man who knows nothing about x and y and who has to make a choice without gathering any further information about the alternatives, he can and will make a rational choice on the basis of this consideration, and any rational man will make the same choice. If on the other hand we take any consideration which mentions the identity or characteristics of any of the individuals in the distribution, then we do not have a consideration which could in principle motivate any rational individual, simply by virtue of his rationality and irrespective of the content of his preferences.

What, then, of the suggested account of the notion of a moral reason? It can best be understood, I think, as a natural development of a particular conception of morality, in which there are five strands.

(i) A moral reason is an impersonal reason, i.e. one that is a reason for any individual whatever his attitudes and preferences. Moral reasons hold *unconditionally* and *uncontingently* for anyone with a capacity for moral agency. An important corollary of this idea is that in acting towards someone on impersonal reasons the agent cannot be taken to be imposing his personal attitudes or preferences on the patient. Nor, for such an action to be acceptable to the patient, would it be necessary that he take over any of the agent's personal attitudes.

(ii) To say that a consideration R is a reason commits one to saying that it would be a *motivating* force for anyone capable of moral action, i.e. to the claim: 'Anyone would be motivated by R under conditions C.' Thus, claims about moral reasons are objective, not simply subjective expressions of personal attitude. (i) and (ii) together thus imply that any moral reason would motivate any moral agent irrespective of the preferences and attitudes he may happen to have. They thus rule out the view that in claiming that R is a moral reason we are simply claiming that the consideration would motivate any human being under certain circumstances because all human beings happen to share some primary form of motivation (e.g. associative sympathy), for this *need* not be shared by all moral agents.

(iii) To claim that R is a moral reason is to be committed to the claim that if anyone is not motivated by R under certain conditions this indicates or constitutes a defect.

(iv) The only acceptable view of the defect is that it is a defect of *rationality*, and this for two reasons. First, rationality is the only aspect of persons' general capacity for moral agency by virtue of which a consideration could motivate all moral agents in the same way. And second, it can be argued that any other account of the defect must proceed from a substantive moral view and is itself morally controversial. The only aspect of a man's practical life which we can identify as defective without reading a particular value system into a concept of a moral reason, is his exercise of practical rationality. Thus, if someone claims that the absence of compassion is a defect because a non-compassionate man fails to realize his nature, we are being asked to accept a particular account of human nature, and the ethical view that it is worth realizing—both disputable.

(v) The only viable notion of practical rationality is the formal notion.

The above is a recognizable and historically significant conception of morality.[13] I cannot, of course, hope to evaluate it here, nor to examine objections that could be brought against it. Besides arguments against the account of the notion of a moral reason, it might also be objected that there are simply no considerations which satisfy the conditions it lays down for counting as a moral reason. This would be to question the possibility of an acceptable general account of rational social choice of the kind Harsanyi or Rawls advances. It would be far beyond the scope of this paper to argue that there are such considerations, or to argue for particular instances. My aim has simply been to indicate how the notion of a moral reason might be analysed in terms of the notion of formal practical rationality and how an account of rational social choice might be supposed to isolate the types of consideration which are moral reasons and to show that they are moral reasons.

Notes

1 See, for example, Arrow, K.J. (1963), pp. 1–6.
2 Arrow, K.J. (1963), ch. VIII. All page references in subsequent discussion of Arrow are to this work. A useful discussion of the theorem can be found in Murakami, Y. (1968), chapters 5, 6.
3 Since there is no simple expression equivalent to 'it is a matter of indifference whether x is chosen or y is chosen', 'x is indifferent to y' will be taken to mean this.
4 Buchanan, J.M. (1954), pp. 116–17.
5 Buchanan, J.M. (1954), Little, I.M.D. (1952), Rothenberg, J. (1953).
6 Buchanan, J.M. (1954).
7 Rawls, J. (1971), pp. 167–75.
8 For a discussion of the rationality of these policies, see Chapter 7, section C, pp. 173–7 of this volume.
9 Harsanyi, J.C. (1955).
10 Rawls, J. (1971). All page references in subsequent discussion of Rawls are to this work.
11 Richards, D.A.J. (1971).
12 Rawls, J. (1971), section 40, particularly pp. 252–3.
13 The main elements of this conception of morality can be found in Kant's ethical works (see bibliography). Some related modern treatments, within the Kantian tradition, of the concept of morality are discussed in Richards, D.A.J. (1971), pp. 79–91. See also Phillips Griffiths, A. (1967).

Bibliography

ARROW, K.J. (1963), *Social Choice and Individual Values*, 2nd edn., New York.
BUCHANAN, J.M. (1954), 'Social choice, democracy and free markets', *Journal of Political Economy*, LXII, pp. 114–23.

BUCHANAN, J.M. (1962), 'The relevance of Pareto optimality', *Journal of Conflict Resolution*, pp. 341–54.

BUCHANAN, J.M. and TULLOCK, G. (1965), *The Calculus of Consent*, Ann Arbor.

COLEMAN, J.S. (1966), 'The possibility of a social welfare function', *American Economic Review*, LVI, pp. 1105–22.

HARSANYI, J.C. (1955), 'Cardinal welfare, individualistic ethics, and interpersonal comparisons of utility', *Journal of Political Economy*, LXIII, pp. 309–21.

HOOK, S. (1967), *Human Values and Economic Policy*, New York.

KANT, I. (1959), *Foundations of the Metaphysics of Morals*, trans. Beck, L.W., New York.

KANT, I. (1964), *The Metaphysical Principles of Virtue*, trans. Ellington, J., New York.

LITTLE, I.M.D. (1952), 'Social choice and individual values', *Journal of Political Economy*, LX, pp. 422–32.

MAY, K.O. (1954), 'Transitivity, utility, and aggregation in preference patterns', *Econometrica*, XXII, pp. 1–13.

MURAKAMI, Y. (1968), *Logic and Social Choice*, London and New York.

PATTANAIK, P.K. (1968), 'Risk, impersonality and the social welfare function', *Journal of Political Economy*, LXXVI, pp. 1152–69.

PHILLIPS GRIFFITHS, A. (1967), 'Ultimate moral principles', in Edwards, P. (ed.), *The Encyclopedia of Philosophy*, New York.

RAWLS, J. (1971), *A Theory of Justice*, Cambridge, Mass.

RICHARDS, D.A.J. (1971), *A Theory of Reasons for Action*, Oxford.

ROTHENBERG, J. (1953), 'Conditions for a social welfare function', *Journal of Political Economy*, LXI, pp. 389–405.

SEN, A.K. (1970), *Collective Choice and Social Welfare*, San Francisco.

TULLOCK, G. (1967), 'The general irrelevance of the General Impossibility Theorem', *Quarterly Journal of Economics*, LXXXI, pp. 256–70.

VICKREY, W. (1960), 'Utility, strategy and social decision rules', *Quarterly Journal of Economics*, LXXIV, pp. 507–35.

Index

Abelson, Robert, views on belief-formation
    discussed, 17–20
action
    formal practical rationality in, 268,
        271–2, 273, 280, 282, 292
    instrumental view of, 184
    irrational, 2–3, 302–4, 387ff
        explanation in political science and,
            247, 248, 250–2, 254, 255
        Hartmann's view of, 147
        political participation as, 252–4
        see also irrationality
    non-rational, 2–3, 106–7, 132, 140,
        149–50, 332–3
        explanation in political science and,
            246, 247
        traditional conduct as, 143–5
        see also affectual conduct; Pareto,
            V.; Parsons, T.; rationality,
            rational/non-rational distinction
    rational
        affectivity and, see affectual conduct
        choice and, see choice
        choice of the best and, 96–8,
            117–19, 120–1
        consistency as condition for, 307–8,
            362, 372ff
        co-ordination and, 361
        'covering assumptions' and, 148
            149, 150, 151
        criteria of, 143, 151–2, 157–8, 176,
            361–3; see also goal-achievement;
            optimality, canons of; rational
            choice criteria of, and theoretical
            determinacy, 158–9, 176, 178f,

180
    deliberate selection of means in,
        361, 369–70, 376–7
    efficiency and, 253
    epistemic requirements for, 96, 117,
        124–9, 143, 268; in Pareto, 136ff,
        143; in Parsons, 140; in technical
        models, 158, 181–4; see also;
        epistemic rationality, unbounded
        rationality in economic theory
    expressive conduct, see expressive
        conduct
    fully, as ideal type, 152
    general accounts of, 2, 4–5, 95–6,
        111–21
    incidence in real life, 104–7,
        121ff, 151–2
    information-processing and, see
        information-processing
    information-search and, see
        information-search
    instrumental, 93–5, 117–19, 224,
        361; see also consequentialism;
        rationality, instrumental
    Oakeshott on, 361–2, 376–7
    ordinary notion contrasted with
        technical models, 6, 16–17,
        117–21, 157–8
    political theory and, 247, chapters
        9–10 passim
    preference and, see preference
    pursuit of ends and, 93–6, 105–9
    rational belief and, 268
    rule-following and, 94, 108–9,
        143–5, 148, 149–50, 361–2,

405

Index

Index

completeness of preference, *see* preference, rational, formal conditions for

conduct, *see* action

confirmation, *see* epistemic rationality, confirmation and

conflict, *see* chicken, game of; game-theory; optimality, canons of, for conditions of strategic interaction; prisoners' dilema

conflict-resolution, theories of, 157

connectedness of preference
condition of rational social choice, 386–8, 390–1
see preference, rational, formal conditions for

connectedness of strategic interactions, *see* strategic interactions

connexity of preference, *see* preference, rational, formal conditions for

consent and political rationality, 250ff

consequentialism
Downs's theory of democracy and, 248, 251
praxeology and, 184–6, 269
see also action, rational, instrumental; rationality, instrumental

consistency
conformity to rules and, 361–2, 372–4
internal, of societies, 374–6
rationality requirement, 52–3, 305–6, 307–8, 361–2, 372ff
see also belief-formation, consistency theory of

constant-sum games, 243 n.30; *see also* zero-sum games

constitutionalism and consent, 250ff, 478ff

constitutions, *see* social decision processes

consumer behaviour, economic analysis of, 200–2, 209, 211

consumer preference, as ideal, 211–12

consumer society, criticism of, 281

contradictions, social, *see* rational societies, Hegel and; rational societies, internal consistency of; rational societies, Marx and

core, *see* game-theory

cost-benefit analysis in political theory, 255ff

decentering, Piaget on, 286

decision, *see* action; choice; preference

decision-making
costs of, 204, 209; *see also* information-search, costs of
praxeological theories of, 159ff
rules-of-thumb in, *see* rules-of-thumb, rationality and

decision procedures, social, *see* social decision processes

decision theory, chapter 7 *passim*

defence, 230–1; *see also* coalition theory,

provision of collective goods in demand, economic theory of, 211; *see also* consumer behaviour; economic theory; economics

democratic systems, rationality of, 364, 372

derivations, *see* Pareto, V.

determinacy of praxeological theories
equilibrium and, 166–7, 181, 208–9
rational belief postulates and, 180–2, 204, 234; *see also* coalition theory, indeterminacy in; predictability in economics; unbounded rationality

deterrence in international relations, 230, 232, 243 n.28

development
concept of, 299
normal, 286–7
conditions for an explanatory theory of, 287–8
moral, of personality, 285
theories of, 286–8

development of human personality
contrasted with biological, 286–7

development of rationality, chapter 12 *passim*

dialectical logic and history, 290–1, 374–5

Diesing, P., 364–5

dominant strategies in game-theory, 217, 260, 261

Downs, A., *An Economic Theory of Democracy*, 6, 188, 247–53, 255, 256

economic theory, neo-classical, chapter 8 *passim*

economics, 16–17, chapter 7 *passim*, chapter 8 *passim*
explanation in, 182–3, 292–3
praxeology distinguished from, 159
scope and methods of, 196, 292–3
subjectivist school of, Schutz, A. and, 142

Edgeworth, F.Y., 212

education, ends in, 270–1

educational psychology, chapter 12 *passim*; *see also* Piaget, J.

elections
coalition theory and, 230–1, 232, 234, 235, 238–9, 243 n.29 and 32, 244 n.49
Downs and rationality in, 249–52

Ellul, J., *The Technological Society*, 379–80

end, natural, of man, *see* telos, man's

end-formation, 265

ends
activities and, 376–7
choice of, 277
conceptually presuppose choice, 284
constitutive of rationality, 12, 100–2
epistemic, 4, 12, 24–5, 49–51, 52–4, 274–5

Index

functional rationality, 369ff

game-theory, 177–81, 184, 212–19, 246–7
    'core', 218, 244 n.46
    dominance in, dominant strategies in
      game-theory
    epistemic problems of, 180, 213
    essential and inessential games, 242 n.7
    imputations, 242 n.12
    n-person, see coalition theory
    recursive games, 244 n.48
    simple games, 242 n.9
    solution of game, 213, 217, 218
    stochastic games, 244 n.48
    three or more person games, 214–18;
      see also coalition theory
    two-person games, 213–14, 218
    unrealistic assumptions of, 219
general will as socially rational, 371–2
Gibson, Q. on rationality in action, 101, 105
gifts in economic theory, 187
goal-achievement, maximizing of, as
    rationality condition, 361, 372, 382 n.1
goal-orientation as a condition for
    meaningful conduct, 135
goals, institutionalized, 249
group rationality, 216; see also coalition
    theory

Habermas, J., *Knowledge and Human
    Interests*, 288–90, 292
Harrod, R., 209
Harsanyi, J., 180–1
Hartmann, H. on irrational conduct, 147, 148
Hayek, F., 365
Hegel, G.W.F., 290–1, 363, 374–6
heteronomy, 283, 284
Hicks, J., 196, 208, 211
history, rational necessity in, 290–1
Hobbes, T., 261, 264
Hobhouse, L.T., 141
Hollis, M, 44
human essence as criterion of rationality in
    institutions, 368, 369, 380–1
human species
    as rational, 290, 381
    as self-creative, 289–90, 291
Hume, D. on reason, 273–4, 275–6, 285
Hurwicz, L., 176

ideal types, Weber's account of rationality in
    terms of, 134
ideas distinguished by Hume from passions,
    274
ideological behaviour
    expressing principles, 255–6; see also
      expressive conduct

incommensurable utilities and, 259
    yielding utilities, 255–6, 258–60,
      267 n.43
imperfect rationality, see practical rationality,
    degrees of; rationality postulates, strong
    vs. week
impersonality as rationality condition, 141,
    276, 282–3, 285, 286, 289, 301–2, 314–20,
    370, 373
inconsistency, toleration of, 48–9
indifference, 161
    curves, 167–9, 201
    symmetry of, 161–3
    weak preference ordering and, 161–2
individualism, 385
inductive inference, probability and
    rationality of, 174
industrial societies, rationality of, 370–1
inference, rational, 13ff, 282; see also belief,
    limited subjective rationality in; mental
    processing rules
information
    complete, Riker's requirement of, 227,
      233, 235, 244 n.35 and 39
    perfect, Riker's requirement of, 227, 229,
      233, 244 n.34
information-processing, 78–83, 98–100
information-search
    costs of, 15–17, 98–100, 183, 199, 202,
      203, 207–8
    rationality in, 183, 198–9, 203–5, 206–8
information transmission and coalition
    theory, 216–17
innovation, Oakeshott on, 377
instincts and residues in Pareto, 138ff
institutions
    ends of, 370–1
    rationality of, 5, 290, 359, 370–1
intellectualism, see belief-systems, evaluation
    of
interest groups, latent, 254, 260
interests
    distinguished from residues in Pareto,
      138
    human, and rational ends, 289–90
international relations, chapter 9 *passim*
interval scales, 171
irrationality, 2–3, 302–4
    of action, see action, irrational
    of belief, see belief, irrational
    explanation of, 313–14
    irrational/unreasonable distinction,
      302–4, 314–16

Jevons, W.S., 159, 169
justificationism, see epistemic rationality,
    justificationist conceptions of

Kafka. F., 373

Index

assimilation and accommodation in, 321–7
homeostatic explanations of, 322–3
egocentric emotions and, 314–16
epistemic, *see* epistemic rationality
evaluative use of concept, 2–3, 270–1, 300–8, chapter 14 *passim*
forms of life and, 45–54
historical relativity of, 25–6
honorific force of, 273, 381
Hume's account of, 273–4
imputed, 148–9, 182, 197
incidence in real life, 104–7, 121ff
limited, 151–2
see also rationality, degrees of
instrumental
in political theory, 246, 248, 249, 251, 253–4, 255–60; *see also* consequentialism; satisfaction-seeking
Parsons's account of, 139–40, 141
Weber's account of, 133–4, 186, 255, 372–3
see also action, rational, pursuit of ends and
intelligence and, 300–3
intercultural comparisons of, 3–4, 5, chapter 2 *passim*
language and, Habermas on, 290, 293 n.26
norms of, 15–16, 18–20, 276, 305–7, 324–7, 363; *see also* action, rational, choice of the best and; rationality, traits of
objectivity and, 304–5, 318–20
of action, *see* action, rational
of belief, *see* belief, rational
of institutions, *see* institutions, rationality of
of social scientists, 6–7
postulates
non-technical, in explanation of action, 100–1, 102–4, chapter 5 *passim*
strong vs. weak, 1–2, 111, 117ff; *see also* belief, limited subjective rationality in; epistemic rationality, degrees of; practical rationality, degrees of
use in explanation of belief, chapter 2 *passim*, chapter 4 *passim*
practical, *see* practical rationality
publicity and, 304–5, 318–20
rational/irrational distinction, 2–3, 132, 302–4, 332–3
rational/non-rational distinction, 2–3, 106–7, 132, 139–40, 332–3, 335–7
rational/reasonable distinction, 302–4, 314–16

reasons and, 2, 12–21, 94–104, 301–4, 306
requirements
strong, 141, 150–1; in game-theory, 217–18; in political theory, 247, 252, 255–6, 265
substantive, 248–9, chapter 11 *passim*; *see also* practical rationality, substantive; role-rationality
weak, 141–2, 148–50; in game-theory, 215ff; in political theory, 255–60, 265
social choice, *see* social choice, rational
social decision processes, *see* social choice; social decision processes, rational choice of
traits of, 3–4, 292–3, 300ff; *see also* practical rationality, trait
transcendence of the present and, 301–2
unbounded, see rationality, degrees of; unbounded rationality
universes of discourse and, 42–5
varieties of, 142ff
Rawls, J., *A Theory of Justice*, 272, 385, 394–6
reality and universes of discourse, 43–5
reason, norms of, *see* rationality, norms of
reasonableness, *see* rationality, rational/reasonable distinction; unreasonableness, explanation of
reasons
for action, *see* action, rational; action, rational, pursuit of ends and; action rational, choice of the best and
for beliefs, *see* belief, reasons for
reflexive behaviour, 133
regulation and external costs, 262
Reichenbach, H., 173
religion as a form of life, 46–8
religious belief, *see* belief, religious
'repressive rationality', 380–1
residues, *see* Pareto, V.
resources, maximization of, 272
revolution and rationality, 377
Riker, W.H., 187–8, 246–7; *Theory of Political Coalitions*, chapter 10 *passim*
Riker, W.H. and Ordeshook, P.C., *An Introduction to Positive Political Theory*, 247, 255–7, 258, 259, 262, 265
risk
choice under conditions of, 170, *see* optimality, canons of, for conditions of risk
distinguished from uncertainty, 175–6
insurance and, 175
optimality and, 158, *see also* optimality, canons of, for conditions of risk
utility and, 169
see also probability

414